Pakistan's Inter-Servic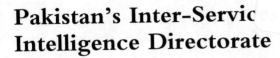 Intelligence Directorate

This book is the first comprehensive study of Pakistan's Inter-Services Intelligence Directorate (ISI).

The rise of Pakistan-backed religious extremist groups in Afghanistan, India and Central Asia has focused international attention on Pakistan's premier intelligence organization and covert action advocate, the Inter-Services Intelligence Directorate or ISI. While ISI is regarded as one of the most powerful government agencies in Pakistan today, surprisingly little has been written about it from an academic perspective. This book addresses critical gaps in our understanding of this agency, including its domestic security mission, covert backing of the Afghan Taliban, and its links to al-Qa'ida. Using primary source materials, including declassified intelligence and diplomatic reporting, press reports and memoirs, this book explores how ISI was transformed from a small, negligible counter intelligence outfit of the late-1940s into the national security behemoth of today with extensive responsibilities in domestic security, political interference and covert action. This study concludes that reforming or even eliminating ISI will be fundamental if Pakistan is to successfully transition from an army-run, national security state to a stable, democratic society that enjoys peaceful relations with its neighbors.

This book will be of interest to students of intelligence studies, South Asian politics, foreign policy and international security in general.

Owen L. Sirrs is Adjunct Professor at the University of Montana, USA, and the author of two previous books, including, most recently, *The Egyptian Intelligence Service* (Routledge 2011).

Pakistan's Inter-Services Intelligence Directorate

Covert action and internal operations

Owen L. Sirrs

Taylor & Francis Group

LONDON AND NEW YORK

First published 2017
by Routledge
2 Park Square, Milton Park, Abingdon, Oxon OX14 4RN

and by Routledge
711 Third Avenue, New York, NY 10017

First issued in paperback 2017

Routledge is an imprint of the Taylor & Francis Group, an informa business

British Library Cataloguing-in-Publication Data
A catalogue record for this book is available from the British Library

Library of Congress Cataloging-in-Publication Data
Names: Sirrs, Owen L., author.
Title: Pakistan's Inter-Services Intelligence Directorate : covert action and internal operations / Owen L. Sirrs.
Description: New York, NY : Routledge, 2016. | Includes bibliographical references and index.
Identifiers: LCCN 2016004564| ISBN 9781138677166 (hardback) | ISBN 9781315559711 (ebook)
Subjects: LCSH: Pakistan. Inter Services Intelligence. | Military intelligence–Pakistan. | Intelligence service–Pakistan.
Classification: LCC UB251.P35 S57 2016 | DDC 327.125491–dc23
LC record available at https://lccn.loc.gov/2016004564

ISBN 13: 978–1–138–49525–8 (pbk)
ISBN 13: 978–1–138–67716–6 (hbk)

Typeset in Bembo
by Wearset Ltd, Boldon, Tyne and Wear

Contents

Illustrations

Figures

Maps

Acknowledgments

The genesis of this book was my two-month stay at the Counterinsurgency Training Center in Kabul, Afghanistan during the summer of 2009. It was there that I learned a great deal more about Afghanistan–Pakistan relations in general and ISI operations in Afghanistan in particular. My thanks therefore to my former boss, Janice Trickel, for sending me there, Mohammed Eshaq for hosting me, and Colonel, USA (retd) John Agoglia for providing me with this opportunity. At the Mansfield Center I would like to thank Major General, USAF (retd) Don Loranger, who built up the Defense Critical Language and Culture Program from truly humble beginnings to the impressive entity it has become today, and Brigadier USA (retd) Joel Cusker, an inspiring boss and friend. I would also like to thank my Afghan colleagues here at the center but, unfortunately, the grim realities of the Afghan war make it impossible to name them in person. It goes without saying that they have given me fresh insights into the tortured history of their country and its difficult relationship with Pakistan. My research was greatly enhanced with the assistance of the Inter-Library Loan librarians at the Mansfield Library of the University of Montana. Without their help, this book would not have been possible. Finally, this book is dedicated to my mother, Margaret, and my wife, Julie, both of whom were there, although at different times.

Abbreviations and Acronyms

AIG	Afghan Interim Government
CAB	Cabinet Papers
CI	Counter Intelligence
CIA	Central Intelligence Agency
CID	Criminal Investigation Department
COAS	Chief of Army Staff
COIN	Counter Insurgency
CPP	Communist Party of Pakistan
CUP	Columbia University Press
DCI	Director of Central Intelligence (U.S.)
DCIA	Director of the Central Intelligence Agency (U.S.)
DEFE	Defence Ministry
DGIB	Director General Intelligence Bureau
DGISI	Director General Inter-Services Intelligence
DGMI	Director General Military Intelligence
DMI	Director Military Intelligence
FATA	Federally Administered Tribal Areas
FBI	Federal Bureau of Investigation
FCO	Foreign and Commonwealth Office
FO	Foreign Office
FRUS	*Foreign Relations of the United States*
GHQ	General Headquarters
HM	*Hezbul Mujahidin*
HuM	*Harakatul Mujahidin*
HUMINT	Human Intelligence
IB	Intelligence Bureau
ISI	Inter-Services Intelligence
JCIB	Joint Counter Intelligence Bureau (ISI)
JCO	Junior Commissioned Officer
JeM	*Jaish-e-Mohamed*
JI	*Jama'at –e-Islami*
JIB	Joint Intelligence Bureau (ISI)
JIC	Joint Intelligence Committee (UK)

JKLF	Jammu and Kashmir Liberation Front
JSIB	Joint Signals Intelligence Bureau (ISI)
LAT	*Los Angeles Times*
LeT	*Lashkar-e-Taiba*
LOC	Line of Control
MI	Military Intelligence
MNF	Mizo National Front
NAP	National Awami Party
NARA	National Archives and Records Administration
NCO	Non-Commissioned Officer
NDS	National Directorate of Security (Afghanistan)
NWFP	North-West Frontier Province
NYT	*New York Times*
OUP	Oxford University Press
PDPA	Peoples Democratic Party of Afghanistan
PIC	Pakistan Intelligence Community
PML	Pakistan Muslim League
PML-Q	Pakistan Muslim League – Quaid
PNA	Pakistan National Alliance
PPP	Pakistan Peoples Party
RAW	Research and Analysis Wing (India)
SIGINT	Signals Intelligence
SSG	Special Services Group
UKNA	United Kingdom National Archives
UTN	*Umma Tamer-e-Nau*
UW	Unconventional Warfare
VCOAS	Vice Chief of Army Staff
WO	War Office
WP	*Washington Post*

Introduction

On the night of 1–2 May 2011, a dark chapter in American history came to an abrupt end with the death of Osama Bin Laden in the Pakistani garrison city of Abbottabad. His killers were US Navy SEALs ferried into the city on state-of-the art helicopters with stealthy features to avoid early warning radars. While some SEALs hauled Bin Laden's body to a waiting helicopter, others scoured his residence for computers, hard drives, flash drives, cell phones and written documents of potential intelligence value. This hunt for information was almost as important as killing the man himself, for it would provide new insight into his terrorist organization called al-Qa'ida. Back in Washington, intelligence analysts hoped Bin Laden's archive would shed light on upcoming al-Qa'ida operations, its links to other terrorist groups, and the extent of its relations with foreign intelligence agencies like Iran's Revolutionary Guards or Pakistan's Inter-Services Intelligence Directorate.

In the United States, news of Bin Laden's death was greeted with joy, relief and an outpouring of national pride. After all, this was the man ultimately responsible for a string of terrorist spectaculars aimed at US citizens that culminated with 11 September 2001 and the deaths of nearly 3,000 people. But now that Bin Laden was dead, American officials and the media began pointing accusatory fingers at the Pakistani government: how did the world's most wanted man reside, almost in plain view, in a city filled with army facilities and retirees, not to mention the national military academy? Indeed, contrary to conventional wisdom in the years after 9/11, Bin Laden was nowhere near the "ungoverned" Pashtun tribal areas of western Pakistan. Some US officials were even asking awkward questions about Pakistan's formidable intelligence apparatus: how much did Pakistan's premier intelligence agency, the Inter-Services Intelligence Directorate – or ISI – know about Bin Laden's hideout?[1] Was ISI in fact secretly supporting al-Qa'ida? After all, ISI had been notorious for backing jihadi groups who were linked to al-Qa'ida, including the Afghan Taliban, *Lashkar-e-Taiba* ("Army of the Pure"), *Harakatul Mujahidin* ("Movement of the Holy Warriors"), and the *Jaish-e-Mohamed* ("Mohamed's Army").

For its part, the Pakistani government was understandably defensive and sullen. Not only were its armed forces not notified by the US in advance of the raid, they had also failed to detect and react to it in time. Several of ISI's domestic critics were even emboldened to ask how Bin Laden managed to hide in a compound close to the Pakistan Military Academy for nearly six years. How much did ISI *really* know about Bin Laden's refuge? Where was the accountability in the Pakistani government? Some speculated that ISI had sheltered Bin Laden after 9/11, although why it would run the risk in doing so was unclear. Some suggested ISI shielded him as a deterrent against future al-Qa'ida attacks on Pakistani targets while others judged that ISI had been grossly incompetent in its failure to find the terrorist leader. The third theory was that rogue ISI elements had hidden the terrorist mastermind without the knowledge of Pakistan's leadership.

What exactly is ISI?

ISI is a military agency. Although a component of Pakistan's "inter-services" (i.e., "joint") military structure, its Director General (DGISI) reports directly to the president. At least he is required to do so constitutionally, but, in reality, the DGISI is an army general who also serves at the pleasure of the most powerful individual in the country – the Chief of Army Staff (COAS). ISI's headquarters is a large structure surrounded by walls, barbed wire and guard towers that is just visible from the Kashmir Highway in Islamabad's G-7/4 Sector. From the outside, the building seems relatively benign, yet in the collective mind of the Pakistani people, ISI has become the country's Orwellian Big Brother. As one Pakistani journalist puts it:

> [ISI] is powerful, ubiquitous and has functioned with so much authority from the central government that it almost became a state within a state. It is not only responsible for intelligence gathering, but also acts as a determinant of Pakistan's foreign policy and a vehicle for its implementation.[2]

In addition, ISI plans and executes Pakistan's proxy war strategy. From Kashmir to Afghanistan, it has created, trained and armed militant groups, some of which have been directly involved in the deaths of American and other coalition soldiers in Afghanistan. Still, with the exception of the 1989 Soviet withdrawal from Afghanistan, Pakistan's proxy strategy has failed to achieve most of its national objectives. Indeed, proxies have created major stresses in Pakistan's foreign policy with the US, UK, Afghanistan, Russia, Iran and even China, all of whom have openly accused ISI of sponsoring terrorist groups against them. Jihadi proxies have also triggered several near wars between Pakistan and India with the risk of nuclear war always looming in the background.

For many Pakistanis, ISI is the dreaded three letter agency with a menacing reputation for omnipotence, omniscience and brutality. Publicized court cases and media revelations provide ample evidence of ISI's role in manipulating elections, bribing politicians, threatening journalists and torturing dissidents. There are also plenty of rumors regarding ISI's ability to "silence" its domestic critics, and the legion of unsolved murder cases with suspected ISI links continues to grow. Thus, ISI is more than just a foreign intelligence and covert action agency: it has a formidable domestic security role as well.

Why this book?

Although ISI has gained considerable international notoriety thanks to its jihadi allies, surprisingly little has been written about it. ISI has not been comprehensively examined from a historical perspective, and the existing secondary literature is often filled with inaccuracies and exaggeration. ISI is deserving of a careful, balanced, systematic investigation since it is a powerful piece on Pakistan's political chessboard with the ability to make or break civilian governments as well as plan and implement proxy wars against neighboring states.

This book is based on the premise that an in-depth study of ISI is essential to understanding Pakistan itself, especially its national security policy and historical attempts at sustained democratization. Indeed, to paraphrase what Sir Alexander Cadogan once wrote about the study of intelligence and diplomatic history, the most recent academic work on Pakistani history, politics and international relations does not adequately address a "missing dimension," namely ISI's prominent role in domestic and foreign policymaking.[3] The following questions provide the framework within which this premise is researched and tested.

1 How has ISI evolved as an institution exercising intelligence and security responsibilities at home and abroad? What were the driving forces behind that evolutionary process?

Starting in the 1980s with ISI's "secret war" in Afghanistan and accelerating in the post 11 September 2001 era, the literature on ISI's unconventional warfare (UW) strategy has exploded; however, we still lack insights into ISI's other mission areas such as espionage, counter intelligence and domestic surveillance.[4] We also do not have an adequate understanding of ISI's origins and how it became one of the most powerful state institutions in Pakistan today.[5] This study therefore details how ISI started out as a modest collection, analysis and counter intelligence agency and then evolved into the intelligence and security empire it is today with extensive responsibilities in both policy formation and implementation.

2 How does ISI fit into the larger Pakistani Intelligence Community?

In a 2004 essay, Len Scott and Peter Jackson highlighted several gaps in intelligence studies, including how national intelligence agencies interact and collaborate with each other.[6] I believe the Pakistani Intelligence Community

(PIC) provides a useful case study in how rival national intelligence agencies interrelate in a state dominated by its military establishment. Indeed, ISI's power within the PIC has grown to such an extent in recent years that the concept of a Pakistani intelligence "community" is something of a misnomer. This book will detail the forces and events that drove the creation of the PIC and how ISI came to dominate it.

3 How has ISI employed UW in support of the state's national security objectives? To what extent has UW been a successful strategy for Pakistan?

There is some disagreement among academics on how unconventional warfare – also known as "covert action" – fits within a common definition of "intelligence." As a policy *instrument*, UW is clearly incompatible with a formulation of intelligence as an activity that facilitates and informs policy, but others argue that UW is fundamental to what many intelligence agencies *do* in addition to their "conventional" collection, analysis and counter intelligence duties.[7] Certainly when it comes to Pakistan, there is little doubt that ISI is a powerful – often *the most powerful* – actor in shaping *and* implementing foreign policy. Theoretical considerations aside, we cannot understand what ISI is and does if we deliberately exclude its use of UW against its neighbors.

4 What is ISI's record in providing accurate and timely early warning intelligence to decision-makers?

There is a growing body of literature on the performance of intelligence communities in strategic surprise scenarios with groundbreaking work done on Pearl Harbor, Hitler's 1941 invasion of the Soviet Union, the 1973 Arab–Israeli war, the 1983 ABLE ARCHER episode and 9/11.[8] Greater awareness of the role that intelligence has played in historical surprise attacks has enabled scholars to probe more deeply into the relationships among national intelligence agencies, the perils of underestimating adversaries or misinterpreting their actions, the reliance decision-makers have placed on intelligence assessments used (or not used) and the frequent politicization of the intelligence process.

India and Pakistan have gone to war three times since their independence in 1947. In 1999, they fought a "half war" over the Kargil peaks that threatened to escalate further until US diplomacy helped calm the waters. Finally, both countries have only narrowly avoided war on a number of occasions, starting with a 1950 mobilization crisis generated by Indian troop movements through the 1986–1987 BRASSTACKS standoff, which eventually led to the mobilization of over one million soldiers, to the 2002 near-war, which was triggered by an attack on the Indian parliament by ISI-linked terrorists. On each occasion, India and Pakistan have backed away from the edge, yet they did so with the assistance of US and other diplomats as mediators. When these individual cases are examined more closely, it is a wonder there have not been four or more Indo-Pakistani wars.

The South Asian experience provides us with useful examples of crisis intelligence, misperception, cognitive dissonance and fears of surprise attack. Since 1986, these stand-offs and mobilization/counter-mobilization cycles have only gained in international significance since both states possess nuclear weapons and the ballistic missiles to deliver them. This study examines how ISI performed providing reliable strategic warning to its masters during several crises with India. US primary sources on the 1990 and 1999 near wars are especially insightful and illustrate the pivotal role that ISI must play if future wars in South Asia are to be prevented or at least contained if and when they do break out.

5 What does the decades-old relationship between ISI and the CIA tell us about the larger US–Pakistan security relationship?

Christopher Andrew has noted how relationships between intelligence communities represent an "understudied" area in the field of intelligence studies.[9] ISI offers a superb example of how the American and Pakistani intelligence establishments have worked together and against each other over the course of nearly 70 years. In addition to a considerable body of primary source reporting on ISI–CIA links in the 1950s and 1960s, post 9/11 revelations have shown how the Central Intelligence Agency (CIA) leveraged its relationship with ISI to aid intelligence collection and conduct "extraordinary renditions" of terrorism suspects. Later, however, that relationship devolved into outright hostility as each openly questioned the motives and reliability of the other.

6 To what extent has ISI disrupted and abused Pakistan's democratic processes?

This study demonstrates how ISI became a pivotal player in domestic politics and an essential tool enabling the army's dominant role in government. During civilian *and* military rule, ISI has bribed politicians, harassed journalists, and employed money and intimidation to forge pro-army coalitions. It is equally notorious for conducting media campaigns against its domestic and foreign adversaries by planting stories in the domestic and international press. Moreover, ISI has reserved for itself the right to determine what constitutes "anti-Pakistan activity" and the punishments to be administered with regrettable consequences for that country's human rights record.

7 Is ISI a rogue agency or a state within a state?

ISI benefits from the so-called plausible deniability of its clandestine operations. This study reveals how ISI's nominally "covert" action efforts have often inhibited India and Afghanistan from carrying out overt reprisals. Moreover, when US officials have been confronted with awkward evidence of ISI subversion, they often resort to the subterfuge that ISI might be a "rogue" agency operating without the knowledge of American "friends" in the Pakistani government. This study tries to puncture the myth of ISI as a "rogue" agency operating beyond the knowledge and consent of the national authorities.

8 Can ISI be reined in and the PIC reformed?

Several newly democratized states have successfully overhauled their powerful military intelligence establishments and harnessed them to a formal constitutional framework. Bearing these examples in mind, what are the prospects for intelligence reform in Pakistan? Can these lessons be applied there or is this country an exceptional case? This study explores historical attempts at reforming ISI and how they have consistently failed to curtail the formidable domestic powers of this agency. It spells out those preliminary actions that would be necessary before any effective reform could be carried out.

Research methodology

Intelligence agencies by their very nature present a tough challenge for researchers since they hide what needs to be hidden, and what little they do reveal is often meant to influence and misinform. For example, ISI's Arab peers are notoriously secretive with regard to historical operations, personnel, structures, politics and missions. By comparison, ISI is a somewhat easier research subject.[10] This may be due to culture and language differences, but it can also be attributed to Pakistan's relatively free press and the revolving door nature of its civilian and military regimes. Unlike Egypt, for example, which has been subjected to military rule since 1952 (with one brief interregnum in 2012–2013), Pakistan's political landscape is more pluralistic and tumultuous. Four military regimes have come and gone over a similar time frame, yet civilian political parties and a vibrant civil society have never been stamped out. This opens the way for a plethora of voices with different political perspectives commenting on ISI and its impact on Pakistani domestic and foreign policy.

It must be admitted, however, that Pakistan's relative openness aside, numerous gaps remain in our knowledge of ISI. Readers will note several shortcomings in this work, including the impact of ISI analysis on leadership decision-making, signals intelligence (SIGINT) and specific human intelligence (HUMINT) operations. On the other hand, this study's heavy focus on UW and domestic operations not only demonstrates the importance of these missions for ISI, it also reflects the relative depth of primary source materials in these areas.

Primary sources provide important and often unique information on ISI's history. For example, memoirs are an invaluable reservoir of information for any student of Pakistani history: the country's generals seem to be a garrulous lot eager to record their opinions and perspectives on historical events.[11] The same could be said for many of their CIA counterparts.[12] The UK National Archives contain material that is particularly valuable in mapping out and assessing ISI's origins while documents at the US National Archives and Records Administration detail how Washington assumed a greater role in Pakistan's national security policy during the mid- to late-1950s. Some declassified State Department cables and CIA reports are accessible on the Internet thanks to State's Foreign Relations of the United States (FRUS) series while George Washington University's National Security Archive website contains a plethora of declassified documents often not found in FRUS. It should be noted that a great deal of information concerning the CIA–ISI relationship has never been declassified, and it is highly unlikely these archives will be opened any time soon.[13] Finally, my research has greatly benefited from the work of journalists such as Syed Saleem Shahzad, Imtiaz Gul, David Sanger, Mark Mazzetti, Eric Schmitt, Adrian Levy, Cathy Scott-Clark, Christina Lamb, and Steve Coll among many others.

This study uses a chronological framework to develop the themes and substantiate the analysis. I have divided the chapters into five parts, which correspond to important dates in ISI's development. Part I covers the first two decades of the Pakistani state from its inception in August 1947 through the coup of 1958 to the 1965 war with India. Part II examines Pakistan's disastrous 1971 war with India, early ISI covert action in Afghanistan, the dramatic rise and fall of Zulfikar Ali Bhutto, and the army-led coup of 1977. Part III is largely devoted to ISI's role in backing the Afghan mujaheddin against the Soviet 40th Army and its Afghan allies. The nine years from 1980 to 1989 mark a golden age of sorts for the agency when it benefited from the infusion of billions of dollars in US and Saudi covert aid. Part IV explores the period from 1990 to the eve of the 11 September 2001 attacks on the United States. It includes ISI's controversial and ultimately unsuccessful role as kingmaker in Afghanistan, its support for insurgency and terrorism in Indian-occupied Kashmir, and its domestic political interference. Part V delves into ISI, Pakistan and the post-9/11 world. This has been a particularly difficult era for the agency as it tries to navigate the myriad contradictions in Pakistan's foreign policy: siding with a US-led coalition against al-Qa'ida and the Pakistan Taliban while quietly maintaining the Afghan Taliban as a valid long-term option for war-ravaged Afghanistan. The study ends with the death of Osama Bin Laden, an event that also coincided with a new, as yet incomplete, chapter in ISI's history.

The picture that emerges is that of an intelligence and security agency whose vast powers pose a formidable obstacle to the long-term viability of Pakistani democracy. Reflecting the siege mentality of its army master, ISI believes it is engaged in an existential war for national survival in the face of India's expanding military capabilities not to mention New Delhi's aspirations for great power status. Reform of the ISI is essential for domestic tranquility

and long-term peace in South Asia; however, any effort to recast ISI or eliminate it altogether will almost certainly be defeated by a military institution
that continues to exercise preponderant power in Pakistan. Much needs to
change in Pakistan before that country stabilizes and achieves a long-term
entente with its neighbors. If that process is to succeed, easing the army back
to its cantonments on a permanent basis and then reforming or abolishing ISI
will be essential first steps.

Notes

1 H. Haqqani, *Magnificent Delusions*, New York: Public Affairs, 2013, 318–319.
2 Z. Hussain, *Frontline: The Struggle with Militant Islam*, New York: Columbia University Press [Hereafter CUP], 2007, 12.
3 D. Dilks (ed.), *The Diaries of Sir Alexander Cadogan O.M. 1938–1945*, London: Faber & Faber, 2010, 21 quoted in C. Andrew and D. Dilks, *The Missing Dimension*, Urbana, IL: University of Illinois Press, 1984, 1.
4 There are several outstanding works on ISI's proxy wars, including S. Coll, *Ghost Wars*, New York, Penguin, 2004; L. Wright, *The Looming Tower*, New York, Vintage Books, 2006; M. Mazzetti, *The Way of the Knife*, New York, Penguin, 2013.
5 The curse of the Internet is that it often perpetuates errors. For example, some commonly accessed websites routinely misspell the name of one of ISI's founding fathers, Sir Walter J. Cawthorn, as Cawthome or Cawthorne, and these are, in turn, carried over into secondary sources. Others carry and repeat extensive line and block charts of ISI's organization without indicating the original source for such information.
6 L. Scott and P. Jackson, "The Study of Intelligence in Theory and Practice," *Intelligence and National Security* [Hereafter INS] 19:2, Summer 2004, 161.
7 For examples of the intelligence – covert action debate see Ibid., 142; L. Scott, "Secret Intelligence, Covert Action, and Clandestine Diplomacy," *INS* 19:2, Summer 2004, 322–323; K. Vrist Ronn and S. Hoffding, "The Epistemic Status of Intelligence: An Epistemological Contribution to the Understanding of Intelligence," *INS* 28:5, 694–716; M. Warner, "Wanted: A Definition of Intelligence," *Studies in Intelligence* 46:3, www.cia.gov/library/center-for-the-study-of-intelligence/csi-publications/csi-studies/studies/vol. 46no3/article02.html [accessed 16/11/15]; M. Lowenthal, *Intelligence: From Secrets to Policy*, Washington, DC: Congressional Quarterly Press, 2002, 8.
8 See, for example, R. Wohlstetter, *Pearl Harbor: Warning and Decision*, Stanford, CA: Stanford University Press, 1962; M.I. Handel, "Intelligence and the Problem of Strategic Surprise," *The Journal of Strategic Studies* 7:3 (1984): 229–281; L. Scott, "Intelligence and the Risk of Nuclear War: Able Archer Revisited," *Intelligence and National Security* 26:6 (2011), 759–777; S. Marrin, "The 9/11 Terrorist Attacks: A Failure of Policy Not Strategic Intelligence Analysis," *Intelligence and National Security* 26:2–3 (2011), 182–202; R.K. Betts, Surprise Attack: Lessons for Defense Planning, Washington, DC: Brookings, 1982; E. Dahl, *Intelligence and Surprise Attack*, Washington, DC: Georgetown University Press, 2013.
9 C. Andrew, "Intelligence, International Relations, and Under-Theorisation," *INS* 19:2, Summer 2004, 173–174.
10 This has been the author's experience researching Egypt's intelligence community. See O. Sirrs, *The Egyptian Intelligence Service: a History of the Mukhabarat*, Abingdon, Routledge, 2010.
11 Still, the limitations of memoirs must be borne in mind. To quote Malcolm Muggeridge: "Diplomats and intelligence agents, in my experience, are even

bigger liars than journalists, and the historians who try to reconstruct the past out of their records are, for the most part, dealing with fantasy." M. Muggeridge, *Chronicles of Wasted Time: The Infernal Grove*, London: Collins, 1973, 149.

12 A sampling since 2011 would find the following in no particular order: M. Morell, *The Great War of our Time* (2015); J. Rizzo, *Company Man* (2014); J. Rodriguez, *Hard Measures* (2012); R. McGeehee, *Deadly Deceits* (2015); A. Trabue, *A Life of Lies and Spies*; H. Crumpton, *The Art of Intelligence* (2012); R. Grenier, *88 Days to Kandahar* (2015); R. Holm, *The Craft We Chose* (2012); S. Methven, *Laughter in the Shadows* (2014); J. Kiriakou, *The Reluctant Spy* (2012).

13 See, for example, G. Miller, "CIA Employee's Request to Release Information 'destroyed my entire career'," *Washington Post*, 4 July 2014, www.washingtonpost. com/world/national-security/cia-employees-quest-to-release-information-destroyed-my-entire-career/2014/07/04/e95f7802–0209–11e4–8572–4b1b969b6322_story.html [accessed 16/11/15].

Part I
ISI's Early Days

1   ISI's Origins

It was late summer 1947. The British had partitioned India, and communal violence was breaking out in the now divided Punjab. A man in his late thirties named Syed Shahid Hamid found himself among the millions of Muslim refugees fleeing their homes in India for the new state of Pakistan. Hamid was an Urdu speaker with family roots in Lucknow, a city with a large Muslim population that now lay inside the borders of independent India. Like many other refugees, reaching the safety of Pakistan was uppermost in Hamid's mind. One thing, however, set him apart from the others: he was a Lieutenant Colonel in the army of the now defunct British Raj, and he was bent on joining the new Pakistani army. He had been trained at Sandhurst and seen war at first-hand in the Burmese jungle fighting against Japan. Most importantly for his future military career, Shahid Hamid was well-connected: he had served as Personal Secretary to Field Marshal Claude Auchinleck, the last commander of the British Indian Army and was linked by family and friendship to the new Pakistani Prime Minister, Liaquat Ali Khan.[1]

Hamid was luckier than most refugees: although forced to leave his wife and children at the hill station of Simla while he prepared their home in Pakistan, he could rest assured that his old boss, Field Marshal Auchinleck, would personally take care of his family when they too moved to Pakistan. In fact, the family reached Pakistan unscathed; however, the experience of Partition left an indelible mark as Hamid recorded in his autobiography:

They passed through armed crowds and jeeps loaded with armed men and saw Muslims being shot and their property burned. At Kalka, the caravan was joined by Colonel Ayub Khan, who was evacuating his family.[2]

An estimated 12 to 15 million refugees were generated as a result of Partition. Perhaps a million were killed.[3] Tens of thousands were slaughtered on trains headed to India and Pakistan, while uncounted more died of starvation, thirst and disease. The aforementioned Colonel Ayub Khan, a future President of Pakistan, later recorded his own impressions of Partition:

This was the unhappiest period of my life. I had never before seen anything so terrible and brutal. Women and children were mutilated and innocent people butchered mercilessly. All human qualities seemed to have been snuffed out and the whole edifice of civilization crumbled.[4]

Hamid and Ayub were equally shocked to see the British Indian Army fracture along communal lines. Another officer named Akhtar Abdul Rahman was escorting a refugee train to Pakistan when Hindu soldiers seized him and tied him up. Akhtar had all but given up hope for his life when some Muslim soldiers rescued him. Thirty years later Akhtar, an inveterate adversary of India, would be appointed Director General of Pakistan's Inter-Services Intelligence Directorate (ISI).[5]

Building a state from scratch

The challenges didn't end when these officers reached Pakistan. Whereas India emerged from Partition with the imperial capital of New Delhi, the facilities of the British Indian Army General Staff and all of the munitions plants, Pakistan inherited precious little. Its new "capital" was a sleepy fishing port of half a million named Karachi. It possessed little in the way of government infrastructure let alone an army that, at independence, existed only on paper. Thousands of its officers were still on their way while others languished in a Lahore transit camp awaiting reassignment. Moreover, all of their relevant personnel records were trapped in New Delhi and would not reach Pakistan until months later. Out of 46 pre-Partition military training establishments, Pakistan inherited seven, including the School of Military Intelligence in Karachi.[6] Army General Headquarters was a makeshift, understaffed operation hastily set up in the city of Rawalpindi. Even office supplies were lacking as Shahid Hamid noted in his diary:

> There is no Government of Pakistan but it is being created overnight. There are no Government offices, no ministries, and no office furniture or stationery. Typewriters are a luxury. It is utter chaos but there is a will to organize all as soon as possible.[7]

Even when the officers still en route to Pakistan were added up, the new army faced a critical officer shortage, especially in technical disciplines like communications and logistics as well as senior ranks; the Pakistanis were forced to hire British officers on short-term contracts even for such posts as Commander-in-Chief.[8] Material and personnel limitations aside, the new army was burdened with more responsibilities than it could possibly handle. Since the civilian bureaucracy barely existed, it was up to the nascent armed forces to provide some semblance of administration in civilian areas while, at the same time, guarding refugee convoys, setting up refugee camps, tamping down civil strife and monitoring the sensitive frontier region bordering Afghanistan.

Other obstacles lay in the army's path. The first and foremost was a resentful Indian neighbor whose population was four times larger. Some Indian politicians were openly hostile toward Pakistan while others eagerly predicted its near-term collapse. Second, New Delhi was reluctant to part with those material and financial resources earmarked for Pakistan after independence. Only a Mahatma Gandhi hunger strike forced the government to hand over some currency reserves, but a lot of military equipment never reached Pakistan. Finally, Pakistan's geography couldn't have been worse from a military perspective given that East Bengal (later Bangladesh) and the western Pakistani provinces were physically separated by over 1,000 miles of Indian territory.

Proxy war in Kashmir

All in all, it was a difficult start for a country with no government, no bureaucracy and no army. Worse was yet to come, however, in a land called Kashmir. When India and Pakistan gained their independence in August 1947, Kashmir's status was uncertain. A mountain kingdom with an overwhelming Muslim majority, Kashmir was ruled by a Hindu maharaja who was contemplating his own independence bid rather than acceding to Pakistan or India. Still, some of the maharaja's Muslim subjects in Gilgit and Baltistan managed to break away and merge with Pakistan; as for the rest, the ruler used his Hindu-dominated army to suppress Muslim revolts.[9] The result was an outbreak of communal violence and yet another refugee exodus into Pakistan (see Map 1.1).

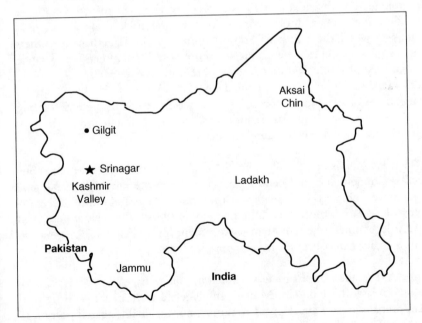

Map 1.1 Kashmir, Summer 1947.

As far as the Pakistani government was concerned, Kashmir's future should never have been in doubt: a Muslim majority area, Kashmir was destined to join Pakistan. Indeed, Pakistanis argued, Kashmir was the "K" in Pakistan. But Indian Prime Minister Jawaharlal Nehru had other ideas. A descendant of Hindu "Pandits" who originally lived in the Kashmir Valley, Nehru was emotionally committed to absorbing Kashmir into his secular Indian state. The longer the maharaja dithered, the more restless the Pakistanis grew, especially as they tried absorbing thousands of Kashmiri refugees over and above the millions still pouring in from India. Not surprisingly, some army officers demanded action, including Colonel Akbar Khan who persuaded Prime Minister Liaquat Ali Khan to order a proxy war and force the maharaja's hand. Liaquat agreed, stipulating that Pakistan's hand in the fighting be kept hidden. Akbar took this as a blank check and proceeded to train and arm Pashtun and Kashmiri insurgents for insertion into Kashmir.[10]

On 22 October 1947, a Pashtun tribal army answered the call for jihad and invaded Kashmir. Among its ranks, and discreetly trying to lead them, were some disguised Pakistani army officers who, if captured, were to say they were "on leave" when they got caught up in the fighting.[11] In this way, a precedent was set for future Pakistan-backed proxy wars: the so-called plausible deniability factor, which let the government maintain a façade of non-involvement in insurgencies that it was covertly backing. At first, the invaders made considerable progress. The maharaja's army was swept away, and the ruler panicked and fled his capital, Srinagar. But then the momentum shifted: the tribesmen's advance stalled outside Srinagar, the maharaja signed an accession agreement with India and Indian forces were flown into the Kashmir Valley. By November, Indian forces were rolling back the Pashtuns and advancing toward the Pakistan-Kashmir border. Colonel Akbar and others struggled to stem the tide by calling for more army "volunteers" to provide much-needed planning, logistics and communications expertise.[12]

The Pakistan government denied any involvement in the conflict, although it was, of course, openly "sympathetic" to the insurgents fighting for a "free Kashmir." It was a difficult façade to maintain as a *Times* of London correspondent discovered in January 1948:

> That Pakistan is unofficially involved in aiding the raiders is certain. Your correspondent has first-hand evidence that arms, ammunition and supplies are being made available to the Azad ["Free"] Kashmir forces. A few Pakistani officers are also helping to direct the operations. And however much the Pakistani government may disallow intervention, moral and material support is certainly forthcoming.[13]

Despite Akbar's best efforts, defeat seemed imminent by April 1948. SIGINT stations operated by Pakistani Military Intelligence were picking up signs of Indian preparations to attack Azad Kashmir, the so-called liberated portion of the original state that still remained in Pakistan's hands.[14] For the country's leadership the consequences of losing Azad Kashmir to India would be dire. First, Indian forces would be ideally placed to carry out an offensive into Pakistan proper. Second, Azad Kashmir would give India the "commanding heights" over sensitive communications lines in northern Pakistan. Third, an Indian occupation of Azad Kashmir would trigger a new wave of refugees into a Pakistan that was already on the verge of collapse. As the Indians drew closer to the border, Indian and Pakistani forces were about to clash directly for the first time. These countries were not even a year old.

Birth of the PIC

The difficult circumstances behind Pakistan's birth provide an essential back-drop to our examination of that country's intelligence community in general and ISI in particular. Pakistan epitomized the term "security state" from its very beginning due to the traumas of Partition, Indian hostility, a contested border with Afghanistan and the Kashmir war. Thus, it is no surprise that the new state desperately needed intelligence on India and Afghanistan. On the domestic front, its leadership faced a host of challenges that required close monitoring. In the North-West Frontier Province (NWFP) and the Federally Administered Tribal Areas (FATA), Pashtun nationalists were demanding a referendum on a separate Pashtun state. Troubles were emerging in East Bengal while Balochi tribal leaders had already declared independence. An Islamic religious party called the *Jama'at-e-Islami* was openly hostile to the cre-ation of Pakistan. All of these dissonant voices reflected the sheer diversity of the new state, which Pakistan's elites tended to see as more of a threat than a boon. Paradoxically, by suppressing diversity in the name of national unity, Pakistan's founding fathers were jeopardizing the long-term stability of their state.

The civilian Intelligence Bureau (IB) was the most powerful agency in the early days of the PIC. It was responsible for internal security, intelligence col-lection and analysis, counter intelligence and UW in Kashmir. It was a lineal descendant of the pre-Partition Delhi IB, a British-run political police that monitored the Raj's many enemies from Communists and Sikh nationalists to religious extremists and the Indian National Congress.[15] At Partition, the Delhi IB's Deputy Director was a Bengali Muslim named Ghulam Ahmed, who opted for Pakistan and brought with him some intelligence files as well as his professional experience.[16] Not long afterwards, Ahmed was appointed as the first Director of Pakistan's IB. As was the case across the bureaucracy, Ghulam Ahmed had to build up the IB virtually from scratch, and his biggest hurdle was acquiring the staff necessary to run a security service (see Figure 1.1).[17]

From its inception, the IB was burdened with too many missions that taxed its very limited capabilities. Its intelligence requirements were over-whelming, ranging from the restless NWFP and Afghanistan to the break-away Balochistan chieftains and numerous domestic opponents. Finally, there was the not-so-covert war in Kashmir for which the IB had little experience and even fewer resources. In short, the IB was overwhelmed, and it could not expect much assistance from the Special Branches that served as the "eyes and ears" of the provincial governors in political matters.[18]

The post-Partition military intelligence establishment was small and equally lacking in staff, doctrine and equipment. Military Intelligence – or army intelligence – was, and remains, the most powerful of the service agencies. A remnant of the British Indian Army intelligence apparatus, Pakistani Military Intelligence started out with a rudimentary infrastructure, no offices and few trained staff officers. In fact, of the pre-Partition Indian Army Intelligence Corps, Pakistan inherited a grand total of ten officers, 27 junior commissioned officers and 102 NCO. This was a fraction of the numbers necessary to meet the army's intelligence requirements.[19] Pakistan did inherit the School of Military Intelligence based in Karachi; however, its British instructors had destroyed most of the teaching materials before departing in 1947.[20]

In March 1948, as the conflict was heating up in Kashmir, Military Intelligence was made a directorate in its own right led by Colonel Mohamed Abdul Latif Khan and responsible for army counter intelligence and security as well as tactical and operational intelligence collection and analysis.[21] Starting in October 1947, it published a monthly intelligence review that examined internal security and regional developments in Iran, Afghanistan, Burma and Tibet.[22] Military Intelligence also inherited some British SIGINT facilities such as the pre-independence Indian Special Wireless Depot in Abbottabad responsible for monitoring Farsi language communications in Afghanistan and Iran.[23] SIGINT was an unusual feature of the first Kashmir war in that both sides not only shared the same languages (English, Urdu-Hindi, Punjabi) but also used the same encryption and broadcast frequencies. Consequently, it was easy for one side to intercept or jam the communications of the other. The Pakistanis first started monitoring Indian communications in December 1947, and they used this data to build up a comprehensive survey of Indian units in Kashmir and Punjab.[24]

In July 1948, Military Intelligence was reduced in size and responsibilities after Pakistan's military intelligence community was reorganized. As of 1950, it had 10–12 officers responsible for counter intelligence and assessing Indian military capabilities and order of battle.[25] By then Military Intelligence had ceded several of its missions to a new, all-military organization called the Inter-Services Intelligence Directorate (ISI) (see Figure 1.1).

Creation of ISI

ISI was the brain child of Major General Sir Walter J. Cawthorn, a former senior military intelligence officer in the British Indian Army, and Shahid Hamid, the well-connected Pakistan army brigadier whom we met at the beginning of this chapter. Cawthorn and Hamid quickly had to find facilities in Pakistan's new capital for their new creation, but this was by no

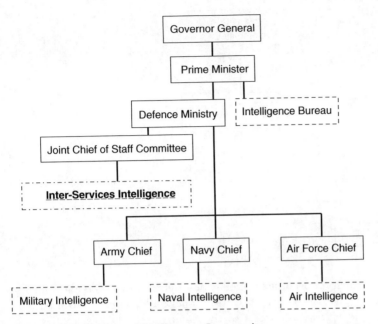

Figure 1.1 Early Pakistani Intelligence Community.

means easy since its population had swelled considerably after independence as refugees flooded into the city looking for residences and jobs. Eventually, a one-storey building was found on the corner of Old Victoria Street and Sir Ghulam Hussain Hidayatullah Road.[26] It was a Spartan outfit: office supplies were still scarce, so packing cases served as chairs and desks. In typical bureaucratic fashion, other military organizations were reluctant to share their scarce staff with a competing agency. All in all, it was a slow start for ISI.[27]

At birth, ISI was comprised of two bureaus: the Joint Intelligence Bureau (JIB) and the Joint Counter Intelligence Bureau (JCIB) (see Figure 1.2). The JIB was modeled after the British JIB, created in 1946 by Major General Kenneth Strong in an attempt to consolidate British military intelligence. Strong's organization was intended to collect intelligence on economics and logistics, military geography, ports, airports, beaches, communications as well as various scientific and technical subjects. In addition, the UK JIB provided strategic analysis for senior military and political leaders. In Strong's vision, the UK JIB would serve as the hub of a Commonwealth intelligence apparatus that would include parallel JIBs in Melbourne, Ottawa, Karachi and New Delhi. In this manner, everyone could pool their resources and area expertise for the benefit of the whole.[28] As we shall see shortly, the notion of Karachi and New Delhi sharing intelligence with each other was a fantasy that never proceeded beyond the planning stage.

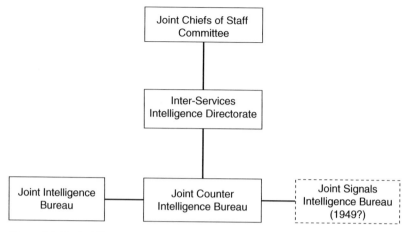

Figure 1.2 Early ISI Organization.

The JCIB supervised counter intelligence operations within the military services. In a conversation with a British colleague, Cawthorn stressed that the JCIB would enjoy "full access to the Civilian IB and its activities." In fact, the JCIB assumed control of those counter intelligence duties that had hitherto been performed by the IB with regard to the armed forces.[29] Its mission was to locate, neutralize and/or double foreign agents; it also conducted interrogations and performed background checks on Pakistani officers. This latter mission didn't exactly endear ISI to the office cadre, and there has always been friction between the JCIB and the service counter intelligence offices.[30] If it had a spy in its ranks, the army naturally wanted to carry out its own investigation (and presumably cover up any embarrassing errors). Consequently, it was agreed that ISI would retain counter intelligence supremacy in cases involving personnel of two or more services; otherwise, the service's own counter intelligence agencies would prevail.[31]

At the outset, ISI suffered from a shortage of technical personnel and managers, so in August 1948, General Cawthorn asked the British Joint Intelligence Committee to help identify "suitable" intelligence officers willing to head up the JIB and JCIB. Cawthorn emphasized that the JCIB director position needed to be filled on an urgent basis. Although he did not say so in his correspondence, Cawthorn believed that UK–Pakistan intelligence sharing depended on Pakistan retaining a British JCIB director. This would alleviate UK concerns about Pakistani information security and counter intelligence capabilities.[32] By April 1949, the UK JIC had identified candidates for both positions; unfortunately their names cannot be found in the declassified UK archives.[33]

While Cawthorn worked his British connections, Shahid Hamid was putting together the nucleus of his team. He benefited from the assistance offered by his friend Ghulam Ahmed, the Director of the IB, in recruiting promising military officers for intelligence work.[34] In fact, Hamid was surrounded by an array of talented young officers in those days such as Sahabzada Yaqub Khan, an erudite scion of a prominent pre-Partition Indian ruling family who was captured by the Germans in North Africa during World War II. While languishing in a POW camp, Yaqub Khan taught himself German, Italian, French and Russian. When he was transferred to ISI in 1948, Yaqub Khan was appointed Director of the JIB instead of the anticipated British candidate. As such, he was the chief of ISI analysis during the last months of the Kashmir war.[35]

Major Mohamed Zahiruddin was another outstanding officer who joined ISI. Most likely, he was Cawthorn's choice, for they had known each other since World War II when Cawthorn recruited him to spy behind Japanese lines in Burma. Zahiruddin bravely served under cover for nearly three years before he was finally captured by the Japanese. When Rangoon fell to the Allies in May 1945, Cawthorn personally sent a plane to bring the newly released Zahiruddin – aka Agent BACKHAND – home with honors. The former spy opted for Pakistan and was appointed Commandant of the School of Military Intelligence from December 1947 to May 1948.[36] When Zahiruddin was transferred to ISI in the fall of 1948, Director Shahid Hamid provided this assessment:

> [Zahiruddin had] great depth of knowledge, sincerity of purpose and dedication. He was most unconventional, an introvert, and morose.... He had an analytical mind, his appreciation of a situation was faultless and his conclusions were always solid.[37]

Shahid Hamid had a unique opportunity to set his personal mark on ISI. He certainly played the political game well given his relationships with important Pakistanis and interactions with Karachi-based diplomats and military attachés. He also took the time to explore the physical layout of Pakistan's future battlefields both in the Northern Areas and the salt marshes of the Rann of Kutch to the south.[38] Still, there are signs that he was frustrated with his ISI assignment. According to a November 1948 British report, "Shahid Hamid is not thought to be making much of his appointment as Head of the Interservices Intelligence Directorate in Karachi."[39] This report doesn't detail the reasons for Hamid's unhappiness, but it probably stemmed from serving in a non-combat agency while his country was at war with India. He was also grappling with the teething problems that afflict new government bureaucracies. No doubt ISI had to fight hard for its share of the pie in a competitive, under-resourced, intelligence community. Then there were the constant demands of the Kashmir war.

ISI struggled with its growing list of tasks and lack of resources. In October 1948, the senior British military representative in Pakistan visited Shahid Hamid at ISI HQ. Hamid's visitor noticed the rudimentary nature of the organization, which he recorded in a report forwarded to London: "It is only just starting and there is a considerable amount of work to be done in the way of alterations to the buildings, etc." Hamid assessed that he needed two more months before his agency would be ready for operations and anticipated an eventual staff of 10–12 Army, 3–4 Navy and 5–6 Air Force officers. At the end of the meeting, Hamid surprised his British colleague when he unveiled a detailed Indian order of battle chart developed by his staff.[40]

In November 1948, ISI produced another assessment of Indian military capabilities entitled *The Expansion of the Indian Armed Forces since 15 August 1947*. The estimate boldly predicted that India would not invade Pakistan "at present"; however, analysts were concerned about the Indian armaments industry believed to be running at full capacity. Since India had inherited all of British India's arms production plants, its self-sufficiency in some weapons categories was to be a long-term ISI obsession.[41]

On 1 January 1949, scarcely five months after ISI was created, a UN-brokered ceasefire brought the first Kashmir war to a halt. Neither party was satisfied with the outcome, which left them each with only pieces of the original state of Kashmir. Pakistan possessed a rump state called Azad Kashmir as well as the lightly populated and remote Northern Areas while India retained the heavily populated Vale of Kashmir, Jammu and Ladakh.

The Kashmir war taught Pakistan's leaders some important lessons such as the need for well-trained, experienced covert action/UW specialists. Colonel Akbar Khan was a brilliant improviser in the field when it came to training and organizing irregular forces, but he lacked a doctrine, a system, a *process* for fighting these kinds of wars. The war also demanded intelligence on a broad range of topics including local cultures, public opinion, Indian military dispositions, Indian intentions and the attitudes of foreign powers like the US, UK and the Soviet Union. Finally, the Kashmir conflict demonstrated that only reliable local allies who knew the terrain and people could execute a successful insurgency campaign. Pakistan would try to address some of these requirements in the future; others were never solved. In any case, in the immediate aftermath of the war the civilian IB – not ISI – owned the portfolio for a new phase of UW in Indian Kashmir.

Notes

1 S. Hamid, *Disastrous Twilight: A Personal Record of the Partition of India*, London: Leo Cooper, 1986, 40, 247.
2 Ibid., 247.
3 See, for example, Y. Khan, *The Great Partition*, New Haven: Yale University Press, 2008, 155–156.
4 A. Khan, *Friends Not Masters*, New York: Oxford University Press [hereafter OUP], 1967, 17.
5 M. Yousaf, *Silent Soldier: The Man Behind the Afghan Jehad*, Lahore: Jang, 1991, 27–32.
6 F.M. Khan, *The Story of the Pakistan Army*, Lahore: OUP, 1964, 48; M. Musa, *Jawan to General: Recollections of a Pakistani Soldier*, Karachi: East and West Publishing Company, 1987, 74–75; S. Nawaz, *Crossed Swords: Pakistan, Its Army, and the Wars Within*, Karachi: OUP, 2008, 30.

7 Hamid, *Disastrous Twilight*, op. cit., 939, 228.
8 S. Cohen, *The Pakistan Army*, Karachi: OUP, 1998, 17.
9 Pakistan's Northern Areas or Gilgit-Baltistan as they are known today.
10 A. Khan, *Raiders in Kashmir*, Islamabad: National Book Foundation, 1975, 19; A. Jamal, *Shadow War: The Untold Story of Jihad in Kashmir*, Hoboken, NJ: Melville House, 2009, 467; S. Riza, *The Pakistan Army: 1947–1949*, Dehra Dun: Natraj Publishers, 1977, 272.
11 Jamal, *Shadow*, op. cit., 45–46.
12 N.C. Behera, *Demystifying Kashmir*, Washington, DC: Brookings, 2006, 74–75; A. Jalal, *The State of Martial Rule*, Cambridge: Cambridge University Press, 1990, 58–59; S.P. Kapur and S. Ganguly, "The Jihad Paradox: Pakistan and Islamist Militancy in South Asia," *International Security* 37:1, Summer 2012, 118.
13 *The Times*, 13 January 1948.
14 D. Ball, "Signals Intelligence (SIGINT) in Pakistan," *Strategic Analysis* 18:2, May 1995, 198.
15 R.J. Aldrich, "American Intelligence and the British Raj: The OSS, the SSU and India, 1942–1947," *INS* 13:1, 1998, 150–151, 159.
16 L.P. Sen, *Slender was the Thread: Kashmir Confrontation*, New Delhi: Orient Longmans, 1973, 26–28; A. Raina, *Inside RAW: the Story of India's Secret Service*, New Delhi: Vikas, 1981, 7–8.
17 S. Hamid, *Early Years of Pakistan*, Lahore: Ferozsons, 1993, 69; S. Chaulia, "The Longest Jihad: India, Pakistan and the Secret Jihad," Book Review, *Asia Times Online*, 5 May 2007, www.atimes.com/atimes/South_Asia/IE05Df02.html [accessed 19/11/14].
18 Aldrich, "American Intelligence," op. cit., 15; Raina, *Raw*, op. cit., 7; Nawaz, *Crossed*, op. cit., 27; Chaulia, "Longest Jihad," op. cit.; H. Haqqani, *Pakistan: Between Mosque and Military*, Washington, DC: Carnegie Endowment, 2005, 29–30; P.C. Joshi, *Main Intelligence Outfits of Pakistan*, New Delhi: Anmol Publications, 2008, 57–59.
19 "History of Corps of Military Intelligence" found in www.pakarmymuseumcom/exhibits/history-of-corps-of-military-intelligence/ [accessed 15/9/14].
20 G.A. Khan, *Glimpses into the Corridors of Power*, Karachi: OUP, 2007, 48–49; Musa, *Jawan*, op. cit., 63–64; Riza, *Pakistan Army*, op. cit., 227–228.
21 Riza, *Pakistan Army*, op. cit., 155; H. Hussain, "The Beginnings – Early Days of Intelligence in Pakistan," *Small Wars Journal*, http://council.smallwarsjournal.com [accessed 12/6/14].
22 See, for example, Army Headquarters Pakistan, *Monthly Intelligence Review*, no. 1, 10 October 1947, found in WO 208/4962, United Kingdom National Archives (hereafter UKNA).
23 A. Stripp, *Codebreaker in the Far East*, Oxford: OUP, 1995, 49–53.
24 Correspondence from A.M. Reed, UK High Commission, Lahore, 30 November 1948, WO 208/4961, UKNA; F.M. Khan, *Story*, op. cit., 91, 118–119; A. Khan, *Raiders*, op. cit., 83.
25 General Headquarters Pakistan, *Monthly Intelligence Review*, no. 4, 10 January 1948, found in WO 208/4962, UKNA.
26 Hussain, "Beginnings," op. cit.
27 Ibid.
28 H. Dylan, "The Joint Intelligence Bureau: (Not So) Secret Intelligence for the Post-War World," *INS*, 27:1, 2012, 27, 31–32.
29 A. Gerolymatos, *Castles Made of Sand*, New York: St. Martin's Press, 2010, 255n9.
30 S.A.I. Tirmazi, *Profiles in Intelligence*, Lahore: Combined Printers, 1995, 5–6, 200.
31 *The Story of the Pakistan Air Force: A Saga of Courage and Honor*, Islamabad: Shaheen Foundation, 1988, 651–652; M.A. Khan, *Trumped Up as An Indian Spy*, Lahore: Mohammad Akram Khan, 2002.

32 Chiefs of Staff Committee, Joint Intelligence Committee, meeting minutes of 24 February 1949, CAB 159/5 PART 1, UKNA; Note prepared by W.J. Cawthorn, 28 September 1948, 2 pages, found in DEFE 11/31, UKNA.
33 Chiefs of Staff Committee, Joint Intelligence Committee, meeting notes for 22 April 1949, CAB 159/5 PART 1, UKNA.
34 Hussain, "Beginnings," op. cit.
35 A. Dil, ed., *Strategy, Diplomacy, Humanity: Life and Work of Sahabzada Yaqub-Khan,* San Diego: Takshila Research University, 2005, 17–18, 39; Riza, *Pakistan Army,* op. cit., 190.
36 Hamid, *Early,* op. cit., 67–68; Hussain, "Beginnings"; N. West, *Historical Dictionary of World War II Intelligence,* Plymouth: Rowman & Littlefield, 2008, 16.
37 Hamid, *Early,* op. cit., 68–69.
38 Ibid., 73.
39 Correspondence from A.H. Reed, British High Commission Office, Rawalpindi, 23 November 1948, WO 208/4961, UKNA.
40 Correspondence from Brig. J.F. Walker, British High Commission, Karachi, 7 October 1948, WO 208/4961, UKNA; Correspondence from Brig. J.F. Walker, British High Commission, Karachi, 6 November 1948, WO 208/4961, UKNA.
41 Correspondence from Brig. J.F. Walker, 6 November 1948, op. cit.

2   ISI and Anglo-American Intelligence

The US Joint Chiefs of Staff define UW as "[a]ctivities conducted to enable a resistance movement or insurgency to coerce, disrupt or overthrow an occupying power or government by operating through or with an underground auxiliary and guerrilla force in a denied area."[1] UW has been a foreign policy tool of the Pakistani state since 1947, although it is usually packaged as "liberation struggle" or "jihad." Kashmir was the arena where Pakistan first honed its UW strategy, and the lessons learned there contributed to the development of a coherent UW doctrine.

Covert wars in Kashmir

Pakistani frustration mounted steadily in the months following the 1949 Kashmir ceasefire, and there was a widespread belief that the United Nations was not doing enough to resolve the dispute. But there was little the Pakistanis could do in terms of conventional warfare since they lacked weapons, supplies and trained personnel. Meanwhile, New Delhi's administrative steps to incorporate Kashmir into the Indian Union were generating concerns in Karachi that Kashmir might be all but lost. Such fears drove the Pakistanis to pursue UW once again, only this time the campaign would be handled by the civilian IB. Thus, what emerged in the early 1950s in Kashmir was a covert struggle between India's and Pakistan's civilian intelligence agencies, where the Pakistan IB infiltrated agents into Kashmir and the Indians tried hunting them down.[2]

The Pakistan IB recruited agents among Kashmiri refugees, some of whom were sent back to Indian Kashmir in order to spy, recruit and conduct sabotage. It helped that in these early years of the conflict Pakistan commanded the sympathies and loyalties of many Kashmiris. According to a former Director of the Indian IB, such sympathizers "formed a useful base for Pakistan to exploit, and as many of them had been sent back deliberately in earlier years for this very purpose, they lent themselves readily to subversion and sabotage, and they formed the links between Pakistani intelligence and the local population."[3]

Mobilization crises

Kashmir aside, Indo–Pakistani rivalries were also aggravated by Pakistan's internal crises. In 1949–1950, communal Muslim-Hindu clashes broke out in East Bengal, and as the violence spread, Hindu Bengalis began fleeing to India for refuge.[4] Indian West Bengal was plagued by internal conflicts of its own, and the arrival of East Bengali refugees only made matters worse. Both Indian politicians and military officers were alarmed: the memory of Partition and its traumas were still fresh in the minds of many, and events in West Bengal seemed to portend a similar communal disaster. These anxieties infected Pakistan as well. In a 13 March 1950 memorandum to Pakistan's Defence Secretary, Major General Cawthorn, warned:

> Certain major troop movements were being carried out in India. Some of them may have considerable significance, in respect of India's intentions. One deduction is that they may be preparatory to political pressure – or even an ultimatum to Pakistan – in connection with either the Kashmir situation or [East Bengal] or both.[5]

General Gracey, Pakistan's Army Commander-in-Chief, was not convinced India was preparing for an attack. Nonetheless, ISI was tasked with searching for key warning signatures such as the movement of Indian armored brigades toward the border or stepped up rhetoric on All India Radio. Eventually, the Pakistanis sent a warning to New Delhi highlighting their concerns about the crisis. The border tensions subsided for a while, but the unrest in East Bengal continued.[6]

In the summer of 1951, the roles were reversed. In May and June, the Indian IB assessed that Pakistan was planning to destabilize Kashmir and force the Indians to the negotiating table.[7] India responded to this intelligence by concentrating forces on Pakistan's Punjab border, reinforcing garrisons in Kashmir and deploying some units to forward positions near East Bengal. ISI detected these deployments, and their assessments of a possible Indian attack triggered alarm bells in Karachi and Rawalpindi. The Punjab provincial government even temporarily moved its capital, since Lahore was too close to the Indian border.[8] For the small ISI staff, monitoring this unfolding crisis was stressful. ISI Director Hamid later recorded that he "had many sleepless nights trying to fathom [Indian] intentions and locate their movements."[9] Lieutenant Colonel Sahabzada Yaqub Khan directed ISI's analytical arm during this crisis, and his staff struggled to locate India's First Armoured Division, normally based at Meerut but now missing some key units. Were the Indians about to launch a surprise attack?[10]

It was Hamid's job to present ISI's threat assessment to Prime Minister Liaquat Ali Khan. ISI believed Indian actions were neither an exercise nor a political demonstration, but a preparation for war. In Hamid's later recollections, Liaquat was attentive, "smoking one cigarette after another." "Are you sure of your facts?" he demanded. Hamid replied: "Sir, I would not have come to you if I were not convinced of the Indian intentions."[11] Hamid's reassurances were apparently all that Liaquat needed, for on 15 July he delivered a speech alleging that 90 percent of the Indian army was deployed along the borders of both Pakistans.[12] On the 16th, Indian Prime Minister Nehru acknowledged his army's deployments, but argued they "had been necessitated by the recent preparations by Pakistan for raids and sabotage in Indian territory."[13] Eleven days later, Liaquat Ali Khan presented his famous "clenched fist" to India, proclaiming that "from today onwards our symbol is this!"[14]

Tensions escalated as both sides issued public threats and deployed more forces to their borders, but then the crisis eased, and by late November units were being withdrawn from the front lines.[15] Another Indo-Pakistan war had been averted for now, but the mobilization crises of 1950–1951 highlighted important features of Indian and Pakistani crisis decision-making that recurred in the future. Both sides lacked accurate intelligence of the other's intentions, thereby giving rise to dangerous misinterpretations and miscalculations. When military deployments *were* detected, the information was rarely sufficient to let analysts definitively answer three crucial questions: (1) *Is this an exercise?* (2) *Is it part of a peacetime redeployment?* (3) *Is it the lead-up to an attack?* The challenge in answering these would haunt ISI decades later, when the consequences of poor analysis could be nuclear war.

Searching for intelligence

ISI's brief exposure to the Kashmir war taught it some important lessons. The success of any UW strategy depends in large part on intelligence. Intelligence of the adversary's intent and capabilities is one major hurdle, but UW practitioners also require information on tribes or similar social groups in the target area, including their leaders, feuds and local histories. In addition, Pakistani leaders needed predictive analysis that would help them gauge how important third parties like the US or China would react to a Pakistan-backed insurgency against India.

In the beginning, ISI lacked well-placed agents and sophisticated SIGINT equipment. After all, it was a startup operation born out of a collapsed empire and lacking trained cadre, operating funds and technical resources. The Joint Signals Intelligence Bureau, formally subordinated to ISI in 1949, had a wireless intercept capability but probably little in the way of deciphering capabilities, since the British had taken the decrypts with them. Ultimately – and ironically – ISI desperately needed the one thing that constituted its raison d'être: timely, reliable and relevant intelligence. Good HUMINT operations require major investments in time and resources, not to mention experienced case officers. Technical surveillance equipment was available in some markets, but it required a skilled staff to set up, operate and maintain. So, where else could a new intelligence agency obtain intelligence? The answer for the Pakistanis lay with their recently departed imperial masters, the British. ISI's approach to the UK intelligence authorities wasn't completely out of left field: Pakistan was a Dominion in the British Commonwealth; it had created a JIB with the expectation of participating in a Commonwealth-wide intelligence network (see Figure 2.1); and it had invited the British to nominate the Director of its JCIB. Finally, Pakistan possessed Major General Bill Cawthorn, a man whose career literally epitomized "British Imperial intelligence."[16]

Security concerns

For ISI, any intelligence was a start. While there could be no expectations of obtaining intelligence on India from the British, the London JIB network might provide information on other threats such as the Soviet Union, Afghanistan, China and regional communist movements. Unfortunately for Karachi, information security was one of the main sticking points blocking Pakistan's access to Commonwealth intelligence. At least that was how London justified it, although one suspects that the newly independent "brown" Pakistanis and Indians were never going to be allowed to join the "White Dominions" intelligence club.[17] A February 1948 security assessment by the UK Joint Intelligence Committee was blunt: the "standard of security"

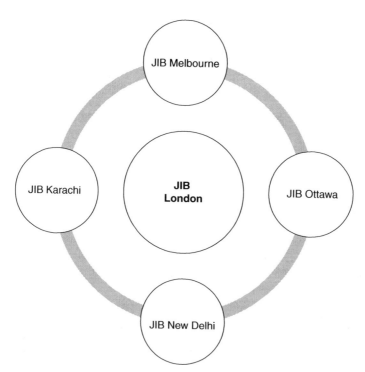

Figure 2.1 Commonwealth Joint Intelligence.

in India and Pakistan "is so low as to be practically non-existent."[18] As a consequence, the British restricted intelligence sharing with both states until they determined their long-term Commonwealth status, demonstrated better security awareness and concluded separate information security arrangements with London.[19] Early British evaluations of Pakistani security were hardly complimentary: the Pakistanis were leaking sensitive information "in all directions" lamented one investigator.[20] There was a concern that Pakistan was highly susceptible to communist infiltration, perhaps even more so than its Indian neighbor.[21] In any case, information security practices were bound to be rudimentary in Pakistan, since it was forced to build its security apparatus literally from the ground up.

Major General Cawthorn went to London in September 1948 to try and reassure his British colleagues about Pakistani security practices. He informed the UK Chiefs of Staff Committee that Pakistan would side with the West in a war with the Soviet Union. He also raised the issue of intelligence sharing, noting that Pakistan wanted to exchange intelligence with the UK on Soviet activities in Afghanistan and communism in Asia. Using a theme that was to be repeated frequently by Pakistani officials in the future, Cawthorn underscored the country's geographical proximity to the USSR as advantageous to UK intelligence. He addressed British information security concerns, arguing that Pakistan should not be considered a security risk:

> The individual sense of the importance of security is, if anything, intensified at present for example by suspicion arising from the state of relations with India, by a strong national pride in their newly won independence and by the political solidarity resulting from practically one hundred per cent adherence to a common religious faith.[22]

Cawthorn insisted that communist activity in Pakistan was minimal and pointed out that Pakistan's civilian IB was responsible for counter intelligence, investigations and enforced security practices. He added that the military's ISI had been created to unify the service intelligence branches, and its JCIB would be led by a British officer. In concluding his pitch, Cawthorn reiterated Pakistan's "great advantages" for SIGINT collection such as good access to Soviet targets.[23] But Cawthorn's overtures did not have the desired effect, because in April 1949, he sent a letter to the British Joint Intelligence Committee, repeating his request for "certain intelligence and information." In its response, the JIC "generally" agreed to share some basic intelligence materials with ISI, such as intelligence summaries and certain military intelligence academic publications like syllabi and lecture notes.[24] All in all, this was pretty thin gruel for the ISI, but at least it was a tentative step in the right direction.

In autumn 1949, ISI Director Hamid spent three weeks in the UK, studying its intelligence structure and security procedures. He spent one week at the Joint Intelligence Bureau, where he was hosted by Major General

Strong and given an introduction to the Commonwealth JIB system, followed by one day visits to the military service intelligence agencies and MI5, Britain's security service. His final stop was the Joint Intelligence Committee, where he argued for closer UK–Pakistan intelligence ties even as he acknowledged British security concerns. He described Pakistan as a unified state, whose people instinctively rejected communism. Information security was not a matter that Pakistanis took lightly, he insisted. As official host of Hamid's visit, Major General Strong noted his recent visit to ISI headquarters, adding that it was "very well organized and had made an excellent start." He predicted that ISI would work well with its Commonwealth counterparts.[25]

The UK played an important role in creating ISI and facilitating its early development. In fact, British concerns were pivotal to ISI's initial structure and missions: a JCIB to alleviate British security concerns and a JIB to "plug and play" in a larger Commonwealth intelligence network. In fact, UK intelligence and security agencies provided technical aid and advice to ISI well into the 1950s. In 1953, for example, the ISI Director asked the British Director General of Military Intelligence for help in creating a Joint Intelligence Committee-type system in Pakistan.[26] Two years later, the UK Joint Intelligence Committee hosted ISI Director-designate Brigadier Malik Sher Bahadur, who had inquired about "joint intelligence methods."[27] Still, the era of UK influence was fading fast because a new, relatively inexperienced, but much wealthier super power was cautiously entering the South Asia power game. The US CIA and its military cousins were soon to become ISI's most important foreign partners and the source of much of its training and equipment.

Red-baiting

On the night of 9 March 1951, security forces in West Pakistan arrested Major General Akbar Khan, a senior Pakistan Air Force officer, and several others in connection with an alleged conspiracy by the Communist Party of Pakistan (CPP). The following morning, Prime Minister Liaquat Ali Khan informed the nation that the conspirators' goal was to "subvert the loyalties of Pakistan's defence forces."[28] This so-called Rawalpindi Conspiracy marked an important turning point in Pakistani history. An alleged military plot had been unearthed for the first time, the CPP had been smashed, torture had been used to extract information, and the government provoked a wave of anti-communist hysteria among the people.

The Rawalpindi Conspiracy was a professional embarrassment for the military intelligence services because it was the civilian Special Branches of the NWFP and Punjab that actually uncovered the plot. After all, it was ISI's mission as well as that of the service intelligence agencies to probe officer loyalty and ensure that the army remained loyal to its political masters. Consequently, the Director of Military Intelligence, Lieutenant Colonel Mohammed Zahiruddin, was subjected to heavy criticism by the new Pakistani Army Chief, General Ayub Khan, and demoted. This was a stinging blow to Zahiruddin, who committed suicide shortly afterwards.[29] The aftermath of the Rawalpindi Conspiracy had a long-term impact on ISI as well. The military leadership had been caught off guard by the conspiracy, and steps were taken to ensure that this would not happen again. Internal security received top priority, and it often entailed spying on outspoken officers and civilian politicians who naturally resented ISI's intrusive surveillance and background investigations. Major General Nawabzada Sher Ali Khan later recalled this period with considerable distaste:

[The Rawalpindi Conspiracy] started a witch hunt and surveillance of Senior Officers of the Army who had any kind of standing and following. And this surveillance was not only confined to people whose normal duty it is to do this kind of work in any state, but a witch hunt within the Army was started and Brother Officer was encouraged to spy on Brother Officer – something unknown and quite wrong in institutions like the Army whose backbone is and must be a strong esprit de corps. It allowed the Senior Officers to be smeared by those [who claimed] to be doing so in the service of the country.[30]

The Rawalpindi Conspiracy had both foreign and domestic policy motives. Early on, the Pakistan government hyped the communist threat to curry favor with the West and obtain US weapons. In addition, there was Pakistan's geopolitical location that the country's founding father, Mohamed Ali Jinnah, argued was its main selling point:

America needs Pakistan more than Pakistan needs America ... Pakistan is the pivot of the world, as we are placed [on] the frontier on which the future position of the world evolves.[31]

This was news to most Americans who couldn't find Pakistan on a map. Still, Jinnah had a point: Pakistan enjoyed proximity to Soviet Central Asia and a China that was about to turn communist. The US Army Attaché in Karachi apparently was swayed by these arguments: in a report sent to the Pentagon he predicted that should Pakistan be invaded by the Soviet Union, the consequences "might be the balancing weight between victory or defeat at the hands of the USSR."[32] In any case, location aside, it was a fact of Cold War international relations that many states in Latin America, Europe and Asia conjured up communist threats as a way of obtaining US political, economic and military backing. The Pakistanis certainly learned to play this game better than most, frequently portraying their country as an "Islamic barrier" against the "Godless Soviets," a theme they were to employ again when the Soviets invaded Afghanistan in 1979.[33]

The IB and ISI were certainly eager to push communist threat assessments on willing CIA officials, diplomats and military attachés. An early IB analysis of the domestic communist threat painted an unlikely picture of a CPP benefiting from cash infusions, a growing staff and expanded links to university student groups and organized labor. Indeed, the government held the CPP responsible for a number of labor strikes when the party's influence was actually minimal.[34] To their credit, some US officials regarded the Pakistani assessments as overblown. In 1949–1950, some in Washington were questioning ISI's "increasingly bizarre reports" on the growing communist threat to Pakistan's stability. The ISI propaganda barrage included one communist pamphlet allegedly found in a Lahore army barracks that warned of "subterranean armies of shock troops" planning "attacks" on "nerve centres."[35] ISI followed these alarmist assessments by requesting US assistance in psychological warfare. The United States Information Service provided the spy agency with counter-propaganda themes as well as prepared pamphlets, newspapers and pre-recorded radio segments. No doubt, the CIA passed its own materials through classified channels.[36]

The PIC shared its assessments on the communist threat with the Commonwealth too. For example, on 20 September 1950, the UK Joint Intelligence Committee discussed a recent ISI report on communism in Pakistan, which some members regarded as too alarmist. The MI5 representative commented that more information was needed about the sources that underpinned ISI's analysis. In any case, the committee did not hesitate to endorse ISI's apparent eagerness to combat communism.[37]

So was the Pakistan communist threat a reality? Despite the government's invoking of a dire communist danger, the CPP was, in fact, debilitated *before* the crackdown. It had some influence over the Pakistan Federation of Trade Unions, and it did enjoy more popularity in East Bengal, where it won four out of 309 seats in March 1954 provincial elections, but this election victory led to the July 1954 decision to ban the party in that province.[38]

What about the Soviet Union, the CPP's ostensible backer? Pakistan's attitude toward Moscow was always ambiguous: on the one hand, the Soviets were the favorite whipping boy to justify approaching the Americans and British for weapons and intelligence. On the other, the Soviets offered leverage in negotiations with the West. They were especially useful in curing the Americans of their occasional infatuation with India, the supposed "prize" in the Cold War struggle for South Asia. Thus, when President Henry Truman invited Nehru to Washington in October 1949, an irritated Liaquat Ali Khan promptly announced that he was ready to go to Moscow for a visit. Liaquat Ali Khan never went to Moscow, but in May 1950, he did visit Truman only weeks after the Soviets appointed their first ambassador to Karachi.

Even as these high-level diplomatic machinations were underway, Pakistan's intelligence community was passing information to the West on Soviet influence-making in Pakistan's labor movement, an upsurge in Moscow-backed peace committees, an increased output in communist propaganda, and renewed CPP activities. On at least one occasion, Pakistan sought MI5 advice on how to monitor and restrict the activities of the Soviet embassy that were posing counter intelligence problems.[39]

The reality of Soviet influence in Pakistan was quite a bit different. In fact, the Soviets found Pakistan to be a tricky and often frustrating intelligence target: the army was clannish and hard to penetrate while the CPP was too small and isolated to be of much value. Communism had no traction in Pakistan's conservative and mainly rural society either. Since the CPP was banned, the KGB *Rezidentura* in Karachi distributed money to smaller secret left-wing groups in Sindh and East Pakistan. The KGB also managed to recruit a few Pakistani assets under false flag in the early 1960s. The most valuable of these worked in the Foreign Ministry, where they had access to diplomatic cables and cypher materials.[40]

Moving on

Within weeks of Liaquat Ali Khan's successful visit to Washington, Director Hamid transferred out of ISI for a new assignment. General Cawthorn and others had tried to convince Hamid to extend his tour but he had grown tired of intelligence work. As he confessed in his autobiography:

> The only distressing thing was that one was 'on duty' all the time and developed a habit of suspecting and believing no one. Every day produced new problems. I was the eyes and ears of the armed forces.[41]

The paranoia and suspicion linked to intelligence work was lamented by other ISI officers in the future. Indeed, from its earliest days, ISI had a dubious reputation in the military for its role in performing background checks and monitoring officer loyalty. This legacy of "spying on brother officers" plagues ISI to this day, not to mention its use of torture and intimidation to keep the politically questionable in line.[42] Decades later, one ISI official described the change in the way his friends and colleagues regarded him after he started working for ISI:

> Overnight you become a different person in the eyes of your peers. Even superiors outside the ISI regard you with deep suspicion, as part of the ISI's function is to keep careful watch on the generals to ensure the reliability of the regime.[43]

Hamid wasn't the only one moving on. In 1951, Cawthorn left Pakistan for Australia, where he became chief of the Melbourne JIB. But he wasn't quite finished with Pakistan, for his government sent him back to that country as Australia's High Commissioner in the mid-1950s, and his many friendships with Pakistani officials made him one of the best-connected diplomats in Karachi.[44] He never quite left the spy business either, serving as Director General of the Australian Secret Intelligence Service from 1960 to 1968. Cawthorn was one of the quintessential, if underrated, spy chiefs in the early Cold War.[45]

The 1950s political scene in Pakistan was marked by a kaleidoscope of civilian governments. The same was true of ISI, which not only lacked funding and clout but witnessed its own revolving door of directors. Hamid's immediate successor appears to have been Brigadier Mirza Hamid Hussain. But Hussain's tenure was a short one, and within a year he was transferred to the Pakistani Foreign Service. Other directors in this time period include Syed Ghawas, Malik Sher Bahadur and Mohamed Hayat Khan. ISI was still a small player in the national security structure, and its dramatic ascent in the future was by no means a foregone conclusion.

US partnership

Pakistani governments came and went, but the country's national security challenges remained the same, and the most potent of these was, of course, India. How could a much smaller Pakistan offset India's population and economic and military advantages, not to mention commanding geopolitical position? How could Pakistan make India yield on the Kashmir problem? If it came down to it, how could Pakistan deter an Indian invasion? The army arrived at two early solutions to these challenges. One was to seek an alliance with the United States. The other was to continue honing the UW strategy first unleashed on Kashmir.

Convincing the US of Pakistan's geographic importance was not too difficult given the context of the Cold War. In May 1954, the US and Pakistan signed a bilateral Mutual Defense Assistance Agreement followed by Pakistan's accession to the Southeast Asian Treaty Organization (1954) and the Baghdad Pact a year later. As it built up its early Cold War containment alliances, the US viewed Pakistan as an important part of its bulwark against communism with Pakistan as a member of two alliances aimed at the USSR and China. Ultimately, however, Pakistan's true worth to the US lay in intelligence. During the early 1950s, the Soviet Union was all but closed off to Western intelligence. Technical intelligence had yet to reach the point where Washington could send spy planes over the USSR with impunity, let alone put an imagery satellite into space. But as the "Bomber Gap" and "Missile Gap" controversies of the late 1950s showed, the US urgently needed intelligence on Soviet intentions, nuclear weapons, ballistic missiles, strategic bombers and the very large conventional military posture Moscow maintained after World War II. China was even more of a mystery to the US intelligence community since there were no American diplomatic missions in that country.

Pakistan presented a partial solution to these early Cold War intelligence problems. Together with Iran (another Baghdad Pact partner), it was well-situated for technical intelligence collection on the Soviet nuclear test site at Semipalatinsk as well as the Tyuratam ballistic missile testing ground.[46] One benefit Iran could not offer was Pakistan's border with China's Xinjiang Province, which contained that country's Lop Nor nuclear weapons test site. Therefore, after the 1954 defense agreement was signed, the US negotiated deals for intelligence collection facilities on Pakistani soil with an ISI delegation led by Brigadier Riaz Hussain. These arrangements enabled the US to place nuclear test monitors, over-the-horizon radars, SIGINT facilities and an airfield for U2 spy planes in Pakistan.[47] In fact, when the American U2 pilot, Gary Powers, was shot down over the USSR on 1 May 1960, the Soviets quickly learned he had taken off from Peshawar. Soon after, Soviet leader Nikita Khrushchev bluntly warned the Pakistanis to shut down the facilities or face "immediate retaliation."

One cannot overstate the importance of these intelligence sites for US assessments of Soviet strategic weapons programs. In a 9 August 1961 letter to Secretary of State Dean Rusk, the Deputy Secretary of Defense, Roswell Gilpatric, laid it all out:

> The Peshawar station is one of a very limited number of important over-seas intelligence gathering stations at which essential information, including warning intelligence can be collected. The Peshawar station enjoys a particularly favorable location with respect to Soviet missile ranges and full exploitation of the intelligence collecting possibilities there is a matter of first importance.[48]

Of course, this arrangement left Washington open to diplomatic pressure by the Pakistanis who understood the importance of these facilities to US national security. Moreover, the nature of the relationship often made ISI suspicious that the US was not sharing all the intelligence gleaned from these sites. Later, a tongue-in-cheek US memorandum commemorating the termination of US SIGINT/ELINT facilities at Badaber outside Peshawar hinted at the diplomatic obstacles linked to intelligence collection in Pakistan:

> Grasping the thorny questions of "participation" and "sharing," which caused so much anxiety among others of its kind around the world, Badaber, quickly and smoothly found a solution which left the ISID [Inter-Services Intelligence Directorate] and the PAF [Pakistan Air Force] happier, wiser and richer therefore. Even at the end of its days it bequeathed its earthly home with many of the wonders and riches therein to these beloved companions.[49]

As the above memorandum hints, there was definitely a quid pro quo for the privilege of basing intelligence facilities in Pakistan, and it was not limited to information sharing alone. When the agreement ended in the late 1960s, some of the equipment at these sites was handed over to ISI for its own use. Nonetheless, what the Pakistanis sought above all else was weapons. Therefore, as the buildings and antenna farms were being erected at Badaber, tanks, jet fighters, medium bombers, and advisors began streaming into Pakistan from the United States.[50] Less visible, but no less important, was a small cohort of US Special Forces soldiers and CIA officers whose mission was to help Pakistan expand its UW capabilities.

Notes

1 US Joint Chiefs of Staff, *Special Operations*, Joint Publication 3–05, 16 July 2014, www.dtic.mil/doctrine/new_pubs/jp3_05.pdf [accessed 29/3/15].

2 India's intelligence community evolved differently than its Pakistani cousin. New Delhi's civilian IB was unquestionably preeminent with domestic and foreign missions. India's military intelligence agencies were no match for the IB in terms of resources and political influence. In fact, India did not create a joint military intelligence organization like ISI until 2002. A. Raina, *Inside RAW: the Story of India's Secret Service*, New Delhi: Vikas, 1981, 9; B. Kasturi, "Military Intelligence in India: An Analysis," *The Indian Defence Review* (1995) www.bharat-rakshak.com/LANCER/idr00001.htm [accessed 29/3/15].

3 Raina, *RAW*, op. cit., 61.

4 East Bengal was the official name for Pakistan's eastern wing until 1955 when it was renamed East Pakistan.

5 S. Riza, *The Pakistan Army: 1947–1949*, Dehra Dun: Natraj Publishers, 1977, 2.

6 Ibid., 2–3.

7 B.N. Mullick, *My Years with Nehru: Kashmir*, Bombay: Allied Publishers, 1971, 55.

8 F.M. Khan, *The Story of the Pakistan Army*, Lahore: OUP, 1964, 103–131; H. Mubashir, *Mirage of Power: An Inquiry into the Bhutto Years, 1971–1977*, Oxford: OUP, 2000, 26.

9 S. Hamid, *Early Years of Pakistan*, Lahore: Ferozsons, 1993, 70.

10 Ibid.

11 Ibid.

12 "Pakistan Protests Indians on Border," *New York Times* [hereafter NYT], 16 July 1951, 4.

13 "Nehru Says Troops Mass for Defense," *NYT*, 17 July 1951, 4.

14 Quoted in Hamid, *Early*, op. cit., 70.

15 Ibid.; F.M. Khan, *Story*, op. cit., 132; N.S.A.K.Pataudi, *The Story of Soldiering and Politics in India & Pakistan*, Lahore: Wajdalis, 1978, 140.

16 Throughout his career, Cawthorn served in a number of British intelligence positions, including chief of the Egypt-based Middle East Intelligence Center, Director of Military Intelligence for the British Indian Army, Director of the Melbourne Joint Intelligence Bureau and head of the Australian Secret Intelligence Service.

17 "White Dominions" once referred to Canada, Australia and New Zealand.

18 Chiefs of Staff Committee, Joint Intelligence Committee, "Disclosure of Information to India and Pakistan," 5 February 1948, CAB 158/3, UKNA.

19 Ibid.

20 Chiefs of Staff Committee, Joint Intelligence Committee, report of 13 April 1948, CAB 158/3, UKNA.

21 A. Gerolymatos, *Castles Made of Sand*, New York: St. Martin's Press, 2010, 192.

22 Note prepared by W.J. Cawthorn, 28 September 1948, DEFE 11/31, UKNA.

23 Ibid.

24 Chiefs of Staff Committee, Joint Intelligence Committee, meeting notes for 7 April 1949, CAB 159/5 PART 1, UKNA.

25 Chiefs of Staff Committee, Joint Intelligence Committee, meeting notes for 16 December 1949. CAB 159/5, PART 1, UKNA.

26 Chiefs of Staff Committee, Joint Intelligence Committee, 23 December 53, CAB 159/14 PART 1, UKNA.

27 Chiefs of Staff Committee, Joint Intelligence Committee, 12 May 55, CAB 159/14 PART 3, UKNA.

28 K.A. Ali, "Of Communists, Couriers and Covert Actions," *The Express Tribune*, 17 May 2011 http://tribune.com.pk/story/169784/communists-couriers-and-covert

actions [accessed 20/3/15]; British Chiefs of Staff Committee, Joint Intelligence Committee, 20 September 1950, "Communism in Pakistan," CAB 159/8 Part 1, UKNA.

29 H. Zaheer, *The Time and Trial of the Rawalpindi Conspiracy*, 1951, Karachi, OUP: 1998, xxi; A. Khan, *Raiders in Kashmir*, Islamabad: National Book Foundation, 1975, 164; S. Nawaz, *Crossed Swords: Pakistan, Its Army, and the Wars Within*, Karachi: OUP, 2008, 83.

30 Pataudi, *Soldiering*, op. cit., 133. This is a view shared by Lt.-Gen. Jahan Dad Khan: J.D. Khan, *Pakistan Leadership Challenges*, Karachi: OUP, 1999, 33–34.

31 M. Bourke-White, *Halfway to Freedom: A Report on the New India*, New York: Simon & Schuster, 1949, 92.

32 Quoted in A. Jalal, *The Struggle for Pakistan*, Cambridge: Belknap Press, 2014, 81.

33 A. Jalal, *The State of Martial Rule*, Cambridge: Cambridge University Press, 1990, 75.

34 Zaheer, *Rawalpindi Conspiracy*, op. cit., 207–207.

35 Jalal, *State*, op. cit., 112–113.

36 Ibid., 115–116.

37 British Joint Intelligence Committee, "Communism in Pakistan," op. cit.

38 H. Zaheer, *The Separation of East Pakistan*, Dhaka: OUP, 1994, 15–16; P.I. Cheema, *Pakistan Defense Policy, 1947–58*, New York: St. Martin's Press, 1990; Zaheer, *Rawalpindi*, op. cit. 204.

39 Minutes to File by H. McEarlean, UK Foreign Office, 19 September 1950, FO 371/86764, UKNA; Jalal, *State*, op. cit., 112.

40 C. Andrew & V. Mitrokhin, *The World Was Going Our Way*, New York: Basic Books, 2005, 341–342.

41 Hamid, *Early*, op. cit., 69.

42 S.A.I. Tirmazi, *Profiles in Intelligence*, Lahore: Combined Printers, 1995, 299–300.

43 M. Yousaf & M. Adkin, *Afghanistan: The Bear Trap*, Havertown, PA: Casemate, 2001, 1–2.

44 In a 3 March 1956 entry in his diary, the former Australian Foreign Minister, R.G. Casey, described Cawthorn in glowing terms: *"Australia is fortunate in having a man like Sir Walter Cawthorn as High Commissioner to Pakistan. He has had a long history of contact with India (including what is now Pakistan) and knows Iskander Mirza, Chaudhury Mohammed Ali (Prime Minister) and General Ayub Khan (C-in-C) all intimately. As a result, although our High Commission is a small one in terms of diplomatic personnel, we are better informed than the much larger diplomatic posts in Karachi. This was confirmed to me by Iskander Mirza, who said to me, 'We have no secrets from Bill Cawthorn.'"* T.B. Millar, ed., *Australian Foreign Minister: The Diaries of R.G. Casey*, London: Collins, 1972, 230–231.

45 Gerolymatos, *Castles*, op. cit., 94; H. Hussain, "The Beginnings – Early Days of Intelligence in Pakistan," *Small Wars Journal*, http://council.smallwarsjournal.com [accessed 12/6/14].

46 J. Richelson, *The Wizards of Langley*, Boulder, CO: Westview, 2001, 36–37, 93.

47 Ibid, 36, 112, 115–116, 127, 188, 367; Memorandum from Assistant Secretary of State for Near East, James P. Grant, Subject: "Circular 175: Request for Authorization to Negotiate an Agreement with the Government of Pakistan Concerning an Expansion of the U.S. Communications Facilities at Peshawar," 14 May 1963, http://nsarchive.chadwyck.com/quick/displayMultiItemImages.do?Multi=yes& ResultsID=147D076B718&queryType=quick&QueryName=cat&ItemID=CH N01236&ItemNumber=20 [accessed 12/9/14]; Airgram from Amembassy Islamabad, 6 October 1969, A-550, "USAF Communications Station, Peshawar," NARA, RG 59, DEF 21 PAK; R.J. McMahon, *The Cold War on the Periphery*, New York: CUP, 1994, 169; Editorial Note found in FRUS, 1958–60, Vol. XV, document no. 291, 615.

48 Letter from Deputy Secretary of Defense (Gilpatric), 9 August 1961, found in http://nsarchive.chadwyck.com/nsa/documents/HN/01128/all.pdf [accessed 12/9/14].
49 Amembassy Islamabad, "USAF Communications Station."
50 D. Kux, *The United States and Pakistan, 1947–2000: Disenchanted Allies*, Washington, DC: Johns Hopkins University Press, 2001, 95–96; Memorandum from Robert W. Komer of the National Security Council Staff, 9 August 1963, FRUS 1961–1963, Vol. XIX, document no. 316, 631.

3   Covert Action in Northeast India

By the mid-1950s, Pakistan's leadership was increasingly fearful that India was creating "facts on the ground" in Kashmir and steadily eroding any local autonomy that remained. Already the Indians had staged fraudulent elections in their portion of Kashmir as the first step toward incorporating it fully into India. In response to its fear of "losing" Kashmir altogether, Pakistan steadily improved its capabilities in UW, and ISI was one of the beneficiaries.

Unconventional warfare

Pakistan's civilian IB ramped up its Kashmiri UW program in response to New Delhi's efforts to assimilate the contested region. The IB began contacting Kashmiri dissidents, including a charismatic politician named Sheikh Abdullah, who originally supported Kashmir's accession to India but later changed his mind and was thrown into prison as a result. In addition, the IB generated anti-Indian propaganda and supplied arms to Kashmiri groups who infiltrated across the ceasefire line to conduct reconnaissance and sabotage missions.[1] By the mid-1950s, though, the Pakistanis were reevaluating their UW program. Overall, the strategy was not achieving its objectives, namely weakening India, forcing a referendum on Kashmir's future and, eventually, incorporating all of 1947 Kashmir into Pakistan. A decision was therefore made to create an elite military unit that specialized in UW.

The army already had some UW experience, and we have already seen how it used Pashtun and Kashmiri proxies against the maharaja of Kashmir in 1947. Furthermore, some training in insurgency and counterinsurgency took place in East Bengal in 1950.[2] Two years prior to that, the famed British Special Operations Executive officer, Colonel Hector Grant-Taylor, established the Close Quarter Battle School in Quetta, which provided commando training. Eventually, it withered on the vine after Grant-Taylor resigned as Commandant in 1950.[3]

Not surprisingly, given the range of military projects covered by their 1954 Defense Agreement, the Pakistanis turned to the US for UW doctrine and training. At the time, the US Army Special Forces approach to UW was based on encouraging and sustaining anti-communist insurgencies and training other countries in counter insurgency. Conceived in the early years of the Cold War, when the Soviets possessed considerable advantages in conventional military power, American UW doctrine envisioned "stay-behind forces" that would conduct crippling guerrilla operations in the Soviet rear once Moscow launched a general offensive into neighboring countries.[4]

Independent of American efforts to create a specialized insurgency/ counterinsurgency force, the Pakistan army sought to develop similar capabilities, especially in the areas of direct action and insurgency support. Under the evolving Pakistani model, direct action commando missions would destroy Indian logistics nodes, ammunition dumps, communications, airfields, and command and control links. In addition, a specialized force would be trained to work alongside, arm and train anti-India insurgents. The anticipated benefits to fighting India through proxies included plausible deniability, tying down Indian forces in counter insurgency and otherwise setting the political conditions for the eventual absorption of Indian Kashmir into Pakistan. At least that was the plan.[5] In 1957, the Pakistan army established the Special Services Group (SSG) with assistance from the CIA and US Army. Directing this new unit was Lieutenant Colonel A.O. Mitha, an émigré from India, who still had a number of close relatives in Bombay.

SSG's creation reflected a broad trend in Pakistani army thinking regarding insurgent warfare. Pakistani military journals of this period examined historical and contemporary insurgent wars in China, Yugoslavia, Algeria and North Vietnam.[6] In one such article published in 1960, an officer named Aslam Siddiq laid out a concise rationale for UW:

> Irregular warfare can help in reducing the crucial nature of the initial battles of Pakistan. It can help in spreading out prolonging action. The essence of this irregular warfare is to deny the enemy targets and keep attacking him again at unexpected places.[7]

SSG and ISI formed close connections from the beginning, and these grew stronger over time as Pakistan fomented insurgencies in India's northeast and Kashmir. ISI often used the SSG to carry out insurgent training, reconnaissance and advisory roles; in fact, the SSG became ISI's "action arm." Consequently, it was no surprise that officers often transferred between these agencies at different stages in their careers, since their unique skills were applicable to both.[8]

The Naga revolt

Kashmir was not the only target of Pakistan's UW efforts. ISI selected some hill tribes in northeast India and, later, the Sikhs of Indian Punjab, as beneficiaries of Pakistani arms, training and safe haven. In fact, ISI exploited the bifurcated nature of their state for their UW campaign: West Pakistan provided access to Kashmir and Punjab while East Pakistan enabled ISI and SSG to tap into active insurgencies in India's remote Assam province. It was in this latter region that Pakistan's military intelligence chiefs discovered a tough and rugged people called the Nagas (see Map Northeast India).

The area called Nagaland bordered directly on Burma but not East Pakistan, yet the latter was close enough to serve as a training base and safe haven for Naga rebels. It is a mountainous and often densely forested area that lends itself to guerrilla warfare as the British and Japanese discovered during World War II. One author describes the setting this way:

> The jungles here can be full of strange shrieks and cries. In the monsoon, the whole of Nagaland appears to turn into a sort of shifting swamp. In the winter, the highlands can be bitterly cold. Insects with powerful bites abound. Valleys are deeply shadowed. For regular army soldiers, there were no 'front lines' in Nagaland.[9]

Living in this formidable environment are the Nagas. Due to the efforts of Christian missionaries in the late nineteenth and early twentieth centuries, many Nagas converted to Christianity and were educated in mission schools. These two facts alone – religion and literacy – served as incubators of a fierce nationalism that would flourish after Indian independence in 1947.[10] India's first Prime Minister, Jawaharlal Nehru, had little patience for Naga independence demands, especially as the British prepared to quit India. In August 1946, he left no doubt that the Naga territories were going to be part of the new Indian state: "it is obvious that the Naga territory in eastern Assam is too small to stand by itself politically and economically ... part of it consists of rather backward people who require considerable help."[11] Such condescending words did not deter some Nagas from trying to achieve their own independence. They formed a Naga National Council led by a man named Angami Zapu Phizo, and on 14 August 1947, hours before India received her own independence, Phizo proclaimed a free Nagaland state. Of course, India did not recognize this state, and the next several years witnessed a series of political skirmishes between New Delhi and its upstart Naga tribes. Meanwhile, the Naga National Council secretly created an army supplied with British and Japanese weapons abandoned in the jungle a decade earlier. In 1954, Phizo once again declared the Sovereign Republic of Nagaland.[12]

Nehru may have been an eloquent proponent of independence for countries under European rule, but he was intolerant of secessionist forces in his own state. After the Naga sovereignty declaration of 1954, Indian army units occupied parts of Nagaland and herded thousands of civilians into guarded camps to "shield" them from the Naga insurgents. Tragically, many died of famine and disease in the squalid conditions of these camps. Indian counterinsurgent operations continued in 1955, and the army was forced to commit more forces to combat the Nagas. Eventually, the tide began to turn, and the beleaguered insurgents were running out of territory, followers and arms. It was at this point that ISI entered the game.[13]

The Pakistanis were tempted by the Naga revolt: if the insurgents liberated Nagaland, their example might inspire other disgruntled Indian minorities to rise up too, including Kashmiri Muslims. Thus, when the Naga leader, Angami Zapu Phizo, reached East Pakistan in early 1956 after a long and hurried flight from his homeland, he encountered a warm reception. ISI put Phizo in a Dhaka safe house and then sent him on to London, where he tried drumming up international support for his cause. Meanwhile, a Naga rebel commander named Kaito Sema evaded Indian forces and reached East Pakistan in 1958 with a band of warriors for training.[14] ISI sent Kaito to the Sylhet area where a camp had been set up with SSG trainers, arms and other supplies. The SSG provided training in insurgency tactics, communications and medical support while the ISI imparted its expertise in intelligence and operational planning.[15] Despite the linguistic and religious differences between the Nagas and their Pakistani trainers, some SSG officers were impressed by the Naga's dedication. Colonel S.G. Mehdi, a veteran SSG officer, praised his Naga trainees years later in an interview with an Indian researcher:

> The Nagas were far better fighters than the Kashmir Mujahids. They were disciplined and dedicated and quickly picked up tactics and weapons skills. They clearly had a cause. The mujahids from Azad Kashmir were unruly. It was clear they had more interest in women and loot waiting for them in the Srinagar Valley. And morale – the mujahid would flee at the first sight of an Indian counter-attack but the Nagas would fight until the bitter end ...[16]

ISI camps in East Pakistan enabled the Naga guerrillas to rebuild their strength and regain much of the initiative lost in 1955–1956. The Indian security forces soon detected the improved capabilities of the Nagas on the battlefield, and a new cycle of accusations and denials ensued between New Delhi and Karachi.[17] For example, Pakistani President Ayub Khan announced in May 1962 that he "categorically" refused to allow a Naga exile government on Pakistani soil.[18] Yet three years later, the Indian External Affairs Minister renewed the accusations in parliament:

> A large gang of Naga hostiles crossed into Burma in October/November, 1964, with the intention of going to East Pakistan. According to reports which have been received recently, this gang, about 1,500 strong, has left East Pakistan and is now on its way back towards Nagaland. It is also reported that the gang has undergone training and collected quantities of arms and ammunition in Pakistan.[19]

The revived Naga revolt fulfilled several Pakistani objectives. At any given time, up to 30,000 Indian soldiers and paramilitaries were policing Nagaland; that meant 30,000 fewer men were facing Pakistan. Not only was the Naga revolt an irritant to the Indian army, it also raised questions about India's reputation as a democratic, socialist and secular state. Pakistan was no doubt pleased to see India's vaunted human rights record take a few hits.

Pakistan was not the only country with a vested interest in aggravating the ethnic, tribal and religious conflicts in Assam. The People's Republic of China disputed the McMahon Line, which constitutes part of its border with India, and in 1962 both fought a brief war that left India humiliated and even more obsessed with its vulnerable northeast than before. Meanwhile, Pakistan was moving toward a rapprochement with Beijing, and this culminated in 1963 with a quasi-alliance that persists to this day. The glue that holds it together is a shared animosity toward India. The Chinese were interested in aiding certain insurgent groups hostile to Indian rule such as the Maoist Naxalites in West Bengal. Not only would assisting these groups weaken India, they would also serve as retaliation for New Delhi's backing of Tibetan rebels against Beijing.[20] Sometime in the mid-1960s, Pakistan and China created a Coordinating Bureau intended to better synchronize their support for insurgencies in Assam.[21] For the Indian army, the challenge was maintaining a vigilant watch on Pakistan *and* China while, at the same time, trying to manage insurgencies within India itself.

The 1965 Indo–Pakistan war (examined in the next chapter) forced a shift in Pakistani support for the Nagas. In the post-war understanding between India and Pakistan, the latter was supposed to refrain from instigating insurgencies against the former. President Ayub thus dismissed as "abstract" allegations that Pakistan and China were training rebels in East Pakistan.[22] His pleas of innocence notwithstanding, something was going on in Nagaland after the 1965 war, and the evidence pointed to ISI. According to a 1968 British assessment, "Pakistan aid in arms and training continues, but it is unlikely to contribute materially to the Nagas' already high native guerrilla capability."[23] Whenever ISI scaled back its material support to the Nagas, the Chinese picked up the slack. For example, in 1966 the first Naga band succeeded in crossing hundreds of miles of Burmese jungles, mountains, and rivers to reach a safe haven in China's southeast.[24] Indian military intelligence estimates that ISI and the Chinese together trained over 5,000 Naga fighters.[25]

The Mizos

August is not a good month in Dhaka. For those not used to the heat, and especially the humidity, the city can be absolutely stifling. And the rain! The monsoon season peaks in August, and with it comes seemingly endless showers. It was in just such an August in 1966 that British diplomats in the East Pakistan capital received an unusual visitor. He gave his name as Lal Thangliana, and his business card revealed that he was "Secretary to the Government of Mizoram in the Ministry of Foreign Affairs on an Ambassadorial Mission." Mr. Thangliana said he had been in East Pakistan since March 1966, and that the Pakistan "Intelligence Department" had provided him with a residence.[26] As the British diplomats questioned him further,

Thangliana explained how the authorities had clamped down on the activities of Mizoram representatives in East Pakistan lest they attract attention. The Pakistanis were reluctant to provide them with visas or passports let alone weapons, and they forbade the Mizos to meet with foreigners. Therefore, Thangliana stated he had come to the British mission in secret.[27] When the diplomats enquired about the purpose of his visit, Thangliana said he sought British aid for the Mizo struggle against India. Pakistan had aided the Mizo National Front (MNF) insurgents, he added, but much of that aid had dried up after the 1965 war, and the movement was in the doldrums. The diplomats politely heard Thangliana's story and then, equally politely, showed him to the door; London was not interested in backing secessionist movements against India.[28]

So who were the Mizos? What was Mizoram? Why did they want to break away from India? Ironically, some of the answers lay in meticulously detailed ethnographic studies that the British themselves had put together when they ruled their Indian empire. The Mizos are found today in northeast India, Bangladesh, and Myanmar. After 1947, the specific area called "Mizoram" was a geographic and cultural entity mainly comprised of Mizo tribesmen inside India and bordering on East Pakistan (see Map 3.1). The Mizos revolted for many of the same reasons the Nagas did: they were physically and culturally isolated from India, many were Christian converts, their literacy levels were relatively high, and nationalist forces had been brewing up for some time. The failure of the Indian government and the provincial Assamese authorities to deal with a famine that swept through Mizoram in the early 1960s led to the creation of the Mizo National Famine Front in 1961.[29] Its leader, Laldenga, had heard about ISI aid for the Nagas and traveled to Dhaka in December 1963 to seek similar assistance. ISI deemed the Mizos a good fit for its proxy campaign against India, so it provided some training and other assistance to Laldenga's MNF fighters.[30] By the end of 1965, the Mizo National Front's Vanapa Battalion of 200 trained fighters was ready for action. It had been given small arms by the ISI, and, before returning to Mizoram, the Battalion had cached its weapons at secret sites on or near the Indian border, because Laldenga was not ready to launch his uprising yet.[31]

After the 1965 Indo–Pakistan war, Karachi deemed it wise to scale back aid to the Nagas and Mizos in keeping with the Tashkent peace deal. Yet peace with India did not mean that the Mizos had ended their quest for sovereignty, and on 28 February 1966, the MNF launched Operation JERICHO, an uprising that overran Indian border posts on the frontiers with Burma and East Pakistan. Eleven towns and villages were captured by the MNF in the Mizo Hills. Nearly one hundred Indian civil and military officials were abducted and spirited away to the East Pakistan border region where the MNF intended to use them as bargaining chips. New Delhi pressed the Pakistanis for their return, and most were repatriated several months later.[32]

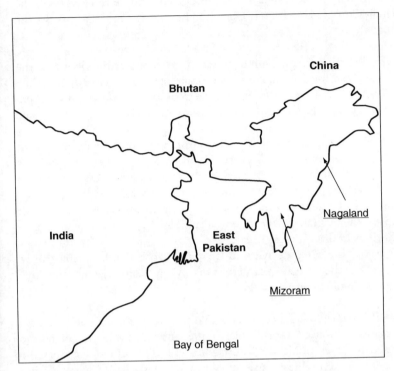

Map 3.1 Northeast India.

The Mizo revolt caught the Indian security apparatus off guard. They lost the initiative at the outset, and months were to pass before the tide began to turn in their favor. Not surprisingly, New Delhi was quick to hold Pakistan responsible for Mizo unrest. In a March 1966 statement, the External Affairs Ministry protested against "the provision of facilities in Pakistan to rebel bands of Mizos for the acquisition of arms and ammunition and for the use of Pakistan's territory as a base from which acts of rebellion and subversion could be carried out."[33] Just as they did earlier with the Nagas, Pakistani officials denied aiding the Mizos. In one such response, Ayub argued that it was India's fault that "Mizo hostiles" were sheltering on Pakistani territory, since Indian forces had driven them there in the first place: "Sometimes the Mizos are driven across the border by the Indians themselves," he said. "What should we do with them? We have no heart to shoot them."[34]

Nonetheless, reports of ISI's involvement in the Mizo conflict continued to pile up. According to one Indian assessment, up to 11 training camps had been set up for the Mizos in the Chittagong Hill Tracts of East Pakistan, and there were sightings of Laldenga in Dhaka.[35] Some said the MNF headquarters was located in a Dhaka safe house and guarded by ISI with the proviso that the MNF abstain from any contacts with foreigners.[36] In December 1966, the British High Commissioner in Rawalpindi pondered the ISI's link to the Mizo rebels:

> [T]here does seem to be some substance to support the view that the authorities in East Pakistan have been giving some help to the Mizo Nationalist Movement.... Perhaps some training.... One wonders where they have obtained these arms, if not from Pakistan.[37]

Once again, the Indian government was confronted with that nagging irritant called "plausible deniability." For every Indian accusation, there was either a smug Pakistani denial or a retort that the Indians were creating their own problems. Adequate proof of ISI complicity in the Mizo revolt was always frustratingly out of reach, and many foreign governments were willing to let Pakistan have the benefit of the doubt. Plausible deniability was to plague India and others in future insurgent wars.

By late 1969, the Chinese were in on the Mizo act too, having gained experience with the Naga guerrillas. One Mizo leader later confirmed Beijing's quiet involvement:

> Senior Pakistani intelligence officers told us we would have no problem so long as we fought India. One of the officers was a brigadier who promised us bases inside the Chittagong Hill Tracts, and said that the Chinese were agreeable to assist us through Pakistan. We were given a number of contact codes and asked to set up groups of volunteers who could be organized for guerrilla warfare on the Naga pattern.[38]

Virtually all aid to the Mizos stopped when Pakistan was defeated by India in the 1971 war because ISI's training camp infrastructure was now in sovereign Bangladesh. Laldenga was on the run, and it would be some time before he resurfaced in Karachi. In the end, the Indians believe that up to 7,000 Mizos were trained by ISI and the Chinese.[39]

With the comfortable distance of nearly half a century, it is easier to assess ISI's UW program in India's northeast. First, the Naga and Mizo independence struggles, no matter how aggressively fought, were little more than sideshows for Pakistan. Pakistan had no territorial claims on India in this part of the world, and the hill tribesmen were certainly not seen as a long-term commitment. It should be noted that India got smarter too when it came to the political angle of counter insurgency. In December 1963, the Indian government created a separate Nagaland state with its own local government. Such political flexibility drained popular support for the insurgents and further isolated the Naga "cooperatives" from the Naga "hostiles."[40] India also had leverage when it came to proxy warfare in the form of Pakistani disgruntled minorities willing to fight with Indian backing. Pakistan's vast yet underpopulated Balochistan province had never been a comfortable fit in the federation, and a new generation of guerrillas was about to emerge there, carrying the torch of independence that had been burning since 1947. There were also Afghanistan's irredentist claims upon the NWFP. In sum, ISI was throwing rocks from a very fragile glass house.[41]

The Naga and Mizo wars show how Pakistan's UW strategy expanded and evolved since the first Kashmir war. Two new agencies, ISI and SSG, were created with specific UW missions. Backing insurgents who didn't even share Islam as a faith nonetheless dispersed Indian forces, mired them in internal security duties, and raised questions about India as a secular and democratic state. UW looked great on paper: it didn't tax Pakistani resources greatly, it distracted and embarrassed the enemy, and it seemed to keep Pakistan safe from reprisals by superior Indian forces. But the greater objective – reuniting all of Kashmir with Pakistan – remained a distant mirage.

Notes

1 B.N. Mullick, *My Years with Nehru: Kashmir*, Bombay: Allied Publishers, 1971, 66–67, 72–75.

2 T.H. Malik, *The Story of My Struggle*, Lahore: Jang, 1991, 19; M.A. Khan, *Trumped Up as An Indian Spy*, Lahore: Mohammad Akram Khan, 2002, 21.

3 S. Riza, *The Pakistan Army: 1947–1949*, Dehra Dun: Natraj Publishers, 1977, 231; A.O. Mitha, *Unlikely Beginnings: A Soldier's Life* (Karachi: OUP, 2003), 161.

4 Mitha, *Unlikely*, op. cit., 176–177.

5 Ibid.; G.A. Khan, *Glimpses into the Corridors of Power*, Karachi: OUP, 2007, 71.

6 S. Cohen, *The Pakistan Army*, Karachi: OUP, 1998, 65–66.

7 Quoted in H. Haqqani, *Pakistan: Between Mosque and Military*, Washington, DC: Carnegie Endowment, 2005, 47.

8 "Remembering our Warriors: Brig (Retd) Shamim Yasin Manto, S.I.(M), S.Bt," *Defence Journal*, www.defence.journal.com/2002/february/manto.htm [accessed 5/8/15].

9 J. Glancey, *Nagaland*, London: Faber and Faber, 2011, 177–178.

10 R. Spur, "Forbidden Kingdom," *Daily Express*, 21 Sept 1956.

11 Quoted in Glancey, *Nagaland*, op. cit., 113.

12 Ibid., 159, 167; S. Bhaumik, *Troubled Periphery: Crisis of India's North East*, New Delhi: Sage Publications, 2009, 95; UK Foreign Office research paper, "Phizo and the Nagas," DO 196/62, UKNA.

13 Glancey, *Nagaland*, op. cit., 4–7, 176; Cable from Malcolm MacDonald, UK High Commissioner in India, 2 July 1956, DO 35/5349, UKNA.

14 Bhaumik, *Troubled*, op. cit., 157; V.K. Anand, *Conflict in Nagaland: A Study of Insurgency and Counter-Insurgency*, Delhi: Chanakya Publications, 1980, 191–192; A. Riaz, *Islamist Militancy in Bangladesh*, London: Routledge, 2008, 66.

15 Riaz, *Islamist*, op. cit., 66; A. Mann, "Naga Tribes Hold Down 30,000 Men," *Daily Telegraph*, 20 March 1957; Bhaumik, *Troubled*, op. cit., 16.

16 Quoted in Bhuamik, *Troubled*, op. cit., 157–158.

17 Ibid., 95–96, 158.

18 *Dawn*, 28 May 1962.

19 Statement by Minister of External Affairs in the Lok/Rajya Sabha on 12 March 1965, DO 39/1069, UKNA.

20 Riaz, *Islamist*, op. cit., 66–67; Foreign and Commonwealth Office, "The Naga Problem," 20 February 1968, FCO 51/52, UKNA; Glancey, *Nagaland*, op. cit., 19; Bhaumik, *Troubled*, op. cit., 161–162.

21 Bhaumik, *Troubled*, op. cit., 17.
22 R. Khan, *The British Papers*, Karachi: OUP, 2002, 550–551.
23 Cable from Freeman, 28 March 1968, no. 622, FCO 37/267, UKNA.
24 Bhaumik, *Troubled*, op. cit., 96–97, 158; Anand, *Conflict*, op. cit., 188.
25 Bhaumik, *Troubled*, op. cit., 159–160.
26 Note by A.B. Moore, British Deputy High Commission, Dacca, 22 August 1966, DO 196/541, UKNA.
27 Ibid.
28 Ibid.
29 Bhaumik, *Troubled*, op. cit., 102–103; S. Bhaumik, *Insurgency Crossfire: North-East India*, New Delhi: Lancer, 1996, 142–144; "War in the Hills," *The Economist*, 18 March 1966 found in DO 196/541, UKNA.
30 Bhaumik, *Insurgency*, op. cit., 145–148.
31 Ibid.; Correspondence from K.R. Crook, Deputy British High Commission, Dacca, 18 May 1966, DO 196/541, UKNA; Meeting notes by A.B. Moore, British High Commission, Rawalpindi, 18 May 1966, DO 196/541, UKNA.
32 Lok Sabha debate proceedings, 9 May 1966, no. 1358, DO 196/541, UKNA; Bhaumik, *Insurgency*, op. cit., 149–150.
33 Correspondence from A.M. Simons, British High Commission, New Delhi, 27 April 1966, DO 196/541, UKNA; Correspondence from A.M. Simons, British High Commission, New Delhi, 30 March 1966, DO 196/541, UKNA.
34 Quoted in Bhaumik, *Insurgency*, op. cit., 158.
35 Correspondence from R.W. Renwick, UK High Commission, New Delhi, 23 February 1967, FCO 37/267, UKNA; Rajya Sabha debate proceedings, 10 May 1966, no. 138, DO 196/541, UKNA.
36 Bhaumik, *Insurgency*, op. cit., 163; Notes of meeting between K.R. Crook, Deputy British High Commission, Dacca, and Rev. M.L. Wenger, 25 April 1966, DO 196/541, UKNA; Note by A.B. Moore, British Deputy High Commission, Dacca, 22 August 1966, DO 196/541, UKNA; Correspondence from K.R. Crook, Deputy British High Commission, Dacca, 25 April 1966, DO 196/541, UKNA.
37 Correspondence from R.W. Purcell, Commonwealth Relations Office, 6 December 1966, D.O. 196/541, UKNA.
38 Quoted in Bhaumik, *Insurgency*, op. cit., 147.
39 Bhaumik, *Troubled*, op. cit., 161.
40 Glancey, *Nagaland*, op. cit., 163, 185.
41 Anand, *Conflict*, op. cit., 186; S.M. Ali, *Cold War in the High Himalayas: the USA, China and South Asia in the 1950s*, New York, NY: St. Martin's Press, 1999, 177–178; Bhaumik, *Troubled*, op. cit., 146.

4 Intelligence and the 1965 War

On the afternoon of 5 August 1965, a shepherd named Mohamed Din was tending his flock in upland pastures near the Kashmir ceasefire line when he saw a column of armed men descending from a ridgeline above him. One normally did not encounter strangers at this altitude, and although these men were dressed in local clothing, they were carrying weapons and walking in military fashion. When the armed men drew near, they offered Din a bribe if he would escort them through the Pir Panjal mountain range. Instead, the bewildered shepherd did something surprising to his visitors: he turned and ran.[1]

It wasn't supposed to be like this. The commanders of the infiltration teams had been told by ISI that Kashmiri Muslims would be relieved to see their Pakistani "liberators." In fact, some of them were supposed to join the infiltrators and help launch the great uprising in Kashmir that everyone in Karachi was waiting for. But more unwelcome surprises were in store. Mohamed Din hastened to inform the local Criminal Investigation Department (CID) about the intruders; cooperating with the enemy so blatantly wasn't anticipated by ISI either.[2] The CID sent a report to the political authorities in Srinagar, who had been receiving similar notifications from other border outposts. Something was definitely taking place near the ceasefire line, so reinforced security patrols were sent into the mountains to intercept intruders.[3] Operation GIBRALTAR, Pakistan's ill-fated bid to force India's hand on Kashmir had begun, but the element of surprise had been lost at the start. Where had the Pakistanis gone wrong?

Unrest in Kashmir

To answer this question we need to briefly examine events in Kashmir that led up to the 1965 war. In the early 1960s, ISI and IB were monitoring promising developments in Indian Kashmir, where an ongoing dispute between New Delhi and the mercurial Kashmiri politician, Sheikh Abdullah, was fueling unrest. In December 1963, the theft of a relic of the Prophet Mohamed from a shrine in Srinagar triggered mass protests that were only suppressed when the Indian army intervened. The relic was eventually returned, but mystery surrounded both its disappearance and sudden restoration.[4] Pakistan's Foreign

Ministry was also studying Kashmir with a keen eye, and some senior diplomats believed the unrest underscored the fragility of Indian rule there.[5] For its part, the IB stepped up infiltrations during and after the Prophet's relic incident in a bid to profit from the unrest.[6] At the same time, though, other Kashmir developments were seen by the Pakistanis as setbacks. India had shown no flexibility on its refusal to hold a referendum; on the contrary, New Delhi was integrating Kashmir into the Union.[7] Moreover, there was that nagging fear in leadership circles that Kashmir was "slipping away," that it was only a matter of time before it would be lost to Pakistan forever. From such anxious perceptions are desperate policies made.[8]

India's first Prime Minister, Jawaharlal Nehru, died on 27 May 1964. A commanding and eloquent leader who was respected at home and on the world stage, Nehru was nonetheless adamant that Kashmir remain in India. As for Nehru's political heirs, the daunting challenge was trying to fill his shoes. In the wake of his passing, ISI Director Brigadier Riaz Hussain confidently assessed that the Indians were demoralized, and therefore the time had come for Pakistan to act.[9] But President Ayub hesitated, creating instead a Kashmir Publicity Committee whose purpose was to monitor events, review existing policy and recommend courses of action.[10] At the outset, the committee was divided between "hawks," led by Zulfikar Ali Bhutto, and "doves," which included senior military officers. The IB had a seat on the committee because it owned the operatives in Indian Kashmir. If the committee were to endorse escalated border infiltrations, the IB would be the agency carrying out the mission.

Bhutto was destined for greater things; however, on the eve of the 1965 war, he was serving as Ayub's Foreign Minister. Intelligent, arrogant, restless and exceedingly ambitious, Bhutto adopted Kashmir as his personal cause. In personal correspondence with Ayub, Bhutto argued that the Pakistani army enjoyed a qualitative advantage over its Indian opponent by a factor of four to one. Moreover, he insisted that India's defeat in a recent war with China gave Pakistan a rare opportunity to "hit back hard ... in such a way as to make it virtually impossible for India to embark on a total war against Pakistan for the next decade or so."[11] During Kashmir Committee meetings, the Foreign Minister urged immediate action because Kashmir "was in revolt." When the doves warned about near-certain Indian retaliation, Bhutto brushed them aside. China, he predicted, would keep the Indians in check by deploying forces to the disputed border with India.[12] For his part, ISI Director Riaz was convinced that although India's Kashmiri Muslims were primed for revolt, they required a spark and a powerful backer before they would act.[13]

GIBRALTAR and GRAND SLAM

Sometime in late 1964, Bhutto's deputy, Minister of State Aziz Ahmed, informed the committee that President Ayub wanted two action plans for Kashmir. The first entailed sabotage missions across the ceasefire line, and the second provided "all-out support for guerrillas" inserted into Kashmir. In a sign of its growing influence on Kashmir, ISI was selected to work with the Foreign Ministry on these plans, not the IB.[14] In February 1965, the Kashmir Committee briefed the two plans to the Cabinet Intelligence Committee, an advisory body with limited oversight of the intelligence community. In attendance were Ayub and the Army Commander-in-Chief, General Musa, among others; however, neither the Air Force nor the Navy commanders were invited. After the Deputy ISI Director, Group Captain T.S. Jan, finished briefing the plans, there was a brief pause as the seniors digested them.[15] Then, according to one account, Ayub unexpectedly rejected it:

> Who authorized Foreign Office and the ISI to draw up such a plan? All I asked them was to keep the situation in Kashmir under review. They can't force a campaign of military action on the government.[16]

It was not long after the Cabinet Intelligence Committee meeting that a crisis flared up between India and Pakistan over the Rann of Kutch, an uninhabited salt marsh near the Indian Ocean. After several clashes, the conflict died down, although the Pakistanis convinced themselves that they had come out as the victors. Maybe the Indian army was weaker than assessed. Perhaps now was the time to strike in Kashmir while the iron was hot and the Indians were down. Even Ayub was swayed by the hawks this time. In July 1965, he told the Kashmir Committee to proceed with both plans.[17]

The Pakistanis believed the Kashmiri opposition leader, Sheikh Abdullah, could help them understand the current situation in Kashmir. After all, the Sheikh had a veritable rolodex of associates, colleagues, contacts and extended family members who might be of assistance to Pakistan down the road. It was with this in mind that Ayub's IB Director met Sheikh Abdullah in Mecca and tried to recruit him as a Pakistani agent; however, the Sheikh astounded his Pakistani interlocutor when he revealed knowledge of key aspects of the close-hold Pakistani war plans for Kashmir. Worse yet, when Sheikh Abdullah returned to India after his pilgrimage, he was promptly arrested by the authorities for conspiring with Pakistani intelligence. Clearly, the Indians had been monitoring the Kashmiri leader's movements in Saudi Arabia, but the real question was – or should have been – how much did the Indian government already know about Pakistan's intent to stoke a crisis in Kashmir?[18]

Despite this leakage of critical information, ISI and the Foreign Ministry blithely proceeded as if no security breaches had taken place. Ironically, tight compartmentalization remained in effect, with the result that an imprisoned Kashmiri opposition leader knew more about Pakistan's plans than either the PAF or Navy chiefs.[19] The designated executive agent of the Kashmir operation, Major General Akhtar Hussain Malik, later tried to justify the intense secrecy surrounding the plan by invoking the Indian espionage threat. Apparently, he had no idea that the voluble Sheikh Abdullah was in Indian custody and witting to important details of Pakistani intentions.[20]

Working under the shaky assumption that the Muslims of Indian Kashmir were ready to revolt, GIBRALTAR was built around three phases. The first involved using the state-run Azad Kashmir Radio and the clandestine *Sada-e Kashmir* (Voice of Kashmir) to beam a steady stream of inflammatory propaganda at Kashmir, encouraging the population to rise up against Indian rule. During the second phase, small teams of guerrillas accompanied by disguised army officers and SSG commandos would cross the ceasefire line and initiate the third phase: attacking Indian logistics nodes, command and control centers, airfields and military bases. It was anticipated that local Kashmiris would eagerly join the cause and accompany the "liberation forces" on their march to Srinagar.[21] It all sounded so neat and simple: the Indian security forces would undoubtedly overreact and crack down on Kashmiri civilians, generating yet more anger and hatred, and thereby fuel a Kashmir-wide revolt. It was assumed that against such popular unrest, the Indians would have no choice but to negotiate a political settlement.[22]

On 13 May 1965, President Ayub reviewed the GIBRALTAR plan with the 12th Infantry Division Commander. As his eyes passed over the operations map, the president focused on Akhnur, a city on the Indian side of the ceasefire line that served as a vital road junction between Kashmir and India. Ayub ordered his army to go for the "jugular" by seizing Akhnur and cutting off India's overland supply route to Kashmir. The result of this second plan was Operation GRAND SLAM, which would only be implemented if GIBRALTAR had succeeded in liberating Srinagar.[23] By the end of July, all the pieces of GIBRALTAR were in place: the guerrillas and the commandos had been positioned along the ceasefire line awaiting orders to cross. Confidence was high as a new chapter in Pakistan's struggle for a united Kashmir began.

The GIBRALTAR plan depended on several untested assumptions. The first and foremost was the belief that Kashmiri Muslims were prepared to risk their lives, families and property in an uprising against their Indian overlords. The second was the expectation (hope?) that Pakistan could hide its involvement by calling the insurgents "freedom fighters" and disguising their officers and SSG men in mufti. Then there was the mistaken belief arising from the Rann of Cutch clashes that Indian forces were demoralized and man-for-man less motivated and capable than their Pakistani counterparts. As a post-hostilities' British military assessment put it, "[a]n air of truculence and considerable over-confidence spread throughout the Pakistan regime accompanied by a contempt for India" on the eve of the 1965 war.[24] Finally, there was the equally shaky proposition that widespread unrest in Kashmir would invite international intervention and ultimately forge a settlement favorable to Pakistan.

Moreover, compulsive operational security turned out to be more of a curse than a blessing. The Air Force and Navy commanders were out of the loop as were Kashmiri Muslim leaders who understood public sentiments in Indian Kashmir better than the committee's members.[25] The irony of course is that many people who should have known about GIBRALTAR didn't, while some who did know shouldn't have. Sheikh Abdullah, for instance, somehow found about the plan early on and apparently leaked like a sieve. CIA learned about the plans from the Kashmiri leader, raising the obvious question: if Sheikh Abdullah and the CIA knew about GIBRALTAR, who else was in the know? India's IB?[26] The lead-up to Pakistan's ill-fated foray into Kashmir was scarred by unquestioned assumptions, a dose of fantasy substituting for careful analysis, and an intensive but poorly functioning security system. The wonder is that Pakistan survived the war as well as it did.

War

But Operation GIBRALTAR failed at the very beginning. Those small bands of paramilitary men and SSG commandos that infiltrated across the ceasefire line often met with wary and even hostile receptions from the locals. Their ability to recruit new insurgents was further hampered by the fact that many of them did not speak the local dialects.[27] On 8 August, the Indian government put four captured infiltrators on All India Radio, where they "confessed" to their mission and its sponsor. As he listened in from Army GHQ in Rawalpindi, the Director of Military Intelligence reportedly exclaimed, "The bastards have spilled the beans!"[28] One Pakistani official later made this wry statement in his memoirs: "In less than twenty-four hours the details of Operation GIBRALTAR, which had been kept secret even from Pakistani officials who were to be directly involved in its execution, were in the possession of the enemy while the people of Pakistan were still in the dark."[29]

Embarrassment was already starting to seep in among those Kashmir Committee hawks who had earlier been so confident of success. When pressed about what was going wrong, ISI Director Riaz replied lamely that all his contacts "had gone underground."[30] As for the propaganda system, it too had broken down at the beginning of the operation. *Sada-e Kashmir* was supposed to announce that a Revolutionary Council had been established in Srinagar in the hope that this would trigger a Kashmiri revolt. But *Sada-e Kashmir* wasn't working properly. On 8 August, the DMI, Brigadier Irshad, approached Ayub's Information Secretary, Altaf Gauhar, with an urgent request: did the secretary happen to have a spare mobile transmitter handy? Better yet, could the Information Secretary take over the whole clandestine radio project? Gauhar tried to refuse, claiming that he had no knowledge of the operation to which Irshad responded: "But that's the beauty of it: even I know very little about it." This is a stunning and rather flippant statement from a senior military intelligence officer who should have been well-integrated into the planning process from the outset. As it turned out, Altaf Gauhar did not have a mobile transmitter of his own, so *Sada-e Kashmir* had to be broadcast on the same frequency as the official Radio Azad Kashmir. This made *Sada-e Kashmir* essentially redundant.[31]

Then the Pakistanis committed their second fatal error. Even though GIBRALTAR had failed to instigate a revolt, the leadership proceeded with

GRAND SLAM whereby regular army units violated the Kashmir ceasefire line on 1 September and tried to seize the Akhnur crossroads. Inevitable delays resulting from a crippling bureaucracy and the "fog of war" meant that the offensive soon stalled, so Akhnur remained tantalizingly out of reach.[32] Pakistan had war-gamed Akhnur-type scenarios repeatedly in the past, and it often anticipated Indian retaliation in one form or another with armed force. This time, however, when the war was a reality and not a game, the Pakistanis inexplicably did not place their Punjab-based units on alert for a possible Indian counterattack there. Likewise, they did not cancel personnel leaves or take other steps that might have prepared them for what lay ahead.[33]

In fact, the Indian army had been preparing a military response ever since infiltrators had been detected during the first week of August. On 15 August, ISI and MI detected Indian troop movements that suggested a substantial force buildup on the Punjab border. Once again, Pakistan Army GHQ debated an old question: were these movements part of an exercise, a display of force, or was India preparing for war?[34] By the end of August, there was a growing consensus inside ISI that an invasion was imminent.[35] On 30 August, ISI's India Desk Chief informed the leadership that ISI had picked up several indications of a pending offensive, including the deployment of units to forward deployment areas at Pathankot and Ahmedabad, dispersals of combat aircraft and the movement of the 1st Armoured Division toward the international border between India and Pakistan.[36] In response to ISI's warning, President Ayub convened a conference to discuss appropriate responses. Foreign Secretary Aziz Ahmed dismissed the ISI assessment: an Indian invasion of Pakistan in response to Kashmir meddling just didn't enter his threat calculations. Army GHQ appeared complacent in the eyes of one observer. Only the Air Force prudently raised its alert status.[37]

But disturbing signals of Indian mobilization and preparations continued to pour in. On 3 September, Indian Prime Minister Lal Bahadur Shastri gave a speech in which he warned his people to be prepared for "hard days ahead" and that India could "suffer damage from air raids."[38] Moreover, the Pakistani High Commissioner to New Delhi received a tipoff from an unnamed contact indicating that India would invade Pakistan on 6 September. Some assert that either Bhutto or his deputy, Aziz Ahmed, suppressed this timely warning since it did not coincide with their more optimistic assessments.[39] Then there was the SSG's ambush of an Indian First Armoured Division dispatch rider with documents confirming that the division was in a pre-assault position just across the border. Yet with all the evidence now in their hands, the Pakistani military leadership assessed that the documents were part of an Indian deception plan.[40] As one Pakistani brigadier later put it, "people had read too much military history and considered this to be a plant by the enemy."[41]

One final confirmation of the leadership's refusal to accept the reality of an imminent Indian attack came via an IB source in the Indian High Commission in Karachi, who warned his handler that the Indian assault would fall on

6 September. When an ISI counter intelligence expert seconded to the IB brought this information to the attention of the IB Director the response was brisk and negative: "Young man, do you want to create panic in the country? Do you know what damage you can cause if this report is accepted and it turns out to be fake? Which it certainly is."[42]

As far as intelligence warnings go, ISI comes out of the 1965 war in a positive light. It repeatedly notified the leadership of the buildup of Indian forces on the border, and it correctly assessed these moves to be aggressive in intent. Real fault seems to lie with the army leadership, which appeared to be oddly complacent in the face of an alarming Indian force mobilization. Yet even here the picture is not so clear cut, for on 4 September at 2230 Army GHQ *did* send out this warning to field formations:

> Latest intelligence reports indicate Indian concentration both on East and West Pakistan and such flash announcement on All India Radio as QUOTE Pakistanis attacking Jammu etc. UNQOUTE indicate their aggressive intention, formations will take defensive measures (.) All Informed.[43]

At 0330 on 6 September 1965, Indian forces invaded Punjab inexplicably catching the Pakistanis by surprise. Ayub himself was notified by the Air Force chief, but when the president called the Army Commander-in-Chief, General Musa reportedly told his boss that he was awaiting "confirmation" of the invasion. Confirmation or not, army units in the Lahore sector were already locked in combat with their Indian adversaries.[44] The senior leadership certainly took its time to meet following the Indian attack. It wasn't until 0900: nearly *six hours* after the offensive began that the chiefs got together at Army GHQ.[45] Per military staff custom, President Ayub asked the DMI, Brigadier Irshad, for a situation update. Irshad had barely begun his briefing when the Chief of the Army's General Staff asked him about the First Armoured Division. Irshad replied that Military Intelligence did not know the exact whereabouts of this division, but his staff was working on it.[46] This unit represented the "mailed fist" of India's attack, and its location would offer a good insight into India's planned line of advance. Army GHQ, MI and ISI had a general sense of its location in the Samba area, but apparently were thrown off the scent when it was inaccurately assessed that some of the relevant intelligence was an Indian deception.

Years later, Zulfikar Ali Bhutto alleged that Ayub dressed down DISI Riaz Hussain in front of the others because ISI had supposedly failed to keep track of the First Armoured Division. Bhutto protested at the meeting that this unit was "not a needle in a haystack," and Ayub piled on, adding that "it is a monster and not a needle." In Bhutto's version, the DISI replied that since "June 1964 Military Intelligence has been given political assignments on elections and post-elections repercussion," making it impossible to carry out some of its other missions such as intelligence collection. Bhutto's narrative cannot be verified, although other reports state it was DMI Irshad who was berated by Ayub and not ISI Director Riaz.[47]

What is beyond dispute, though, is that the Indian invasion caught a complacent leadership completely off guard, even though it had raised the stakes in the first place by infiltrating soldiers into Indian Kashmir followed by a general assault across the ceasefire line. The key players like Ayub, Bhutto, Aziz Ahmed, and General Musa seemed to possess fixed opinions about what India would and would not do, and refused to admit their mistake until it was too late. This miscalculation directly influenced soldiers at the lowest ranks as the British High Commissioner at the time noted:

> Astonishingly the Pakistanis were taken by surprise: their troops had not been alerted and were asleep in their barracks. Some of them left with their weapons for the front lines in their pyjamas for want of time to put on battle-dress.[48]

A 23 September ceasefire put an end to the war, as both sides had run out of ammunition. In 1966, Ayub and Indian Prime Minister Lal Bahadur Shastri were invited to Tashkent by Soviet Premier Alexei Kosygin where they concluded a peace agreement. Shastri died of a heart attack as the last details of an accord were being hammered out. Although Ayub returned to Rawalpindi very much alive and in control, his political career was entering its own death throes. A new phase in Pakistan's political history was about to begin.

Notes

1 P. Swami, *India, Pakistan and the Secret Jihad: The Covert War in Kashmir, 1947–2004*, London: Routledge, 2007, 145.
2 Ibid.
3 Ibid.
4 B.N. Mullick, *My Years with Nehru: Kashmir*, Bombay: Allied Publishers, 1971, 151.
5 A. Gauhar, *Ayub Khan: Pakistan's First Military Ruler*, Karachi: OUP, 1996, 205; G.H. Khan, *Memoirs of Lt. Gen. Gul Hassan Khan*, Karachi: OUP, 1993, 113–114.
6 Gauhar, *Ayub*, op. cit., 205; M. Musa, *My Version*, Lahore: Wajidalis, 1983, 2.
7 Musa, *Version*, op. cit., 2–3.
8 Gauhar, *Ayub*, op. cit., 318–319; G.H. Khan, *Memoirs*, op. cit., 115–117; A.H. Amin, *The Pakistan Army Till 1965*, Arlington, VA: Strategicus and Tacticus, 1999, 219.
9 Gauhar, *Ayub*, op. cit., 167–168.
10 Musa, *Version*, op. cit., 4–5; Gauhar, *Ayub*, op. cit., 208–209.
11 Bhutto correspondence cited in A. Jalal, *The Struggle for Pakistan*, Cambridge, MA: Belknap, 2014, 118–119.
12 S. Wolpert, *Zulfi Bhutto of Pakistan*, New York: OUP, 1993, 48.
13 S. Riza, *The Pakistan Army: War of 1965* (Dehra Dun: Natraj Publishers, 1977), 19; Musa, *Version*, op. cit., 3–5.
14 S. Nawaz, *Crossed Swords: Pakistan, Its Army, and the Wars Within*, Karachi: OUP, 2008, 206.
15 K.M. Arif, *Khaki Shadows*, Karachi: OUP, 2001, 47; Gauhar, *Ayub*, op. cit., 209–210.
16 Gauhar, *Ayub*, op. cit., 320–321.
17 Ibid., 205–206; M. James, *Pakistan Chronicle*, New York: St. Martin's Press, 1993, 128–129.

18 A. Jamal, *Shadow War: The Untold Story of Jihad in Kashmir*, Hoboken, NJ: Melville House, 2009, 81; A. Gauhar, "How Intelligence Agencies Run Our Politics," *The Nation*, 17 August 1997; Mullick, *My Years*, op. cit., 64–65.

19 Nawaz, *Crossed Swords*, op. cit., 208; *The Story of the Pakistan Air Force: A Saga of Courage and Honor*, Islamabad: Shaheen Foundation, 335.

20 H. Abbas, *Pakistan's Drift into Extremism*, Armonk, NY: M.E. Sharpe, 49–50.

21 N.C. Behera, *Demystifying Kashmir*, Washington, DC: Brookings, 2006, 77; V. Schofield, *Kashmir in Conflict*, London, I.B. Tauris, 2003, 108; Jamal, *Shadow*, op. cit., 83.

22 UK Ministry of Defence, *The India–Pakistan War 1965*, DEFE 44/102, UKNA.

23 Gauhar, *Ayub*, op. cit., 210–211; G.H. Khan, *Memoirs*, op. cit., 223.

24 *The India–Pakistan War 1965*, op. cit.

25 P.N. Bazaz, *Kashmir in the Crucible*, New Delhi, Pamposh Publications, 1967, 133.

26 D. Clarridge, *A Spy for All Seasons* (New York: Scribner, 1997), 103–105.

27 Nawaz, *Crossed Swords*, op. cit., 208; *India–Pakistan War 1965*, op. cit.; Behera, *Demystifying*, op. cit., 78; Gauhar, *Ayub*, op. cit., 214.

28 Gauhar, "How Intelligence," op. cit.

29 Gauhar, *Ayub*, op. cit., 208.

30 Gauhar, "How Intelligence," op. cit.

31 Ibid.

32 *India-Pakistan War 1965*, op. cit.

33 A. Khan, *Generals in Politics: Pakistan 1958–1982*, New Delhi, Vikas, 1983, 209.

34 S. Riza, *The Pakistan Army: 1947–1949*, Dehra Dun: Natraj Publishers, 1977, 133.

35 Nawaz, *Crossed Swords*, 222.

36 *Story of the Pakistan Air Force*, op. cit., 342, 350–351.

37 Ibid., 350–351; Gauhar, *Ayub*, op. cit., 223.

38 Quoted in Gauhar, *Ayub*, op. cit., 223.

39 G.A. Khan, *Glimpses into the Corridors of Power*, Karachi: OUP, 95; S. Bhattacharya, *Nothing But! What Price Freedom*, New Delhi: Partridge, 2013, 484.

40 Riza, *Pakistan Army*, op. cit., 133–134, 483; Nawaz, *Crossed Swords*, op. cit., 222; Arif, *Khaki*, op. cit., 72.

41 Quoted in Nawaz, *Crossed Swords*, op. cit., 227–228.

42 S.A.I. Tirmazi, *Profiles in Intelligence*, Lahore: Combined Printers, 1995, 14–15.

43 Quoted in Riza, *Pakistan Army*, op. cit., 134–135.

44 Musa, *My Version*, op. cit., 18; James, *Chronicle*, op. cit., 136; Bhattacharya, *Nothing But!* op. cit., 484; Gauhar, *Ayub*, op. cit., 224.

45 Bhattacharya, *Nothing But!* op. cit., 482.

46 Ibid.

47 Z.A. Bhutto, *If I Am Assassinated*, New Delhi: Vikas, 1979, 62–64; Wolpert, *Zulfi*, op. cit., 91.

48 Quoted in Schofield, *Kashmir*, op. cit., 110.

Part II
ISI at War

5 ISI's Domestic Missions under Ayub

In its earliest years, the PIC's hierarchy and mission "lanes of the road" were fairly well established. The ISI reported through the Joint Service Commanders' Committee to the civilian government in Karachi. Military Intelligence was responsible for operational and tactical intelligence as well as army-specific counter intelligence matters; it reported to the Army Commander-in-Chief via the army staff structure in Rawalpindi. The Air Force and Navy service agencies were much smaller and focused on their own service-centric missions. Then there was the civilian IB, which dominated the intelligence community as long as civilians ruled in Karachi. The IB possessed both internal and external intelligence responsibilities, primacy in counter intelligence, and it retained the Kashmir UW portfolio. Access to power is power itself, and the IB had the undisputed advantage of reporting directly to the civilian Prime Minister, giving it a leg up on its military rivals. This hierarchy remained in place provided that a civilian government possessed clear authority over the armed forces. But the army was rising in political power in the mid-1950s, its ascendancy fueled by the political ambitions of its leadership and a host of domestic challenges, which civilian governments seemed utterly incapable of resolving.

Fragile state

It was always going to be a steep climb for Pakistani democracy in any case. We've seen how Pakistan was born out of Partition with no infrastructure or standing bureaucracy and a military built from scratch. The country had been founded on the questionable premise that religion alone constituted a nation, regardless of language, culture or ethnicity. But some political parties were demanding more than just a state for Muslims: they wanted an "Islamic state" based on the application of Islamic law – or *Sharia*. Because of these disputes over Islam and language politics, Pakistan did not have a constitution until 1956, nearly a decade after its founding.

One of the sharper conflicts eating at the essence of Pakistan was its bifurcated territory. From the outset, the western provinces dominated their eastern sister, even though the latter possessed more people and a jute crop that was Pakistan's greatest foreign currency earner. In 1948, the founder of Pakistan, M.A. Jinnah, made what was arguably the biggest political mistake of his career when he insisted on Urdu becoming the "national language" of Pakistan. Few residents in either wing even spoke Urdu. Moreover, unlike the ethnically fractured West, East Pakistan could claim that the vast majority of its people spoke one language – Bengali – and shared a single culture and customs. These features gave the Bengalis a national identity and the foundations for a nation state of their own.

Pakistan also suffered from an acute deficit in senior leadership. Its politicians were more interested in feathering their nests and winning power struggles than actually running the country. In this vacuum, the civilian bureaucracy and army saw an opportunity for power and seized it. In fact, it was a creeping military dictatorship, one that was all but imperceptible to the politicians, who underestimated the danger of a powerful army working in a system lacking viable political parties and strong civilian leadership. Army supremacy was boosted by several factors. The first of these was the literal "tyranny" of distance: the government of Pakistan was based in Karachi, but army headquarters was nearly a thousand miles away in Rawalpindi. Geographical distance exaggerated differences in perspective between the government and its army, and the former allowed the latter to run its own show, largely independent of civilian oversight. Then there was General Ayub Khan, Pakistan's first native Army Commander-in-Chief, who harbored political ambitions of his own. Finally, there was the brief imposition of martial law in Lahore in 1953, when the army was called in to suppress demonstrations against a minority religious sect. Martial law gave many senior officers their first taste of power, and they never forgot it.[1]

As Ayub's power base expanded, and that of the civilian politicians contracted, the relative power positions inside the intelligence community began to shift as well. In his rise, Ayub used ISI against his adversaries. Though weak when it came to domestic intelligence, ISI was eager to take on this mission and the increased authority that was almost certain to follow.[2] On 7 October 1958, amid a stream of alarmist intelligence reports indicating rising Indian influence in East Pakistan, President Iskander Mirza abrogated the 1956 constitution and declared martial law with General Ayub's backing.[3] In the first few weeks following the takeover, tensions mounted between Mirza and Ayub, creating an atmosphere of suspicion and sullen anger. A 15 October 1958 cable from the American Embassy in Karachi captures this sentiment:

> Uneasiness and even nascent fear have in past few days begun to make their appearance.... Telephones are being tapped on an extensive scale; martial law agents and inspectors are beginning to appear – or to be suspected – everywhere; number of 'intellectuals' (editors, newspaper writers, professors, some civil servants, even judges) privately admit they [are] feeling distinctly nervous under increasing degree of police control.[4]

In the first decade of Pakistan's existence, its politics were often lively, bois-terous, chaotic and even violent, but now the army and its intelligence agency acolytes were imposing a straight-jacket on the government, stifling civilian politics, and bottling up pressures in an already volatile society. In the lead-up to the second coup, the intelligence community was divided against itself for the first time. Trapped in the fetid humidity of coastal Karachi, President Mirza leaned on the IB to inform him about Ayub's moves and intentions.[5] As for Ayub, he had not one but two military intelligence ser-vices spying on Mirza. According to one reliable account, either MI or ISI had succeeded in intercepting a phone call between Mirza and a cabinet minister in which the president reportedly asserted that he would "sort Ayub Khan out in a few days." Of course, Ayub assumed the worst and made his move against Mirza on 27 October 1958. Mirza and his wife were bundled on a plane to London with only the then Australian High Commissioner, Bill Cawthorn, there to see them off.[6]

ISI under Ayub

The 1958 coups accelerated the trend toward greater centralization of power, and it was under this rubric that ISI was given more domestic intelligence duties.[7] In an unprecedented move, Ayub ensured that the three dominant intelligence agencies – the IB, ISI and Military Intelligence reported directly to him.[8] This meant that each agency was now fiercely competing with its peers for the favor of the new strongman of Pakistan. But it was never a contest of equals: Ayub was a quintessential general who didn't trust civilian rulers or bureaucrats let alone a civilian-run political police like the IB. According to Jahan Dad Khan, then a captain in the army on assignment to ISI's Lahore Detachment, Ayub "used to openly express his displeasure of the civilian intelligence agencies."[9] Not surprisingly, Ayub preferred ISI, since it was led by army officers personally selected by and beholden to him.[10]

Over time, Ayub expanded ISI's domestic mission while the MI focused mainly on the Indian military threat. Ayub also asked ISI to expand surveil-lance and internal security missions in East Pakistan because he did not trust the IB's subsidiary office in Dhaka.[11] As one author notes of ISI's expanded powers during this period: "the ISI began to function like intelligence organi-zations in other dictatorships, tapping the phones of opposition figures, har-assing critics of the military regime, conducting media campaigns, intimidating influential citizens, and carrying out occasional assassinations."[12]

To solidify this transformation of ISI missions, Ayub removed ISI's Director, Brigadier Mohamed Hayat Khan, and replaced him with Brigadier Riaz Hussain, an Ayub confidant.[13] Unlike his predecessors, Riaz would enjoy a long tenure (1959 to 1966) at ISI during which he presided over an expansion of its capabilities in internal security, intelligence collection and UW. He can be con-sidered one of the top three ISI directors in terms of influence, for he pioneered this agency's rise to preeminence within the intelligence community.[14]

Pakistan was a dictatorship, and it is axiomatic that dictatorships require some kind of political police to stay in power. In Pakistan, Ayub used his three primary intelligence and security services – ISI, MI and IB – to monitor his political opposition and assess the loyalty of military officers to his regime. All three were tasked to spy on disgruntled civilian politicians, media personalities, trade union activists and religious groups as well as secessionist movements in East Pakistan, Balochistan and the Pashtun frontier.[15]

After creating a new constitution and an election system aimed at keeping him in power Ayub ordered presidential elections in 1964. A victory would give him the pretense of a popular mandate that he still lacked. Prior to the elections the IB's Director confidently predicted that Ayub would win over 75 percent of the carefully screened "electors" in the indirect vote for president.[16] Meanwhile, ISI was making its first foray into assessing domestic elections, but its reports were dismissed by one official as no more than "simple gossip."[17] As was to occur frequently in the future, Ayub's intelligence agencies told him what he wanted to hear by accentuating the positives and downplaying the negatives of his campaign. At the same time, the hitherto dismissed opposition parties coalesced around a surprise candidate, Fatima Jinnah, sister of the deceased founder, whose campaign caught Ayub's minions off guard and forced them to rely on electoral shenanigans to win. Wavering electors were strong-armed into voting for Ayub. The Combined Opposition Parties front was infiltrated with intelligence agents, who reported on its meetings and aggravated its leadership feuds.[18] Ayub "won" his election, but it was not a ringing endorsement of his policies. Having to resort to vote rigging in a system designed to keep him in power was a humbling let down for the president and his advisors. It was also a sign that political pluralism was still alive in some sectors of Pakistani society. Fortunately for Ayub, the 1965 Indo-Pakistani war temporarily silenced his critics.

ISI was focused heavily on internal threats as a result of the new missions Ayub had assigned it. As a member of Ayub's inner circle, ISI Director Riaz's top priority was ensuring that anti-Ayub elements did not emerge within the armed forces. His was a position requiring absolute trust as a 1966 British assessment made clear:

> [Riaz is the] one man in the whole of Pakistan who Ayub must have felt to be completely loyal to him, for apart from his normal intelligence duties it is he who has been responsible for the internal security of the Armed Forces and thus for making sure that no officer should be in a position to topple the Government by a coup.[19]

Intelligence reform

Following the 1965 war, Ayub made changes to his intelligence community. The consensus among the leadership was that the community had performed poorly during the war, and as one researcher put it, military intelligence (ISI and MI) suffered from "almost unbelievably bad intelligence procedures."[20] Foreign observers thought so, too. In a post–war assessment the British military attaché in Karachi argued that a lack of intelligence was one of the contributing factors to Pakistan's lackluster performance in the war. For example, the failure to track India's First Armoured Division prior to hostilities was then compounded by India's "surprise" attack on 6 September.[21]

Altaf Gauhar was Ayub's Information Secretary during this time as well as a close presidential confidant. He later recalled a conversation with Ayub in which the president criticized ISI Director Riaz for making false promises of ISI capabilities before the war when the results showed, using Gauhar's words, a "complete black out of intelligence gathering. The intelligence agencies cannot perform their core missions of collection and analysis," Gauhar continued, adding that "[t]hey have no idea of intelligence work.... All they can do is investigative work like sub–inspectors of police, tapping telephone conversations and chasing the suspects."[22]

If Riaz was, in truth, part of the problem, then he would have to be removed, but the challenge lay in easing him out of intelligence work without allowing his apparent failures to reflect poorly on Ayub. The answer was the time–honored bureaucratic solution of kicking the culprit into a more senior position with fewer responsibilities. Thus, in May 1966, Riaz Hussain was promoted to Major General and sent off to command a division at Sialkot.[23]

The new ISI chief was, in the words of a contemporary, "a tall and extremely handsome individual" named Mohammed Akbar Khan. He previously had gained some UW experience when he helped train Kashmiri guerrillas for Operation GIBRALTAR. Akbar's transfer to ISI came at a particularly sensitive time for Ayub and the intelligence community because discontent in Pakistani society was spilling over into the officer corps. As noted, one of ISI's most important duties was monitoring the officers for dissent and disloyalty.[24]

Replacing the ISI Director was only one step in Ayub's effort to shore up his intelligence agencies. In March 1967, he ordered his deputy, General Yahya Khan, to head up a committee tasked with examining the intelligence agencies and issue recommendations on improvements.[25] Ayub was especially concerned about recent unrest in the Navy as he made clear in his diary:

> DIG [Deputy Inspector General – a civilian police position] and his associates have done an excellent job whilst the Naval Intelligence and ISI were fast asleep. It just shows that we are babes in intelligence work. This is why I have set up a committee under General Yahya to consider the problem and suggest methods of revamping the system.[26]

Other members of Yahya's committee included Altaf Gauhar – apparently since he had been so voluble on intelligence reform – and the Director of the IB, Ayub Bukhsh Awan. The initial focus of the committee was the IB itself. Ayub was particularly displeased with it, lamenting that it was "still working on old lines" and not devoting enough attention to communists, student activists and outspoken mullahs. Ayub told the committee that he wanted better early warning intelligence of domestic threats so he could avoid being constantly caught by surprise.[27]

Over time, Yahya's committee expanded its investigation to include the ISI and MI. The committee's final report is still classified, making it difficult to reach any conclusions about the problems it identified and the solutions it proposed. We can make educated guesses about some of the recommendations based on changes that took place in ISI during this time. For example, sometime in 1968, the "Director" of ISI became a "Director General." This boost in bureaucratic status was accompanied by an automatic promotion from brigadier to major general. Yahya also sought to expand ISI's authority by posting its officers to the civilian-run district administrations, but Gauhar and Awan resisted this, viewing it as a blatant attempt by the military to meddle in the IB's business.[28] Finally, the committee proposed the creation of a military intelligence corps that would permit professionalization at all ranks through standardized procedures, school houses and, above all, training.[29]

Ayub was dissatisfied with the Yahya committee's final report. It accomplished little, Ayub lamented, "apart from tinkering here and there."[30] The Yahya committee encountered many of the same obstacles that were to befall similar efforts in the future, for intelligence is ultimately an exercise in power, and any attempt to reform it faces a phalanx of entrenched interests and jealously guarded turf. The failure of the Yahya committee should have been a salutary lesson for the future, but it wasn't.

President Ayub tried reforming his intelligence apparatus to obtain better early warning of internal unrest. But it was too little too late, for the last year of Ayub's rule was shaken by near-constant student and labor unrest not to mention growing tensions in East Pakistan. The country was set to blow, and it would take Ayub along with it.

Disenchantment and discontent

When the 1965 ceasefire ended the war, Pakistanis were convinced their armed forces had won a stunning victory. After all, as hostilities progressed, they had been exposed to an endless stream of propaganda extolling Pakistani victories and humiliating Indian defeats. For example, on 7 September – 24 hours after the Indians unleashed their assault on West Pakistan – the Karachi *Morning News* crowed that a "sneak thrust on Lahore" had been "decisively repulsed."[31] Another daily carried a banner headline, full of bravado: "We will not concede an inch."[32] Two weeks later, as a UN-brokered ceasefire came into effect, the public was told that "a battered India [had begged] for [a] ceasefire."[33]

Given all this triumphalism and patriotism, a wave of disillusionment swept over the country after the details of the 1966 Tashkent deal were announced. The war had ended with a whimper; all of Pakistan's gains in India were swapped for territory captured by India. Most bitterly of all, Kashmir's status remained unchanged, with no referendum in sight. No wonder many Pakistanis were confused and angry, and some began to openly voice their criticism of the regime. Sensing an opportunity, the savvy Zulfikar Ali Bhutto broke with Ayub at this time and in 1967 formed the Pakistan Peoples Party (PPP). Bhutto scored points by blasting the Tashkent settlement as a "sellout," an unnecessary compromise of Pakistan's legitimate interests in Kashmir. In response to these and other challenges, Ayub ordered his intelligence and security agencies to step up monitoring and harassment of domestic critics.[34] Within weeks of the end of the 1965 war, a senior Pakistani official informed US diplomats in Karachi that a "semi-police state atmosphere" had settled on Pakistani society.[35] Ayub's so-called benevolent dictatorship wasn't looking so benevolent anymore, and it was rapidly losing its legitimacy.

As it entered the late 1960s, Pakistan was primed for an internal explosion. Too many disruptive forces were culminating at the same time, making it impossible for the internal security apparatus to monitor them. The luster of Ayub's Basic Democracy system was wearing off amid widespread allegations of corruption involving members of his family. Wages were stagnant or declining, yet food prices were climbing, and already impoverished families were being asked to do more with less. West Pakistan's largest constituent ethnic groups were chafing at the One Unit policy, which denied them the separate, provincial status they had previously enjoyed. In the face of all this, the tone deaf regime erred when it spent $30 million on a nationwide celebration of its first decade in power.[36]

In 1968, a wave of protests and demonstrations swept across East and West Pakistan. Students filled city streets calling for political reform and an economy that could employ them when they graduated. Labor unrest broke out in Karachi, Lahore, and Dhaka based on demands for better working conditions and higher wages. But the most significant challenges to the regime were found in East Pakistan, where there was widespread discontent with the regime's failure to raise the standard of living or give the people political representation commensurate with their numbers. It didn't help that the Indian government had set up a clandestine radio station promoting the independence of East Pakistan as a separate state called Bangladesh.[37]

Notes

1 H. Haqqani, *Pakistan: Between Mosque and Military*, Washington, DC: Carnegie Endowment, 2005, 20–21.
2 A. Gauhar, "How Intelligence Agencies Run Our Politics," *The Nation*, 17 August 1997; I. Malik, *State and Civil Society in Pakistan*, London: Macmillan, 1997, 290n9.
3 A. Jalal, *The Struggle for Pakistan*, Cambridge, MA: Belknap, 2014, 97.
4 Telegram from Amembassy Karachi, 15 October 1958, found in Foreign Relations of the United States (hereafter FRUS) 1958–60, Vol. XV, document 328, 674–676.
5 A. Khan, *Friends not Masters*, New York: OUP, 1967, 75.
6 Ibid., 75.
7 Jalal, *Struggle*, op cit.

8 F. Grare, *Reforming the Intelligence Agencies in Pakistan's Transitional Democracy*, Washington, DC: Carnegie Endowment for International Peace, 2009, 17.
9 J.D. Khan, *Pakistan Leadership Challenges*, Karachi: OUP, 31.
10 P.C. Joshi, *Main Intelligence Outfits of Pakistan*, New Delhi: Anmol Publications, 2008, 15, 125.
11 Ibid., 15; P. Tomsen, *The Wars of Afghanistan*, New York: PublicAffairs, 2011, 238–239.
12 Tomsen, *Wars*, op. cit., 239.
13 T.H. Malik, *The Story of My Struggle*, Lahore: Jang, 35.
14 R. Khan, *The British Papers*, Karachi: OUP, 2002, 524–526.
15 Grare, *Reforming*, op. cit., 17.
16 Gauhar, "How Intelligence," op. cit; A. Gauhar, *Ayub Khan: Pakistan's First Military Ruler*, Karachi: OUP, 1996, 176.
17 Gauhar, "How Intelligence," op. cit.
18 Ibid.; Malik, *State*, op. cit., 293n41; H. Feldman, *From Crisis to Crisis*, Karachi: OUP, 1972, 72.
19 Telegram from UK High Commission in Rawalpindi, 5 May 1966, FO 371/188919, UKNA.
20 N.C. Behera, *Demystifying Kashmir*, Washington, DC: Brookings, 2006, 79.
21 UK Ministry of Defence, *The India-Pakistan War 1965*, DEFE 44/102, UKNA.
22 Gauhar, "How Intelligence," op. cit.
23 Telegram from UK High Commission in Rawalpindi, 5 May 1966, op. cit.
24 Ibid., M.A. Khan, *Trumped Up as an Indian Spy*, Lahore: Mohammad Akram Khan, 2002, 196–197; S. Wolpert, *Zulfi Bhutto of Pakistan*, New York: OUP, 1993, 183.
25 C. Baxter, ed., *Diaries of Field Marshal Mohammad Ayub Khan 1966–1972*, Karachi: OUP, 2007, 69.
26 Ibid., 98–99.
27 Ibid., 69.
28 Gauhar, "How Intelligence," op. cit.
29 "History of Corps of Military Intelligence" found in www.pakarmymuseumcom/exhibits/history-of-corps-of-military-intelligence/ [accessed 9/15/14].
30 Baxter, *Diaries*, op. cit., 422.
31 "India attacks: Sneak thrust on Lahore repulsed," *The Morning News*, 7 September 1965, 1.
32 "We will not concede an Inch," *The Daily News*, 7 September 1965, 1.
33 "Bravado gone: A battered India begs for ceasefire," *Morning News*, 21 September 1965, 1.
34 James, *Chronicle*, op. cit., 152.
35 Cable from Amembassy Office Rawalpindi, "Indo-Pak Crisis – SC Kashmir," 19 September 1965, no. 84, found in R. Khan, *The American Papers*, Karachi: OUP, 1999.
36 Feldman, *Crisis*, op. cit., 89.
37 R. Khan, *British*, op. cit., 466–468.

6 Intelligence Failures in East Pakistan

When Major Nurul Islam defected to the *Mukti Bahini* guerrillas in March 1971, he did so because his employer, the Pakistan army, had left him and other Bengali officers little choice. Ironically, Nurul Islam was the kind of officer who advertised what was best about United Pakistan: commissioned into the 2 East Bengal Regiment in 1962, he had ably served in both ISI and MI. As a Bengali, he could have offered his West Pakistani commanders valuable insights into the culture, customs, opinions and grievances of his people. Indeed, such insights might have helped prevent the crisis that led to the army's war against its own people, the ensuing defeat at the hands of India and the secession of East Pakistan. Instead, Nurul Islam defected, and he took his valuable knowledge of intelligence operations with him.[1]

Enter Yahya

Ayub resigned as president on 25 March 1969, when he could not suppress the demonstrations that were destabilizing Pakistan. His replacement was his deputy, General Yahya Khan, who immediately imposed martial law, but also promised to hold elections by November 1970. But the army was gambling with elections. After all, in a worst case scenario, it could be driven from power by a Bengali-dominated government intent on decentralizing the governing system and weakening the armed forces. So why did Yahya risk it? The consensus of his intelligence agencies like ISI was that no single party would win an outright majority in the National Assembly, thereby leaving room for buying and selling representatives and creating alliances to form cabinets. The army, it was reasoned, could stay on top of the political game through a mixture of mediation and manipulation.[2]

There were three major political parties entering these elections. Mujibur Rehman's Awami League was expected to do well in East Pakistan, where his Six Points platform of greater provincial autonomy was especially popular. Zulfikar Ali Bhutto's PPP was something of an unknown factor. True, Bhutto was a charismatic speaker, but what kind of support did he really enjoy outside his native province of Sindh? As for the Muslim League, that old war horse was going through lean times, torn by factional disputes and lacking public support in East Pakistan.

On the eve of the 1970 elections, the intelligence community was undergoing some changes of its own. First, General Yahya had created a National Security Council headed by a former MI Director, Major General Ghulam Omar. It was General Omar's responsibility to harness and coordinate the capabilities of ISI and the other intelligence agencies and use them to fight the regime's battles in the domestic and foreign arenas.[3] Second, the IB clearly was no longer first among equals in the community, having yielded up its monopoly on domestic intelligence to ISI and MI. Indeed, both military agencies were monitoring election candidates, polling public opinion and trying to predict election outcomes. Although it was on a downward trajectory in terms of relative power, the IB nonetheless retained considerable expertise in East Pakistani politics on account of an experienced cadre of Bengali officers steeped in their language and culture.[4] Unfortunately, the government did not make better use of this expertise; had it done so, the East Pakistan crisis might have turned out differently.

Yahya assigned the IB the task of creating a weak, pro-army civilian government. In practical terms, this meant organizing a new, reinvigorated, Muslim League capable of draining votes from the other parties and thereby serve as a "king's party" in the legislature.[5] The IB and ISI tried aggravating centrifugal forces within the Awami League by funding Abdul Hamid Khan Bhashani, a socialist activist who was a thorn in Mujibur Rehman's side. As we shall see, this effort to divide and weaken the League failed with catastrophic results for Pakistan.[6]

On elections' eve, ISI was led by Major General Mohamed Akbar Khan, a hardliner in Yahya's inner circle who vehemently opposed any power transfer to civilians.[7] Paradoxically, although Ayub had ordered ISI to pick up assignments in East Pakistan back in the 1950s, the organization still had a thin bench of Bengali expertise. ISI's Punjabi and Pashtun leadership viewed the lush delta basin and the jungle-covered Chittagong Hills of the east wing as literally an alien world apart.[8] Such expertise as ISI possessed on East Pakistan was found in officers of Bengali origin such as Major Nurul Islam Shishu and Captain Sadekur Rahman Choudhury, both of whom went on to serve in the Bangladesh army.[9]

Polling public opinion was one of ISI's most important missions in the lead-up to elections. This was certainly a non-traditional assignment for military intelligence; even so, ISI officers were sent down to provincial districts, where they tried ferreting out local sentiment. The information they obtained was transmitted back to ISI HQ where it was compiled and collated before forwarding to the leadership. These ISI assessments downplayed the Awami League's chances in the election, calculating that it would be unable to win enough seats in the legislature to unilaterally form a government. ISI situation reports like these were routinely sent to the Chief Martial Law Administrator (Yahya), the Joint Service Commanders Committee and the Minister of Defence.[10]

Another important pre-election task for ISI was reaching out to Islamist parties. Again, the objective was to weaken the Awami League and the PPP by siphoning of some of their votes. ISI's favored Islamist party at the time was the *Jama'at-e-Islami* (JI), a disciplined, well-funded organization intent on establishing *Sharia* as the law of the land. In general terms, the JI was not popular in either wing of Pakistan; however, its reputation was especially poor in East Pakistan because it opposed the "divisive" autonomy arrangement desired by many Bengalis.[11] ISI tended to overestimate the JI's popularity in East Pakistan. For example, ISI's Dhaka Detachment forwarded one assessment of a JI rally under the wordy title "Massive Show on Shaukat-e-Islam Day by Muslims Indicating Their Unflinching Faith in Islamic cum Pakistan Ideology." Such ringing endorsements of ISI's Islamist ally did more harm than good, because what the government really needed was actual, on-the-ground facts, not overblown assessments of JI's supposedly surging popularity. The Awami League was the real player to watch, but the "agencies" downplayed its election chances.[12]

Though underestimated, the League was not spared from ISI surveillance. Former Ayub confidant, Altaf Gauhar, recalled that ISI's Akbar Khan approached him for the names of prominent Bengali intellectuals and journalists because ISI was trying to infiltrate the camp of Mujibur Rehman, head of the Awami League.[13] According to several sources, ISI planted a bug in a conference room, where Mujib informed colleagues that any pre-election agreements made with Yahya would be null and void once the League was in power. "Who could challenge me once the elections are over?" Mujib was recorded as saying. Needless to say, once he was informed of Mujib's comments, Yahya lost whatever remaining trust he had in the League.[14]

The Awami League was well aware that Yahya's spies were trying to infiltrate its ranks and sow the seeds of dissension. In a June 1970 meeting with US diplomats, Mujib complained about ISI and IB meddling, alleging they were shaking down Pakistani industrialists for money to fund pro-government parties and intimidating East Pakistanis into voting against the League. In a message he clearly wanted transmitted to Islamabad, Mujib warned that ISI interference would not be tolerated: "I will proclaim independence and call for guerrilla action if the army tries to stop me."[15]

In the days leading up to the election, ISI stood by its assessment that the Awami League was not going to win as many seats as League leaders expected. One ISI estimate maintained this veneer of unrealistic optimism by asserting that there were "[u]nmistakable signs of some disillusionment in East Pakistan people with Sheikh Mujib and his Awami League."[16] It went on to predict that the League could only form a government in a coalition with other parties. That fact alone, the Director General of ISI (DGISI) Akbar Khan reasoned in a meeting with Yahya, should give the army plenty of room to mediate, adjudicate, intimidate and facilitate a cabinet responsive to army interests.[17]

Political crisis

The results of Pakistan's first free and fair national election stunned the army and the intelligence community. The Awami League won an outright majority, enabling it to form a cabinet without a coalition. It won 160 of 162 delegate seats from East Pakistan, yet it had no representation in West Pakistan. Bhutto's PPP took a respectable 81 out of 138 seats in West Pakistan, but none in the east wing. As for ISI's Islamist allies, they put in an unimpressive performance, with the JI winning four seats and the *Jamiat Ulema-e-Islam* seven. Almost all of the intelligence community's pre-election predictions were dead wrong, leading policymakers to question the agencies' competence. Viewing events from retirement, Ayub recorded his own perspective of their deficiencies:

> The trouble with our intelligence agencies and especially the Director, Intelligence Bureau, is that they tell stories after the event which can be picked up from any newspaper. What they don't do is give advance warning which can only be obtained by infiltrating into subversive organisations and finding out their plans. I always had my doubts whether the policemen were the correct people to man such as organisation. You need people with much more flexible and subtle minds for a job like that.[18]

Still, it's worthwhile asking the question: if the IB and ISI possessed the "flexible and subtle minds" that Ayub sought, would the policymakers have listened to the analysis? What if those Bengali IB officers who knew their community like no West Pakistani could, produced an assessment forecasting a big Awami victory? Would Yahya, Akbar and company have believed it? Probably not, for it was easier to dismiss the IB as being overly influenced by Bengalis. The failure to accurately gauge the 1970 election outcome is an indictment of the political system as much as the intelligence agencies. So large was the Awami League's margin of victory that the Yahya junta was virtually paralyzed and rapidly lost whatever initiative it had left.

One cannot envy Yahya's predicament after the elections, for he was confronted by an impossible conundrum: how to keep East Pakistan in the Union without weakening that Union and the army's dominance within it? Yahya could simply accept the results, transfer power to Mujib and wash his hands of the whole affair, accepting that Mujib would make Pakistan a weaker, more loosely united confederation. Alternatively, Yahya could reject the results, impose martial law and move on; however, the risk in doing this was the near certainty of civil war.

Critical decisions like these required good advisors, a willingness to entertain contrary opinions and reliable intelligence. Yahya lacked all of the above. Only a small number of his advisors like former East Pakistan governors, Vice Admiral Ahsan or Sahabzada Yaqub Khan understood the

Bengali situation best, but they were dismissed as being too sympathetic to the "bingos." In fact, Yahya relied too much on his intelligence community for information and advice on East Pakistan even though the leaders of the two most important agencies – the IB and ISI – were not Bengalis themselves. Both were headquartered in the West and, over time, the ISI in particular had marginalized those Bengali officers in its ranks who might have offered some useful pointers about East Pakistan. The result of this fundamental lack of information was misunderstanding and lousy estimates. Two American researchers put a finer point on this in their history of the 1971 Indo-Pakistan War:

> Regardless of the way intelligence was evaluated and presented, it still did not adequately reflect the intensity of Bengali sentiment or the scope of the public support enjoyed by the Awami League. Government intelligence services had poor access to the Awami League and relied increasingly on non-Bengali groups.[19]

DGISI Akbar Khan was one person in Yahya's entourage who could have shaped the leader's thinking on East Pakistan in a more constructive manner. Tragically though, for all concerned, Akbar was the *worst* person to provide Yahya with unbiased views on the crisis, for he was a known hardliner who adamantly rejected the election results. "We will not hand over power to these bastards!" he is recorded as saying.[20] Like so many other West Pakistani officers, Akbar believed the Bengalis were a "non-martial race" who, when coerced, would be "respectful and obedient" to their masters.[21]

So it was in this manner that Yahya's government entered the worst crisis in Pakistan's history: essentially blind and deaf, living in a world of dangerous fantasies and misplaced optimism. A lot of people were going to pay with their lives for the illusions and delusions of his leadership. Civil war, foreign invasion and, ultimately, the dismemberment of Pakistan itself were just around the corner.

Suppression and civil war

On 1 March 1971, Yahya announced that he was suspending the Awami-League-dominated National Assembly indefinitely. After weeks of inconsequential talks and secret meetings between the army and the politicians, the long wait was over; Yahya was not going to let the League take power. Predictably, the latter responded with mass demonstrations in Dhaka and other cities. Cries of betrayal were in the air, long pent up frustrations were finally being expressed; this was the real Pakistan that Bengalis had long known existed: a country and regime unwilling to let elections take their course, because the result would be governance by the despised Bengalis.

With East Pakistan paralyzed by unrest, the army planned a province-wide crackdown ostensibly to restore order but also to intimidate the population and teach it a lesson. Reinforcements were flowing in from the west wing, cantonments were a hub of activity, and the security apparatus was being stealthily purged of its Bengali officers.[22] On 25 March 1971, these preparations culminated with Operation SEARCHLIGHT, which included disarming East Pakistan Rifles troops, arresting Awami leaders, and an assault on the hotbeds of Bengali nationalism like Dhaka University. After the soldiers had made their arrests, ISI conducted the interrogations of the captives and obtained information on the whereabouts of other League leaders. ISI's performance during this period was mixed: on the one hand, it captured Mujibur Rehman and hauled him off to an ISI safe house in West Pakistan; on the other, the security forces failed to identify and arrest several other opposition leaders, most of whom fled to India.[23] But ISI was mainly working behind the scenes. It was the army's actions in Dhaka that outraged world opinion and galvanized Bengalis into full-scale revolt. Murder, pillaging and rape were rife amid the flames of burning buildings, while the screams of terrified civilians only seemed to spur the soldiers to greater violence and mayhem. It was probably the darkest period in the history of Pakistan's armed forces.[24]

Some foreign correspondents were in Dhaka when the blow fell, but their reporting could not reach overseas editors because ISI had cut the phone and telex lines; intelligence officers were also rounding up the journalists and shipping them out on the next available plane.[25] Yet ISI failed to stifle news of the massacres, for within days, the first wave of what would eventually amount to several million refugees flooded into India, bearing stories of the tragedy unfolding in their country. In addition, diplomats were witnessing the sacking of Dhaka with their own eyes, and the tone in their correspondence home was one of shock. The Australian Deputy High Commission, for example, noted that "[the army] had one purpose and one purpose only – to strike terror as widely and deeply as possible. This was to be done by killing as many Bengalis as they could find in what they regarded as 'suspect' areas."[26]

International horror of what was taking place was communicated to the government in Islamabad through diplomatic channels. Since the foreign military attaché corps was officially accredited to him, DGISI Akbar Khan served as the army's front man in answering some of their questions. Unfortunately for the Yahya junta, Akbar turned out to be a public relations disaster, not only because of his dealings with the more discreet military attachés, but his press interviews as well. For instance, on 27 March, two days after SEARCHLIGHT commenced, Akbar briefed the attachés from Canada, the UK and the US at his office in Islamabad. His message was strident and unyielding: the army would not let Pakistan disintegrate by allowing the Awami League to take power, implement its Six Points, and essentially tear the country to pieces. Akbar adopted an optimistic stance that other officials would take in the days to come: "Everything is now under control and all is calm not only in [Dhaka] but throughout East Pakistan," he asserted. Akbar admitted that a few students had been shot for "resisting arrest," but the situation had stabilized and the evacuation of foreign nationals was no longer necessary. The DGISI insisted that compromise with the League was imposs- ible: give Mujibur Rehman one compromise, he warned, and he would want three more. Akbar also rode hard on the foreign press:

> [T]here will be no freedom of the press in this country for a very long time to come. Nearly everything in the press is misrepresented and the foreign press has been thoroughly malicious. They talk of genocide when the army kills only 27 people in a thoroughly restrained manner.... We have seen what freedom of the press can mean, particularly of the correspondents based in Delhi, where they absorb only the Indian viewpoint.[27]

In a separate conversation with a British diplomat, Akbar stated that the Bengali intelligentsia represented the real enemy:

> I personally talked to the intellectuals and left them in no doubt that the Army could and would step in. They obviously refused to believe that we would make mincemeat out of 70 million Bengalis, even though I said we would, if necessary, bring in the entire Army from West Pakistan.[28]

Akbar sneered that Mujibur Rehman was "blubbering hysterically" after his capture by SSG commandos, adding that the Awami leader was ready to state that everything he stood for was "all a mistake." Of course, what induced Mujib to make such statements – if in fact he did – is left unsaid, although torture is a distinct possibility.[29]

The DGISI's denials notwithstanding, atrocities were taking place, and some were later recorded by a Pakistani commission under Justice Hamoo- dur Rehman. The report, for example, narrates that "going to Bangladesh" was a term widely used by police and other security officials to describe the summary execution of Bengali prisoners. One civilian official who had been in the east wing lamented that "army officers who were doing intelli- gence were raw hands, ignorant of the local language and callous of Bengali sensibilities." DGISI Akbar was recorded as saying that "no commanders should be afraid to be called a butcher if that is the demand of the hour." In the end, no ISI spin master could disguise the sheer number of terrified refugees flowing into India every hour.[30] Within weeks, the number had climbed from tens of thousands to hundreds of thousands and, eventually, to millions. The refugee camps, with their squalor, filth, disease and starva- tion, triggered worldwide condemnation of Pakistan and a memorable "Concert for Bangla Desh" organized by George Harrison and Ravi Shankar. The fact that a majority of the refugees were Hindu cast a sec- tarian pall over the disaster.

As an unnatural calm settled over Dhaka, SEARCHLIGHT seemed to have accomplished its short-term goals. The League was beheaded and direc- tionless, while its activists were either in hiding, dead or in Indian refugee camps. The army extended its presence to those areas it could reach by road and boat; however, the complicated riverine terrain of central Bangladesh inhibited movement, especially for heavy vehicles. Even so, the army estimated that it had suppressed 50 percent of the resistance by May 1971.[31] But it was a deceptive calm, for actual control over the population was very limited. Coercion could only go so far: it brought grudging, fearful but temporary support, and when the insurgents showed up at many villages, the population often welcomed them with open arms. The army harbored no illusions that it controlled East Pakistan by night, when its soldiers huddled in their garrisons and stirred nervously at every unusual noise coming out of the darkness around them. For all intents and purposes, the insurgency was at a military and political stalemate until India entered the fight.[32]

Indian intervention

India was directly affected by SEARCHLIGHT because the influx of East Pakistani refugees rapidly overwhelmed local means of support in its West Bengal province. A Maoist insurgency called the Naxalites had been disrupting this troubled area for some time, and the presence of a large refugee population was only making the security situation worse. Finally, there was concern that West Bengali unrest might tempt ISI, since it always liked to fish in troubled waters when Indian security was at stake.[33]

In the beginning, India's main objective was to prevent the splintering, weakening and possible radicalization of the Awami League, since this could affect Indian stability as much as, if not more than, that of Pakistan. India also wanted to recast the League both as a Bangladesh government-in-exile and an insurgent movement, so on 17 April 1971, League leaders in India announced the creation of the Sovereign People's Republic of Bangladesh. The next day, Radio Free Bangladesh began broadcasting into East Pakistan.[34]

Developments took place on the clandestine front as well. An Indian-sponsored black – or covert – radio station transmitted pro-Bangladesh propaganda into East Pakistan from a ship anchored in the Hooghly River near Calcutta.[35] At the same time, an insurgent army was set up with help from the India Border Security Force (BSF) that was eventually called the *Mukti Bahini*. The BSF ran camps that trained, armed, and sustained *Mukti Bahini* operations inside East Pakistan until Indian intelligence took over the operation.[36] By November 1971, ISI estimated 59 camps were preparing Muktis for insurgent warfare.[37]

India's objectives were threefold: spread out the Pakistan army and distract it with onerous internal security duties; further degrade and delegitimize government authority; set conditions for the eventual independence of Bangladesh and the weakening of what was left of Pakistan.[38] It was no coincidence that these goals were very similar to those of ISI in Kashmir against India: it was payback time, and India intended to exact its revenge in full.

ISI and counter insurgency

The task of an intelligence agency is to reduce the risk of surprise, whether it is technological (a new weapon, for example), strategic (a surprise attack *à la* Pearl Harbor) or political (an unexpected victory or coalition). When it came to East Pakistan, it was ISI's job to warn of a pending mass uprising, help identify the kind of war the army was fighting – in this case an insurgency – and provide information on insurgent goals, capabilities, foreign supporters and leadership. In addition, West Pakistani soldiers and officers needed to know more about the people they were supposedly defending from the guerrillas – their history, customs, and language. Tragically, all of the above were in short supply during the 1971 crisis.

Some of the information was available to those looking for it, and residual expertise in things Bengali could still be found in agencies like the IB, which, as far back as 1961, had its finger on the pulse of East Pakistan:

> The people in this province will not be satisfied unless the constitution ensures them in reality equal and effective participation in the management of the affairs of the country, equal share of development resources and, in particular, full control over the administration of this province. The intelligentsia would also like to see a directive principle in the constitution to increase speedily East Pakistan's share in the defence services as well as equal representation of East Pakistanis in the central services.[39]

Unfortunately, cogent analysis like this probably wasn't read by the leadership and, even if it was, it would probably have been dismissed as the ravings of a civilian intelligence agency tainted by treasonous Bengalis in its ranks. It was a self-fulfilling prophecy because many of those Bengali IB officers who were shunted aside during the crisis eventually defected to the *Mukti Bahini* where their skills were in high demand.[40] Predictably, as its confidence in the IB diminished, the junta turned to ISI and MI for interpreting the East Pakistan crisis; however, both lacked expertise, sources and understanding of the insurgency and its causes. The problem was particularly acute in the ISI's senior ranks, which were overwhelmingly West Pakistani and a thousand miles away from the front. According to one account, when the Army Chief of Staff was asked whether Yahya knew what was happening in the east wing, the glib reply was "[h]ow can he ever, when he has three Punjabis as his intelligence chiefs."[41]

The importance of HUMINT in counter insurgency (COIN) cannot be overstated. Good COIN requires excellent knowledge not only of the adversary but, more especially, of the population, its social structure, leadership, linguistic and religious divisions as well as its attitudes toward the insurgency. For military intelligence agencies traditionally focused on order of battle, technical intelligence, and military personalities, switching to a COIN environment where the priorities include tribal structures, local customs, and religious affiliations, the transition can be very difficult. ISI HUMINT in East Pakistan failed to adapt to COIN requirements. A reasonably competent HUMINT collector when it came to the Indian military, ISI was overwhelmed by the insurgency because it possessed few officers familiar with the culture or proficient in the language. Senior leaders were blinded by prejudice and an inability to understand Bengali grievances and sensibilities. What few Bengali spies ISI did possess disappeared after the March–April 1971 atrocities or as a result of *Mukti Bahini* counter intelligence.[42] The senior Pakistani commander in the East, Lieutenant General Amir Abdullah Khan Niazi later recorded in his memoirs: "We never really succeeded in establishing an intelligence setup which could be helpful to us. Some arrangements were made but there were a lot of handicaps due to language difficulties and the hostility of the local population."[43]

The ISI tried compensating for these deficiencies by relying on the ethnic minorities and religious parties of East Pakistan like the Biharis, an Urdu-speaking people who emigrated to the east wing after Partition, and the *JI*. Together, members of these were formed into militias called *Razakars*, which tried to intimidate the population into non-cooperation with the Muktis, and obtain intelligence on insurgent operations. Still, the very nature of the *Razakar* militias meant that their knowledge of the Bengali majority (both Muslim and Hindu) wasn't much better than their sponsors. They had little insight into *Mukti Bahini* insurgent operations that could be of much value to the authorities.[44] In fact, ISI and MI had only limited success infiltrating the Muktis. First, there was the challenge of recruiting spies who were both Bengali and willing to work for the army. Next was the dangerous task of infiltrating the insurgent camps in India, where they could be sniffed out by *Mukti Bahini* CI officers, whose declared mission was the "liquidation of enemy agents, informers and collaborators."[45]

As far as COIN goes, SIGINT can facilitate counter-leadership strikes, ambushes, or attacks on important individuals or supplies. On the other hand, SIGINT usually offers less insight into cultures and religious practices as well as adversary intentions. The Indians followed better communications security practices in 1970 than they did in 1965; they reportedly used more encryption and tried to eliminate "chatter" over open lines. Still, the Pakistanis intercepted Indian tactical communications that helped to build up detailed order of battle charts.[46] They also intercepted some *Mukti Bahini* wireless communications; however, given the nature of their dispersed, autonomous operations, the Muktis didn't rely much on wireless.[47]

East Pakistan was a "black hole" for ISI, and this meant that the army's eyes and ears were increasingly blind and deaf to ground realities. In fact, East Pakistan, a constituent part of the state, had become a "denied area" for the army and its intelligence services: the garrisons were isolated, the Muktis owned the countryside, reconnaissance patrols were frequently ambushed, and local intelligence sources were neutralized. Poor assumptions plus lousy sources often yield equally lousy analysis. In the case of ISI and the 1971 crisis, many analysts automatically assumed the Bengalis were poor fighters who would run in the face of determined army opposition. Ironically, it was also assumed that most Bengalis were loyal Pakistani citizens, whose moderate voices were being drowned out by a few extremists.[48]

As the East Pakistan crisis escalated in spring 1971, ISI analysis remained deficient. It did pick up early signs of the *Mukti Bahini* formations in India, but analysts believed India would not let the Muktis get too strong lest they overwhelm the Pakistanis and trigger an India–Pakistan war. ISI also assessed the *Mukti Bahini* intended to set up a government in a "liberated area" of East Pakistan backed by Indian artillery and air power.[49] The ISI chief had his own "spin" on East Pakistan, which he shared with army leaders and diplomats alike. Akbar denied a civil war was taking place in East Pakistan and argued that the Bengalis as a whole were loyal to Pakistan; they were even helping the army crush the Muktis. Indeed, he argued that the "rebellion" would have been crushed within weeks were it not for the Indian army.[50]

Later in the summer of 1971, ISI briefed the senior leadership on Indian army order of battle and military capabilities. The analysts warned that the Indians were forward deploying their forces to the borders of both East and West Pakistan, but tempered their alarm with a confident prediction that India probably would not attack Pakistan. Still, as the Indian buildup continued, it was getting harder for ISI to ignore the obvious signs of an imminent Indian invasion.[51]

If the policymaker uses intelligence assessments to help frame decisions – and this is by no means certain – then it is logical to conclude that bad assessments often lead to bad policies. Sometimes, assessments reinforce bad policies by creating the illusion that said policies are working when they're not. In the case of Pakistan, no one in the intelligence community appeared to be speaking truth to power.[52] The Army Chief of General Staff, Lieutenant General Gul Hassan Khan, captured the overall problems posed by intelligence collection and analysis in the east wing:

> First, our intelligence system had broken down completely. The Bengalis, who dominated our intelligence services, had either elected to join the rebels or fed us information which was not authentic for fear of reprisals at the hand of anti-government elements. In fact, we knew next to nothing except for the reports initiated by our troops, and these mainly touched upon field intelligence of immediate tactical value. There was no information that could aid us in constructing an overall scenario on which we could build our own plans.[53]

The COIN mission in East Pakistan clearly exceeded ISI's capabilities, particularly in the area of HUMINT operations; however, ISI was able to provide adequate warning to the leadership when the Indian government decided to intervene militarily in the crisis in December 1971.

Notes

1   A. Habibul, *Brave of Heart: the Urban Guerrilla Warfare of Sector-2 during the Liberation War of Bangladesh*, Dhaka: Academic Press and Publishers Library, 2006, 31, 36.
2   A. Siddiqi, *East Pakistan: The Endgame*, Karachi: OUP, 2004, 42–43; J. Marker, *Quiet Diplomacy: Memoirs of an Ambassador of Pakistan*, Karachi: OUP, 2010, 115.
3   A. Shah, *The Army and Democracy*, Cambridge, Harvard University Press, 2014, 108.
4   A.A.K. Niazi, *The Betrayal of East Pakistan*, Karachi: OUP, 1999, 96–97.
5   H. Zaheer, *The Separation of East Pakistan*, Dhaka: OUP, 1994, 124; I. Malik, *State and Civil Society in Pakistan*, London: Macmillan, 1997, 293n41.
6   Siddiqi, *East Pakistan*, op. cit., 45–46; Malik, *State*, op. cit., 293n41.
7   L. Ziring, "Militarism in Pakistan: the Yahya Khan Interregnum," *Asian Affairs* 1:6, July-August 1974, 411.
8   K. Matinuddin, *Tragedy of Errors: East Pakistan Crisis, 1968–1971*, Lahore: Wajdalis, 1994, 476.
9   "List of the Persons in the Agartala Conspiracy Case," http://soc.culture.bangladesh [accessed 8/4/15].
10 Matinuddin, *Tragedy*, op. cit., 151.
11 H. Feldman, *From Crisis to Crisis*, Karachi: OUP, 1972, 65.
12 Matinuddin, *Tragedy*, op. cit., 141, 151, 476; G.A. Khan, *Glimpses into the Corridors of Power*, Karachi: OUP, 2007, 124.
13 A. Gauhar, "How Intelligence Agencies Run Our Politics," *The Nation*, 17 August 1997.
14 G.W. Choudhury, *The Last Days of United Pakistan*, London: C. Hurst, 1974, 98.
15 Cable from Amconsul Dacca, "East Pakistan: Sheikh Mujib in Serious Mood," no. 306, found in R. Khan, *The American Papers*, Karachi: OUP, 1999, 367.
16 Matinuddin, *Tragedy*, op. cit., 151.
17 Ibid., 141, 150.
18 C. Baxter, ed., *Diaries of Field Marshal Mohammad Ayub Khan 1966–1972*, Karachi: OUP, 2007, 422.
19 R. Sisson and L. Rose, *War and Secession: Pakistan, India, and the Creation of Bangladesh*, Berkeley: University of California Press, 1990, 108.
20 Ziring, "Militarism," op. cit.
21 Matinuddin, *Tragedy*, op. cit., 171–172.
22 Zaheer, *Separation*, op. cit., 166–167.
23 Ibid. 167; A.O. Mitha, *Unlikely Beginnings: A Soldier's Life*, Karachi: OUP, 2003, 349; Cable from Army Military Attaché, Deputy British High Commission, Dacca, 29 March 1970, FCO 37/879, UKNA; Matinuddin, *Tragedy*, op. cit., 267.
24 Telegram from Amconsul Dacca, 28 March 1971, no. 959, "Selective Genocide," NARA, RG 59, POL 23–9 PAK.
25 Telegram from Assistant Military Attaché, Dacca, 27 March 1971, FCO 37/879, UKNA; Telegram from Assistant Military Attaché, Dacca, 29 March 1971, FCO 38/879, UKNA.
26 Correspondence from J.L. Allen, Australian Deputy High Commission, Dacca, 30 March 1971, no. 54, FCO 37/880, UKNA.
27 Cable from British High Commission, Islamabad, 28 March 1970, no. 404, FCO 37/879, UKNA.
28 Correspondence by A.A. Halliley, Deputy British High Commission, Dacca, Islamabad, FCO 37/884, UKNA.
29 Ibid.; Cable from Pickard, British High Commission, Islamabad, 27 March 1971, no. 404, FCO 37/879, UKNA.
30 Government of Pakistan, *Hamoodur Rehman Commission Report*, nd www.pppusa.org/Acrobat/Hamoodur%20Rahman%20Commission%20Report.pdfs [accessed 17/5/11].

31 Niazi, *Betrayal*, op. cit., 70.
32 Zaheer, *Separation*, op. cit., 171; Choudhury, *Last*, op. cit., 187.
33 Sisson and Rose, *War*, op. cit., 145–146; S. Nawaz, *Crossed Swords*, Karachi: OUP, 2008, 284.
34 Sisson and Rose, *War*, op. cit., 142–143.
35 Zaheer, *Separation*, op. cit., 276; K.M. Arif, *Khaki Shadows*, Karachi: OUP, 2001, 130.
36 Niazi, *Betrayal*, op. cit., 69; G.J. Bass, *The Blood Telegram: Nixon, Kissinger and a Forgotten Genocide*, New York: Knopf, 2013, 181; Sisson and Rose, *War*, op. cit., 143–144; A. Raina, *Inside RAW: the Story of India's Secret Service*, New Delhi: Vikas, 1981, 56.
37 Sisson and Rose, *War*, op. cit., 183–184.
38 Raina, *RAW*, op. cit., 59.
39 Quoted in Gauhar, *Ayub*, op. cit., 98–99.
40 Niazi, *Betrayal*, op. cit., 96–97.
41 Siddiqi, *East Pakistan*, op. cit., 29–30.
42 D.K. Palit, *The Lightning Campaign*, New Delhi: Thomson Press, 1972, 155.
43 Niazi, *Betrayal*, op. cit., 96–97.
44 H. Haqqani, *Pakistan: Between Mosque and Military*, Washington, DC: Carnegie Endowment, 2005, *Pakistan*, 77.
45 Sisson and Rose, *War*, op. cit., 184–185; Bass, *Blood*, op. cit., 186–187.
46 Niazi, *Betrayal*, op. cit., 131.
47 G.H. Khan, *Memoirs of Lt. Gen. Gul Hassan Khan*, Karachi: OUP, 1993, 313.
48 Sisson and Rose, *War*, op. cit., 162–163.
49 Ibid.
50 Siddiqi, *East Pakistan*, op. cit., 121–122.
51 Mitha, *Unlikely*, op. cit., 350.
52 Siddiqi, *East Pakistan*, op. cit., 152–153, 173.
53 G.H. Khan, *Memoirs*, op. cit., 301.

7   Intelligence and the 1971 War

At the outset the war in East Pakistan was an internal one, pitting the *Mukti Bahini* insurgents and their Indian supporters against the Pakistani armed forces, paramilitaries, and militias. Until the Indians commenced military operations at the end of November 1971, the struggle for East Pakistan was unconventional, characterized by insurgency and COIN, information warfare, and intelligence operations. ISI was not equipped to handle the requirements of COIN, and when India invaded in December 1971, the intelligence apparatus in East Pakistan had broken down completely.

UW in East Pakistan

ISI exercised broad responsibility for UW in the east wing, and the same limitations that hampered its intelligence mission there affected its UW campaign as well. East Pakistan was virtually a foreign country for ISI's UW practitioners: the people spoke a different language, and their culture was, in many respects, a mystery. ISI's problems in recruiting spies among the Bengali population held true for the UW effort as well. ISI recruited heavily among the minority ethnic Bihari community to form militias aimed at policing the majority Bengalis and neutralizing the *Mukti Bahini* insurgency. Speakers of Urdu, the Biharis had earlier benefited from their loyalty to Pakistan by appointments to the district- and provincial-level administration of East Pakistan. This generated considerable resentment, envy and hatred among Bengalis who felt like an aggrieved majority inside their own country.[1]

Then there were the religious parties of which the *JI* was the clear ISI favorite. Vehemently opposed to the idea of Bangladesh and the socialist, secular platform of the Awami League, the JI viewed Pakistan's potential breakup as yet a further weakening of the *Umma* – the worldwide community of Believers. ISI helped fund the JI newspaper in East Pakistan called the *Dainik Shangram*, while the JI's student wing provided cadres for two anti-Mukti militias named after early Islamic battles: *al-Badr* and *al-Shams*. These militias gave the JI and ISI additional muscle; they were also notorious for torturing and killing those they deemed "disloyal" to Pakistan.[2]

The militias served a useful purpose for ISI inside East Pakistan, but they were not going to be effective waging proxy wars inside India. In that arena, ISI responded to India's backing of the *Mukti Bahini* with proxies of its own, such as the Nagas, Mizos and possibly the Maoist Naxalites. In a November 1971 press conference, Lieutenant General Amir Abdullah Khan Niazi, the senior commander in East Pakistan, admitted that recent train derailments in India's Assam Province had been caused by Pakistani-trained saboteurs. Ultimately, though, Pakistan's proxy strategy failed to deter India from meddling in the east wing, let alone absorb large numbers of Indian forces in COIN duties.[3]

ISI's poor understanding of the motives behind Bengali unrest meant that information operations in the field were often crude. For example, in May 1971, the Eastern Command Chief of Staff (and future Director General of ISI (DGISI)), Brigadier Ghulam Jilani, emphasized the need for an army "hearts and minds" campaign during a staff conference in Dhaka. Oddly, his proposed method for winning these hearts and minds was to eliminate the alleged "Hindu" aspects of East Pakistani culture by substituting the Arabic alphabet for the traditional Devanagari one in the written Bengali language. In Brigadier Jilani's opinion (shared by many others in the army), Bengali intellectuals were responsible for the East Pakistan crisis, because they were "un-Islamic" and corrupted the minds of the vulnerable youth with Bengali nationalism.[4] For his part, Niazi, the senior officer in Eastern Command, prided himself on his information operations, which consisted in part of dropping radios into rural East Pakistan programmed to receive only government stations. He optimistically believed that such radios would help offset Indian propaganda and the Muktis' repeated calls for Bangladesh.[5]

But Pakistan's leadership was living in a dream world, where human rights abuses could be disguised by simply denying journalists access to the most troubled areas. It was impossible to prevent news of the atrocities from spreading even inside Dhaka itself, where the journalists that remained learned about events from multiple sources. One observer later recalled that "[i]n fact, a foreigner could get complete information in the [Dhaka Intercontinental] hotel from its staff and the room bearers who acted as the couriers of the rebels to the foreign guests."[6]

Information controls aside, ISI became one of the government's de facto spokesmen as it conveyed its assessments of the situation to the domestic and foreign media. Although DGISI Akbar preferred staying out of the limelight, East Pakistan forced him into a public relations role for which he was ill-suited.[7] It has already been noted that Akbar was one of the more vocal hardliners in Yahya's inner circle, and he did not hesitate to share his sentiments with foreigners as well, including the Western media that he was supposed to cultivate. In the summer of 1971, for instance, he met a member of the British Council in Dhaka, where he proceeded to denounce the BBC for its "lies" about East Pakistan. "Let there be no mistaking what we can do for British citizens in Pakistan if this continues," he added, ominously. His British guest asked him why the Pakistani government refused to grant journalists' access to the east wing and thereby obtain a more accurate picture of the situation. Akbar's response was characteristically blunt: "We do not care about world opinion," he said. "We have a job to do and we will do it no matter what anyone says."[8]

Despite Akbar's dislike of the media, he nonetheless held several press conferences throughout the crisis, where he tried to maintain a steady drumbeat of criticizing the Awami League, the Muktis, and India. He reiterated that the Six Points were a blueprint for secession, Mujib's real objective was independence, and the East Pakistan situation was not a civil war but a "rebellion" against constitutional authority. In the end, as far as the DGISI was concerned, all roads led back to India: "The root cause of the Indo-Pakistan trouble is that India has never really accepted the fact of Pakistan."[9]

Counter intelligence problems

In addition to collection, analysis and UW, ISI was responsible for counter intelligence (CI) in East Pakistan. At the best of times, CI is a difficult, painstaking discipline that requires patience and attention to detail, yet the nature of the fighting in East Pakistan added new layers of complexity to the CI task. By their very definition, civil wars are messy affairs where loyalties are often dangerously unclear. *Who do you trust? Who is loyal to the enemy?* In this context, ISI's challenges were nearly insurmountable: there were pro-Mukti sympathizers in the civilian bureaucracy, the official paramilitary units like the East Pakistan Rifles, and even the intelligence apparatus itself. Then there were those who had already defected to the *Mukti Bahini*, including one Bengali staff officer who provided the Indians with valuable order of battle data for the Pakistan army.[10] Last, but certainly not least, were pro-Mukti officials who stayed at their official Pakistani posts, and provided India's Research and Analysis Wing (RAW) with war plans, order of battle, and diplomatic traffic.[11] Lieutenant General Gul Hassan Khan discussed the defector problem in his memoirs:

> They not only divulged the details of our defence layout, including the extent of our minefields, etc., but took whatever equipment they could carry. At the best of times it is never a simple task to fight an enemy four to five times superior in numbers, but it is positively a hopeless undertaking when he is also in possession of our plans.[12]

It has been asserted that India possessed "excellent local intelligence" on the general situation in East Pakistan, Pakistan military capabilities, morale, senior command conflicts and troop movements.[13] Some of this came from Bengali switchboard operators, who eavesdropped on conversations and wrote down what they heard for their Mukti and RAW handlers.[14] All in all, the Indians and the Muktis possessed a proficient intelligence organization which ran circles around ISI:

The highly educated personnel of the Mukti Bahini readily understood what information was required, where and how to get it, and how and when it should be conveyed for maximum utility and effectiveness. Indian forces ... were almost invariably in possession of detailed information regarding enemy locations, moves and even intentions.[15]

ISI's inability to adequately protect its secrets and its agents was one consequence of the army's oppressive policies in East Pakistan. Whereas the Mukti Bahini could count on the local population for shelter, supplies and information, ISI and the army as a whole were regarded as agents of an alien occupation.

Collapse

In September, DGISI Akbar Khan was rotated out to command 12th Infantry Division in West Pakistan.[16] His replacement as DGISI was newly promoted Major General Ghulam Jilani Khan, the previous Chief of Staff for Eastern Command.[17] As DGISI, it was Jilani's task to inform Yahya and Niazi about Indian military deployments near the East Pakistani border, stepped up Mukti operations and ongoing Soviet arms shipments to India. By early October, under his watch, ISI assessed that a war with India was likely and imminent. As more intelligence became available, ISI was able to predict that the Indian assault would take place in the last week of November. On 19 November, Army GHQ sent the latest ISI assessment to General Niazi in the east wing, which provided a detailed breakdown of the Indian order of battle and predicted that the invasion would take place on 20 November. This valuable information was based on a "reliable" source who may have been an Indian officer with access to the GHQ war plans.[18]

On the night of 20–21 November, Indian units began probing Pakistani defenses with supporting artillery fires, yet India avoided declaring war, and launching its assault until Pakistan acted first.[19] Pakistan obliged, and 36 hours after Pakistani fighters conducted a preemptive strike on Indian Air Force bases, India invaded the east wing with overwhelming force. On 5 December, only hours before the assault began, the Pakistani Army Chief of Staff notified General Niazi in Eastern Command that: "It is now evident from all sources including intelligence channels that INDIANS will shortly launch a full-scale offensive against EAST Pakistan ..."[20]

The outcome of this phase of the war in East Pakistan was pre-ordained. Arrayed against eight fully equipped and supported Indian divisions were three under-strength and demoralized Pakistani ones, two of which lacked heavy equipment such as tanks and artillery. Rather than tackle each Pakistani fortified position in turn, the Indians masked them instead, and advanced rapidly toward Dhaka, their main objective.[21] Pakistani command and control rapidly broke down, and Eastern Command Headquarters soon lost contact with subordinate field units.[22] Tactical intelligence could not be sent to HQ for further analysis, and the same was true of HQ efforts to push needed intelligence down to troops in the field. For its part, ISI HQ in Islamabad was all but cut off from its subordinate detachments in the East.[23]

On 16 December, Pakistani forces in Dhaka surrendered to their Indian counterparts. Although Pakistani accounts generally do not mention this, the surrender of some 90,000 soldiers must have posed a daunting operational security nightmare for ISI. How much valuable material, including intelligence data, encryption machines and cyphers were the Indians able to salvage from the defeated Pakistani army? Some ISI officials who were still in East Pakistan when Dhaka fell, tried to go underground or flee to Burma rather than subject themselves to likely abuse by the Indians or, worse, the angry *Mukti Bahini*.[24]

The 1971 defeat devastated the rump Pakistani state that remained. Overnight, the country lost 53 percent of its population, not to mention the rich agricultural lands of East Pakistan and the jute crop. The loss of the Bengalis also meant that their more pluralistic and heterodox approach to Islam would no longer check the tendencies of the more fundamentalist version found in the west wing.[25] Indeed, one consequence of defeat was a quest among many West Pakistanis for a more "authentic" Islam, which they believed provided better answers to their country's myriad problems than the army's worn-out secular ideology.[26]

ISI's performance

ISI emerged from the war in relatively good shape. On the positive side, it had situational awareness of the Indian armed forces and their operational planning up until the actual invasion. On the negative side, the ISI's inability to fathom the anger and frustration simmering in East Pakistan meant it failed to predict the vehemence of Bengali resistance, the formation of the *Mukti Bahini* insurgency in India, and the near total unwillingness of the people to cooperate with the army. There was an enormous gulf between the delusions of a West Pakistani ISI leadership, which preferred to believe the fantasy of a passive, pro-Pakistan majority in the East, and the stark reality that this same people viewed the army as a brutal and alien occupying force.

ISI's alliance with the *JI* was solidified during the war, and this had portentous consequences for Pakistani politics. As historian Stephen Cohen put it: "Thus began a long and sordid history of the Pakistani state and its intelligence services using Islamist radicals to terrorize regime opponents, ethnic separatists, the moderate politicians, and, where necessary, radical Islamists."[27] This alliance was to manifest itself repeatedly in the future both in ISI's manipulation of domestic politics and foreign policy.

A more immediate concern for ISI and MI was the discontent brewing in the army since the defeat. On 19 December, a mutiny broke out in two army divisions based at Gujranwala, whose senior officers demanded an immediate power transfer to civilian leadership. Yahya had to go, they insisted or they would march on Rawalpindi and do the job themselves. DGISI Jilani and the Director of Military Intelligence hastened to Gujranwala to meet the rebellious generals and talk them back from the edge. But they failed in this, and the consensus among senior generals was to put Yahya under house arrest, and make him the scapegoat for the defeat. As for civilian rule, it was conceded in GHQ that the time had come to transfer power, and the only viable candidate was the second-place winner in the 1970 election: Zulfikar Ali Bhutto.[28]

Zulfikar Ali Bhutto

On 20 December 1971, Bhutto became the fourth President of Pakistan and Chief Martial Law Administrator. His was the first civilian-run government since 1958, and it would be fair to say that the army had handed him a mess of epic proportions. Unquestionably intelligent, Bhutto had a knack for communicating with the people on their own terms and in their own dialect, but he was also intensely ambitious and arrogant, quick to dismiss those he felt were not his intellectual or social equals.[29] Such condescension was going to cost him dearly in the future. Former British High Commissioner to Pakistan, Sir Morrice James, later captured some of the contradictions in Bhutto's character:

> Bhutto certainly had the right qualities for reaching the heights.... But there was — how shall I put it? — a rank odour of hellfire about him.... He was a Lucifer, a flawed angel ... I sensed in him a ruthlessness and capacity for ill-doing which went far beyond what is natural.[30]

Bhutto was chronically suspicious of close friends, colleagues and relatives. According to one of his associates, he reveled in the "dirt" dished up by the intelligence agencies on his cabinet ministers and political opponents since this gave him material to manipulate, cajole and intimidate them.[31] His instructions to his spies were to monitor "every barb, every harsh word, every 'lie and falsehood' aimed at himself or his Pakistan Peoples Party (PPP)."[32] Given his suspicious, even paranoid, nature it is not surprising that Bhutto placed a premium on intelligence. In fact, he was an avid intelligence consumer, and what he wanted the intelligence community inevitably provided, whether it was election predictions and biographies of foreign leaders or "gossip" reports on friends and associates.[33] At the same time, Bhutto feared foreign intelligence machinations, especially those he believed were managed by the CIA. When an expose of the CIA called *The Invisible Government* was published in 1964, he reportedly distributed 300 copies to other government officials.[34] A year later, when he was serving as Ayub's Foreign Minister, Bhutto warned his boss about permitting American Peace Corps volunteers into Pakistan: "They are in our hair, under our nails — they are to be found everywhere." The US government was determined to oust Bhutto and "even the President [Ayub] himself."[35]

Zulfikar Ali Bhutto was also wary of his own intelligence community, which he referred to as an "invisible power" (there must have been a link with the Wise/Ross book here); as early as 1974 he told colleagues the "agencies" were bugging his Karachi residence telephones.[36] Some PPP stalwarts wanted to get rid of the intelligence agencies altogether, having suffered torture and prolonged imprisonment at its hands during the Ayub and Yahya eras.[37] Yet, in the end, Bhutto did not dismantle any of the agencies, for he well understood their utility for his own political objectives: the intelligence community would help him stay in power; it would also foil plots hatched by foreign adversaries, such as India and Afghanistan. Finally, Bhutto regarded himself as an expert in international relations and believed he needed better assessments of overseas developments than his Foreign Ministry was providing him. This created an opening for ISI to move in and shape the president's thinking on important foreign policy problems such as Afghanistan, Iran and relations with the Arab world.[38]

Several of Bhutto's earliest associates believed the intelligence community deliberately fed his paranoia by giving false or "half true" information to heighten his fears and suspicions. One such associate was Mubashir Hassan, who later reiterated his belief that "[t]he major goal of the intelligence community is still to wean the Prime Minister away from the principal members of his team, his old political comrades, and his favourites from the services."[39] In fact, by 1976, Bhutto had broken with many old colleagues such as his first cousin, Mumtaz Bhutto, whom he suspected was trying to kill him. Another one of the original PPP founders, Miraj Mohammed Khan, was equally alarmed by the marginalization of the PPP "old guard":

> I told [Bhutto], you're being taken over by Intelligence. J.A. Rahim was pushed out, Dr. Mubashir Hassan was pushed out, so was I – all the founding members, all of us the most radical elements. Intelligence would send him reports saying we were plotting to kill him . . .[40]

Zulfikar Ali Bhutto wanted the intelligence community to serve *his* objectives not the state's, unless those goals happened to coincide, and mission number one in his playbook was keeping the army under his thumb. How ISI was supposed to do this when it was part of the military establishment and led by an army general was a question that was never really answered. Indeed, the problem persists to this day. Having the civilian IB screen all army officers for "anti-state activities" was one way of keeping the army in check; however, this was firmly rejected by the army chief, Lieutenant General Gul Hassan Khan, who argued that assessing officer loyalty was an inherent ISI task.[41] Still, Bhutto was nothing if not a savvy bureaucratic infighter, and he secretly set up a special IB cell under a retired Colonel named Mukhtar Ali Khan, that compiled files on all senior officers in the military.[42] One Bhutto associate later recalled that: "Mukhtar pieced together facts, fiction, rumours, and juicy reports to please Mr. Bhutto. His appointment undermined the time-tested intelligence system which Bhutto trusted on a selective basis."[43] As it turned out, ISI and MI discovered Mukhtar's cell and quietly neutralized it; Bhutto's power over the armed forces definitely had its limits.[44]

Just as future civilian Pakistani leaders would do, including his daughter, Benazir, Zulfikar Ali Bhutto tried counterbalancing ISI's growing domestic power by reviving the IB. He appointed Mian Anwar Ali as IB Director, but personnel assignments were not going to change the fact that the IB could never match the budget and reach that the army conferred on ISI and MI. The days of the IB's status as lead agency in the community had come to an end, and the ISI had taken its place.[45]

Bhutto used another method of containing the army and this was the time-tested technique of creating parallel security forces to serve as a Praetorian Guard. The Federal Security Force (FSF) and the Federal Investigation Agency (FIA) were established with the idea of civilianizing certain functions previously performed by ISI and/or the MI such as counter terrorism and CI. Moreover, FSF and FIA retained intelligence capabilities of their own.[46] According to Shuja Nawaz, "Bhutto had set up a system of intelligence gathering and control parallel to that of the Pakistan Army, one that was reporting directly to him."[47]

Given his suspicious nature, it is not surprising that Bhutto wanted to make sure that "his" people staffed the most important government posts. Yet DGISI Ghulam Jilani Khan was one of only a handful of senior officials who not only predated Bhutto's presidency, but were also present in the same post when Bhutto was ousted by the army in 1977. This is even more remarkable when we consider the highly sensitive nature of Jilani's position and Bhutto's habitual mistrust of subordinates. In fact, Jilani was one of the first officials Bhutto summoned after becoming President and Chief Martial Law Administrator, because the new president sought Jilani's advice on flag officers in the armed forces: who should be removed? Who should be retained?[48] Moreover, Bhutto gave the DGISI authority to vet all senior officer promotions for any information that might bring that individual's morality or political reliability into question. This was a tremendous amount of power to be placed in Jilani's hands, for it effectively meant he could weigh in on the selection of the COAS, his ranking superior. Bhutto was going to deeply regret the day he gave his DGISI such authority over promotions, because one of the officers Jilani endorsed for advancement was Lieutenant General Zia ul-Haq.[49]

Ghulam Jilani Khan

So who was Ghulam Jilani and how did he achieve such a powerful position in Pakistan's national security apparatus? Born in 1924 and commissioned into the British Indian Army in 1944, Jilani opted for Pakistan at Partition. After proving his mettle as a volunteer in the Kashmir resistance against the Indians in 1947–1948, Jilani was given the plum assignment of Assistant Military Attaché to Washington, DC in 1952.[50] He was appointed DGISI in October

1971, when Pakistan's fortunes were approaching their lowest ebb. For reasons that will be evident in the following pages, a good argument can be made that Ghulam Jilani is the true father of the modern ISI as we know it today, for it was during his six-year term as Director General that ISI became one of the most powerful and feared agencies in Pakistan with an extensive domestic agenda and expanded covert action operations in Afghanistan.

Jilani quickly discovered that Bhutto was highly susceptible to flattery and he used this to gain the president's trust. An example of Jilani's sycophantic behavior can be found in a 1977 memorandum to Bhutto:

> There is no alternative leadership of [Mr. Bhutto's] standing and stature, or near his standing and stature, available in the field ... Mr. Bhutto is the only leader with an international standing and image, who has pro-found knowledge and experience of the inter-play of international power politics. He has done a yeoman's service to Pakistan. He is the symbol of Pakistan's stability and integrity.[51]

No wonder Zulfikar Ali Bhutto enjoyed Jilani's company so much. Indeed, he trusted him like he trusted few others. He extended Jilani's tour as DGISI, promoted him to Lieutenant General, and accepted Jilani's recommendation that Zia ul-Haq be promoted COAS.[52] Years later, as he sat in a prison cell contemplating his future, Bhutto penned his last testament called *If I Am Assassinated* in which he described with some regret how Jilani had access to his thinking on politics, politicians, army generals, foreign policy initiatives, as well as plans to consolidate the PIC after the 1977 elections.[53]

Balochistan

Bhutto's first serious domestic challenge was the restless province of Balochistan, which is populated mainly by autonomous Baloch and Pashtun tribes. Balochistan has always been something of a square peg in Pakistan's round hole: it is lightly inhabited, impoverished, marginalized and remote from Punjab, the province that makes the country run. In fact, Baloch tribal leaders have been a thorn in Pakistan's side from 1947 when the Khan of Qalat declared independence and formed an army to defend it. A quarter century and three rebellions later, Balochistan was simmering over once again. The example of East Pakistan's successful – if bloody – secession from the Union convinced some Balochi leaders that the time was ripe for their revolt, so they sought backing from neighboring countries.[54] One interested sponsor was Afghanistan, where an ambitious cousin of the King named Daud Khan tried to undermine Pakistan by promoting Pashtun and Balochi nationalism. In 1972, Daud authorized the construction of several camps in Kandahar province that not only housed Balochi refugees but trained men and boys in insurgent warfare as well.[55] Joining the guerrillas in the field were Marxist-leaning Pakistani students eager to take up arms against the oppressors and free Balochistan from the "parasitical"

Pakistani state. The presence of these leftist students enabled Islamabad to assert that there was a Soviet hand in the revolt. Indeed, agencies like ISI were convinced the USSR, India, Afghanistan and Iraq were jointly supporting the Baloch insurgents with the goal of weakening Pakistan.[56]

But why Iraq? Baghdad did not have a particular ax to grind with Islamabad at the time, although Pakistan was irritated when Iraq recognized Bangladesh in August 1972. Iraq was engaged in a proxy war of its own with Iran in the early 1970s, when it armed Iranian Balochis in retaliation for the Shah's assistance to Iraqi Kurds. Whether the Baloch were Iranian or Pakistani really was of little concern to Iraqi Intelligence Service officers, whose primary concern was to tie down Iranian security forces in COIN duties. Iraq allowed the transnational Baluch Liberation Front to set up headquarters in Baghdad and gave it transmitters to beam pro-Baloch propaganda into Iran and western Pakistan. Needless to say, the Pakistani authorities were annoyed by the radio broadcasts, but there was little they could do other than to work more closely with Iran.[57]

Eventually, however, Iraq crossed the line. In February 1973, an ISI surveillance team picked up signs that a substantial arms shipment had been delivered to the Iraqi Embassy in Islamabad for unknown purposes. DGISI Jilani briefed a committee consisting of President Bhutto, COAS General Tikka Khan, and others, providing pictures of the shipment taken by ISI officers.[58] The committee ordered the SSG to raid the Iraqi Embassy and the residence of the Iraqi Military Attaché where they discovered a small arsenal of machine guns, hand grenades, 100,000 rounds of ammunition and communications equipment.[59] At first, ISI stated to the US Army Attaché that it could not determine the weapons' destination, although it did not rule out the Balochi resistance.[60] However, Bhutto had already decided that the arms were intended for Pakistan's Baloch rebels, obligating the ISI to alter its assessment to coincide with the president's.[61] So Bhutto had ISI roped in, but meanwhile his IB Director was informing US diplomats that it made little sense for Iraq to arm the Baloch via Pakistan since the more direct route was via the largely unguarded Makran coast of Iran and Pakistan.[62]

Of course, there was a political angle to Bhutto's analysis as well, for the Iraqi arms affair gave him an opportunity to settle political scores with the provincial governments of Balochistan and NWFP. ISI had been telling the president for some time that the National Awami Party (NAP) government in Balochistan had been planning to revolt against the central government. Acting on this information, Bhutto dismissed the Balochistan Government on 12 February 1973 and placed the province under president's rule.[63] It was all tied together, a "grand design" as Bhutto wrote US President Richard Nixon, whereby the NAP, the Soviet Union, Iraq, Afghanistan and India were all working together to destroy Pakistan.

In the end though, the real issue was not foreign meddling in Pakistan's internal affairs, but a failure by the government to acknowledge – let alone address – the grievances of its Baloch population.[64] Just as Ayub was suspicious of Bengali IB officers, so too did Bhutto shun his Pashtun and Baloch IB experts on Balochistan and the NWFP in favor of an ISI whose senior leadership he felt he could trust. He ordered ISI to create "political cells" in both provinces to monitor NAP activities and keep tabs on the tribes as well. In doing so, he had given ISI yet another grant of power that it would use in the future against civilian governments.[65] Meanwhile, an increasingly assertive Zulfikar Ali Bhutto was focusing on reforming his intelligence community.

Notes

1 H. Haqqani, *Pakistan: Between Mosque and Military*, Washington, DC: Carnegie Endowment, 2005, 79.

2 S.V.R. Nasr, *The Vanguard of the Islamic Revolution: The Jama'at-i Islami of Pakistan*, Berkeley, CA: University of California Press, 1994, 66–67; S. Cohen, *The Idea of Pakistan*, Washington, DC: Brookings, 2004, 104–105; A. Jamal, *Shadow War: The Untold Story of Jihad in Kashmir*, Hoboken, NJ: Melville House, 2009, 108; A.R. Siddiqi, "View: Intelligence Fault lines: East Pakistan Endgame II," *Daily Times*, 3 September 2012 http://archives.dailytimes.com.pk/editorial/03-Sep-2012/view-intelligence-fault-lines-east-Pakistan-endgame-ii-a-r-siddiqi [accessed 3/11/14]; A. Geromylatos, *Castles Made of Sand*, New York: St. Martin's Press, 2010, 200.

3 Correspondence from J.D. Hennings, British High Commission, Islamabad, 18 November 1971, FCO 37/894, UKNA; A.A.K., *The Betrayal of East Pakistan*, Karachi: OUP, 1999, 66.

4 A.R. Siddiqi, *East Pakistan: The Endgame*, Karachi: OUP, 2004, 103–104.

5 Ibid., 154.

6 H. Zaheer, *The Separation of East Pakistan*, Dhaka: OUP, 1994, 201.

7 A.R. Siddiqi, "ISI: Changing of the Guard," *Dawn*, 9 May 1993.

8 Correspondence by A.A. Halliley, Deputy British High Commission, Dacca, FCO 37/884, UKNA.

9 Siddiqi, *East Pakistan*, op. cit., 120–121; Siddiqi, "View: Intelligence Fault lines," op. cit.; L. Ziring, "Militarism in Pakistan: the Yahya Khan Interregnum," *Asian Affairs* 1:6, July–August 1974, 412.

10 G.H. Khan, *Memoirs of Lt. Gen. Gul Hassan Khan*, Karachi: OUP, 1993, 335–336.

11 A. Raina, *Inside RAW: the Story of India's Secret Service*, New Delhi: Vikas, 1981, 52–53; R. Sisson and L. Rose, *War and Secession: Pakistan, India, and the Creation of Bangladesh*, Berkeley: University of California Press, 1990, 313n32.

12 G.H. Khan, *Memoirs*, op. cit., 278.

13 Sisson & Rose, *War*, op. cit., 214; Niazi, *Betrayal*, 74, 114, 156; G.H. Khan, *Memoirs*, 319.

14 Bhaumik, *Troubled*, 164; Niazi, *Betrayal*, 55.

15 Palit, *Lightning*, 154–155.

16 Wolpert, *Zulfi*, 161; Mitha, *Unlikely*, 325; Telegram from Amembassy Islamabad, "Pak Civilian Intelligence Chief on Iraqi Arms," 23 February 1973, no. 348, R. Khan, *The American Papers*, Karachi: OUP, 1999, 897–899.

17 Niazi, *Betrayal*, op. cit., 50–51; S. Nawaz, *Crossed Swords*, Karachi: OUP, 2008, 269.

18 G.H. Khan, *Memoirs*, op. cit., 305–306; S. Wolpert, *Zulfi Bhutto of Pakistan*, New York: OUP, 1993, 161; G.W. Choudhury, *The Last Days of United Pakistan*, London: C. Hurst, 1974, 197; K.M. Arif, *Working with Zia*, Karachi: OUP, 1995, 32.

19 Nawaz, *Crossed*, op. cit., 292–293; G.H. Khan, *Memoirs*, op. cit., 319–320.

20 Government of Pakistan, *Hamoodur Rehman Commission Report*, nd www.pppusa. org/Acrobat/Hamoodur%20Rahman%20Commission%20Report.pdf [accessed 17/5/11], 97.
21 Raina, *RAW*, op. cit., 60; Arif, *Working*, op. cit., 31.
22 Siddiqi, *East Pakistan*, op. cit., 195.
23 G.H. Khan, *Memoirs*, op. cit., 328.
24 A. Gauhar, "How Intelligence Agencies Run Our Politics," *The Nation*, 17 August 1997.
25 Cohen, *Idea*, op. cit., 9.
26 Z. Hussain, *Frontline: The Struggle with Militant Islam*, New York: Columbia University Press, 2007, 20–21.
27 Cohen, *Idea*, op. cit., 194.
28 Zaheer, *Separation*, op. cit., 358, 429–431; G.H. Khan, *Memoirs*, op. cit., 342–344.
29 Arif, *Working*, op. cit., 410.
30 M. James, *Pakistan Chronicle*, New York: St. Martin's Press, 1993, 110.
31 R. Raza, *Zulfikar Ali Bhutto and Pakistan*, Karachi: OUP, 1997, 302; Wolpert, *Zulfi*, op. cit., 178; F. Bhutto, *Songs of Blood and Sword*, New York: Nation Books, 2010, 124; G.A. Khan, *Glimpses*, op. cit., 149.
32 Wolpert, *Zulfi*, op. cit., 267.
33 R. Anwar, *The Terrorist Prince: The Life and Death of Murtaza Bhutto*, London: Verso, 1997, 227n2; H. Mubashir, *Mirage of Power. An Inquiry into the Bhutto Years, 1971–1977*, Oxford: OUP, 2000, 202–203.
34 H. Haqqani, *Magnificent Delusions*, New York: Public Affairs, 2013, 117.
35 Cited in A. Jalal, *The Struggle for Pakistan*, Cambridge, MA: Belknap, 2014, 120–121.
36 Mubashir, *Mirage*, op. cit., 279–282
37 Ibid, 203–204; Haqqani, *Pakistan*, op. cit., 109–110.
38 A. Nazir, "The Inside Story," *Herald Annual*, 1991, 29; Wolpert, Zulfi, op. cit., 279.
39 Hassan, *Mirage*, op. cit., 208.
40 F. Bhutto, *Songs*, op. cit., 119–120.
41 G.H. Khan, *Memoirs*, op. cit., 360.
42 B. Cloughley, *War, Coups and Terror: Pakistan's Army in Years of Turmoil*, New York: Skyhorse, 2008, 8–9.
43 Arif, *Working*, op. cit., 128.
44 Ibid., 43–44, 123; Tirmazi, *Profiles*, op. cit., 235–236.
45 Mubashir, *Mirage*, op. cit., 265.
46 K.M. Arif, *Khaki Shadows*, Karachi: OUP, 2001, 284; Arif, *Working*, op. cit., 178–179; Wolpert, *Zulfi*, op. cit., 273.
47 Nawaz, *Crossed*, op. cit., 339.
48 Raza, *Zulfikar*, 143.
49 Arif, *Khaki*, 156.
50 P.C. Joshi, *Main Intelligence Outfits of Pakistan*, New Delhi: Anmol Publications, 2008, 157–158.
51 Z.A. Bhutto, *If I Am Assassinated*, 58–59.
52 Ibid., 59.
53 Ibid., 58.
54 Cable from Pumphrey, British High Commission, Islamabad, "Baluchistan Disturbances," 8 December 1972, FCO 37/184, UKNA.
55 US NATO Delegation, "Baluchistan," 20 May 1980, FCO 37/2362, UKNA; Haqqani, *Pakistan*, 170, 174; A. Hyman, *Afghanistan under Soviet Occupation, 1964–1981*, New York: St. Martin's Press, 1982, 67–68.
56 Cable from Ramsbotham, British Embassy, Tehran, 24 May 1972, no. 455, 24 May 1972, FCO 37/184, UKNA; Arif, *Working*, 171.
57 Wolpert, *Zulfi*, 211; Foreign and Commonwealth Office, "Pakistan and the Islamic World," 12 July 1974, FCO 37/1506, UKNA.

58 Raza, *Zulfikar*, op. cit., 268–269.
59 Ibid.; Haqqani, *Magnificent*, op. cit.,195; S. Harrison, *In Afghanistan's Shadow: Baluch Nationalism and Soviet Temptation*, Washington, DC: Carnegie Endowment, 1981, 35; Letter from President Zulfikar Ali Bhutto to President Richard Nixon, 14 February 1973, found in R. Khan, *American*, op. cit., 888–889; S. Saeed, "Caught! (But What?)," *The Friday Times*, 4 March 2011, www.thefridaytimes. com/04032011/page26.shtml [accessed 24/11/14].
60 Arif, *Working*, op. cit., 172; Saeed, "Caught!"; Telegram from Amembassy Islamabad, "Iraqi/Soviet Arms: The Web of Speculation," 24 February 1973, no. 182, R. Khan, *American*, op. cit., 900–902.
61 Arif, *Working*, op. cit., 172.
62 Telegram from Amembassy Islamabad, "Pak Civilian Intelligence Chief," op. cit.; Saeed, "Caught!"
63 Haqqani, *Pakistan*, op. cit., 169.
64 Cable from Amembassy Islamabad, "Bhutto on Current Problems with Indians, Afghans and Soviets," 10 April 1974, no. 6835, http://aad.archives.gov/aad/creat epdf?rid=82083&dt=2474&dl=1345; Action Memorandum from NEA (Joseph J. Sisco), nd, "President Bhutto's Proposals for Closer Military Collaboration with the U.S.," R. Khan, *American*, 809.
65 Joshi, *Main*, op. cit., 31–32.

8   ISI under Zulfikar Ali Bhutto

The Balochistan insurgency persisted throughout much of Zulfikar Ali Bhutto's term in office mainly because he was unwilling to countenance any serious peace overtures to the guerrillas. Balochistan was an unwanted obstacle for Bhutto, a man anxious to reform the state and cement his hold over the government. His interest in intelligence has already been noted, so it was logical that one of his earliest reforms involved the intelligence community.

Intelligence reform?

In 1975, Bhutto appointed an Intelligence Reform Commission under a PPP stalwart named Rafi Raza whose purpose was to conduct an in-depth study of the community, identify its shortcomings, and recommend changes. When the commission concluded its investigation, it noted a number of deficiencies such as the PIC tendency to report *everything* to the leadership, including unevaluated intelligence reports and the failure of the agencies to share information and coordinate operations and assessments.[1] When it came to reforms, some felt the commission didn't go far enough in advocating an overhaul of the PIC. Tellingly, Rafi Raza himself later wrote that "the system needed complete revamping, but nothing was done."[2] Still, "complete revamping" aside, changes *were* made to ISI's missions, including domestic affairs. Sometime in 1974–1975, Bhutto signed an executive order establishing an ISI office responsible for all of the agency's domestic activities; the commission essentially endorsed this office and gave it some legitimacy.[3] But the creation of this "Internal Wing" (if that was indeed its name) was not a revolutionary expansion of ISI powers because ISI had been meddling in politics since the 1950s.

Under Bhutto, ISI's Internal Wing monitored communists, the minority Shia and Ahmadiyya populations, cabinet ministers, opposition parties, and PPP members of both the national and provincial assemblies. It conducted "elections management" such as forecasting, vote rigging, buying off politicians, forming and breaking coalitions, and intimidating opposition parties.[4] Yet Bhutto's decision to "legitimize" ISI's internal missions carried what one author has rightly called "long-term serious consequences" for future civilian rule in Pakistan.[5] It is a paradox that while future civilian governments would rail against ISI's domestic meddling, none was willing to take serious action against it. This was partly due to civilian fear of the army, but it can also be attributed to the fact that, once in power, civilian governments were eager to use ISI's powers against their enemies.

The Intelligence Reform Commission gave ISI its formal charter, established "lanes of the road" responsibilities within the community and defined ISI's reporting chain to include the Joint Services Secretariat, the military services chiefs and the head of government.[6] The charter gave ISI 24 specific tasks, and although they remain classified, an observer can ferret out the more obvious missions, including (1) armed forces CI; (2) strategic and operational analysis; (3) HUMINT collection; (4) coordination of the services' analysis and collection branches; (5) UW; (6) domestic political activities as directed by the Chief Executive; (7) production and dissemination of SIGINT; (8) supervision of technical intelligence requirements; (9) creation and enforcement of unified security procedures across military intelligence; (10) provision of security for the Chief Executive; (11) responsibility for the foreign military attaché community in Pakistan; (12) acquisition of sensitive technologies overseas, including nuclear components and materials; and (13) supervision over the Army Corps of Intelligence, which supervises training and establishes joint doctrine. It was the creation of this Corps that gave Ghulam Jilani his third star; henceforth, all ISI Director Generals would be Lieutenant Generals, a rank that allowed them to attend corps commanders conferences, where vital state security decisions are made.[7] Finally, the Intelligence Reform Commission created a National Intelligence Board to coordinate assessments. Led by Rao Rashid, the board filtered the myriad assessments and raw reports that previously fell haphazardly on the Chief Executive's desk. It also empowered Rashid, since he was now gate keeper for most intelligence products to reach Bhutto.[8]

Counter intelligence

CI is one of the least understood disciplines in the espionage business and yet, as an old CIA saying has it, an intelligence service is only as good as its counter intelligence capabilities.[9] In other words, one or two moles inside your intelligence agency can reverse all the good work performed by hundreds of case officers and their clandestine assets. When it comes to CI, the public tends to concentrate on the defensive aspects such as identifying and eliminating spies in one's own service or other sensitive state agencies and ensuring that what passes for intelligence is not, in fact, disinformation. But there is another, more offensively oriented, aspect of CI where identified foreign-controlled spies are "doubled" and employed against their original masters both to collect useful intelligence on the adversary's service and to pass deceptive information that could impact decision-making.

ISI has always handled the overall armed forces CI mission, which is vested in its JCIB. As we have seen, the founders of ISI understood that to obtain intelligence from the UK, they would have to demonstrate an awareness of security and the threat posed by hostile intelligence services. In short, the JCIB originally was intended to be ISI's entrée to the world of Commonwealth intelligence. What little is known about the JCIB can be partly found in the memoir of a former JCIB director, Brigadier Syed A.I. Tirmazi. Although some of Tirmazi's assertions cannot be verified, his is nonetheless a unique glimpse into the world of Pakistani CI.

Tirmazi's memoir reveals ISI's proficiency in CI. He reports that the agency would routinely "dangle" false agents in front of known or suspected Indian spies in order to learn more about the Indian espionage apparatus and its officers.[10] We also know from other sources that the JCIB did not hesitate to use harassment, intimidation and sometimes physical violence against suspected spies in order to deter, dissuade and double. Not surprisingly, some Indian RAW case officers did not want to be assigned to Pakistan because of its stifling CI environment.[11]

Although many Pakistanis might disagree vehemently, Tirmazi complained about the inadequacies of ISI's existing phone tap equipment: "I am sure we must have missed a lot," he wrote, "for want of better equipment and facilities." Predictably, ISI had tapped the phones of the resident Indian Military Attaché in Islamabad and once even caught a Pakistani army major offering the Indians sensitive information over an open line. Tirmazi does not indicate whether this officer was doubled by ISI and used to feed the Indians disinformation, but it would have been a logical course of action.[12]

Tirmazi's memoirs also highlight the incessant rivalries, backbiting and feuds that beset Pakistan's national security bureaucracy of the 1970s and 1980s. ISI and the Foreign Ministry routinely squabbled over the number of ISI officers posted overseas under diplomatic cover. When relations with India were restored after the 1971 war, the Foreign Ministry overrode ISI objections and allowed the Indians to open a consulate in Karachi before Pakistan could open one of its own in Bombay. With an eye to CI concerns, ISI had demanded that both consulates be opened at the same time, but this argument did not carry the day. On another occasion, the Foreign Ministry stiff-armed the JCIB's request for photographs, names and biographical data of diplomats assigned to the Soviet Embassy in Islamabad; later it turned out the Ministry had never asked the Soviets for this information in the first place.[13]

Since the JCIB shared the CI mission with the service intelligence agencies, there were bound to be turf wars and jurisdictional fights. In principle, the JCIB exercised the preponderant voice in most military CI matters, although pushback from the service CI branches was inevitable. As an example, Tirmazi highlighted the case of Group Captain Cecil Choudhury, a Pakistani Air Force officer and air ace from the 1965 and 1971 wars, who had been designated Air Attaché (AIRA) to Moscow. The JCIB tried to stop the appointment on the basis that Choudhury had been seen contacting the Soviet AIRA in Islamabad. For its part, the PAF Intelligence Branch did not share ISI's concerns, and recommended the appointment move forward. In the end, Choudhury was sent instead as AIRA to Iraq and, upon his return, was informed that he would not be promoted further.[14]

In his book, Tirmazi chides the Pakistani public for being unhelpful in catching spies and contrasts this with Israel where, he asserts, civilians work hand in glove with the security services to identify and expose intelligence agents. To reinforce his argument, Tirmazi records one ISI attempt to recruit a Pakistani employee at the US Embassy who refused because, if caught, he/she would lose the perks of working for the Americans such as an air conditioner, a refrigerator and the prospects of permanent residency in the US.[15]

Tirmazi doesn't spare the armed forces either when he describes their negative attitudes to CI. Echoing statements made by others in the organization's history, Tirmazi notes how officers routinely viewed ISI as a disreputable agency full of snitches. Tirmazi asserts that such disregard for ISI was expressed in officer promotions, where in one year no ISI Majors were promoted to Lieutenant Colonel. Being passed over like this on account of the job rather than the man was bound to have a negative impact on morale.[16]

ISI and the bomb

The 1971 defeat at the hands of India dealt a tremendous shock to Pakistan, but another blow came three short years later when India tested its first nuclear weapon. The 18 May 1974 test was not a complete surprise to the Pakistani establishment because ISI had been warning for some time that the Indians were approaching a nuclear weapons capability. In a meeting with a US official shortly after the test, the Deputy Director of ISI stated that India's motivation was prestige, influence and, ultimately, regional hegemony. He did not believe India would use nuclear weapons against Pakistan but rather as leverage for contentious issues like Kashmir. Trying to allay US concerns about a Pakistani nuclear weapons program, the Deputy Director stated his country lacked the human, technical and financial resources necessary for a crash program. Indeed, such a project would bleed the economy dry at a time when the state was desperately struggling to recover from the war. Pakistan's only alternative, the ISI official concluded, was to modernize its conventional military in the hope this would be enough to deter India.[17]

The Deputy Director was lying. Pakistan *was* developing a bomb, and US intelligence agencies knew it. Indeed, Islamabad's top priority after the Indian test was acquiring the bomb, and Bhutto ordered his scientists and intelligence officers to spare no effort in acquiring a nuclear deterrent.[18] One ISI challenge was keeping the program secret lest the international community impose sanctions or other punitive measures. It was also ISI's responsibility to recruit scientists and engineers with knowledge of nuclear technology and acquire the necessary materials and technologies abroad.

Coincidentally (or not) a Pakistan-born metallurgist named Abdul Qadir Khan was working for a European consortium called URENCO at this time, and he had access to many of the technologies that Pakistan so desperately needed. URENCO researched and developed high speed gas centrifuges capable of producing enriched uranium for the European nuclear energy industry. While URENCO centrifuges were configured to enrich uranium for civilian uses, there were no substantial technical hurdles in adapting them to produce highly enriched uranium for nuclear weapons.[19] The part ISI played in Khan's decision to return home with stolen centrifuge designs is unknown. Did he volunteer his services to Pakistan out of anger at the 1971 defeat? Did ISI talent spot him through the Pakistani émigré community in Europe or via intercepted letters from the homesick scientist to relatives at home? There is no evidence to support either assertion. In any case, A.Q. Khan was soon put in contact with an ISI officer in Belgium, who taught him basic espionage tradecraft and served as the conduit through which Khan passed blue prints of centrifuge designs and lists of European companies providing technology and materials to the URENCO effort.[20]

Sometime in 1974, the Pakistani scientist met Zulfikar Ali Bhutto for the first time during a trip home. As usual, Bhutto asked ISI for background information on Khan, and ISI's character description was not very flattering. Based on interactions with the scientist, ISI officers sensed he lacked maturity and tended to exaggerate his personal accomplishments; but, they conceded, Khan did have access to some technologies necessary for the bomb effort.[21] Khan's meeting with Bhutto was to launch Pakistan on its successful path to a nuclear weapon, and 20 years later the scientist was lauded throughout the country as the Father of the Pakistani Bomb.

Another ISI task was providing security for the uranium enrichment facility at Kahuta, such as conducting employee background checks and keeping unauthorized personnel away from the plant. One French ambassador and a subordinate learned this the hard way in July 1979 when their car was stopped near Kahuta and the two diplomats beaten by villagers. The head of ISI CI later claimed the diplomats were beaten because the villagers thought they were photographing local women, but the fact that the incident took place near Kahuta was certainly no coincidence.[22] The Americans too were detected snooping around the plant, but the ISI apparently was more circumspect in dealing with them. In one instance, the CIA planted a package of sensors disguised as a rock near Kahuta, but it was accidentally discovered and handed over to ISI, where it reportedly serves today as an exhibit at headquarters.[23]

ISI and Bhutto's demise

Undoubtedly, the biggest mistake of Zulfikar Ali Bhutto's political career was following his ISI chief's advice in selecting General Zia ul-Haq as COAS. At this point in their professional relationship, Bhutto relied heavily on Jilani for his judgment on military matters and believed the Director General of ISI (DGISI) was loyal. It is unclear if Jilani played the preponderant role in convincing Bhutto to choose Zia; however, three years later, as he awaited sentencing, Bhutto made much of Jilani's position as his close, confidential advisor.[24] At the time of his appointment, Zia was something of a dark horse in the COAS sweepstakes, for he was junior to six other generals, including Jilani; if appointed, Zia would automatically supersede these generals and possibly force their retirement. But Zia appealed to Bhutto on several levels: he projected a placid, laid back demeanor that often tricked people into believing he lacked grit and a mind of his own. He was also willing to play sycophant to Bhutto, much the same way that DGISI Ghulam Jilani, did.[25]

Bhutto's second mistake was listening to Jilani play up his reelection chances in 1976 and 1977. In fact, ISI became one of Bhutto's most trusted pollsters, possibly because its analysts were telling him virtually everything he wanted to hear.[26] During the period from March to June 1976, ISI Headquarters ordered its nationwide detachments to poll public opinion on Bhutto, the PPP, and the opposition parties. It is unlikely that these surveys were conducted with any attention to scientific accuracy, but their data were nevertheless compiled at ISI HQ and served as the foundation for some of ISI's early polls.[27] One estimate passed to Bhutto in April 1976 recommended he renew his mandate by holding national elections soon. Others flowed across his desk in the ensuing months, and some of these presciently warned him that the hitherto enfeebled and divided opposition might form a coalition against the PPP.[28] On 5 October, Jilani forwarded a 53-page assessment to Bhutto entitled "General Elections" in which ISI judged that Bhutto should hold elections sooner rather than later. Predictably, the paper heaped praise on Bhutto for uniting Pakistan after the 1971 war: "[H]is leadership proved to be a breadth [sic] of fresh air in the acrid and suffocating political atmosphere, a dawn of hope in the dark days of economic chaos.... He has given back the 'soul' to the people ..."[29] The adoration didn't stop there, for the paper went on to affirm that no one in Pakistan could challenge Bhutto who was the "only Pakistan leader with an international standing and image." The paper predicted Bhutto should win between 75 percent and 80 percent of the Sindh vote as well as 70 percent of the crucial vote in Punjab.[30]

Such was the sycophantic language in ISI analysis that some later suspected darker motives. The former Pakistani diplomat and scholar, Hussain Haqqani has written that "the ISI's keenness in advising Bhutto to go to the polls is significant in light of later events," while some PPP stalwarts also alleged ISI malfeasance in convincing Bhutto to hold elections.[31] At the same time, though, it was widely believed that the prime minister would easily win reelection so how would it be advantageous to push him into elections? Indeed, the ISI would have been incredibly clairvoyant to accurately plan and guide the tragic sequence of events that ultimately led to Bhutto's 1977 downfall.

As Zulfikar Ali Bhutto pondered election strategy in late 1976, trouble was brewing in the army. On 3 December, DGISI Jilani sent a memorandum to General Zia ul-Haq and copied to Bhutto, warning of Islamist forces in the ranks. Crude posters had been found in a Multan Barracks calling for an "Army Revolution." ISI's assessment included the following:

[T]he personnel are more susceptible to religious appeal. The mullah is omni-present in our units. The mullah has his own brand of religious affiliations,... Above all, there is the influence of the JI [Jama'at-e Islami] and the JUI [Jamiat Ulema-e-Islam] ... [T]he JI and JUI have been making ingresses into the armed forces.[32]

In the margin of this report, Bhutto wrote an accurate prediction of how Zia's religious temperament would affect the army: "such teachings become dangerous only when the Chief of the Army gives them official blessings and respect. This will boomerang ... that is why I told [Zia] in my first letter that I do not want a 'mullah army.' ..."[33]

The opposition parties, hitherto dismissed as in a "sorry state" by Bhutto's advisors, staged a surprise on 5 January 1977 when they formed a coalition called the Pakistan National Alliance (PNA).[34] ISI had warned that an opposition front was possible, but Bhutto nonetheless faulted it for failing to warn him of this development. The *Jamaa't-e Islami* was an important force behind the PNA, not so much because of its electoral appeal (it never garnered more than single digit percentages in a national election) but rather on account of its organization skills, funding from wealthy donors, ability to generate street protests and a youth wing that provided muscle as necessary.[35] On 7 January, Bhutto announced that elections would be held in two months, hoping to limit the time in which the PNA could prepare a platform and start to campaign. He ordered ISI to step up monitoring of the opposition and, in the four weeks preceding the election, Bhutto received an average of two intelligence assessments per day on election matters.[36]

Prior to the PNA's announcement, the prime minister assumed he would be running against a divided opposition, and this would allow him to win a two-thirds majority in the National Assembly. This was the number necessary to make amendments to the 1973 Constitution, and some observers believed Bhutto wanted to change back to a presidential system which would give him more personal power.[37] With the PNA, however, all bets were off regarding that two-thirds majority, unless the intelligence agencies could manipulate the elections through covert means. Bhutto's first priority was to ensure that all PPP candidates for national and provincial assemblies were vetted by ISI and the IB to determine their loyalty to him; for the more independent-minded ones, the "agencies" would assess whether they could be bribed or blackmailed into at least backing his agenda.[38] At the same time, he unleashed the ISI and IB on the opposition: politicians were kidnapped before they could register their candidacies, banks were strong-armed into filling the PPP's war chests, and some candidates bribed to vote with the PPP caucus. When bribery failed, the intelligence officers fell back on black mail, scanning each candidate's past for embarrassing peccadilloes or, more commonly, income tax evasion which was and is something of a national pastime.[39]

ISI analysts still predicted a PPP victory with 70–80 percent of the National Assembly seats, partly because they assessed the PNA was too faction-ridden to be effective.[40] A 19 February 1977 joint ISI–IB estimate predicted a "clear win" for the PPP.[41] One month later, and only three days before voters went to the polls, the IB/ISI team predicted Bhutto would win at least 122 out of 200 seats in the National Assembly.[42] Still, Bhutto and his aides left nothing to chance. On election eve, ISI field detachments were sending a steady stream of election-related data to a 24-hours operations center at headquarters. Throughout Election Day on 7 March, as Bhutto aides clamored for up-to-date results, ISI observers hovered around the polling stations, trying to ascertain the public mood. At 0200 hours on 8 March, Bhutto called his DGISI for the latest estimates, and the latter replied that the vote was swinging strongly in the PPP's favor. Jilani also updated the prime minister on the law-and-order situation across the country.[43]

When the final results came in, the extent of the PPP's victory surpassed all expectations, for it had captured 155 out of 200 seats, while the PNA took a measly 36. Not only did Bhutto have a solid majority, he had a super majority which gave him more than enough seats to rewrite the constitution. But there was widespread speculation that the election had been rigged, and the PNA was soon staging mass demonstrations, demanding Bhutto's resignation and new elections.[44] In the meantime, the prime minister huddled with his advisors to plan a response. Rafi Raza, recommended that new elections be held at once to defuse the anger and restore a sense of normalcy to the country. DGISI Jilani sided with Raza, pointing out that post-elections' ISI analysis revealed that 33 PNA candidates had lost their seats due to "unfair means" (whatever those were). If new elections were held in at least these contested districts, Jilani advised, some of the PNA outrage might dissipate.[45] The DGISI later insisted he had told Bhutto on two separate occasions (8 March and 19 March 1977) to hold new elections, but the prime minister was "too proud" to concede election fraud and preferred to wait until the PNA backed down.[46] But events defied Bhutto's "wait-it-out" strategy, for the internal situation continued to deteriorate as the anti-government protests grew in size and spread across the country.[47]

Bhutto was unwilling to publicly admit his party had engaged in egregious vote fraud. There was always going to be someone else to blame, and the Americans were an irresistible target for the latest conspiracy theories. On 26 April, Bhutto met with various intelligence agency chiefs, Foreign Ministry officials, and others to discuss the CIA's role in the turmoil; however, the intelligence chiefs declared they had nothing in their files to support his allegations of US interference.[48] Bhutto persisted, and on 28 April delivered a blistering attack on the US in a speech before the National Assembly, alleging a "foreign hand" was behind the PNA in a "vast, colossal, huge international conspiracy." He cited a communications intercept of a phone conversation between two American diplomats on elections eve, where one told the other that a certain dinner party was over. Bhutto took it another way: "The party's over, the party's over," he thundered, "He's gone … well, gentlemen, the party is not over!"[49] The prime minister continued to press his staff for

evidence of foreign meddling, and during a May cabinet meeting, he criticized the intelligence community for not warning him of the PNA's supposed reliance on foreign funds. No evidence was forthcoming. Bhutto had
fallen into a trap of his own making, and few were willing to make up stories
to get him out.[50]

Bhutto also contemplated using the army to suppress the riots, and he sent
the head of ISI's Public Relations Wing to Sindh to determine how the
public there might react to the imposition of martial law.[51] For his part,
the DGISI, Ghulam Jilani, counseled against martial law on the grounds that
the public still showed "open contempt" for soldiers because of the 1971
debacle. If the army was brought in to crush the protests, Jilani cautioned,
martial law duties would preoccupy it for a long time. The only path out was
negotiations with the PNA.[52] Bhutto wasn't worried about the army's popularity as much as the possibility it would overthrow his government. He was
not a Napoleon Bonaparte enthusiast for nothing, and an army coup was no
doubt on his mind in May and June 1977 when he ordered ISI to monitor
the ranks for potential coup plotting.[53]

Negotiations with the PNA sputtered on until late June, when it seemed
as if a settlement was in sight. Two important Bhutto advisors – Rafi Raza
and Ghulam Jilani – urged him to sign a deal quickly, because rumors were
circulating of secret army negotiations with the PNA. It was whispered that
Zia had met his corps commanders, and they had voiced their own discontent with the political impasse. Indeed, some were seeking a "military option"
to the crisis.[54]

Caught in the middle of a besieged civilian government on the one hand,
and an increasingly restless army on the other, the DGISI faced some tough
choices. He warned Bhutto that the army was in the advanced stages of a
coup, prompting the prime minister to call each of the corps commanders in
turn to determine the truth; but no one was revealing anything. At some
point in this complex minuet, Jilani threw in his lot with the army and
managed to come out of the July 1977 coup unscathed. Once again, his survival instincts had served him well.

On 5 July 1977, the army ousted the Bhutto government. Citing the supposed breakdown in negotiations between the PPP and the PNA as justification for the coup, General Zia ul-Haq went on television to make the same
flaccid promises about elections and an immediate return to civilian rule that
another general was to make in the future. Meanwhile, the prime minister
was under house arrest and most of his key functionaries rolled up. The status
of the DGISI was unknown.[55] Indeed, decades after the 1977 coup, questions
remain regarding Ghulam Jilani: was he a loyal subordinate of the prime
minister or was he really working all along for Zia, a man he helped promote
to the highest position in the army? After all, the COAS was not only his
boss by military rank but also the officer who evaluated his fitness for further
promotion. Some later alleged that the idea of Jilani working against Bhutto
was a contrivance of embittered PPP veterans.[56] In support of this argument,

one must concede that the DGISI's pre-coup advice to Bhutto was sound. Recall that he had counseled the prime minister to order fresh elections immediately and thereby ease the crisis with the PNA. Note that he had urged Bhutto to sign a deal with the opposition to ward off a rumored coup. It is difficult to see how a disloyal Jilani would advise his boss to defuse a confrontation and warn of an imminent coup by the army (of which he was a ranking member).[57] Still, Jilani was later appointed Governor of the powerful Punjab province under Zia.

While Jilani survived the coup without a scratch, the same could not be said for the IB chief and his immediate predecessor, both of whom were arrested and interrogated by the army. Some allege the DGISI was playing a double game, building up trust with Bhutto while working behind the scenes to derail any PPP-PNA reconciliation.[58] Another charge is that Jilani somehow made an already tense Bhutto-PNA relationship worse to ensure that no rapprochement would take place between the political parties.[59] Still others suggest that the DGISI warned Zia that he was about to be removed from office, and armed with this knowledge, Zia acted first.[60] None of these charges can be proven, and the most plausible answer seems to be that Jilani was loyal to the prime minister up to the moment it became patently obvious that a coup was inevitable. In any case, Ghulam Jilani Khan had survived another regime change while still holding one of the most sensitive positions in the Pakistan military. This was quite an accomplishment.

Notes

1 R. Raza, *Zulfikar Ali Bhutto and Pakistan 1967–1977*, Karachi: OUP, 1997, 302.
2 Ibid.
3 F. Grare, *Reforming the Intelligence Agencies in Pakistan's Transitional Democracy*, Washington, DC: Carnegie Endowment for International Peace, 2009, 18; I. Malik, *State and Civil Society in Pakistan*, London: Macmillan, 1997, 97.
4 A. Nazir, "The Inside Story," *Herald Annual*, 1991, 29; S. Wolpert, *Zulfi Bhutto of Pakistan*, New York: OUP, 1993, 279; H. Mubashir, *Mirage of Power: An Inquiry into the Bhutto Years, 1971–1977*, Oxford: OUP, 2000, 294.
5 K.M. Arif, *Khaki Shadows*, Karachi: OUP, 2001, 358.
6 Ibid., 357–358.
7 Government of Pakistan, *Abbottabad Commission Report*, http://webapps.aljazeera. net/aje/custom/binladenfiles/Pakistan-Bin-Laden-Dossier.pdf [accessed 15/4/14], 194; P.C. Joshi, *Main Intelligence Outfits of Pakistan*, New Delhi: Anmol Publications, 2008, 136.
8 Raza, *Zulfikar*, op. cit., 308.
9 R. Helms, *A Look Over my Shoulder*, New York: Presidio Press, 2003, 154.
10 S.A.I. Tirmazi, *Profiles in Intelligence*, Lahore: Combined Printers, 1995, 120–123.
11 V.K. Singh, *India's External Intelligence*, New Delhi: Manas, 2007, 120.
12 Tirmazi, *Profiles*, op. cit., 107–109.
13 Ibid. 95.
14 Ibid., 175–176; "Obituary: War Hero Cecil Chaudhry passes away," *The Express Tribune*, 14 April 2012, http://tribune.com.pk/story/364519/obituary-war-hero-cecil-chaudhry-passes-away/ [accessed 25/11/14].
15 Tirmazi, *Profiles*, op. cit., 41.

16 Ibid., 18–19.
17 Cable from SecState, "Pakistan's Reaction to Indian Nuclear Explosion," 22 May 1974, no. 106703, http://aad.archives.gov/aad/createpdf?rid=82083&dt=2474&dl =1345 [accessed 28/11/14].
18 D. Frantz, "From Patriot to Proliferator," *Los Angeles Times* [hereafter LAT], 23 September 2005, http://articles.latimes.com/2005/sep/23/world/fg-khan23/2 [accessed 20/4/15].
19 A. Levy & C. Scott-Clark *Nuclear Deception: The Dangerous Relationship Between the United States and Pakistan*, New York: Walker & Co., 2008.
20 Ibid., 21, 32; D. Frantz & C. Collins, *The Nuclear Jihadist*, New York: Hachette, 2007, 38, 40–41.
21 Levy & Scott-Clark, *Deception*, op. cit., 21.
22 Tirmazi, *Profiles*, op. cit., 44–47.
23 Ibid., 57–59; Frantz & Collins, *Jihadist*, op. cit., 134–135. Former DGISI, Lieutenant General Asad Durrani denies any ISI security role in the Pakistan nuclear program. It is difficult to accommodate his denials given the extensive body of reporting explicitly linking ISI to Kahuta security. See *Talk Back with Wajahat Khan*, "Interview with Lieutenant General (Retd) Asad Durrani." www.youtube.com/watch?v=DdxZzmldc4s [accessed 14/1/15].
24 Z.A. Bhutto, *If I Am Assassinated*, New Delhi: Vikas, 1979, 58–59.
25 K.M. Arif, *Working with Zia*, Karachi: OUP, 1995, 43; H. Haqqani, *Magnificent Delusions*, New York: Public Affairs, 2013, 219.
26 Raza, *Zulfikar*, op. cit., 322.
27 Tirmazi, *Profiles*, op. cit., 224.
28 Ibid., 224.
29 H. Haqqani, *Pakistan: Between Mosque and Military*, Washington, DC: Carnegie Endowment, 2005, 114–118, 346n73.
30 Ibid., 117.
31 Ibid., 115; Wolpert, *Zulfi*, op. cit., 275.
32 Wolpert, *Zulfi*, op. cit., 280–281.
33 Ibid.
34 Raza, *Zulfikar*, op. cit., 358–359; F.A. Chishti, *Betrayals of Another Kind: Islam, Democracy and the Army in Pakistan*, Lahore: Jang Publishers, 1996, 76–77.
35 V.R. Nasr, *The Vanguard of the Islamic Revolution: The Jama'at-i Islami of Pakistan*, Berkeley, CA: University of California Press, 1994, 66–67.
36 Tirmazi, *Profiles*, op. cit., 228; Wolpert, *Zulfi*, op. cit., 279.
37 Wolpert, *Zulfi*, op. cit., 279–280.
38 Raza, *Zulfikar*, op. cit., 322; Mubashir, *Mirage*, op. cit., 297.
39 Arif, *Working*, op. cit., 62–63.
40 Haqqani, *Magnificent*, op. cit., 220; Tirmazi, *Profiles*, op. cit., 222.
41 Wolpert, *Zulfi*, op. cit., 279.
42 Bhutto, *If I Am Assassinated*, op. cit., 74–76.
43 Tirmazi, *Profiles*, op. cit., 225–226.
44 Raza, *Zulfikar*, op. cit., 321.
45 Ibid., 336; Arif, *Working*, op. cit., 67–68, 87–88; Tirmazi, *Profiles*, op. cit., 226.
46 Arif, *Working*, op. cit., 87–88.
47 Wolpert, *Zulfi*, op. cit., 290.
48 Raza, *Zulfikar*, op. cit., 363.
49 Arif, *Working*, op. cit., 76–77; Haqqani, *Magnificent*, op. cit., 222–223.
50 Arif, *Working*, op. cit., 78.
51 Haqqani, *Pakistan*, op. cit., 124.
52 Tirmazi, *Profiles*, op. cit., 230–231; Arif, *Working*, op. cit., 71.
53 Arif, *Working*, op. cit., 80–85.
54 Ibid., 85–88; Raza, *Zulfikar*, op. cit., 354, 375n45.

55 A.H. Amin, "Remembering our Warriors: Lt. Gen. Imtiaz Waraich, SJ," *Defence Journal,* www.defencejournal.com/2001/october/imtiaz.htm [accessed 24/4/15].
56 Raza, *Zulfikar,* op. cit., 162n1.
57 Ibid., 354, 375n45; Arif, *Working,* op. cit., 86, 88.
58 Bhutto, *If I Am Assassinated,* op. cit., 57–58.
59 Haqqani, *Pakistan,* op. cit., 124–125.
60 Malik, *State,* op. cit., 97.

Part III

Overreach

9   Zia ul-Haq, Afghanistan and ISI

The son of a religious scholar, Zia ul-Haq was personally observant, shunned alcohol and was drawn toward the *JI*.[1] Significantly for the future of Pakistan, Zia didn't keep his faith to himself, but imposed it on the army by creating a Directorate of Religious Education, establishing officers' tests on Islam, mandating attendance at Friday prayers and letting a proselytizing organization called *Tablighi Jama'at* operate inside army cantonments. The Raj-era tradition of whisky night caps at the regimental mess was gone for good.[2]

Bhutto's execution

Zia's first conundrum was deciding the fate of the man he had just ousted from power. There was little doubt Bhutto would win reelection despite the March 1977 vote fiasco, and that he would go after Zia with a vengeance. Probably fearing this possibility, Zia put Bhutto on trial for trumped up murder charges and, following a sham trial, the former prime minister was sentenced to execution by hanging. Foreign leaders as disparate as Jimmy Carter and Libya's Muammar Qadhafi asked Zia to grant clemency, but what concerned him more was Pakistani public opinion: how would Pakistanis react to news of Bhutto's execution? Would there be riots? It was with these considerations in mind that Zia asked ISI to survey public opinion. Based on its findings, ISI advised against executing Bhutto.[3] Later, the former JCIB chief, Syed A.I. Tirmazi, denied an ISI role in Bhutto's death:

> The ISI, it needs to be emphasized, has no role to play either in the imprisonment, hanging or ultimate burial of [Bhutto].... We were neither the king makers nor the manipulators for any party. We were neither sycophants nor yes-men of [Bhutto] or General Zia. Our reports were candid, unbiased and honest to the last letter.[4]

Tirmazi protests too much to be convincing. In any case, ISI involvement or not, Zulfikar Ali Bhutto was hanged on 4 April 1977.

ISI leadership change

So what happened to Bhutto's Director General of ISI (DGISI), Ghulam Jilani, after the coup? As discussed above, he was not punished for his service to Bhutto, and this fact alone contributed to rumors regarding his loyalty. When the military junta tried justifying its coup in a white paper, it alleged that the prime minister used and abused ISI "exclusively for the personal political use."[5] Still, Jilani's time was up at ISI – he had served nearly six years after all – so he was "promoted" to the ceremonial position of Secretary General of Defence. In May 1980, Zia gave Jilani the highest political reward for his services by appointing him Governor of Punjab, Pakistan's most important province.[6]

The new DGISI, Mohamed Riaz Khan, had a reputation for being religiously inclined, and this made him a logical choice to serve as Zia's intelligence chief. Such was his piety that Riaz asked a subordinate if intelligence was even permitted under *Sharia*. The question was referred to the new Religious Directorate at Army GHQ, and the answer came back in the form of a booklet issued to all ISI employees. In brief, the Directorate judged that intelligence was a "noble profession" sanctioned by the Qur'an and the Sunna (Prophet Mohamed's sayings and actions). Shortly afterward, posters appeared in ISI HQ with Qur'anic verses linked to security and intelligence themes.[7]

Riaz Khan claimed to be surprised by the ISI assignment because he lacked an intelligence background and had not even completed the basic MI course at Murree. Still, he made an honest effort to learn what his job entailed by visiting ISI's provincial field detachments in Quetta, Peshawar, Lahore and Karachi. He also toured the individual directorates of his headquarters such as the Internal Wing, CI, the JIB and the Joint Signals Intelligence Bureau.[8] After six years of Ghulam Jilani Khan as head of ISI, some ISI officers welcomed the change at the top. As one of them wrote, "there was a new wave of life, and fresh red blood started to run through the ISI arteries."[9] Unfortunately for Riaz supporters, the respite was short lived, for in June 1979, he died of a stroke in his office.[10]

ISI's domestic and foreign roles

The 1977 coup triggered a shift in ISI's domestic missions. Now Zia's enemies became ISI priorities, and these included Sindhi separatists, Shi'a militants stirred up after the 1979 Iranian Revolution, the PPP, and the Bhutto family.[11] ISI's military security task didn't go away either now that the generals were in power, for in 1980, it neutralized a conspiracy led by Major General Tajammal Hussain Malik. Tajammal had been captured by India in 1971, and the traumas of defeat plus several months in a POW camp brought about a fundamental change in his outlook on life, for he had rediscovered Islam. In 1980, Tajammal secretly put together a Revolutionary Command with a plan to overthrow the government while the COAS and DGISI were attending a senior officers' conference. Unfortunately for Tajammal, the ISI detected his plot and arrested him on 6 March 1980. He was subsequently sentenced to 14 years for conspiring against the state.[12]

Zia's foreign policy was substantially different from that of his predecessor. He was not a jet-set diplomat, although he did emphasize Islam as a foreign policy element, especially when it came to Afghanistan.[13] As we will examine later, Islam was the principal motivating factor behind the ISI-backed Afghan resistance, who called themselves "Mujahidin" – or "Soldiers of God." When it came to the US, Zia backed away from Bhutto's occasional anti-US diatribes and declarations of non-alignment by attempting a cautious rapprochement. Such tentative moves were derailed by Bhutto's 4 April 1979 execution and the 21 November 1979 sacking of the US Embassy in Islamabad that was prompted by the seizure of the Grand Mosque in Mecca by militants.

One theme of this history is that the US–Pakistan intelligence relationship does not necessarily parallel the ups and downs of the conventional diplomatic one. For example, in 1979, while diplomats quarreled over human rights and Pakistani nuclear weapons, the US was quietly installing some SIGINT collection equipment in Pakistan's Northern Areas that monitored Soviet communications. The new US–Pakistan SIGINT relationship was never going to replicate the scale of the 1960s operation at Badaber, but it did permit joint collection and intelligence sharing of Soviet and Afghan communications.[14] The importance of the Northern Areas SIGINT sites was reaffirmed in late December 1979, when the Soviet 40th Army invaded Afghanistan. The ISI–CIA relationship was about to be reinvigorated in a remarkable way as they digested the implications of the ominous new Soviet presence in Afghanistan. Indeed, the invasion marked the beginning of a critically important phase in ISI's development, and one with which the Pakistan, the US, and Afghanistan continue to grapple.

The Afghan problem

Pakistan's problems with its other neighbor, Afghanistan, were every bit as intractable as the Indo-Pakistan ones, but on a different order of magnitude. As far as Pakistan's leadership was concerned, one conflict could not be separated from the other, for it was an article of faith that India and Afghanistan were allies, intent on destroying what remained of Pakistan. In fact, Afghanistan was openly hostile to Pakistan from the moment the latter achieved its independence in 1947; it was not long after the Pakistan flag was first raised over Government House that Kabul announced it would not recognize its border with the new state. Furthermore, the Afghan government claimed it was the natural guardian of Pakistan's Pashtun population, most of which lived in the NWFP and the FATA (see Map 9.1). To Islamabad's great irritation, Kabul openly backed the Pashtunistan movement, which called for an independent Pashtun state carved out of Pakistan and attached to Afghanistan. At times, the Afghans armed and instigated the more volatile FATA tribes like the Wazirs and Mehsuds against Pakistan.[15]

Map 9.1 Northern Pakistan.

In July 1973, an already tense bilateral relationship took a turn for the worse when the Afghan King was ousted in a bloodless coup led by his cousin and son-in-law. The new self-appointed president, Daoud Khan, was an intensely ambitious and headstrong politician, who never disguised his antipathy for Pakistan; he was also one of the more fervent proponents of Pashtunistan. At first, Daoud tacked to the left in his politics, because he owed much of his coup's success to army officers affiliated with the Marxist PDPA. ISI reports at the time warned of the dangers posed by the Daoud–PDPA relationship for Pakistan and predicted greater Soviet involvement in Afghanistan.[16] In fact, Daoud reignited the simmering Pashtunistan issue, resumed covert aid for FATA tribes and sheltered Balochi secessionists fleeing the Pakistani army crackdown on their homeland.[17]

Bhutto was determined to respond to Daoud's provocations; however, his country was in disarray, the army was licking its war wounds, and new weapons were scarce. In the summer of 1973, at the time of the Daoud coup, Bhutto created an Afghan Cell within the Foreign Ministry whose purpose was to explore policy alternatives and provide recommendations to the leadership.[18] One policy action shut down Afghanistan's duty free corridor to the port of Karachi; however, greater Afghan–Soviet trade cushioned some of the impact. Islamabad stepped up radio broadcasts in Dari and Pashto, the two dominant languages of Afghanistan, and much of the program content was focused on Islamic themes. The Pakistani authorities believed then (as they do now) that a pan-Islamic identity could offset a more parochial Afghan, Pashtun or Baloch nationalism pushed by Kabul.[19] But the most enduring policy advocated by the Afghan Cell was recruiting, training and arming Afghan proxies and directing them against Kabul. Bhutto, the ever-calculating strategist, assessed:

> Two can play at the same game.... We know where their weak points are, just as they know ours. The non-Pushtuns there hate Pushtun domination. So we have our ways of persuading Daoud not to aggravate our problems.[20]

Pakistan already possessed the tools, doctrine, and experience for this type of warfare. First and foremost was ISI, with its network of informants in the border region as well as extensive experience with UW. Second were the officers and NCOs of the SSG, who handled the mission of training and arming insurgents. Last, but not least, was the Frontier Corps, a paramilitary militia comprised of fighters from Pashtun tribes, whose greatest advantage for Pakistan was their intimate knowledge of the local dialects and tribal politics.

Islamabad's plan for waging a covert war by proxy against Afghanistan was divided into four phases. Phase one was stepping up intelligence collection in that country, including ferreting out potential Afghan allies and weaknesses in the Daoud regime. Under phase two ISI operatives contacted the exiled Afghan King in an unsuccessful bid to have him lead an anti-Daoud resistance movement.[21] Phase three involved joint anti-Afghan operations with Iran, since both the Shah and Bhutto regarded the PDPA as a threat to the regional balance of power. Iran's intelligence service, SAVAK, backed several anti-Daoud groups unilaterally, but ISI wanted to entice the Iranians into joint missions against the Afghans. The last phase in ISI's game plan was also the most important: recruiting an insurgent army from the growing number of anti-Daoud Afghan exiles in Pakistan.[22] Of these, ISI was most interested in a small band of former students, university professors and intellectuals who espoused the agendas of the Egypt-based Muslim Brotherhood and Pakistan's *JI*. This group was to include many future Afghan insurgent commanders and political leaders like Ahmed Shah Massoud, Burhanuddin Rabbani, Sibghatullah Mojadeddi, Gulbuddin Hekmatyar, Jalaleddin Haqqani and Abd al-Rasul Sayyaf. Although each shared the goal of creating an Islamic state in Afghanistan, they inevitably quarreled over the details. From ISI's point of view, this feuding band was the perfect riposte to Daud's Pashtunistan and Balochistan strategies.[23]

ISI valued its émigré Afghan Islamists in varying degrees, but the bearded, glowering Hekmatyar was always the clear favorite. A Ghilzai Pashtun from northern Afghanistan who briefly attended the engineering college at Kabul University, Hekmatyar was an Islamist rabble rouser at a time when Afghan university campuses were shaken by clashes between Marxist and Islamist student groups. Hekmatyar was ideal for ISI's purposes: he was young, power hungry and fanatical, and he was willing to accept Pakistani guidance.[24] He also was a paid ISI asset from the early 1970s, according to Graham Fuller, a CIA case officer assigned to Afghanistan at that time:

> We had good information that [Hekmatyar] was being directly funded by Pakistan.... This was critical because the Soviets had provided a range of assistance to individuals such as Daoud. Hekmatyar was Pakistan's answer to Daoud.[25]

So how did these bickering Afghan Islamists end up in Peshawar? In 1973, shortly after he had seized power, Daoud cracked down on his Islamist problem with the result that many fled to Pakistan and ISI shelter. ISI also did what it could to extricate the families of some of the more important exiles to Pakistan while supporting those left behind. The more promising emigres were transferred to the Frontier Corps, which served as cover for ISI and SSG activities. The Inspector General of the Frontier Corps at the time was an army brigadier named Naseerullah Babar, a Pashtun from the Pakistan side of the border, who had a good rapport with the exiles.[26] He also served as Z.A. Bhutto's Frontier expert, with a "taste for clandestine operations" of the sort planned by ISI and the SSG.[27]

SSG instructors like Major Sultan Amir Tarar trained the most promising Afghans at SSG's base in Cherat.[28] Tarar had passed the SSG qualification course in 1970 and, four years later, attended a US Army Special Forces course at Fort Bragg. For the Afghan project he and other SSG officers were supposed to cultivate and train the Afghan rebels by living, working, eating, and training with them.[29] The program objectives were clear: use the proxies to dissuade Afghanistan from meddling in Pakistan's internal affairs, and preserve them as a hedge should Afghanistan's political system implode. Naseerullah Babar stated later that "[w]e took them under our wing because we knew that someday there would be trouble in Afghanistan. We wanted to build up a leadership to influence events."[30]

The year 1975 was a watershed in Afghan–Pakistan relations. First, there was tribal unrest in Pakistan's Bajaur Agency, which Islamabad attributed to Kabul's agents. Then, on 5 July, a Pakistan International Airways B707 was bombed at the Islamabad airport in an incident DGISI Ghulam Jilani blamed on the banned NAP and a "neighboring country." At the same time, President Daoud confronted several short-lived ISI-backed uprisings across eastern Afghanistan, including the Panjsher Valley, where an exile named Ahmed Shah Massoud gained his first experience in insurgent warfare. Kabul attributed these revolts to the ISI and the Muslim Brotherhood; in another move, it mobilized and forward deployed some forces to the border with Pakistan.[31] ISI sources reported cancellations of officers' leave, unprecedented Army and Air Force exercises, stepped up activities on the border, an influx of Soviet arms, and the presence of disguised Indian army advisors in Kabul. Whether these reports were true or not, the rule of thumb was (and is) that such information was to be treated as factual until proven otherwise: Pakistan could not afford to be strategically surprised by either India or Afghanistan.[32]

Revolution

In early 1976, Afghanistan–Pakistan relations suddenly improved. Sensing the growing power of the communists inside his government, Daoud began repairing his bridges with Iran and Pakistan. By October 1976, DGISI Jilani was informing a US diplomat that the Afghans were no longer fomenting unrest in Pakistan and that ISI was pleased with the new phase in bilateral relations.[33] Unfortunately, that rapprochement was short lived, for on 27–28 April 1978, the PDPA staged a bloody coup in Kabul that resulted in the murder of thousands, including Daoud and his family. Literally overnight, Pakistan's threat perspective on Afghanistan shifted from cautious optimism to outright alarm since all the gains made with Daoud were now reversed. The PDPA promptly reignited the Pashtunistan and free Balochistan rhetoric amid calls for a revolution in Pakistan itself.[34]

Confronted by the new threat on his western border, Zia turned to the Afghan Islamist proxies who had languished in exile since the Daoud entente. At first, Zia ordered all Afghan-related covert operations transferred officially to ISI (which had been controlling most of them all along) and reactivated the Afghan Cell. The cell reviewed defense plans, revisited the neglected proxy program, and explored the possibility of attracting foreign aid for the anti-PDPA guerrilla movement.[35] Still, one cell member later downplayed its impact, asserting that more substantive debates, such as covert action, were handled in a separate, secret channel.[36]

Meanwhile, the PDPA leadership was in a hurry. Ignoring the counsel of their Soviet advisors, the Afghan communists plunged into a program of land reform, universal education, nomad resettlement and national conscription that shocked and enraged a conservative and largely rural society. That society started doing what generations of Afghan villagers did when Kabul overstepped its bounds: they took up arms. An action-reaction cycle ensued: every time the regime imposed "progressive" policies, the people responded with protests and revolts. To enforce its program the PDPA turned its internal party security apparatus into a nationwide secret police that went through several metamorphoses before it became the dreaded *Khadamat-e Etla'at-e Dawlati* – or KhAD.[37] On the regional front, Afghan President Nur Mohamed Taraki confidentially told Soviet leader Leonid Brezhnev that he wished to revive the "liberations movement" in Pakistan: "[w]e must not leave the Pakistani Pashtun and Balochi in the hands of the imperialists. Already now it would be possible to launch a liberation struggle among these tribes and include the Pushtun and Baloch regions in Afghanistan."[38] Consequently, Baloch training camps in Afghanistan were reopened, and word was spread throughout the Baloch community that Kabul was again offering arms and aid.[39]

Part of ISI's response to this renewed threat was relying on the personnel, organization, and ideology of the *JI*, a Pakistani political party that gained from the July 1977 coup. We have already seen how the JI compensated for its lack of popular support by making itself the most organized, disciplined and well-funded of Pakistan's political parties. In addition, the JI had ideological affinities with Afghan Islamists in general and with Gulbuddin Hekmatyar's *Hezb-e Islami* (Islamic Party) in particular. A three-way relationship consisting of the *Hezb*, JI and ISI emerged that was to endure for nearly two decades.[40]

Fortunately for ISI, the PDPA was stricken by disunity from the outset. Moscow had been worried for some time about the worsening situation in Afghanistan. First, Soviet advisors could not restrain the more radical PDPA elements from imposing reforms that enraged most of the population. Second was the turbulence within the PDPA itself, where factional fighting broke out within days of the April 1978 Saur Revolution. Things seemed to reach an all-time low for the Soviets when the first Afghan communist president, Nur Mohammed Taraki, was murdered by his ambitious deputy, Hafizullah Amin. As the PDPA ripped itself apart in Kabul, the rest of the country was sliding inexorably toward civil war.

Soviet invasion

Moscow responded to the Afghan crisis by sending in more military and intelligence advisors to Kabul. By late November 1979, the Politburo believed it had run out of all options to salvage Afghanistan save one: rescuing the tottering PDPA with Soviet soldiers and air power. In late December 1979, the Soviet 40th Army invaded Afghanistan and Hafizullah Amin was gunned down by Soviet *Spetsnaz* soldiers in the Taj Beg Palace south of Kabul. A new government – Afghanistan's fourth in little more than two years – was literally hoisted into power on the tips of Soviet bayonets.[41]

Along with the USSR, Pakistan was the neighboring state with the greatest national security stakes in Afghanistan. With Soviet soldiers in Kabul, Islamabad faced the alarming prospect of an emboldened Soviet Army invading Pakistan itself, rolling down the Indus Valley to a warm water port on the Indian Ocean. No wonder the Pakistani leadership believed it was surrounded, what with the Red Army to the west and the age-old Indian nemesis (and Soviet ally) to the east. Within hours of the invasion, Zia ul-Haq had turned to his DGISI, Akhtar Abdur Rahman, for ISI's estimate of future Soviet moves and how Pakistan should respond to them. By the time ISI's assessment was completed it had expanded into a lengthy research paper that explored, among other matters, Afghanistan's geography, peoples and cultures. The history of the disputed border was raked over yet again. ISI analysts also considered variables that could impact Soviet decision-making such as the aftershocks of the Iranian Revolution, US responses to the invasion, and India's close ties to both the USSR and the Afghan government.[42]

But the heart of the paper was its assessment of Soviet intent and projected moves in the future. Akhtar and his staff believed the Soviet move was not defensive in nature, but rather the prelude to future Soviet adventurism in the Persian Gulf and South Asia. ISI assessed that over the next year or so, the Soviets would focus on propping up the PDPA while, over the long term, Moscow would seek to exert control over Iran and the Gulf Arab states. The outstanding variable was whether the Soviet army could transfer most internal security duties to a reconstituted Afghan army. If that were possible, the analysts reasoned, the Soviets would be able to free up forces for an invasion of Pakistan, starting with the destabilization of the NWFP, the tribal agencies, and Balochistan.[43]

As for recommended courses of action, ISI put UW first, since it had Afghan Islamist proxies at hand. In reality, Pakistan had no other viable choice: its conventional forces were no match for a Soviet Army while its diplomacy could never leverage the USSR out of Afghanistan unless Islamabad was backed by one or two great power allies plus Soviet instability at home, a superpower confrontation in Europe, or a broader East–West "grand bargain."[44] One thing was indisputable: Pakistan had to respond in a way that would prevent the Soviets from consolidating their gains in Afghanistan. Otherwise, the only remaining alternative was adopting a pro-Moscow foreign policy. Neither Zia nor Akhtar were prepared to accept "Finlandization" just yet, so their UW plan envisioned using the Afghan mujahidin as Pakistan's "forward defense" against the Soviets. It was hoped that an Afghan insurgency could bog the 40th Army down indefinitely and thereby thwart any Soviet planning to subjugate Pakistan.[45] "Plausible deniability" – i.e., the fanciful notion that the Afghan mujahidin had no backing from any official Pakistan source – was the thin screen behind which Islamabad hoped to wage a proxy war against Afghanistan and avoid Soviet military retaliation.

Zia agreed with ISI's proposal to step up Afghan operations, but he never tired of repeating his mantra to Pakistanis and foreigners alike: "The water in Afghanistan must be made to boil at the right temperature. It must not be allowed to boil over into Pakistan."[46] In other words, ISI had to carefully calibrate the guerrilla campaign against the USSR, lest the latter retaliate against Pakistan by armed force. It was a delicate, high wire balancing act. The wonder is that Islamabad was able to pull it off.

Akhtar Abdur Rahman

Now we can turn to one of the most important players in Pakistan's Afghan insurgency campaign: Lieutenant General Akhtar Abdur Rahman. Appointed DGISI in June 1979 to replace the deceased Mohammed Riaz, Akhtar served in this post until 1987, the longest term yet for an ISI chief. Like several of his predecessors, Akhtar did not have an intelligence background, but this did not stop him from becoming the most famous (or infamous, depending on one's point of view) Director General in ISI's history.[47] One admiring subordinate was to write later that Akhtar was the "only general to take on the Soviet military machine since the end of World War 2 – and win."[48] We also know more about Akhtar than any of his predecessors or successors thanks to hagiographic biographies written by former associates and accounts by former CIA officers who worked with him against the Soviets in Afghanistan.

Born in 1924, Akhtar Abdur Rahman was one of the last officers commissioned into the British Indian Army in 1947. After choosing Pakistan at Partition – his experiences during that period were briefly chronicled at the beginning of this book – Akhtar went on to fight in the 1948, 1965 and 1971 wars. Then his career entered something of an eclipse: after his promotion to brigadier, Akhtar was consistently passed over for every subsequent rank. Yet somehow, in the end, he managed to obtain his second and third stars until his path to COAS was blocked by the Zia ul-Haq promotion in 1976.[49]

When it comes to personality descriptions, there is a consensus that Akhtar was a harsh task master. Brigadier Mohammed Yousaf admired Akhtar, having served under him in ISI during the 1980s. As Yousaf later recorded in his memoirs:

> [Akhtar] looked a soldier. His physique was stocky and tough, his uniform immaculate, with three rows of medal ribbons denoting service in every campaign in which Pakistan has fought since partition from India in 1947. He had a pale skin, which he proudly attributed to his Afghan ancestry, and he carried his years well.[50]

Yet even Brigadier Yousaf conceded that Akhtar had a "daunting reputation" and was motivated by a "hatred of India" that dated back to Partition.[51] Others who interacted with Akhtar both feared and disliked him intensely for being obsequious to his superiors yet abrasive to subordinates.[52] Syed A.I. Tirmazi described Akhtar as a "hard-task master, a sadist and a yes-man."[53] Another officer, Mahmood Ahmed, served under Akhtar when he helped train Afghan mujaheddin on the Stinger anti-aircraft system. His perspective was similar to Tirmazi's:

> He had a fearsome reputation. Those of us at the lower and middle level joked that he ate subalterns and captains for breakfast. He rarely smiled, remained mostly aloof and cold, was a hard taskmaster, but frankly, we never saw him lose his temper, especially with junior officers.[54]

Yet Akhtar was an ideal spy chief in other ways. Not one to cultivate close friendships – his colleagues called him "inscrutable" and "secretive" – he avoided the diplomatic cocktail circuit and press interviews. He was a teetotaler, who shunned cigarettes and any outward signs of ambition, traits that appealed to Zia.[55] Indeed, there was never any question of loyalty to Zia and, as one former CIA Station Chief stated "[i]f Zia said, 'It is going to rain frogs tonight,' Akhtar would go out with his frog net."[56] He also shared Zia's vision of a post-Soviet "Islamic Confederation" composed of Pakistan, Afghanistan, Kashmir and even the states of Soviet Central Asia.[57] These were fanciful dreams in the early 1980s. No one could have predicted a near-term Soviet withdrawal from Afghanistan, the outbreak of a nationalist revolt in Indian Kashmir, let alone the 1991 collapse of the Soviet Union itself.

Saudis enter the game

Pakistan's poverty, lack of development, corrupt bureaucracy, illiteracy and lop-sided military budgets were another formidable impediment to Zia's goals. The country had been relying on foreign development aid to fill in some of these gaps, but after the 1977 coup and Bhutto's execution, Pakistan became an international pariah. Thus, when the USSR invaded Afghanistan in December 1979, Pakistan was especially vulnerable because of its diplomatic isolation. Still, Islamabad could always count on one ally with considerable financial resources and a shared perspective on the Soviet threat: the Kingdom of Saudi Arabia (KSA). Within hours of the Soviet invasion, King Khaled called Zia to exchange views on the new threat.[58] Then DGISI Akhtar was sent to Riyadh for talks with the head of the General Intelligence Directorate (GID), Prince Turki al-Faisal. Turki would later recall that this visit set a new precedent in the KSA–Pakistan intelligence relationship since the IB had been the GID's Pakistani partner up until that point.[59] In this way, a new KSA–Pakistani intelligence alliance was launched. The normally irascible Akhtar put on his best face when dealing with Prince Turki, because the GID chief had the financial resources Pakistan needed to fight its Afghan proxy war.[60] Over time, a routine was established where Turki or his deputy would travel to Islamabad with suitcases of cash, eat sumptuous meals at ISI HQ, and discuss Afghanistan and the Soviet Union while ISI brigadiers counted the money in a backroom. On occasion, the Saudis would tour the border area, review progress in roads and depot construction, or interview rebel commanders.[61]

Cash was the greatest GID contribution to the war. It was transferred through several channels, including the official GID–ISI one and a separate GID network that funneled money directly to clients such as the Saudi-trained Islamic scholar-turned-mujahidin leader, Abd al-Rasul Sayyaf.[62] Lastly, there were private fundraising efforts inside Saudi Arabia that passed funds through various charities to Afghan refugees, the Peshawar-based exile politicians and commanders inside Afghanistan.[63] It should be understood that, images of brave warriors chanting *"Allahu Akbar!"* notwithstanding, the Afghan jihad was fueled by money – and lots of it. It was used to purchase weapons, ammunition, food and other supplies as well as the loyalty of field commanders. Finally, ISI leaned heavily on the GID at times for cash infusions to cement alliances among the Afghan resistance parties.[64] Nominally separate from the official GID-ISI channel were the so-called Arab Afghans, volunteers for jihad who fought alongside the Afghans or provided refugee support in Peshawar. Leading these volunteers was an Islamic scholar of Palestinian origin named Abdullah Azzam, who set up the "Services Bureau" in Peshawar to assist newly arrived Arab jihadists.[65] It was some of these Arab jihadists who were to leave their mark on the larger world outside Afghanistan in the 1990s and beyond.

Notes

1   K.M. Arif, *Khaki Shadows*, Karachi: OUP, 2001, 154.
2   Z. Hussain, *Frontline: The Struggle with Militant Islam*, New York: Columbia University Press, 2007, 19–20; Z. Hussain, *The Scorpion's Tail*, New York: Free Press, 2010, 54–55.
3   S.A.I. Tirmazi, *Profiles in Intelligence*, Lahore: Combined Printers, 1995, 237.
4   Ibid.
5   Quoted in Z.A. Bhutto, *If I Am Assassinated*, New Delhi: Vikas, 1979, 57.
6   A.D. Ahmad, "Intelligence Agencies in Politics," *The Nation*, 25 Aug 1992.
7   Tirmazi, *Profiles*, op. cit., 21–23.
8   Ibid.
9   Ibid., 21.
10 Ibid., 23.
11 F. Grare, *Reforming the Intelligence Agencies in Pakistan's Transitional Democracy*, Washington, DC: Carnegie Endowment for International Peace, 2009, 18; B. Bhutto, *Daughter of Destiny*, New York: Simon & Schuster, 1989, 168.
12 Tirmazi, *Profiles*, op. cit., 238–251; Arif, *Khaki*, op. cit., 159–162; I. Malik, *Pakistan: Democracy, Terrorism and the Building of a Nation*, Northampton, MA: Olive Branch Press, 2010, 237–240.
13 D. Isby, *Afghanistan*, New York: Pegasus Books, 2010, 72–73.
14 A. Gauhar, "How Intelligence Agencies Run Our Politics," *The Nation*, 17 August 1997; J. Ranelagh, *The Agency: The Rise and Fall of the CIA*, New York: Simon and Schuster, 1987, 666–667.
15 A.O. Mitha, *Unlikely Beginnings: A Soldier's Life*, Karachi: OUP, 2003, 222.
16 A. Dil, ed., *Strategy, Diplomacy, Humanity: Life and Work of Sahabzada Yaqub-Khan*, San Diego: Takshila Research University, 2005, 356–357.
17 H. Haqqani, *Pakistan: Between Mosque and Military*, Washington, DC: Carnegie Endowment, 2005, 101.
18 Ibid., 103–104; S. Nawaz, *Crossed Swords*, Karachi: OUP, 2008, 368.
19 A. Hyman, *Afghanistan under Soviet Occupation, 1964–1981*, New York: St. Martin's Press, 1982, 68–69.
20 D. Cordovez & S. Harrison, *Out of Afghanistan: The Inside Story of the Soviet Withdrawal*, New York: OUP, 1995, 61–62.
21 Haqqani, *Pakistan*, op. cit., 103–104; 173–175; K.M. Arif, *Working with Zia*, Karachi: OUP, 1995, 306.
22 Cordovez & Harrison, *Out of Afghanistan*, op. cit., 16.
23 R. Khan, "Babarnama: Interview with Naseerullah Babar," *The News*, 18 February 2007; www.qissa-khwani.com/2013/12/babarnama-interview-with-naseerullah.html [accessed 10/12/14].
24 S. Coll, *Ghost Wars*, New York: Penguin, 2004, 119; O. Roy, *Islam and Resistance in Afghanistan*, Cambridge: Cambridge University Press, 1990, 230.
25 Quoted in S. Jones, *In the Graveyard of Empires*, New York: W.W. Norton, 2009, 33.
26 E.R. Girardet, *Afghanistan: The Soviet War*, New York: St. Martin's, 1985, 166; I. Gul, *The Most Dangerous Place*, New York: Viking, 2010, 2–3.
27 Gul, *Dangerous*, op. cit., 2–3.

28 Ibid.; A. Davis, "How the Taliban Became a Military Force," in W. Maley, ed., *Fundamentalism Reborn?* New York: NYU Press, 1998, 44–45; Haqqani, *Pakistan,* op. cit., 172–173.

29 S. Shah & J. Landay, "Pakistan's Former Spymaster: Taliban Leader is Ready to Talk," McClatchy Newspapers, 25 January 2010; Y.A. Dogar, "Colonel Imam as I knew Him," www.academia.edu/7490637/Colonel_Imam_As_I_know [accessed 26/4/15].

30 Quoted in I. Akhund, *Trial and Error: The Advent and Eclipse of Benazir Bhutto,* Karachi: OUP, 2000, 169–170.

31 P. Tomsen, *The Wars of Afghanistan,* New York: PublicAffairs, 2011, 108; Hyman, *Afghanistan,* op. cit., 67–68; Girardet, *Afghanistan,* op. cit., 166–167; Cable from Amembassy Kabul, "Year-End Afghan Internal Assessment," 31 December 1975, no. 8458, http://aad.archives.gov/aad/createpdf?rid=82083&dt=2474&dl=1345 [accessed 14/2/14]; Cable from Amembassy Islamabad, "Explosion on PIA Aircraft," 12 August 1975, no. 7381, http://aad.archives.gov/aad/createpdf?rid=8208 3&dt=2474&dl=1345 [accessed 14/2/14].

32 Cable from Amembassy Islamabad, "Pak-Afghan Relations," 29 December 1975, no. 11902, http://aad.archives.gov/aad/createpdf?rid=82083&dt=2474&dl=1345 [accessed 14/2/14].

33 Cable from Amembassy Islamabad, "Pak-Afghan Relations," 5 October 1976, no. 10334, http://aad.archives.gov/aad/createpdf?rid=82083&dt=2474&dl=134 5 [accessed 14/2/14].

34 Gul, *Dangerous,* op. cit., 4.

35 Arif, *Working,* op. cit., 307.

36 R. Khan, *Pakistan: A Dream Gone Sour,* Karachi: OUP, 2000, 96–97.

37 KhAD stood for *Khadamat-e Atalat-e Dawlati* (State Information Services).

38 Wilson Center, Cold War History Project, "Soviet Invasion of Afghanistan," http://digitalarchive.wilsoncenter.org/collection/76/soviet-invasion-of-afghanistan [accessed 6/8/15].

39 Correspondence from P.R. Fearn, British Embassy Islamabad, 7 January 1979, FCO 37/2130, UKNA.

40 Haqqani, *Pakistan,* op. cit., 172–173; A. Jalal, *The State of Martial Rule,* Cambridge: CUP, 1990, 317.

41 The road to the Soviet involvement in Afghanistan is brilliantly narrated in Gregory Feifer's *The Great Gamble: The Soviet War in Afghanistan,* New York: HarperCollins, 2009.

42 M. Yousaf, *Silent Soldier: The Man Behind the Afghan Jehad* (Lahore: Jang, 1991), 40–42.

43 Ibid.

44 Ibid. M. Yousaf, M. and M. Adkin, *Afghanistan: The Bear Trap,* Havertown, PA: Casemate, 2001, 25.

45 Yousaf and Adkin, *Afghanistan,* op. cit., 25.

46 G. Crile, *Charlie Wilson's War,* New York: Grove, 2004, 128.

47 Tirmazi, *Profiles,* 24.

48 Yousaf, *Silent Soldier,* op. cit., 16–17.

49 Ibid., 27–32.

50 Ibid., 25.

51 Yousaf & Adkin, *Afghanistan,* op. cit., 22–23.

52 H. Abbas, *Pakistan's Drift into Extremism,* Armonk, NY: M.E. Sharpe, 2005, 99–100.

53 Tirmazi, *Profiles,* op. cit., 24.

54 M. Ahmed, *Stinger Saga,* Xlibris, 2012, 67.

55 Yousaf, *Silent Soldier,* op. cit., 25; Coll, *Ghost,* op. cit., 64, 84.

56 Quoted in Coll, *Ghost Wars,* op. cit., 64.

57 Cordovez & Harrison, *Out of Afghanistan*, op. cit., 162; I. Akhund, *Trial and Error: The Advent and Eclipse of Benazir Bhutto*, Karachi: OUP, 2000, 149.
58 K. Lohbeck, *Holy War, Unholy Victory*, Washington, DC: Regnery, 1993, 18; E. Margolis, *War at the Top of the World: The Struggle for Afghanistan, Kashmir and Tibet*, New York: Routledge, 2000, 42–43.
59 Coll, *Ghost Wars*, op. cit., 81; Nawaz, *Crossed Swords*, op. cit., 372–373.
60 Yousaf, *Silent Soldier*, op. cit., 87–88; L. Wright, *The Looming Tower: Al-Qaeda and the Road to 9/11*, New York: Knopf, 2006, 99–100.
61 Nawaz, *Crossed Swords*, op. cit., 375; Coll, *Ghost*, op. cit., 72, 156–157.
62 Coll, *Ghost*, op. cit. 81–82.
63 Tomsen, *Wars*, op. cit., 196–198.
64 Nawaz, *Crossed*, op. cit., 373–340.
65 M.A. Zahab & O. Roy, *Islamist Networks: The Afghan-Pakistan Connection*, New York: CUP, 2004, 14–15; Tomsen, *Wars*, op. cit., 248–249.

10 ISI's Afghanistan War

His name was Engineer Ghaffar, and his mission was to shoot down Soviet aircraft with a new weapon called the Stinger. A former Afghan army engineer, Ghaffar was a member of Gulbuddin Hekmatyar's *Hezb-e-Islami* when ISI selected him for Stinger training at Ojhri Camp. It was rumored among the mujahidin that this weapon could reliably and consistently shoot down aircraft, and in September 1986, Ghaffar led a small mujahidin band into the hills near Jalalabad to find out if the Stinger lived up to its reputation. On 26 September at around 1600, as the heat of the day was just starting to ease, Ghaffar heard the familiar thump-thump of MI-24D/HIND attack helicopters as they approached the airport at low altitude. The MI-24 had been the bane of the mujahidin for years because it was armored, difficult to shoot down and armed with rockets and guns. It often flew fast and low, ambushing refugee columns, inserting Soviet *Spetsnaz* men behind insurgent lines and wreaking havoc on guerrilla logistics. Ironically, given the legend that soon grew up around it, the first Stinger missile was a dud, impacting the ground about 300 yards away. Nonetheless, Ghaffar's team had been well-trained: they stood their ground and fired once again at the helicopters. Within minutes, three helicopters lay in cinders outside Jalalabad's airport.[1]

It was a stunning blow, a defining moment of the Cold War combining Afghan courage, American technology and Pakistani guidance to bring down one of the most formidable war machines of the Soviet military. Now that they were effectively denied the tremendous advantages of air power, the war weary Soviets began contemplating a withdrawal from Afghanistan. The path to this tremendous accomplishment was littered with the blood of many Afghans, demoralizing setbacks and, at times, the prospect of defeat at the hands of the Soviets and their Afghan allies.

Intelligence alliances

US–Pakistan diplomatic relations had all but collapsed during 1979, yet the CIA and ISI continued exchanging intelligence on Afghanistan and the Soviet Union. Moreover, the CIA began sending non-lethal aid to the mujahidin via ISI as early as July 1979 – five months before the Soviet invasion.[2] After the invasion, the CIA forged a new agreement with ISI under which it funneled money and weapons to ISI for onward distribution to the resistance. At first "plausible deniability" was the name of the game, so the CIA scrounged up Soviet weapons from several sources to maintain the fiction that the rebels obtained their arms from Soviet and Afghan troops. Once the weapons were acquired overseas, they were shipped to Karachi, where ISI took possession of them.[3] In this way, ISI became the middle man in the effort to get the Soviets out of Afghanistan. It handled the transport of weapons from Karachi to Ojhri Camp in Rawalpindi, where cargoes were divided by intended recipients before being shipped to Peshawar for distribution to the resistance. A smaller stream of weapons was sent directly from the Karachi docks to ISI warehouses in Quetta, where they were parceled out to mujahidin groups fighting in southern Afghanistan (see Map 10.1).[4] Hindsight is 20/20, and many have criticized the CIA for empowering the ISI and letting it favor the more extremist parties such as *Hezb-e-Islami*. Yet implicit in the CIA–ISI deal was the understanding that Pakistan ran the greatest risk of Soviet retaliation for aiding the Afghan rebels; so in return for accepting the possibility of Soviet attack, Islamabad had final say on where the weapons went.

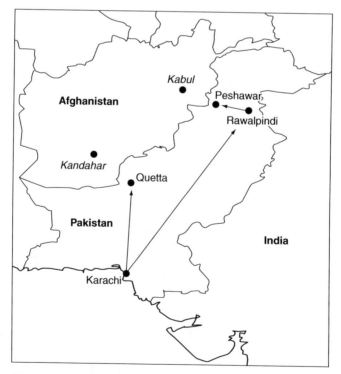

Map 10.1 ISI Logistics, 1980s.

The 1980 election of Ronald Reagan brought about significant changes in the scope and nature of the CIA–ISI partnership. Reagan and his new Director of Central Intelligence (DCI), William Casey, were determined to strike back at the Soviets by aiding anti-communist resistance movements in Nicaragua and Afghanistan. Indeed, the mujahidin fit in well with the Reagan–Casey vision of a more assertive US policy toward the Soviets and, for the next several years, "aid for the muj" commanded bipartisan support on Capitol Hill. DCI Casey built up a rapport with his ISI counterpart, Akhtar Abdur Rahman, over a series of face-to-face meetings right up until Casey's death in 1986. Casey would periodically fly into Islamabad at night in his darkened C-141 Starlifter, greet the various ISI dignitaries waiting on the tarmac and then get whisked away by limousine to ISI headquarters. If a government agency's influence can be measured by the quality of its surroundings and furnishings, then ISI did not come up short. The headquarters facility was surrounded by carefully tended gardens and lawns. In the Director General's office and conference room were teak paneling and paintings of the most exquisite Arabic calligraphy. When Casey and his team took their seats, liveried servants quickly and efficiently appeared with appetizers, the main course and the dessert, all in a well-choreographed performance. Long after the dishes had been swept away, the conversations would continue, lubricated with copious amounts of tea.[5]

Casey's restless imagination was not limited solely to giving the Soviets a bloody nose in Afghanistan. He wanted a more aggressive approach that would extend mujahidin operations into Soviet Central Asia itself. From ISI's perspective, Casey's proposal was loaded with risks since Pakistan would no doubt bear the brunt of Moscow's wrath. On the other hand, by taking the war to Central Asia, ISI would be helping to fulfill Zia's dream of an anti-India Islamic Union consisting of Pakistan, Afghanistan and the liberated states of Soviet Central Asia. Therefore, a decision was made to proceed, albeit with the caveat that ISI could terminate these operations at any time.[6]

ISI's Afghan Bureau led the close-hold planning for Casey's Central Asia initiative, which started out on a modest scale with smuggling anti-Soviet propaganda and Uzbek-language Qur'ans into Central Asia. The next phase involved the covert transport of weapons across the Amu Darya River for future use by the mujahidin.[7] Eventually, operations reached a point where ISI was planning to blow up the Friendship Bridge, a critical bottleneck on the Soviet logistics line into Afghanistan. If the bridge was destroyed, the Soviets would almost certainly retaliate against Pakistan with covert and/or conventional military means. Zia cancelled this operation in 1985, following his dictum that ISI's proxy war should never have the Afghan pot boiling over into Pakistan.[8] But Zia's cautious instincts aside, ISI continued supporting attacks inside the USSR. For example, in April 1987, guerrillas launched rockets onto an airfield near the border town of Termez. Around the same time, another insurgent band attacked a convoy and factory inside Uzbekistan. Smuggling Qur'ans was one thing, but taking the Afghan war into Soviet territory definitely crossed Moscow's red line. As a consequence, the Soviets sent a direct warning to the Pakistanis stripped of the usual diplomatic politesse: if Pakistan continued to sponsor attacks on Soviet soil, the Soviet Union would retaliate with conventional military force. Zia got the message: ISI ordered a halt on raids into the "soft underbelly" of the USSR.[9]

In the end, though, ISI profited handsomely from American and Saudi support for the mujahidin by skimming off its "management fee" from the money, weapons and other supplies transferred by the CIA and GID. This tremendous influx of resources transformed ISI in other ways too: its staffing increased exponentially during the course of the Afghan war, and its facilities were upgraded as well. ISI probably was the best-funded arm of the Pakistani government at the time, a fact that made many non-ISI army officers envious and resentful.[10] ISI benefited in other ways as well. For instance, it was on the receiving end of CIA intelligence equipment and training on new US weapons systems like the Stinger surface-to-air missile.[11] Finally, the US shared more intelligence with ISI than it had in the past, including, as one ISI veteran put it, "verbal intercepts of the Afghans and Soviets in our area of interest."[12]

For its part, Washington quietly applauded the Pakistanis for their success in tying down 100,000+ Soviet soldiers in a senseless war. This was the peak of the bilateral relationship, when both countries shared an enemy, and the US willingly ignored troublesome developments in Pakistan like narcotics trafficking and nuclear weapons. Another facet of the CIA–ISI liaison was the joint exploitation of Soviet weapons, sensors and other equipment left behind on the battlefield. Milt Bearden, Islamabad Station Chief in the late 1980s, records in his memoirs how a Soviet Su–25 strike aircraft was shot down over Pakistan and ultimately made its way into US hands via the ISI.[13]

But it wasn't all sweetness and light: while ISI and the CIA were maximizing their mutual benefits from the Afghan war, their relationship was often marred by mistrust. For example, ISI resented the CIA's occasional probes into its accounting practices; it also suspected the CIA was recruiting assets among ISI and regular military officers training in the US.[14] Apparently, one useful CIA recruiting pitch was to offer US university education for the children of targeted officers. As a result of these real and potential breaches in security, ISI tried imposing basic guidelines for official interactions with the CIA. Among these were the following: (1) meetings required prior authorization from higher levels; (2) at least two ISI officers had to be present at any meeting; and (3) meeting notes were to be sent to headquarters as soon as possible.[15] There were some cultural differences as well, and, predictably, these often centered on alcohol, women and religion. Still, as one ISI officer pointed out years later, Americans were not always blind and deaf to Muslim sensibilities: "The American officers, before they took up their assignments, were well briefed in our customs, habits, and what was to be their conduct and line in official matters, much unlike our officers, who learned things mostly on the job."[16]

There were other irritants, such as persistent rumors that ISI was linked to narcotics trafficking. The CIA Station avoided looking into these too much: there was no sense irritating an ally when higher objectives like defeating the Soviets in Afghanistan were at stake. But some in Washington policy circles began asking awkward questions about drugs and Islamic extremists, and the CIA apparently was not divulging much. Years later, former US Ambassador to Pakistan, Robert Oakley, offered an evasive answer to a question regarding ISI and drug trafficking: "My belief was then and still is that [CIA] wanted to protect their contacts in Pakistani intelligence. We were convinced the ISI was involved but we could not get any hard evidence of it."[17]

Ultimately, it's a tribute to leaders on both sides that the ISI–CIA alliance on Afghanistan worked as well as it did for as long as it did. There were bound to be divergent opinions in some areas, but in the end there was an understanding that ISI was in the driver's seat when it came to managing the Afghan insurgency. After all, the war was fought with Afghan blood, paid for with American and Saudi money, and managed by ISI with the constant risk of Soviet military retaliation against Pakistan.

UW in Afghanistan

The infrastructure underpinning ISI's supposedly "covert" action program in Afghanistan was the product of experience, trial and error, and the lessons learned from earlier insurgencies in Kashmir and northeast India. It was built on a foundation previously laid by the Frontier Corps with ISI supervision and SSG instructors in the mid-1970s. ISI headquarters handled overall strategy, planning and guidance for the Afghan program. The Director General of ISI (DGISI) was personally involved at times in the Machiavellian world of intra-mujahidin politics, mediating feuds, forging new alliances and disciplining the more independent-minded parties by withholding weapons from them.[18] The ISI Director of Administration, located at headquarters, dealt with accounting procedures (such as they were), supervised the cash flow, conducted creative financing to cover shortfalls and otherwise managed the budget.[19]

The next level in the hierarchy was the Afghan Bureau, housed at Ojhri Camp near Rawalpindi. At the time, Ojhri was a conglomeration of World War II-era barracks, mess halls, warehouses and training grounds where mujahidin weapons were sorted and stored before onward transfer to Peshawar.[20] The Afghan Bureau was composed of three branches each led by a Colonel. The Training and Operations Branch was the most significant in terms of mission, manpower and budget, for it supervised the vast training infrastructure that put thousands of Afghan men and boys onto the battlefield every year. This branch also recruited ISI volunteers to staff teams inside Afghanistan, where they advised the mujahidin and collected intelligence on the Soviets, the Afghan regime and even the resistance itself.[21] As of 1984, there were 11 such teams inside Afghanistan, and each was composed of a Major, a junior commissioned officer and a non-commissioner officer. They grew full-length beards and dressed in mufti so that they could blend in with the population; at least one team member had to be fluent in Pashto. Given the nature of the mission, its hardships, and the infinite patience required in mediating mujahedin disputes, SSG men were the most common volunteers accepted for this assignment.[22]

ISI's Afghan Bureau also possessed a logistics branch, which handled the storage, allocation and delivery of weapons, ammunition and other supplies. All of the problems routinely linked to moving goods across a rugged, mountainous terrain with few roads and lots of land mines were compounded by the need for plausible deniability, even if this was just a façade. Interminable factional rivalries often meant that shipments never reached their intended destinations, and the standard transit time for mule- and horse convoys was usually measured in weeks or months.[23] The former Afghan Bureau chief, Brigadier Mohamed Yousaf, appreciated the difficulties inherent to mujahidin logistics:

> The task of my logistics Colonel was certainly the most unenviable within my bureau, if not within the entire ISI organization. His was the daily grind of keeping supplies moving, of worrying about ship or aircraft arrivals, lack of manpower, late supply railway wagons, insufficient vehicles, mechanical breakdowns, and above all security – preventing any leaks as to what we were doing getting to the public, or over-inquisitive journalists and enemy agents.[24]

The third and final branch within the Afghan Bureau was responsible for psychological warfare which, in the Afghan context, consisted of printed media (leaflets, night letters, etc.) and radio stations. Given the widespread illiteracy in Afghanistan, radio likely had greater impact – at least in those areas where its broadcasts could be received.[25] At its peak in the late 1980s, the Afghan Bureau was staffed by 60 officers, 100 junior officers, and over 300 non-commissioned officers.[26]

Many of the time-sensitive tasks were delegated by the Afghan Bureau to ISI Detachments in Peshawar and Quetta. The Peshawar office was the more important of the two, because this city served as the headquarters for the seven officially recognized mujahidin parties. Peshawar was also ground zero for a bewildering array of charities, news organizations, inquisitive diplomats, foreign fighters and, of course, spies. Quetta, on the other hand, was advantageous to ISI because of its proximity to Afghan refugee camps and the city of Kandahar, capital of Afghanistan's influential southern Pashtuns. By the mid-1980s, Sultan Amir Tarar, whom we last encountered as an SSG officer training the earliest generation of Afghan mujahidin, was now a Lieutenant Colonel working for ISI in Quetta. It was here that he trained mujahidin, some of whom eventually constituted the Taliban of the mid-1990s.[27] Nicknamed "Colonel Imam" by his trainees, this officer was one of those ISI experts who lived and breathed in that hall of broken mirrors called Afghan tribal politics. He knew the right people and how to get things done, both inside southern Afghanistan and also in the Pakistani tribal areas as well (see Figure 10.1).[28]

Over time, Zia ul-Haq dumped more responsibilities on ISI because the spy service was wealthier, more efficient and less corrupt than civilian agencies. Consequently, ISI took on two big missions related to the Afghan war that had previously been managed by civilians. One was providing food and clothing for mujahidin groups training or recuperating inside Pakistan, while the other involved provisioning the camps as *millions* of refugees flooded into western Pakistan. Managing all this was a staggering task.[29] Converting illiterate Afghan tribesmen and pastoralists into combat savvy insurgents was ISI's primary task, since it enabled the larger goal of dissuading the Soviets from invading Pakistan. The camps were multifaceted in the kinds of training on offer. A basic two- to three-week course on light weapons and rudimentary tactics was sufficient for most mujahidin. The camps also offered a comprehensive curriculum for more promising recruits that ranged from bomb-making, urban warfare and sniper school to the use of the Soviet SA-7, British Blowpipe and American Stinger anti-aircraft missiles. The camps were

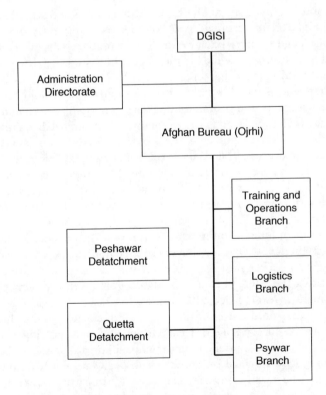

Figure 10.1 ISI's Afghan Bureau.

an open secret, but that did not deter ISI from making strenuous efforts to disguise them. Communications security was a nagging problem that was never solved: the garrulous mujahidin were notorious for their lack of discretion over open lines, and the Soviets were only too happy to listen in.[30]

In the end, ISI's greatest accomplishment was not training guerrilla fighters, but rather manipulating Afghan exiles in Peshawar to form pro-Pakistan parties. After all, the Afghans were notoriously prickly when it came to outside pressure, and this was especially true when it came to Pakistan. The mujahidin leadership came from three sources: (1) those already in Pakistan at the time of the Soviet invasion like Burhanuddin Rabbani and Hekmatyar; (2) those who arrived after the Soviet invasion; and (3) those who decided to remain inside Afghanistan. In the beginning, the exiled leaders reflected the diversity of Afghan politics, for they included royalists, Afghan nationalists, Pashtun nationalists, Pashtun tribal elders, other ethnic groups, socialists, mystic brotherhoods, Islamists and even Maoists. Peshawar literally became an Afghan Babel of languages, ethnicities, sects, and political agendas that rarely – if ever – cooperated for long.

Managing the Muj

In forging a new and improved mujahidin for combat against the Soviets and the Afghan army, ISI had to reconcile two contradictory objectives: unity versus control. Challenge number one was creating a unified political front out of all these disparate groups while, at the same time, ensuring that this front remained under ISI control. For instance, in 1980, some Afghan exiles formed a *jirga* (conference), which sought to build a consensus around four objectives: (1) a specific rejection of Islamist doctrines; (2) espousal of a non-sectarian, "big tent" Islam; (3) local autonomy instead of centralized, Kabul-focused control; and (4) non-alignment in the Cold War. While this agenda would have sounded quite reasonable to most Afghans, it nonetheless posed a clear threat to ISI prerogatives, for it smacked too much of Afghan independence with a disturbing hint of the old Pashtunistan poison that irritated the Pakistanis so much in the past.[31] As we have seen, the Pakistan army (and, by extension, ISI) wanted a pro-Pakistan Islamist regime in Kabul when the Soviets left and the communist government overthrown. In pursuit of that goal, ISI disrupted the 1980 *jirga* by buying off factions with cash and weapons, and aggravating disagreements between the ethnic groups, tribes and parties. As a result, the effort to create an Afghan consensus, and perhaps an Afghan government-in-exile, failed at the outset.[32]

Control was ISI's top priority, even if this came at the expense of mujahidin unity and efficiency. In 1984, DGISI Akhtar and the Saudi intelligence chief took the first step toward consolidating the mujahidin parties and, at the same time, increasing ISI's leverage over them. In order to receive weapons and humanitarian aid, the existing, chaotic sprawl of Afghan parties was eventually pared down to seven. Not surprisingly most of the so-called ISI-7 were

Islamist with a few weak moderates added as window dressing. None of the ISI-7 represented the interests of Afghanistan's Hazara, Uzbek, Turkmen and Nuristani communities. In fact, the seven parties had no demonstrable pre-invasion support inside Afghanistan, but were nurtured instead in the hot-house of Peshawar exile politics.[33]

Eventually, ISI would only provide to the seven parties and they, in turn, distributed it to affiliates in the refugee camps and commanders inside Afghanistan. This ability to apportion guns, food, shelter and employment gave the ISI-7 significant power over the refugee camp population. To the extent that commanders inside Afghanistan relied on the parties for their weapons, the ISI-7 influence extended into that country as well.[34] Further-more, ISI did not treat the seven parties equally. Those willing to toe the ISI line received more supplies, and they included the *Hezb-e-Islami* party of Hekmatyar, the *Hezb-e-Islami* of Yunus Khalis, the *Ittihad-e-Islami* of Saudi proxy, Sayyaf, and the *Jamiat-e-Islami* led by Rabbani. Thus, there was defi-nite incentive for commanders inside Afghanistan to embrace one of those parties since they had the most money, weapons, ammunition and other necessities to sustain the insurgency.[35] Even so, there were some commanders on the "inside" whom ISI regarded as too independent-minded, because they resisted its attempts at control. One was the veteran Panjshir Valley guerrilla leader, Ahmed Shah Massoud, and another was the eastern Pashtun com-mander, Abdul Haq. ISI tried but usually failed to bring these and other inde-pendent commanders into line by withholding money, arms, ammunition, food and medical supplies from them.[36] Over the long term, this policy built up a bitter hatred for Pakistan and ISI among many Afghans.

Of significance for the future, the 1980s Afghan war gave ISI valuable experience in UW. While it is true that ISI had already been in the UW business for years, having trained Kashmiris, Nagas and Mizos, it was the sheer scale of the program and the risks of Soviet retaliation it entailed that made the Afghan campaign so different from the earlier ones. New skills were developed in insurgent recruitment and training, and ISI established contacts with the burgeoning world of jihadi extremists who flocked to the war and formed a sort of "Islamist International." Such contacts paid off when ISI initiated new UW campaigns in Kashmir and Afghanistan in the 1990s.

ISI owns the Afghan file

ISI drove Pakistan's approach to Afghanistan in a process that continues to the present day. Under Zia ul-Haq, ISI was given authority over an Afghan policy that normally would have been the Foreign Ministry's domain.[37] While it is true that Zia reintroduced the concept of an Afghan Cell, where the principal players from the president's office, the Foreign Ministry, the army staff and ISI met to shape policy, the cell was *not* empowered to discuss ISI's covert support of the mujahidin, arguably the most important single element within Pakistan's strategy for Afghanistan.[38] The cell debated a future Afghan government; however, ISI's backing of an Islamist regime defeated the Foreign Ministry's more nuanced approach of a broad-based coalition. When Zia backed the ISI position on this vital issue, he effectively condemned Afghanistan to decades of civil war after the Soviet withdrawal.[39]

United Nations' efforts to mediate a peace settlement in Afghanistan were another bone of contention between ISI and the Foreign Ministry. ISI was predictably skeptical and pressed hard for an outright mujahidin victory rather than a messy compromise deal with the Afghan communists. Zia's Foreign Minister, Sahabzada Yaqub Khan, often complained to the president about ISI's encroachment on his turf, but Zia did nothing, so ISI continued its open-ended UW effort in Afghanistan. In the end, the UN's Geneva Process defied all predictions and actually yielded a settlement in 1988, whereby the Soviets agreed to pull out of Afghanistan by early 1989.[40]

Curse of corruption

ISI's rise to the top of the intelligence community came with some costs, especially in the areas of graft and corruption. As ever greater amounts of cash and weapons flowed into ISI every year to support the mujahidin effort, the opportunities for making personal fortunes grew as well. There were some ISI officers with fewer moral scruples and considerable street smarts who could not resist personal aggrandizement.[41] Some of these corruption problems briefly surfaced in 1983, when three ISI officers at the Quetta Detachment were court-martialed for taking bribes from mujahidin in exchange for weapons. As a consequence, DGISI Akhtar implemented changes in the way ISI supplied arms to the resistance. Brigadier Raza Ali, the Afghan Bureau chief, was sacked and replaced by Brigadier Mohamed Yousaf, while Colonel Salman Ahmed, aka "Colonel Faizan," was appointed the new chief of Quetta Detachment. An SSG officer who helped train Afghan dissidents in 1973–1974, Faizan stayed at his post for seven years, and along with his deputy, Lieutenant Colonel Sultan Amir Tarar ("Colonel Imam"), he gained an unrivaled knowledge of the complicated tribal dynamics of southern Afghanistan.[42]

Akhtar's exit

By 1987, Akhtar Abdur Rahman had been DGISI for eight years – an unprecedented feat that has not been matched before or since. But in March of that year, Zia decided he wanted a change at ISI, so he kicked Akhtar upstairs into the ceremonial job of Chairman of the Joint Chiefs of Staff Committee. Although Zia's motives in doing so were never clear, he did tell his Vice COAS that Akhtar "deserved to be compensated" for his many years of service at ISI.[43] Akhtar left an impressive legacy at ISI, especially in the UW arena where he built a solid foundation for future campaigns of this nature. A deep pool of jihadi recruits had been created, and many of them were willing to fight wars at ISI's direction whether the target was Afghanistan, Kashmir or elsewhere. A vast training infrastructure had been created, and although some camps were later moved to Afghanistan in the late 1990s, others remained in Pakistan, ready to accept a new stream of recruits after 9/11. Finally, thanks to these camps, ISI had established contacts with numerous jihadi groups from Pakistan's own *Sepah-e-Sihaba Pakistan* to the *Abu Sayyaf* group in the Philippines, *Hezb-ut-Tahrir* in Central Asia, *Hezbul mujahidin* in Kashmir, and al-Qaeda, to name a few.

Akhtar's replacement was the serving Director General of Military Intelligence (DGMI), Major General Hamid Gul, a short, forceful, charismatic man, who never failed to leave a strong impression on those who dealt with him. Ambassador Peter Tomsen, who served as President George H.W. Bush's envoy to the Afghan resistance, remembered Gul as "dynamic and devious ... peppery and brutal" while CIA Station Chief, Milt Bearden, left this account: "After a few meetings, I thought I spotted a side of Hamid Gul that could make the slide from 'daring and bold' to plucky and even harebrained, and much later I would find that I was right."[44]

Hamid Gul inherited the nearly impossible job of keeping the conflict-ridden mujahidin coalition welded together long enough to provide a credible government after the Soviets quit Afghanistan. But the ISI-7 kept letting him down, and Gul's determination to ensure an absolute mujahidin victory collided with the final stages of the Geneva Talks, where negotiations over a government of national unity were foundering.[45] Like his patron, Zia ul-Haq, Gul was wedded to the dream of an Islamic coalition led by Pakistan and directed against India. As he once put it: "It's a strategic depth concept that links Pakistan, Iran, Turkey, and Afghanistan in an alliance. It would be a jeweled Mughal dagger pointed at the Hindu heart."[46] He also advocated the "liberation" of subject Muslim peoples in other states like Eritreans, Bosnians, Rohingyas, Uzbeks and even the Uighurs of western China.[47]

Soviet withdrawal

Throughout much of the 1980s, the Soviets paid lip service to United Nations peace efforts in Afghanistan because the Red Army General Staff was confident that a military victory could be achieved there with the right amount of firepower, innovative combat tactics and some political maneuvering. Therefore, ISI analysts were safe in their assessment that Moscow would not abandon Kabul but would push harder for that elusive "decisive victory" over the mujahidin. In 1986, however, there were significant changes in Moscow's attitude toward the war that were driven mainly by the new Soviet leader, Mikhail Gorbachev, who once described the Afghan conflict as a "bleeding wound."[48] Other factors were at work too, such as the introduction of the American Stinger surface-to-air missile system to the mujahidin, which forced changes in Soviet close air support doctrine and, ultimately, operational planning as well. ISI estimated that the Stinger downed 274 aircraft, including 101 helicopters, from the time of its first use in 1986 to the final pullout of Soviet forces in February 1989.[49]

On 14 April 1988, in an event that no one would have predicted two or three years earlier, the Geneva Accords were signed by the governments of Afghanistan and Pakistan, with the US and USSR standing in as guarantors. Along with pledges of non-intervention by all sides, the Accords provided for a complete Soviet military withdrawal by February 1989; however, the Accords were ominously silent on the future status of the Afghan government, leaving the communist leader, Najibullah, in power while the ISI-7 bickered on the sidelines.

Suspiciously, just four days before the Geneva Accords were signed, the huge ISI arms depot at Ojhri Camp in Rawalpindi exploded, showering mortar rounds, ammunition, battlefield rockets and other ordnance onto the camp and nearby civilian areas, killing dozens and injuring over a thousand. ISI's Afghan Bureau offices were damaged and five ISI officers killed, but Brigadier Afzal Janjua and Colonel Imam survived, and they supervised the evacuation of the camp until the fires were suppressed.[50] An inquiry into the Ojhri incident determined that human error caused the explosion, but many were not satisfied with this answer. There was more to it, skeptics argued, and the list of possible perpetrators extended from the CIA and even ISI itself to the Afghan KhAD; however, in the absence of any definite evidence, we are left with the most plausible – albeit less exciting – explanation of human error.[51] Brigadier Yousaf, previous head of the Afghan Bureau, described the shoddy conditions and poor security practices at the arsenal prior to the explosion:

> Lying in the open, in piles, under an arched roof were all types of small arms, mortars, rocket launchers and recoilless rifles, together with their ammunition. Just about every safety rule I had ever been taught for arms storage was being broken, and this within a densely populated area.[52]

When the Soviets initiated their withdrawal shortly after the Geneva Accords were signed, both ISI and the CIA were confident that regime change in Kabul would take place. Few gave Najibullah much of a fighting chance when the last Soviet soldier left his country. This perception of weakness affected the ISI-7 as well, for that fictitious alliance stitched together with Saudi money and ISI pressure was again disintegrating as everyone suspected the other of secretly conspiring to unilaterally seize power in Kabul.[53]

As the Soviet withdrawal accelerated, unexpected political developments took place in Afghanistan that were not well-received at ISI HQ. In September 1988, the communist governor of Kandahar began negotiating a settlement with local tribal and mujahidin leaders. When ISI spies heard about this there was great concern in Islamabad that talks were taking place without ISI-7 participation. In response, ISI increased arms deliveries to Hekmatyar and Sayyaf's *Ittihad-e-Islami* in order to gain more influence in the south and scupper the talks.[54] A similar process was taking place in Herat, where a prominent mujahidin commander named Ismail Khan was making arrangements with local communist officials to share power in Herat City. ISI had always regarded Ismail Khan as "too independent" for its tastes, and it immediately cancelled his $500,000 annual subsidy and sharply reduced his arms shipments.[55] ISI ultimately succeeded in thwarting any separate peace process inside Afghanistan but this "success" helped doom the country to long-term civil war.

In February 1989, the last Soviet troops departed Afghanistan over that same Friendship Bridge the ISI planned to destroy just a few years earlier. The CIA and ISI claimed their share of the victory, even if the war had been fought by Afghans who died in the hundreds of thousands. In 1989, the newly elected President Bush gave Colonel Imam a piece of the Berlin Wall with a plaque that read: "In recognition of being the first to strike the blow."[56] Unfortunately for Afghanistan and its beleaguered people, the Soviet withdrawal did not end the war, which instead entered a new stage pitting the disparate mujahidin factions against a surprisingly resilient communist regime.

Zia's death

It is an irony of history that neither Zia nor DGISI Akhtar lived to see the day when the last Soviet soldier officially left Afghanistan. Both were killed in a 17 August 1988 plane crash that also took the lives of the US Ambassador to Pakistan and the chief of the US Military Advisory Group.[57] Once again, Pakistan lived up to its dismal reputation as the country where high-level assassinations were never adequately explained. ISI investigated the crash and, in the words of a critic, "its efforts appeared less than enthusiastic."[58] Curiously, autopsies were not conducted, even though this would have been routine in a high-level political murder; others alleged that the evidence had been tampered with.[59] What the investigators did find were traces of substances pointing to an explosion inside the aircraft.[60] One favorite theory was that a device for dispensing a nerve agent was hidden in a basket of mangos and placed on board the C-130 just before takeoff.[61] Set to go off at a certain altitude, the bomb detonated in the cockpit, incapacitated the pilots, and thereby caused the plane to crash.

As for the culprits, the list is a veritable who's who on Zia's enemy list, including the KGB, KhAD, and RAW, as well as Zulfikar Ali Bhutto's son, Mir Murtaza.[62] Some retired ISI officers like Hamid Gul, Colonel Faizan and Mohamed Yousaf believe the CIA did it to get rid of the troublesome, independent Zia. At any rate, the circumstances surrounding Zia's death are about as murky as those linked to the assassination of Liaquat Ali Khan in 1951 or Benazir Bhutto in 2007. Pakistan investigators apparently are chronically unable or unwilling to carry out effective inquiries into any high visibility political crimes.

While the remnants of Zia's plane lay smoldering on the ground, the Vice COAS, Lieutenant General Mir Aslam Beg, returned to Islamabad and handed over power to an interim civilian president named Ghulam Ishaq

Khan.[63] Elections were scheduled for 16 November, and to give them more legitimacy, the army allowed the PPP to participate. It was widely anticipated by many – and feared by some too – that the PPP would easily win a majority in the National Assembly and enact substantial changes in civil–military relations. After more than a decade of military rule, the often unheard Pakistani voter was seeking an alternative.

Notes

1 S. Coll, *Ghost Wars*, New York: Penguin, 2004, 148–149; M. Ahmed, *Stinger Saga*, Xlibris, 2012, 47–50, 55.
2 "Brzezinski: "Oui, la CIA est entrée en Afghanistan avant les Russes," *Nouveau Observateur*, 15–21 Janvier 1998, 76.
3 Coll, *Ghost*, op. cit., 63; P. Tomsen, *The Wars of Afghanistan*, New York: Public Affairs, 2011, 247; M. Yousaf and M. Adkin, *Afghanistan: The Bear Trap*, Havertown, PA: Casemate, 2001, 84; L. Wright, *The Looming Tower: Al-Qaeda and the Road to 9/11*, New York: Knopf, 2006, 111.
4 K.M. *Working with Zia*, Karachi: OUP, 1995, 386–387; S. Coll, *On the Grand Trunk Road*, New York: Penguin, 2009, 386–387.
5 M. Bearden and J. Risen, *The Main Enemy*, New York: Random House, 2003, 233, 237–240; G. Crile, *Charlie Wilson's War*, New York: Grove, 2004, 127–128; Coll, *Ghost Wars*, op. cit., 63.
6 Yousaf & Adkin, *Bear Trap*, op. cit., 197.
7 Ibid., 189, 193; Bearden and Risen, *Main Enemy*, op. cit., 294–296; Coll, *Grand Trunk*, op. cit., 240.
8 Yousaf and Adkin, *Bear Trap*, op. cit., 197–198.
9 Ibid., 200,205; Coll, *Ghost Wars*, op. cit., 103–104, 161–162.
10 Yousaf and Adkin, *Bear Trap*, op. cit., 93–96; Ahmed, *Stinger*, op. cit., 11, 119.
11 Yousaf and Adkin, *Bear Trap*, op. cit., 95–96.
12 Ahmed, *Stinger*, op. cit., 119.
13 Ibid., 103, 113; Yousaf and Adkin, *Bear Trap*, op. cit., 92–93; Bearden and Risen, *Main Enemy*, op. cit., 339–341; Coll, *Ghost Wars*, op. cit., 134.
14 Coll, *Ghost Wars*, op. cit., 66–67.
15 Ibid., 66–67; Crile, *Charlie Wilson's War*, op. cit., 458–459; Ahmed, *Stinger*, op. cit., 108–110.
16 Ahmed, *Stinger*, op. cit., 100.
17 Quoted in G. Peters, *Seeds of Terror*, New York: Thomas Dunne, 2009, 46–47.
18 Yousaf and Adkin, *Bear Trap*, op. cit., 39.
19 Ibid., 81–83.
20 Ibid., 26–27.
21 Ibid., 113–114.
22 Crile, *Charlie Wilson's War*, op. cit., 151; B. Riedel, *Deadly Embrace*, Washington, DC: Brookings Institution Press, 2011, 24; M. Yousaf, *Silent Soldier: The Man Behind the Afghan Jehad*, Lahore: Jang, 1991, 59; Ahmed, *Stinger*, op. cit., 86.
23 Yousaf and Adkin, *Bear Trap*, op. cit., 29; Yousaf, *Silent Soldier*, op. cit., 16–17; Ahmed, *Stinger*, op. cit., 86.
24 Yousaf and Adkin, *Bear Trap*, op. cit., 98.
25 Ibid., 29; Yousaf, *Silent Soldier*, op. cit., 16–17; Ahmed, *Stinger*, op. cit., 86; Coll, *Ghost Wars*, op. cit., 156.
26 Yousaf and Adkin, *Bear Trap*, op. cit., 28–29.
27 A. Davis, "How the Taliban Became a Military Force," in W. Malley, ed., *Fundamentalism Reborn?* New York: NYU Press, 1998, 45.

28 Y.A. Dogar, "Colonel Imam as I knew Him," www.academia.edu/7490637/ Colonel_Imam_As_I_know [accessed 26/4/15].

29 Yousaf & Adkin, *Bear Trap*, op. cit., 29.

30 Ibid., 117–118; Coll, *Ghost Wars*, op. cit., 132, 144; K.M. Arif, *Working with Zia*, Karachi: OUP, 1995, op. cit., 318; Coll, *Grand Trunk Road*, op. cit., 238–239; Ahmed, *Stinger*, op. cit., 24, 26; D. Cordovez, and S. Harrison, *Out of Afghanistan: The Inside Story of the Soviet Withdrawal*, New York: OUP, 1995, 194.

31 Cordovez & Harrison, *Out of Afghanistan*, op. cit., 62–63.

32 Ibid., 63.

33 Yousaf, *Silent Soldier*, op. cit., 65, 67; A.S. Zaeef, *My Life with the Taliban*, ed. Alex Strick van Linschoten and Felix Kuehn, New York: CUP, 2010, 104–106; Yousaf & Adkin, *Bear Trap*, op. cit., 39.

34 Tomsen, *Wars of Afghanistan*, op. cit., 254; Crile, *Charlie Wilson's War*, op. cit., 225.

35 Tomsen, *Wars of Afghanistan*, op. cit., 220, 302; Peters, *Seeds*, op. cit., 33–34.

36 Tomsen, *Wars of Afghanistan*, op. cit., 220, 302.

37 Yousaf, *Silent Soldier*, op. cit., 33–34.

38 D. Kux, *The United States and Pakistan, 1947–2000: Disenchanted Allies*, Washington, DC: Johns Hopkins University Press, 2001, 265; Arif, *Working with Zia*, op. cit., 322.

39 R. Khan, *Untying the Afghan Knot*, Durham, NC: Duke University Press, 1991, 200–201; Cordovez and Harrison, *Out of Afghanistan*, op. cit., 154, 161, 163, 231–232, 256, 368n108.

40 Arif, *Working with Zia*, op. cit., 320; Cordovez & Harrison, *Out of Afghanistan*, op. cit., 161, 197, 231–232; I. Akhund, *Trial and Error: The Advent and Eclipse of Benazir Bhutto*, Karachi: OUP, 2000, 148n23.

41 Quoted in A. Levy and C. Scott-Clark, *Nuclear Deception: The Dangerous Relationship Between the United States and Pakistan*, New York: Walker & Co., 2008, 130–131.

42 Tomsen, *Wars of Afghanistan*, op. cit., 255; Yousaf and Adkin, *Bear Trap*, op. cit., 21–22, 38–39; Coll, *Ghost Wars*, op. cit., 67; A. Rashid, *Taliban: Militant Islam, Oil and Fundamentalism in Central Asia*, New Haven: Yale University Press, 2000, 120–121.

43 K.M. Arif, *Khaki Shadows*, Karachi: OUP, 2001, 432–435.

44 Tomsen, *Wars of Afghanistan*, op. cit., 245, 255; Bearden and Risen, *Main Enemy*, op. cit., 291–294; 309, 367.

45 C. Lamb, *Waiting for Allah: Pakistan's Struggle for Democracy*, London: Hamish Hamilton, 1991, 221–222.

46 Quoted in D. Frantz and C. Collins, *The Nuclear Jihadist*, New York: Hachette, 2007, 159.

47 S. Cohen, *The Idea of Pakistan*, Washington, DC: Brookings, 2004, 172.

48 S. Schmemann, "Gorbachev says U.S. arms note is not adequate," *NYT* (26 February 1986), www.nytimes.com/1986/02/26/world/gorbachev-says-us-arms-note-is-not-adequate.html [accessed 4/5/15].

49 Ahmed, *Stinger*, op. cit., 57.

50 Bearden and Risen, *Main Enemy*, op. cit., 333; Riedel, *Deadly Embrace*, op. cit., 38; Ahmed, *Stinger*, op. cit., 71–72; R. Khan, *Untying the Afghan Knot*, op. cit., 282–283.

51 Lamb, *Waiting for Allah*, op. cit., 42, 223–224; S. Nawaz, *Crossed Swords*, Karachi: OUP, 2008, 393; Ahmed, *Stinger*, 63; Levy and Scott, *Nuclear Deception*, op. cit., 132; Bearden & Risen, *Main Enemy*, op. cit., 333–334.

52 Yousaf & Adkin, *Bear Trap*, op. cit., 28.

53 Tomsen, *Wars of Afghanistan*, op. cit., 254; Lamb, *Waiting for Allah*, op. cit., 231–232.

54 Lamb, *Waiting for Allah*, op. cit., 226; R.D. Kaplan, *Soldiers of God*, Boston: Houghton Mifflin, 1990, 215–216.

55 Tomsen, *Wars of Afghanistan*, op. cit., 324.

56 Ahmed, *Stinger*, op. cit., 87.

57 Levy & Scott, *Nuclear Deception*, op. cit., 174.
58 Yousaf & Adkin, *Bear Trap*, op. cit., 14.
59 K. Lohbeck, *Holy War, Unholy Victory*, Washington, DC: Regnery, 1993, 256.
60 Arif, *Working with Zia*, op. cit., 407.
61 H. Abbas, *Pakistan's Drift into Extremism*, Armonk, NY: M.E. Sharpe, 2005, 126.
62 Bearden & Risen, *Main Enemy*, op. cit., 351–352.
63 Nawaz, *Crossed Swords*, op. cit., 412–413.

Part IV
Adrift

11 Intelligence and Democracy
1988–1999

The 11 years between 1988 and 1999 in Pakistan witnessed a sadly comical merry-go-round of civilian governments, each dismissed by the presidency, which was backed by the army. The parties were not given time to gain the experience and legitimacy necessary to challenge the army in domestic politics. As a subordinate arm of the military – although it reported to civilian leaders on paper – ISI was prominent in manipulating Pakistani politics throughout the 1990s. Generally speaking, it opposed Benazir Bhutto's PPP, since she was the only politician with the charisma and popularity to undermine the army's hold on power. The problem with the other civilian leader, Mian Nawaz Sharif, was that he was more independent-minded than ISI had reckoned with when it helped him enter national politics.

ISI and domestic politics

The ISI chiefs during this period differed in character, politics and outlook from their predecessors. Hamid Gul has already been examined as an ambitious, outspoken general prone to conspiracy theories and an expansive Islamist vision. Another Director General of ISI (DGISI) of the 1990s was Javed Nasir, the first openly jihadist DGISI, who nearly put Pakistan on the US State Sponsors of Terrorism list. Then there was Mahmud Ahmed, a "born again Muslim," political chameleon and master of deceit. In the days following 9/11, he promised the US ISI's whole-hearted support while at the same time he urged the Taliban to defy Washington over Osama Bin Laden.

ISI remained dominant within the intelligence community during the 1990s despite efforts by both Bhutto and Sharif to empower the IB at ISI's expense. Both prime ministers appointed "their" DGsISI without the customary concurrence from the COAS. The inevitable result was that the COAS froze the DGISI out of army-related decision-making. The COAS also transferred certain ISI missions to his direct subordinate, the DGMI.

The 1988 national elections posed a significant challenge to the army, because the PPP was almost certain to win. If Benazir became Prime Minister, she would undoubtedly challenge the army's chokehold on domestic politics. Somehow, the PPP would have to be checked, and the most likely means of doing this was creating a rival coalition. To carry out this delicate task, Hamid Gul relied on Brigadier Imtiaz Ahmed, ISI's Additional Director of National Security (ISI's Internal Wing) whose staff identified the core weaknesses behind Bhutto's candidacy.[1] First of all, she was a woman from Sindh, one of the smaller provinces of Pakistan with nothing close to the clout of Punjab, and, secondly, her Islamic credentials were flimsy given that her father had been an avowed socialist not to mention a non-practicing Shi'a.[2] It was with these weaknesses in mind that ISI helped create the *Islami Jamhoori Ittihad* (IJI)("Islamic Democratic Alliance"), a coalition of nine parties, including the JI, the JUI and a revived Muslim League. IJI's leader was Nawaz Sharif, scion of a wealthy Lahore industrialist who reportedly was talent-spotted by the Punjab Governor, Lieutenant General (retd) Ghulam Jilani Khan. A former DGISI under Zulfikar Ali Bhutto, Jilani retired from the army and entered politics in 1985.[3]

ISI worked with the JI on a dirty tricks campaign that included pamphlets and newspaper ads denigrating Benazir, and alleging that she was a tool of the Americans who would sell her country to India. At times, the campaign descended into the crude and infantile such as pictures of Benazir and her mother, Nusrat, superimposed on bikini models. Another widely distributed picture was of Nusrat Bhutto dancing with US President Gerald Ford, which was intended to offend conservative sensibilities.[4] ISI also ensured that money flowed into the IJI's campaign coffers. For instance, former Military Intelligence chief Asad Durrani would later reveal that COAS Mir Aslam Beg had ordered him to transfer 340 million rupees (around $18 million) to IJI in 1988.[5]

When the election results came in the PPP won 94 out of 215 seats in the National Assembly versus 56 for the IJI. Normally, the PPP would have been given the first opportunity to form a government since it had the most seats, but Pakistani politics are rarely normal. Instead, General Beg and ISI's Hamid Gul went to President Ghulam Ishaq Khan and asked him to delay the formation of a PPP government while ISI tried cobbling together a new coalition consisting of the IJI and several other parties. But these efforts failed, and after two weeks of intense backroom negotiations, the PPP formed a government with Benazir Bhutto as Prime Minister. Nawaz Sharif remained Chief Minister of Punjab, where the IJI had done well in provincial elections; the expectation was that as head of Pakistan's most powerful province, he would serve as a brake on Benazir's power. The results of the 1988 elections represented a success story from ISI's perspective. It had blatantly influenced an election and, in so doing, probably cost the PPP a parliamentary majority. ISI had also helped ensure that Nawaz Sharif led a de facto government-in-waiting from his Chief Minister post in Punjab.[6] It was with acts like these that an unelected, legally ambiguous intelligence agency became the tacitly acknowledged kingmaker in Pakistani politics. The consequences for that country's democracy were profoundly disheartening.

Intelligence reform revived

Still, majority or not, Bhutto was determined to press ahead with her agenda in the face of army opposition. At stake in this power struggle was the future course of Pakistan's foreign and domestic policy. ISI and MI ratcheted up the pressure on the prime minister by bugging her residences and offices as well as keeping her under constant surveillance. When Benazir asked General Beg about this persistent shadowing by intelligence officers, he replied that it was for her own "protection."[7] But Bhutto was a clever politician in her own right. Taking a page from her father's play-book, she set up a committee to examine the sensitive issue of intelligence reform. The intent was obviously to weaken ISI, strengthen the IB and reshape Pakistani intelligence to serve her own interests. It was an opening salvo in a civilian-military struggle for control of the intelligence community that was to continue throughout the rest of the decade.

The Intelligence Reform Commission was established in March 1989, literally within weeks of Benazir's swearing in as prime minister. Led by retired Air Marshal Zulfikar Ali Khan, the commission's task was to identify intelligence community shortfalls and propose improvements. The areas of particular concern were ISI's domestic political role, community coordination, training, recruitment, and oversight by the executive and legislative branches.[8] When the Zulfikar Ali Khan Commission issued its findings, dismantling ISI's Internal Wing was at the top of the list of recommended reforms. As a result of its investigation into the Internal Wing's activities, the commission determined that:

> Arrogating to themselves the exclusive right to patriotism, it is understood that they tried to manipulate the results in favor or against certain political parties by threats and coercion, persuasion and offers of bribes. Subsequently, efforts were made to destabilize the government duly established by law and these agencies tried to act as virtual King-makers. No responsible government can allow this to continue.[9]

The commission also endorsed the idealistic notion of separating intelligence agencies from the temptations and pitfalls of policymaking:

> Facts have no politics and intelligence agencies must interpret facts without fear or favour. In fact, to be useful to its political masters an intelligence agency must be absolutely free from any political bias or influence, its supreme role and concern being the defence of the state.[10]

The commission advocated foreign covert operations and even listed some of those it approved, such as black propaganda and financial backing of political parties, labor unions, businesses and student organizations.[11] It also called for the termination of some unspecified operations then underway in India. The commissioners touched on the sensitive issue of creating a National Security

Council (NSC) under the prime minister and consisting of the Foreign, Defence, and Interior Ministers, the Chairman of the Joint Chiefs of Staff Committee, and the individual armed forces services chiefs. Among other tasks, the NSC would supervise a proposed Joint Intelligence Committee (JIC) that was intended to improve coordination across the intelligence agencies. The commission members were especially critical of the overlapping missions among the intelligence agencies and sought to establish a clearer set of "lanes of the road" to reduce redundancy. JIC membership would consist of the Secretaries of Foreign Affairs, Defence, Interior, and Finance plus the heads of the IB and ISI. A Permanent Chairman would supervise the JIC's day-to-day activities and have a chair on the NSC as well.[12]

Not surprisingly, the commission also stressed the importance of strengthening the IB vis-à-vis ISI and MI by transferring ISI CI to the IB. Moreover, the IB would return to its old role of performing missions at home and abroad, although it was acknowledged that it currently lacked crucial experience in HUMINT and technical surveillance operations. At the same time, the commission recommended that the IB not be given a role in domestic politics other than analysis.[13]

One innovative solution proposed by the commission was to reduce the army's dominance over ISI by rotating the Director General slot among the three services. In acknowledgment of the army's dominance, however, that service would be allowed to appoint directors for two consecutive terms. A recommendation was made to appoint at least 20 civilians to ISI posts in order to give the agency more of a civilian flavor.[14] These were all sound recommendations and would have accomplished a great deal in reforming the intelligence community and making it more accountable to civilian rule. But the creation of an NSC reporting to the prime minister would have been especially contentious since it challenged the army's self-appointed role as sole policy-maker in the national security realm. Many have proposed reforming and empowering the IB relative to ISI, but such recommendations have had little traction since they required political will, not to mention financial and human resources that the non-military ministries lack. IB had neither, whereas ISI could fall back on the armed forces for staffing and funds not to mention ample reserves of weapons and facilities. Unfortunately, just as other proposed reforms of the intelligence community foundered, this one too was shelved. The reasons are not clear, although one can surmise that Benazir, with the limited political capital at her disposal, was unwilling to challenge the army over intelligence reform. It was an opportunity lost. Nonetheless, the commission's report still stands as one of the better models for reforming Pakistan intelligence today.[15]

New ISI chief

Intelligence reform aside, Benazir had other fish to fry, including her not-so-loyal DGISI, Hamid Gul, who never disguised his contempt for her. Her national security advisor, Iqbal Akhund, later provided this description:

"[d]ark browed and intense in appearance, Hamid Gul was one of the new breed of army officers – a pseudo-ideologue, class conscious, ambitious, with a head full of simplistic political solutions for the country's problems."[16] A clash between Bhutto and Gul was inevitable, yet the DGISI believed he could always rely on the COAS, General Mir Aslam Beg, to back him up. This was true as long as Gul's professional reputation was not contested, but when an important Afghan mujahidin offensive failed in Jalalabad in 1989, Gul suddenly looked vulnerable. Then rumors surfaced that he was plotting against Benazir along with Nawaz Sharif and a Peshawar-based Saudi named Osama Bin Laden.[17] On 24 May 1989, Bhutto made arguably the boldest move of her first term in office when she fired Hamid Gul. When Gul heard the news of his dismissal, he reportedly exclaimed: "I think India has won."[18]

Unlike her predecessors, Bhutto did not consult her COAS when she selected her new DGISI. In fact, the announcement was made while she was on an official visit to Turkey, leaving her conveniently distant from the political repercussions of her move.[19] The new DGISI – Bhutto's DGISI – was a *retired* Lieutenant General named Shamsur Rahman Kallue, who had resigned several years earlier over Zia's effort to Islamize the army. Benazir's political calculation was starkly obvious: to gain control over ISI by appointing her own Director General, a retired officer, who would lack an institutional powerbase of his own. It was a de facto "civilianization" of the ISI from the very top. Benazir Bhutto would later write:

> To the dismay of the intelligence officers, the PPP chose to pick a retired general as the head of the powerful Inter-Services Intelligence. A retired general was free of threats that could otherwise be made to serving officers by reporting to the general headquarters.[20]

General Beg fought fire with fire. As soon as he learned of the Kallue appointment, Beg removed all sensitive files from ISI's Internal Wing and transferred them to MI. Beg also transferred parts of the Afghan program from ISI to MI, and appointed Hamid Gul as his "special advisor" on Afghan affairs. These moves were intended to ensure that the army retained the last say on Afghan policy, including any political settlement. In a pointed snub, Beg did not invite Kallue to gatherings of senior army officers, which often dealt with political issues. Whatever Kallue's personal qualities were, he was never going to be allowed to run ISI: ISI was owned by the COAS not the prime minister. As DGISI, he found that his chain of command was not functioning as it should. For example, subordinates were not reporting to him, and he soon realized that key issues pertaining to his agency were being deliberated by subordinates without his knowledge. The COAS refused to meet him, while the DGMI, Major General Asad Durrani, enjoyed greater power within the intelligence community than any previous DGMI had in the past.[21]

Intelligence wars

With her coup de main in appointing a retired general as DGISI, Benazir tried to make herself a player in the struggle for Pakistan's intelligence apparatus. On one side was the civilian prime minister who had direct authority over the relatively weak IB and nominal control over ISI. On the other was the COAS, General Mir Aslam Beg, who exercised direct control over the MI and key parts of ISI. Thus, ISI was effectively divided against itself, torn between the needs of its two adversarial masters, and this split became evident in a plot against Benazir's government.[22] In September 1989, ISI's Internal Wing, now working for General Beg, launched Operation MIDNIGHT JACKAL, an effort to unseat the Bhutto government by buying off some of her parliamentary backbenchers. The conspirators believed that if they purchased enough votes, Benazir could be defeated in a no-confidence vote that would force new elections. At the head of the plot was Brigadier Imtiaz Ahmed, former Additional Director of ISI's Internal Security Wing, and a retired officer named Amir Khan. MIDNIGHT JACKAL backfired on its sponsors, however, for unbeknownst to Imtiaz or Amir, the IB secretly videotaped them trying to bribe two PPP parliamentarians. The effort to trigger a no-confidence vote failed, but the conspiracies against Benazir continued. ISI's Internal Wing next struck at Bhutto through her Achilles Heel: her notoriously corrupt husband, Asif Ali Zardari. He was an easy target, and ISI did not have to work too hard to plant leaks in the press about Zardari's reputation as "Mr. Ten Percent." In the 1990 elections, the IJI would use such stories for political gain.[23]

When repeated efforts to dethrone Bhutto failed, her opponents opted for outright dismissal of her government by President Ghulam Ishaq Khan. In July 1990, the president worked out a plan with COAS Beg and the DGMI, Asad Durrani, to dissolve the government based on the prime minister's corruption. Benazir found out about the plot when her cabinet ministers informed her that MI officers had already urged them to defect before the government was brought down. But it was too late for her to act on the information. On 6 August 1990, Bhutto's enemies celebrated her dismissal as prime minister and the dissolution of the National Assembly on the president's orders. MI seized the television studios and radio broadcasting facilities, while the IB offices were locked up and sensitive IB files transferred to MI headquarters. With radio and TV denied her, Benazir convened a press conference in which she alleged that "military intelligence forced the President to make this decision." But it was all too little, too late.[24]

The coup was carried out efficiently and with no blood shed. The Director General of Benazir's IB was arrested and interrogated in an ISI safe house where he confessed to "improprieties." COAS Beg dismissed Kallue from ISI and replaced him with his trusted co-conspirator, the DGMI, Asad Durrani.[25]

The cerebral DGISI

Asad Durrani was a career artillery officer whose close ties to General Beg gave him considerable influence. A fluent German speaker, Durrani had previously served as a military attaché at the Pakistani Embassy in Bonn, giving him international exposure that most of his predecessors lacked. Unlike the outspoken Hamid Gul, Durrani preferred a lower profile. As one colleague later wrote, "Durrani was not verbose.... He was decisive and a notch or two above the best of his colleagues in the province of the mind."[26] For several months, Asad Durrani held the positions of both DGMI and DGISI; not only was this a clear example of the trust that Mir Aslam Beg placed in him, it also demonstrated that Durrani's priority mission was restoring ISI to army discipline.

Enter Nawaz Sharif

They may have dismissed her government, but neither Ghulam Ishaq Khan nor the army was willing to ban Benazir from participating in the 1990 national elections. Now more than ever, they were determined to prevent another PPP election victory, so they established an Election Cell, whose sole purpose was ensuring Bhutto's defeat. ISI undoubtedly helped fix the 1990 election, and although much is still unknown, a few revelations have emerged in court trials since. For example, ISI set up a specific account where money was stashed away as a slush fund for bribing PPP politicians, while the Pakistani Habib and Mehran Bank loaned $3 million to DGISI Durrani for use in the election against Benazir.[27]

Not surprisingly, Nawaz Sharif ended up winning this election. Yet despite what the army might have hoped, he was not going to be anyone's stooge. A shrewd operator, Sharif bided his time while he laid his own plans to enhance his power at the army's expense. Like Benazir before him, Sharif tried counterbalancing ISI with an empowered IB. IB bugs were placed in the offices and residence of the new COAS, General Asif Nawaz Janjua; additional taps were placed on the telephones of IJI and opposition politicians as well as judges and journalists.[28]

When General Beg retired as COAS in August 1991, DGISI Durrani lost a valuable protector. Moreover, Nawaz Sharif's Director General of the Intelligence Bureau (DGIB) was none other than the same retired Brigadier Imtiaz Ahmed, who, as head of ISI's Internal Wing, tried derailing Benazir Bhutto's 1988 election campaign. The DGIB reportedly set up Durrani for a fall by planting doubts in the prime minister's mind about rumored coup plots within the army. Thus prompted, Sharif summoned Durrani for a read out of a recent corps commanders' conference, where the most senior generals routinely discussed army matters. When the DGISI replied that nothing of interest took place in the conference, the prime minister's doubts about his loyalty were confirmed. If what the DGIB said was true, then it was Durrani's duty to warn Sharif of any conspiracies in the ranks. A few days later, Nawaz Sharif informed the COAS General Asif Nawaz that Durrani had to go. On 2 March 1992, Sharif named a new DGISI, reportedly on the recommendation of Imtiaz Ahmed and not the COAS, who was traveling when the announcement was made. Thus, for the second time in three years, a civilian tried to seize control of the ISI by appointing a DGISI without consulting the army first.[29]

The bearded DGISI

Nawaz Sharif's choice as DGISI was Javed Nasir, an officer of Kashmiri origin whose career was spent in the Army Engineering Corps. Javed Nasir reportedly rediscovered Islam in 1986 because of the Afghan war, and he became a member of the *Tablighi Jama'at*, a Deobandist organization dedicated to propagating Islamic revivalism worldwide. As a visible demonstration of his faith, Nasir grew out a long, untrimmed beard that emulated the practice of the Prophet Mohamed. Javed Nasir's close ties to the DGIB, Imtiaz Ahmed, were highlighted by an article in the Pakistan daily, *The News*, which asserted that ISI and IB cooperation had already improved as a result of Javed Nasir's appointment. According to the article, both Nasir and Ahmed had Kashmiri origins and were "committed Rightists," previous rivalries between these agencies were now being resolved in an effective manner.[30]

Javed Nasir put his beliefs to work as soon as he took over ISI by ordering the agency to expand its covert action programs beyond Afghanistan and Kashmir to other beleaguered Muslim communities such as Bosnians, Chechens, Uighurs, Myanmar Rohingyas and Uzbek militants. But it wasn't just Muslim causes that interested Javed Nasir, for under his watch ISI worked with Tamil and Sikh extremists against the common Indian adversary. While efforts to expand Pakistan's proxy wars did not accomplish much, they did complicate Pakistan's relations with several countries, including the Central Asian states, Russia, India, Egypt, Algeria and the US.[31]

In March 1993, a Bombay underworld don named Dawood Ibrahim ordered his gang to bomb several sites in retaliation for the destruction of a mosque in the Indian city of Ayodhya by Hindu nationalists. Investigators later determined that Ibrahim had extensive ties to the ISI and may have conducted the bombings on Islamabad's orders. The Bombay attacks, combined with ongoing unrest in Kashmir, served as the catalyst for India's request that the US pressure Pakistan into throttling back its proxy wars. Consequently, US diplomats warned the Pakistanis that if ISI continued to support secessionists in India, Washington would put Pakistan on the State Department's list of terrorist sponsoring countries. It was a blunt threat, and Islamabad did the minimum necessary to ensure that US demands were met – at least on the surface and only until the Americans were distracted by other foreign policy priorities.[32]

Javed Nasir's aggressive jihad policy did raise two fundamental questions in foreign capitals: was the DGISI acting without the knowledge of the prime minister and/or the COAS? If not, who ordered him to execute this proxy offensive and why? Some foreign diplomats found it expedient to label ISI a "rogue" agency if only to postpone difficult policy decisions on handling a Pakistani government that employed terrorism as an instrument of state policy.[33] The "rogue" theory would be repeatedly used in the future to explain Pakistani behavior that otherwise seemed illogical and inexplicable.

In many respects, DGISI Javed Nasir faced many of the same institutional obstacles that disrupted Shamsur Rahman Kallue's tenure in that position. There was no question the "jihadi DGISI" enjoyed the backing of the prime minister and that his effort to ramp up covert action abroad was approved by the COAS and/or the prime minister. Nevertheless, senior army officers were wary of Nasir and isolated him; he was not "their" man in ISI but the prime minister's stooge. Taking his cue from his predecessor, the COAS, General Asif Nawaz, excluded the DGISI from corps commanders' conferences. Lack of access to Army GHQ thinking meant the DGISI would be of limited value to Nawaz Sharif when it came to assessing army opinion.[34]

But as it turned out, the COAS and the army were the least of Nawaz Sharif's problems, for in spring 1993 tensions between the prime minister and the president, Ghulam Ishaq Khan, mounted. As the crisis wore on, the president contemplated dismissing Sharif on the familiar charges of mismanagement, corruption and nepotism. One sign of the decline in Sharif's authority came on 3 May 1993, when DGISI Javed Nasir was dismissed and retired from the army allegedly as a result of US pressure. In July 1993, Nawaz Sharif stepped down as prime minister after a three-month legal wrangle with the president, but his resignation did not mean he was exiting politics – far from it. Even so, his failure to complete the term of his government was cementing a bad precedent in Pakistani politics.

The reformist DGISI

With Nawaz Sharif gone and new elections yet to be held, the COAS seized the opportunity to select a new DGISI who would represent the army's corporate interests. His choice was a former DGMI, Javed Ashraf Qazi, whose prior position gave him the background and experience to take over the ISI post. Qazi's instructions were unambiguous: clean out ISI's Augean Stables and, in the words of one observer, "make ISI invisible again."[35] He also set out to repair bridges to the CIA that had been damaged by his predecessor's religious zeal. Shuja Nawaz describes in his book, *Crossed Swords*, how the new DGISI was shocked when he entered his headquarters for the first time and saw many officers in *shalwar qameez* instead of uniforms. Some proudly wore the long, shaggy beards favored by their previous boss while still others vanished from their desks for scheduled and unscheduled prayer times. Qazi was also troubled by the lack of accountability for the large amounts of cash that routinely flowed through the agency on its way to vague destinations. As if all this wasn't enough, there was a much abused chain of command, where junior officers routinely circumvented their supervisors and demanded meetings with the most senior chiefs of the agency. Not surprisingly then, Qazi ordered all ISI officers to wear uniforms and trim their beards while some of the more blatant Islamist officers were retired or transferred out. The Afghan Bureau was especially hard hit with personnel transfers, staff cuts and greater headquarters scrutiny of its budget. Qazi also decided to terminate some of the more controversial operations underway, including an unspecified one in Southeast Asia. ISI had lost its way, he decided, sacrificing its intelligence role for the phantoms of covert action.[36]

In retrospect, DGISI Qazi's reforms were more form than substance, their primary objective keeping Pakistan off the US terrorism sponsors list. Operations deemed essential to Pakistan's national security like Afghanistan actually escalated under Qazi as did the Kashmir proxy war. The appearance of reform was enough to disguise the reality of very little change beneath the surface. US support for Pakistan continued.[37]

President Ghulam Ishaq Khan resigned along with Sharif in May 1993, yielding to an interim government that ruled until October 1993 elections. For once, ISI did not manipulate, cajole, purchase, sell or otherwise abuse the election process, but ISI was, of course, prepared to play the kingmaker role if the election results permitted this. DGISI Qazi later affirmed in an interview that "[t]he ISI did not take part in the election process. It was absolutely free and fair."[38] As it turned out, the PPP and its leader, Benazir Bhutto, won a new mandate. Bhutto had learned a lesson or two from her first term, and one of these was to steer clear of army prerogatives like nuclear weapons, Afghanistan, and Kashmir. In fact, she sought an entente with the COAS and DGISI, an effort made easier by the fact that Javed Ashraf Qazi's personality was more conciliatory than that of her first term *bête* noire, Hamid Gul.[39]

Strengthening the IB

In the end, though, Bhutto was a politician, and this meant she was loth to rely on fragile understandings with the army when it came to her political future, so she hedged her bets by trying once again to strengthen the IB as a counter to the military agencies. She reappointed Masood Sharif Khan Khattak as DGIB, a post he had held during her first term, and expanded the IB's staff and capabilities. Bhutto then unleashed "her" IB on adversaries by tapping the telephones of President Faruq Leghari's family, spying on the corps commanders, keeping an eye on ISI and MI, and monitoring politicians and retired army officers.[40] Meanwhile, everyone could rest assured that MI and probably ISI too were spying on the prime minister and her aides. As the journalist Kamran Khan later wrote:

It would have been much more fruitful for the health of the country if all the intelligence agencies could have focused on tracking the activities of extremist outfits who were creating havoc in the country rather than spying on each other.[41]

But such hopes were in vain. In September 1995, the DGMI, unveiled a coup plot within the army organized by a Major General named Zahir ul-Islam Abbasi. Like so many other officers of his generation, Abbasi was profoundly influenced by the 1980s Afghan war, when he served as an ISI liaison officer to the mujahidin. He rediscovered Islam and became a member of *Tablighi Jama'at*, which, as we have seen, exercised a powerful influence on Javed Nasir. Abbasi also was once posted as military attaché to New Delhi, but the Indians expelled him for espionage.[42] For his conspiracy, Abbasi had recruited 40 army officers, including a brigadier and fighters from the jihadi group *Harakatul Ansar*. The plotters planned to seize army headquarters and kill all those senior generals present at a promotion board. The coup would be announced on television, and Abbasi would proclaim his intention of making Pakistan a true Islamic state. Once again, observers of the Pakistan army, both foreign and domestic, were left wondering to what extent Islamist ideologies were now influencing the officer cadre.[43]

The wheel turns again

On 5 November 1996, President Leghari dismissed Bhutto for corruption and then, in the interim before elections, he reorganized the IB. An army major general was appointed as DGIB, and several retired army officers were assigned to the agency's senior leadership positions. A future civilian administration was not going to be allowed to use the IB against the army again.[44] On 3 February 1997, Nawaz Sharif was elected Prime Minister for the second time. The extent of his election victory (he won 137 out of 207 seats) convinced Sharif that he had a mandate for sweeping changes in domestic and even foreign policy. His most important decision was selecting a new COAS. Like Zulfikar Ali Bhutto before him, Nawaz Sharif was looking for a COAS who would concentrate on army matters and let the civilians run the government. As luck would have it, however, the prime minister managed to choose a general whose temperament was diametrically opposed to what Sharif sought in a COAS: Pervez Musharraf.[45]

Within days of selecting the COAS, Nawaz Sharif named his new DGISI without consulting Musharraf in advance. His choice was Khwaja Ziauddin Butt, colorfully described by one author as "a stocky man, about five feet nine inches tall, and his face looked as if it had been boxed around a few times."[46] Curiously, Ziauddin resembled Sharif's previous choice as DGISI, Javed Nasir, in that he was a career engineering officer as opposed to the combat arms backgrounds of most ISI directors. It was also rumored that Ziauddin was linked to Sharif either by family or political and business ties.[47]

Musharraf soon revealed that he was not a good choice to be Nawaz Sharif's COAS. He was brash, brazen and often showed no tolerance for the foibles of civilian governments. It was not long before the COAS and the prime minister were plotting against each other, waiting for the propitious moment to strike. One result of this power struggle was that the DGISI once again found himself in an ambiguous position, trying to serve two very different masters. Sharif needed Ziauddin to keep him up to date on conditions within the army including the loyalty of its officers. Meanwhile, Musharraf locked the DGISI out of army leadership gatherings. This was starting to develop into a regular pattern. One quirk this time, though, was that Ziauddin's deputy, Major General Ghulam Ahmed, was reporting to Musharraf behind his boss's back, and was in on the plans to oust the prime minister.[48]

On 12 October 1999, the conflict between Sharif and Musharraf came to a head when the General was flying back from an official visit to Sri Lanka. While Musharraf was still in the air, Sharif dismissed him and appointed DGISI Ziauddin in his place. Musharraf learned of his dismissal when the Karachi air traffic control tower refused to let his plane land. Fortunately for Musharraf, Lieutenant General Mahmud Ahmed, commander of X Corps, was on his side. Subordinate to X Corps was the pivotal 111 Brigade based in the Islamabad area, which Ahmed used to round up the Sharif loyalists, including the would-be COAS General Ziauddin, and stifled the takeover. Musharraf's plane was allowed to land, the prime minister was packed off to Saudi Arabia and a new military dictatorship seized the reins of power.[49]

Musharraf

Musharraf quickly changed the leadership of both the IB and ISI in order to cement his powerbase. The former DGIB, Major General Rafi Ullah Niazi, who had been dismissed by Sharif in September 1997, was restored to his position. More importantly, Musharraf believed ISI needed another purging of officers whose loyalties to the army he deemed suspect. Musharraf also imposed new limits on ISI–CIA cooperation, which had expanded considerably under Ziauddin. Finally, as a reward to the X Corps Commander for backing him in the coup, Musharraf appointed Mahmud Ahmed as DGISI.[50]

Some continuity was maintained in ISI as the Deputy DGISI, Major General Ghulam Ahmed Khan, retained his post under the new regime. Ghulam Ahmed occasionally served as de facto spokesman for ISI in press interviews. In one such interview, in February 2000, he tried to put a positive spin on ISI's reputation:

> People think ISI is a state within a state, but there are tight checks and controls, and there are certain scruples.... We have an Islamic system here which does not permit terrorism. We must put the record straight. It is wrong to blame this organization. There is a lot of scrutiny on us.[51]

In this same interview, the DDGISI asserted that ISI did not have the degree of control over foreign militant groups that outsiders believed. As for Kashmiri groups, he fell back on the well-worn but false story that ISI was only providing "political and moral backing." The main threats to Pakistan, he concluded, were Afghan refugees, poverty, sectarianism, lack of land reform and law-and-order problems. It was a refined, sophisticated exposition on all the right things ISI was doing, even though many of its liaison partners must have seen it as yet another example of ISI duplicity.[52]

Like his most recent predecessors, Sharif and Bhutto, Musharraf toyed with that elusive mirage called intelligence reform. One proposal only briefly under consideration was to give the Ministry of Interior the authority to coordinate the PIC's activities, designate lanes of the road and otherwise nudge the agencies toward greater collaboration. Not surprisingly, given the military equities involved, this idea was quickly scrapped.[53] Musharraf did carry out one innovative reform, although this was motivated by politics more than government efficiency. A National Accountability Bureau (NAB) was created to investigate official corruption. DGISI Ahmed was heavily involved in setting up the NAB in its early days, and ISI and IB information was used as leads for further inquiries. Eventually, the NAB created its own Central Investigation Team staffed in part with retired ISI personnel. This power to expose and pillory became useful when Musharraf wanted to intimidate and punish his opponents.[54]

Notes

1 G.A. Khan, *Glimpses into the Corridors of Power*, Karachi: OUP, 2007, 205; H. Haqqani, *Pakistan: Between Mosque and Military*, Washington, DC: Carnegie Endowment, 2005, 207; C. Lamb, *Waiting for Allah: Pakistan's Struggle for Democracy*, London: Hamish Hamilton, 1991, 59.

2 Haqqani, *Pakistan*, op. cit., 207; I. Malik, *State and Civil Society in Pakistan*, London: Macmillan, 1997, 98.

3 Lamb, *Waiting for Allah*, op. cit., 58–59; Haqqani, *Pakistan*, 201; H. Abbas, *Pakistan's Drift into Extremism*, Armonk, NY: M.E. Sharpe, 2005, 134, 147; Malik, *State*, op. cit., 98; S. Nawaz, *Crossed Swords*, Karachi: OUP, 2008, 411–412; K.M. Arif, *Working with Zia*, Karachi: OUP, 1995, 238.

4 Lamb, *Waiting for Allah*, op. cit., 39, 68.

5 P. Tomsen, *The Wars of Afghanistan*, New York: PublicAffairs, 2011, 256.

6 Z. Hussain, *Frontline: The Struggle with Militant Islam*, New York: CUP, 2007, 23.

7 Abbas, *Pakistan's Drift*, op. cit., 255n5; S. Coll, *Ghost Wars*, New York: Penguin, 2004, 191–192; I. Akhund, *Trial and Error: The Advent and Eclipse of Benazir Bhutto*, Karachi: OUP, 2000, 301n1.

8 J. Kifner, "Bhutto Ousts Powerful Intelligence Chief," *NYT*, 26 May 1989, www.nytimes.com/1989/05/26/world/bhutto-ousts-powerful-intelligence-chief. html [accessed 27/4/10]; Akhund, *Trial and Error*, op. cit., 140.

9 R. Shahzad, "How to Control Intelligence Agencies," *The Friday Times*, 16–22 March 2012, www.thefridaytimes.com/beta2/tft/article.php?issue=20120316&page =5.2 [accessed 1/2/15]; "Zulfikar Agency Certified Agencies' Political Operations", *The News*, 10 March 2012, www.thenews.com.pk/Todays-News-2–96944-Zulfikar-Commission-certified-agencies-political-operations [accessed 11/1/2015].

10 "Zulfikar Agency Certified Agencies' Political Operations," op. cit.
11 Ibid.
12 Ibid.; N.Iqbal, "Zulfikar Commission Suggested Law to Legalise IB Working," *Dawn*, 31 March 2012, www.dawn.com/news/707007/zulfikar-commission-suggested-law-to-legalise-ib-working [accessed 1/2/15].
13 "Zulfikar Agency Certified Agencies' Political Operations," op. cit.
14 Ibid.
15 Ibid.; Akhund, *Trial and Error*, op. cit., 134–135.
16 Akhund, *Trial and Error*, op. cit., 138–139; A.R. Siddiqi, "Background on Intelligence Chief Given," *The Nation*, 9 April 1992.
17 D. Kux, *The United States and Pakistan, 1947–2000: Disenchanted Allies*, Washington, DC: Johns Hopkins University Press, 2001, 300; Abbas, *Pakistan's Drift*, op. cit., 203; H. Muñoz, *Getting Away with Murder*, New York: W.W. Norton, 2014; Hussain, *Frontline*, op. cit., 24.
18 M. Ahmed, *Stinger Saga*, Xlibris, 2012, 84.
19 K.M. Arif, *Khaki Shadows*, Karachi: OUP, 2001, 364; Tomsen, *Wars*, op. cit., 291; Giffner, "Bhutto Ousts Powerful Intelligence Chief," op. cit.; Siddiqi, "Background on Intelligence Chief Given," op. cit.
20 B. Bhutto, "The Rise of the Intelligence Officer," *The Nation*, 29 August 2000.
21 B.M. Chengappa, "The ISI's Role in Pakistan's Politics," www.idsa-india.org/an-feb00–2.html [accessed 1/2/13]; A. Levy and C. Scott-Clark, *Nuclear Deception: The Dangerous Relationship Between the United States and Pakistan*, New York: Walker & Co., 2008, 199–200; Malik, *State and Civil Society*, op. cit., 100–101; Lamb, *Waiting for Allah*, op. cit., 256–257; Arif, *Khaki Shadows*, op. cit., 364; Nawaz, *Crossed Swords*, op. cit., 425–526; Tomsen, *Wars*, op. cit., 291.
22 S. Coll, *On the Grand Trunk Road*, 2nd edition, New York: Penguin, 2009, 126; Lamb, *Waiting for Allah*, op. cit., 113.
23 Malik, *State and Civil Society*, op. cit., 99–101, 291n19; I. Talbot, *Pakistan: A Modern History*, New York: Palgrave Macmillan, 2009, 309; A.D. Ahmad, "Intelligence Agencies in Politics," *The Nation*, 25 August 1992; Haqqani, *Pakistan*, op. cit., 218.
24 R. Khan, *Pakistan: A Dream Gone Sour*, Karachi: OUP, 2000, 109; Akhund, *Trial and Error*, op. cit., 306–307, 134; Malik, *State and Civil Society*, op. cit., 101; B. Cloughley, *War, Coups and Terror: Pakistan's Army in Years of Turmoil*, New York: Skyhorse, 2008, 55.
25 R. Rashid, "Pakistan IB: Bureaucracy's Mine-Field," quoted in P.C. Joshi, *Main Intelligence Outfits of Pakistan*, New Delhi: Anmol Publications, 2008, 64; B. Bhutto, *Reconciliation*, New York, Harper, 2008, 202; Malik, *State and Civil Society*, op. cit., 101–102; Nawaz, *Crossed Swords*, op. cit., 433–434.
26 Quoted in Abbas, *Pakistan's Drift*, op. cit., 147.
27 Arif, *Khaki Shadows*, op. cit., 359–360; Haqqani, *Pakistan*, op. cit., 219; *Talk Back with Wajahat Khan*, Interview with Mirza Aslam Baig, 18 May 2011, www.youtube.com/watch?v=Q2YpVnOBmD0 [accessed 3/2/15].
28 Nawaz, *Crossed Swords*, op. cit., 438; Malik, *State and Civil Society*, op. cit., 289n5; Haqqani, *Pakistan*, op. cit., 223; Joshi, *Main Intelligence Outfits*, op. cit., 35.
29 G.A. Khan, *Glimpses*, op. cit., 226; Chengappa, "ISI's Role;" *The News*, 11 April 1992; Nawaz, *Crossed Swords*, op. cit., 451–452.
30 Malik, *State and Civil Society*, op. cit., 102; Cloughley, *War, Coups, and Terror*, op. cit., 76; Arif, *Khaki Shadows*, op. cit., 365; Nawaz, *Crossed Swords*, op. cit., 456.
31 S.A.I. Tirmazi, *Profiles in Intelligence*, Lahore: Combined Printers, 1995, 130; Levy & Scott-Clark, *Nuclear Deception*, op. cit., 220; Siddiqi, "Background on Intelligence Chief," op. cit.; Abbas, *Pakistan's Drift*, op. cit., 148–149; Nawaz, *Crossed Swords*, op. cit., 502n6.
32 Petition filed by Lt Gen (Retd) Javed Nasir, Former Director General, Inter-Services Intelligence, Pakistan, before the Anti Terrorism Court, Lahore, no. 107,

23 October 2002 found in www.satp.org/satporgtp/countries/Pakistan/document/papers/petition.htm [accessed 14/3/14]; Z. Hussain, *The Scorpion's Tail*, New York: Free Press, 2010, 58; Haqqani, *Pakistan*, op. cit., 292; Nawaz, *Crossed Swords*, op. cit., 467.

33 Hussain, *Frontline*, op. cit., 26.

34 Nawaz, *Crossed Swords*, op. cit., 456–457; A.R. Siddiqi, "ISI: The Political Dimension," *The Nation*, 30 July 1997.

35 Quoted in Haqqani, *Pakistan*, op. cit., 229.

36 Nawaz, *Crossed Swords*, op. cit., 467–469; Ahmed, *Stinger*, op. cit., 95; I. Gul, *The Unholy Nexus*, Lahore: Vanguard, 2002, 16–17; Hussain, *Frontline*, op. cit., 27; Coll, *Ghost Wars*, op. cit., 467–468.

37 Haqqani, *Pakistan*, op. cit. 297.

38 Quoted in Nawaz, *Crossed Swords*, op. cit., 473.

39 Ibid., 474; Coll, *Ghost Wars*, op. cit., 289; Bhutto, *Reconciliation*, op. cit., 481.

40 Nawaz, *Crossed Swords*, op. cit., 482; Abbas, *Pakistan's Drift*, op. cit., 157–158.

41 Quoted in Abbas, *Pakistan's Drift*, op. cit., 157.

42 Levy and Scott-Clark, *Nuclear Deception*, op. cit., 253; Muñoz, *Getting Away with Murder*, op. cit., 171; Hussain, *Frontline*, op. cit., 74; Arif, *Working with Zia*, op. cit., 222; Nawaz, *Crossed Swords*, op. cit., 477; S. Cohen, *The Pakistan Army*, 1998 edition, Karachi: OUP, 169–170.

43 Abbas, *Pakistan's Drift*, op. cit., 152–153.

44 I. Banerjie, «Pakistan's Inter-Services Intelligence in Afghanistan,» SAPRA *India Monthly Bulletin*, 20 September 2001; Joshi, *Main Intelligence Outfits*, op. cit., 41–42.

45 Nawaz, *Crossed Swords*, op. cit., 500; Coll, *Ghost Wars*, op. cit., 480.

46 Coll, *Ghost Wars*, op. cit., 439.

47 Ibid., 438.

48 Cloughley, *War, Coups, and Terror*, op. cit., 114; Coll, *Ghost Wars*, op. cit., 477; "Sharif Removed Musharraf after a Phone Call: Gen Butt," *Dawn* 12 October 2010, www.dawn.com/news/848878/sharif-removed-musharraf-after-a-phone-call-gen-butt [accessed 18/11/14]; Abbas, *Pakistan's Drift*, op. cit., 175, 180.

49 Abbas, *Pakistan's Drift*, op. cit., 176; O.B. Jones, *Pakistan: Eye of the Storm*, New Haven: Yale University Press, 2003, 39, 41, 47–48; I. Sehgal, "The Army and the ISI," *Shafaqna Pakistan*, Pakistan.shafaqna.com/featured/.../24365-the-army-and-the-isi.html? [accessed 2/12/14]; "Sharif Removed Musharraf after a phone call: Gen Butt," op. cit.

50 Coll, *Ghost Wars*, 480, 504–505.

51 P. Constable, "Pakistani Agency Seeks to Allay U.S. Terrorism," *Washington Post* [Hereafter WP], 15 February 2000, A17.

52 Ibid.

53 Gul, *Most Dangerous Place*, op. cit., 180.

54 R. Grenier, *88 Days to Kandahar*, New York: Simon & Schuster, 2015, 50; Abbas, *Pakistan's Drift*, op. cit., 185–188.

12 Insurgency in Kashmir and Punjab

Throughout the 1980s, the Afghan war occupied most of the ISI's time and resources. Still, Zia ul-Haq and the ISI leadership kept an eye on Kashmir, dreaming of uniting it under Pakistan rule while, at the same time, avenging the humbling loss of East Pakistan to India. Pakistan had gone to war in 1965 to break the status quo in Kashmir, yet the referendum issue had languished in UN filing cabinets ever since. The bottom line was that Islamabad still lacked the diplomatic, military and economic means to expel the Indians from Kashmir. ISI hoped to change that. While Kashmir always received top priority, ISI backed other, non-Muslim secessionist forces in India, including the Sikh extremist secessionist movement.

Renewed focus on Kashmir

It was in light of Pakistan's deficiencies in weapons, allies and nuclear weapons that ISI had returned to its strategy of UW in the 1970s. Compared to wars fought with conventional arms, proxy wars are relatively inexpensive. Handled in the right way, they could give Pakistan sufficient plausible deniability to undercut the legitimacy of any Indian retaliation. The strategy had certain other advantages too, such as tying down large numbers of Indian soldiers in COIN, and ultimately weakening New Delhi's resolve to hold on to the territory. Deny India its hold on Kashmir, optimistic Pakistanis reasoned, and the whole edifice of democratic, secular India would come crashing down.[1] Then DGMI Hamid Gul likened a Pakistan victory in Kashmir to creating "centrifugal tendencies" that would tear India apart.[2] It sounded promising in theory: an insurgent war would be sparked in Kashmir, the Indians would have to pour more forces into the state to contain the guerrillas, and eventually, New Delhi would tire of the war and give up. The practice, however, was quite different as the Pakistanis realized at great cost to Kashmiris by the end of the 1990s.

Sometime in the early 1980s, ISI set up the Kashmir Bureau, which was collocated with the much larger Afghan Bureau at Ojhri Camp in Rawalpindi. The Kashmir Bureau presumably resembled its Afghan counterpart in its structural layout with separate branches handling administration, operations, logistics, and psychological warfare. One thing the Kashmir Bureau lacked, however, was Kashmiri proxies that were dependable, effective and willing to follow ISI's lead. Similar to the Afghan mujahidin, Kashmiri insurgents were disunited and fractious. On the one hand, such internal divisions made it relatively easy for ISI to infiltrate and pit the groups against each other, but on the other, they hampered insurgent capabilities. It was the same old challenge of unity versus effectiveness that the ISI had tried surmounting with the seven party mujahidin "alliance" in Peshawar.[3]

Searching for proxies

In keeping with Zia's religious proclivities and ISI's record of working closely with Islamist parties, the *JI* and the *JUI* were natural allies of choice for working with Kashmiri insurgents. In 1980, Zia met the JI chief for Azad Kashmir, Maulana Abdul Bari, in Rawalpindi to discuss how his party could work with ISI on future insurgency operations in Kashmir. Under the proposed deal, ISI would provide money, trainers and camps in return for JI recruits, intelligence assets, propaganda, fundraising and other political support. ISI also sought information on the public mood in the Vale of Kashmir. For example, how did the Kashmiri Muslims feel about a union with Pakistan? Would they support a Pakistan-sponsored insurgency?[4]

Maulana Abdul Bari conveyed Zia's proposal to the JI branch based in Indian Kashmir, but the response was skeptical. The JI members needed more convincing before committing to a deal that could end up with them serving time in an Indian jail or worse. Therefore, ISI officers met the JI activists from Indian Kashmir during the annual pilgrimage to Mecca, but still failed to overcome Kashmiri caution. This prompted Zia to host their leaders in May 1983 and push the negotiations forward. During these talks, the JI for Indian Kashmir (JIK) wanted to impose certain conditions on the proposed partnership, including minimizing ISI's role to that of training, weapons and money. The Kashmiris did not want ISI to exercise any operational control over any planned operations.[5]

ISI balked at these conditions, sensing the JIK was too passive to launch an effective revolt against India.[6] Fortunately for ISI, another option emerged from a quite unexpected direction: the Jammu and Kashmir Liberation Front (JKLF). A creature of its times, the JKLF was guided by a secular, nationalist ideology, which emphasized the independence of Kashmir above union with Pakistan or India. This fact alone meant that JKLF was not going to be a good match for ISI's long-term goal of a united Kashmir under the Pakistan banner. Still, in lieu of any viable alternative, the JKLF was the best short-term expedient for ISI plans. Some in Islamabad hoped that an ISI–JKLF cooperative relationship would force the JIK to seek a similar arrangement.[7]

Meetings between ISI representatives and the JKLF leadership took place in 1984 at ISI HQ and possibly during the Haj season in Mecca as well. Yet the talks with the JKLF were contentious, requiring the personal intervention of the DGISI to break the logjam.[8] For example, JKLF leader Amanullah Khan was deeply suspicious of ISI motives: "How could we trust and cooperate with the ISI, which has stabbed us twice in the past?" Amanullah also rejected the ISI's strong emphasis on Islam as a guiding principle of the Kashmir cause: "As a Muslim I believe in the Kalima [Muslim profession of faith]; as a Kashmiri, I believe in a sovereign Kashmir."[9]

Yet these differences were set aside, and in 1986 an agreement was finally reached between ISI and the JKLF. Under its terms, the JKLF agreed to provide insurgent recruits while ISI supplied the training facilities, funds, and operational support. More importantly from the JKLF's perspective, ISI at least nominally pledged non-interference in the movement's internal politics.[10] JKLF and ISI agreed on the slogan *"Azadi"* ("Freedom"), but the unanswered question was freedom for whom? The JKLF interpreted *Azadi* to mean an independent Kashmir, incorporating all the lands of pre-Partition Kashmir, and free of Indian or Pakistani control. ISI regarded it as incorporating all of Kashmir into the Pakistan state.[11]

In spring 1987, the JKLF began recruiting young men inside Kashmir for ISI camps in Pakistan. Building on the successful model employed with the Afghan mujahidin, ISI built several training camps around Muzaffarabad, capital of Azad Kashmir.[12] The regime was later described in an account of one trainee named Javid:

> Uniformed instructors who everyone murmured with respect were members of the ISI or from the Pakistan military, taught Javid how to strip down a Kalashnikov and assemble a rocket launcher. Once a week he ate slivers of fatty mutton; the rest of the time it was cold bread, rice and daal scoffed down while squatting on the ground.[13]

Meanwhile, events in Kashmir looked promising for the ISI–JKLF program, for in 1987, a blatantly rigged election in that state triggered a cycle of demonstrations and government reprisals. Thousands of young men crossed the Line of Control into Azad Kashmir, demanding guerrilla training to fight India. This influx of would-be insurgents overwhelmed the camps: there were insufficient arms, ammunition, food, space and instructors to handle the overflow. As a result, many Kashmiris were sent to camps run by Gulbuddin Hekmatyar's *Hezb-e Islami* in Pakistan's NWFP and Afghanistan.[14]

Revolt in Kashmir

One year later, on 13 July 1988, the JKLF formally launched its revolt with a series of bombings in Srinagar. Some suggest that ISI impatience with perceived JKLF back peddling finally drove the movement to war. Indeed, it was reported that ISI threatened to expose the JKLF's senior leadership to Indian intelligence if the campaign wasn't launched soon.[15] This was clearly not a match made in heaven. Whether it was coerced into action or not, the

JKLF was pushing on an open door in Muslim Kashmir, where many people were fed up with corrupt administrators, rigged elections and security forces repression. The result was persistent unrest in the heavily populated Kashmir Valley, some of which could be attributed to JKLF, but a lot of which was home-grown.[16] According to one estimate, the number of riots in Indian Kashmir skyrocketed from 390 in 1988 to 4,000 in 1990, a fair measure of the spiraling violence confronting the Indian government.[17] All in all, ISI had to be pleased with the way things were turning out, but it was nonetheless wary of the JKLF's popularity and the fact that most of its recruits were originally from Indian-occupied Kashmir. It was that old effectiveness versus control debate again, where ISI was uncomfortable backing groups it could not dominate. One ISI officer tellingly revealed that Islamabad did not want to create a "Kashmiri PLO," a reference to the Palestine Liberation Organization, which gradually became more powerful than the Jordanian and Lebanese authorities hosting it.[18]

ISI was further emboldened by the Soviet departure from Afghanistan in 1989, reasoning that if the Soviet superpower could be defeated then leveraging India out of Kashmir was not far-fetched as it once seemed.[19] After all, ISI already had the infrastructure in place to conduct a stepped up UW campaign in Kashmir, including camps, trainers, doctrine, weapons and experience. It also possessed a cadre of foreign jihadis spoiling for a new fight now that the Afghan war was entering a different phase. DGISI Hamid Gul put it this way:

> We wanted to mirror the mujahideen's success in Afghanistan by sending them into Indian-administered Kashmir to manipulate the Kashmiri people's anger at India's refusal to grant them autonomy. We would train the freedom fighters. We would arm them.[20]

As a result of decisions taken at the senior-most levels of the army, if not the civilian government, ISI's provision of training, weapons, and money to JKLF and smaller Kashmiri groups increased. There was a sense of optimism in Islamabad that a solution had been found at last for India's continued occupation of much of Kashmir.[21] Yet there was one cloud on the horizon as far as ISI's shadow warriors were concerned: they still lacked a viable Islamist proxy in Kashmir that could replace the JKLF. Indeed, JKLF's secular nationalist agenda was never going to be compatible with ISI's goals, especially since the movement's independent Kashmir initiative would also include Pakistan's Azad Kashmir and the Northern Areas.[22]

Islamist movements

ISI finally found the Islamist Kashmir insurgency group it was looking for when the *JI* affiliate in Indian Kashmir finally threw its hat in the ring with an affiliated insurgent group, the *Hezbul Mujahidin* (Party of the Holy Warriors)

(HM). Created in 1989, HM was, essentially, the equivalent of Hekmatyar's *Hezb-e-Islami* in Afghanistan, which was linked to the JI as well. Like the JKLF, HM was "overwhelmingly Kashmiri" as far as its cadre went, but it rejected the JKLF's nationalist agenda in favor of an Islamist one. What this meant in theory was that the party saw nothing that was doctrinally incorrect in joining and thereby strengthening Pakistan. As soon as it became apparent that the HM was a promising fighting force, ISI began cutting off money and weapons to the JKLF, causing the latter to fracture. Sensing it now had more leverage over a weakened JKLF, ISI demanded the group drop its "sovereignty" plan in favor of a vague "self-determination" one instead. It also wanted an observer seat on the JKLF's Central Committee meetings. JKLF leader Amanullah Khan rejected both demands and tried to circumvent ISI by appealing to Prime Minister Benazir Bhutto instead. ISI thwarted this initiative too, and proceeded to shut down the JKLF camps and hand them over to the HM.[23]

As the dismantling of the JKLF apparatus inside Kashmir continued, JKLF officials alleged that some of their leaders and top fighters were being assassinated by the HM. JKLF leader Amanullah Khan told a press conference in December 1991 that "Hizbul Mujahideen not only liquidates JKLF fighters, it also informs the Indian army of our hideouts."[24] Another JKLF leader based in Muzaffarabad spoke anonymously for obvious reasons:

> The ISI had actually given Hizbul Mujahideen the task of completely liquidating JKLF from occupied Kashmir. This was because the JKLF demanded an autonomous Kashmir and also because it was the largest Kashmiri organization.[25]

Perhaps bearing in mind some lessons learned from the 1980's Afghan war, ISI never put all its eggs in one basket. JKLF could be sacrificed on the altar of expediency, but HM was not going to be allowed to dominate the Kashmir arena either. Although HM possessed definite advantages relative to JKLF, especially in the area of ideology, ISI was not entirely comfortable with HM either. First of all, HM's parent organization, the *JI* had shown disturbing signs of recalcitrance during the mid-1980s negotiations with ISI. Moreover, HM's core of Kashmiri fighters wasn't seen by ISI as necessarily a good thing either, because in the eyes of ISI's operatives, Kashmiris lacked "martial ardor."[26] For example, HM sometimes rejected Pakistani orders to kill Kashmiri Hindus or punish Muslims collaborating with the Indians.[27]

ISI's preference was for groups that were unambiguously close to Pakistan and willing to take its orders. This was due in part to mistrust of "independent" insurgent outfits, but it also had to do with ISI's belief that Kashmiri-dominated groups were more susceptible to penetration by RAW.[28] With the end of the Soviet war in Afghanistan, the Pakistanis had a number of transnational jihadi groups to choose from, but one gained prominence quite rapidly, the *Harakatul Mujahidin* (Movement of the Mujahideen), whose acronym, HuM, was added to the bewildering array of names already crowding Kashmir's complex underground war.

HuM emerged during the Soviet phase of the Afghan war, and it became ISI's alternative to that other group with a similar name, the *Hezbul Mujahidin*. Whereas the latter was aligned with the JI, HuM was affiliated with the sometime rival *Jamiat Ulema-e-Islam* (Society of the Scholars of Islam) or JUI for short. HuM appealed to ISI, not only because it represented an alternative to the HM, but also due to the large numbers of foreign fighters in HuM ranks. ISI apparently believed that foreign fighters made up for many of the perceived shortfalls in Kashmiris as jihadis.[29]

But ISI continued searching for new proxies, and what it boiled down to was control – ISI control that is – and the degree of Islamic militancy demonstrated. It is with these characteristics in mind that ISI forged its own jihadi outfit in the late 1980s called *Lashkar-e-Taiba* ("Army of the Pure") (LeT) that trained in Afghanistan's remote northeast before turning to Kashmir.[30] LeT's modus operandi was substantially different from that of the *Hezbul Mujahidin* or even HuM. It was more of an "International Islamic" fighting organization in the sense that it recruited Pakistani Pashtuns and Punjabis as well as foreign fighters from around the world, trained them in Afghanistan for combat experience, leavened their ranks with some retired army and ISI personnel, and then sent them into the Kashmir conflict. Given their well-deserved reputation for brutality, LeT's fighters were resented by Kashmiris, who had seen their secular nationalist struggle hijacked by militant Islamic groups allied with Pakistan.[31]

Funding became an unexpected problem for ISI as the Kashmir campaign escalated. In the early years, ISI could dip into funds provided by the CIA and the Saudis that were earmarked for Afghanistan; however, after the Soviet withdrawal, the CIA rapidly downsized its mujahedin operations. Soon the Pakistanis found themselves in the unenviable position of funding two proxy wars on a shrinking budget even with steady Saudi funding.[32] ISI either had to find other funding sources or reduce its commitments in Afghanistan and/or Kashmir. There are numerous allegations that ISI as an institution exploited the Afghan opium trade and used the proceeds to fill empty coffers. One estimate put the total at $2.5 billion, a figure which could go some way toward offsetting the money previously supplied by the CIA.[33] In fact, Nawaz Sharif later alleged that in February 1991 then COAS, Mir Aslam Beg, and DGISI Asad Durrani, requested a meeting with him to discuss some current ISI operations. During this meeting both officers emphasized the funding problems hampering the growth of ISI's UW campaign and, as a solution, recommended profiting from the narcotics trade. Sharif said he rejected the plan outright, and presumably no more was heard about it. Beg and Durrani deny Sharif's claim, with Durrani describing it as "preposterous." To muddy the waters even further, Nawaz Sharif later retracted his statement.[34]

Brigadier Badam

In the mid-1990s, the Director of ISI's Kashmir Bureau was a Brigadier known to us only by his nom de guerre, "Badam" or "almond milk," which he apparently enjoyed drinking in large quantities. During this period, Brigadier Badam reported to the ISI Deputy Director General in charge of the External Wing, Major General Syed Iftikhar Hussain Shah, who provided overall direction for the Kashmir effort and conducted sensitive political discussions with Kashmiri politicians and insurgent commanders. Brigadier Badam (whose real name may have been Mohamed Saleem) was a veteran with 30-plus years in the army, some of which were spent in ISI. At one point in his career, he handled the difficult logistics branch of the Afghan Bureau, and became, as one account describes it, an "expert in unconventional warfare."[35] He certainly understood the value of a good information operations campaign, for he made sure that articles of Indian atrocities in Kashmir were published every week in a HuM magazine called *Voice of the Mujahid*. The goal was to stir up anti-Indian sentiments among the Muslims of Kashmir, India and Pakistan by spotlighting alleged human rights abuses by the Indian security forces.[36]

Brigadier Badam's number one challenge in managing Pakistan's scarcely covert war in Kashmir was the disunity afflicting all the militant groups. He would have been familiar with this having previously dealt with the notoriously fractious Afghans. ISI's preferred clients aside, literally hundreds of groups emerged in the late 1980s which as one observer noted wryly, bore names of "the Prophet's This and the Army of that, the Fight-for-Something-or-Other and the Battle-of-Some-Such, nominal names for national outfits whose members on average had a battlefield life expectancy of less than six months."[37]

Pakistan's Kashmir war and the US response

As the violence in Kashmir spiked in the early 1990s, India raised the decibel level of its denunciations of Pakistan. Just as Islamabad did when it came to its perennial Balochistan problems, New Delhi usually attributed chronic violence in Kashmir to foreign interference. This time there were differences, though: genuine discontent in Kashmir aside, the rising tide of violence could not be attributed to internal dissent alone. Pakistan was fanning the flames and radicalizing the conflict in a manner which ironically would redound to India's benefit. But the Indians did not know this yet in 1990. What they did know was that the violence was escalating, and they had enough evidence to pin the blame on Pakistan. The Indians presented their findings to the Americans hoping that Washington would pressure Pakistan to reduce, if not cease, its covert war in Kashmir. Up to this point, the US had turned a blind eye to Pakistan's proxy offensive against India. The Pakistanis were good friends, it was reasoned, they had withstood Soviet pressure when it came to arming the Afghan mujahidin, and they shared the glory when the last Soviet soldier left

Afghanistan. It was far easier to say that the US government could neither confirm nor deny reports that ISI was backing the Kashmir resistance movement and leave it at that.

When Washington did act, it preferred to raise the issue with Islamabad via diplomatic channels. But it was a dialogue of the deaf: the Americans would politely issue their warning and the Pakistanis would smile, deny, seemingly yield and then obfuscate. An example of this pattern can be found in 1990 when the US Undersecretary of State for Political Affairs, Robert Kimmit, discussed Kashmir with Benazir Bhutto's national security advisor, Iqbal Akhund. True to form, the Pakistani side reiterated that the true source of unrest in Kashmir was Indian repression. The US must do more, the Pakistanis argued, to stop Indian human rights abuses. Kimmit fired back, with a "friendly warning" that some members of the US Senate were becoming vocal about ISI's terror campaign in Kashmir. If this opinion prevailed, he added, the Senate could go after the US aid program for Pakistan. But Kimmit also offered the Pakistanis a way out: perhaps the Pakistani government did not know what ISI was doing?[38]

A year later, the issue of Pakistani interference in Kashmir came up again when Deputy National Security Advisor Robert Gates met General Mir Aslam Beg. This time, however, the Pakistanis took a different line: Beg admitted that Pakistan had trained "thousands" of militants to fight in Kashmir; however, the 37 camps on Pakistan soil were now shut down. This *mea culpa* enabled the Pakistanis to argue that, yes, there were camps, but now they were closed, so end of story. Any reports to the contrary were either "old news" or Indian propaganda.[39] In its annual report on terrorism, the US State Department was less diplomatic in detailing Pakistani backing of terrorist groups in Kashmir:

> There were continuing credible reports throughout 1991 of official Pakistani support for Kashmiri militant groups engaged in terrorism in Indian-controlled Kashmir.... This support allegedly includes provision of weapons and training.[40]

The US may have calculated that since the Pakistanis were ignoring warnings in diplomatic communications, perhaps a "leak" or two and the annual terrorism report might goad Islamabad into action. For its part, Pakistan fell back on a predictable pattern of denial and demand. In meetings with US officials, the cry rang out "show us your evidence," which, of course, translated to "show us your intelligence sources and methods." Then, sometimes, the Pakistanis might budge a little: any militant activities in Kashmir were due to "unofficial groups" with no connection to ISI or any other state authority. As a "concession" the Pakistanis would agree to shut down the "unofficial camps" that were training these "unofficial militants."[41]

If the Pakistanis thought they could finesse their way out of this controversy or delay it until after the US presidential election cycle, they miscalculated. On 10 May 1992, Secretary of State James Baker sent a private letter to Prime Minister Sharif with a blunt message: if the ISI continued providing support to Kashmiri and Sikh militants, then the US might put Pakistan on the list of terror sponsoring countries, joining the who's who of America's gallery of rogues: Libya, Syria, Iran, Iraq, North Korea and Cuba.[42] To add further emphasis, the bearer of the message, US Ambassador Nicholas Platt, handed over his talking points that were even more strident:

> We are very confident of our information that your intelligence service, the Inter-Services Intelligence Directorate, and elements of the Army are supporting Kashmiri and Sikh militants who carry out acts of terrorism.... This support takes the form of providing weapons, training, and assistance in infiltration.... We're talking about direct, covert Government of Pakistan support. There is no doubt in our mind about this.... This is not a case of Pakistani political parties, such as Jamaat-e Islami, doing something independently, but of organs of the Pakistani government controlled by the President, the Prime Minister and the Chief of Army Staff. Our information is certain. Please consider the serious consequences to our relationship if this support continues.... You must take concrete steps to curtail assistance to militants and not allow their training camps to operate in Pakistan or Azad Kashmir.[43]

It is noteworthy that this warning contained no reference to ISI activities in Afghanistan. In any case, it was sufficient to trigger a debate within the government, where the Foreign Ministry highlighted the disastrous consequences for the economy of US sanctions. The DGISI at the time was the bearded, born again fundamentalist, Javid Nasir, who insisted that Pakistan not abandon its Kashmiri allies. It was the "Indo-Zionist" lobby in the US that was generating this most recent flap, he said. "We have been covering our tracks so far and will cover them even better in the future."[44] The DGISI concluded that the Americans would never risk designating Pakistan as a state sponsor of terrorism. Nawaz Sharif's official response to the US warning was that covert aid would cease. Characteristically, Sharif asked the US to assume a direct role in resolving the Kashmir dispute.[45]

ISI was reined in for the moment, but it was only for show.[46] ISI was still involved, but its aid to the militants was more carefully disguised now and moved through cut-outs. Some ex-ISI and MI officers used the religious parties as cover for their terrorist support efforts, in a move that may mark the beginning of ISI's Directorate S, a secret cell planted within an intelligence agency that uses tight compartmentalization, rigid communication security procedures and a network of former intelligence officers to aid militant groups and conduct plausibly deniable operations.[47]

In the end, Javed Nasir was right about one thing: the US government never did place Pakistan on its list of terrorist supporting states. Instead, American officials pursued another chimera of non-action in the face of reality: the "ISI reconstruction" argument. After Javed Nasir was sacrificed in 1993 to preserve American–Pakistani amity, one unnamed US official was quoted as saying that the Pakistanis were reorganizing ISI. They needed more time, it was argued, to clean up house.[48] Reforming the ISI became another justification for US inaction in the future too. As far as the Pakistanis were concerned, this argument allowed ISI to buy time, keep the country off the terrorism list and more carefully disguise its support for militants.

Still, as much as Pakistan and the US wanted to get past the jihadi issue by ignoring it, papering it over or agreeing to disagree, the problem just wouldn't go away. ISI-linked militants were emerging in a broad swath of Asia from the Central Asian states through Xinjiang in Western China to Kashmir and the Philippines. Consequently, the Pakistani government probably was not greatly surprised when former US Ambassador to Islamabad, Robert Oakley, arrived in Pakistan with another warning message from the US government. This time, the US was concerned about the foreign fighter phenomenon: Arabs, Afghans, Pakistanis and others who were now turning up in Kashmir. Oakley's interlocutor on this occasion was Benazir Bhutto, then in her second term as Prime Minister.[49] In Bhutto's recollection, there appears to be a considerable amount of selective memory at work:

> I called in my ISI chief, General Javed Ashraf Qazi. I asked: 'Why were there armies of foreigners being sent into Kashmir and being trained in our camps?' Qazi with a straight face told me, 'Because the Indians have killed all the Kashmiris.' These military guys and the intelligence agencies were living in a world of their own.[50]

DGISI Ashraf Qazi decided to take a more aggressive stance when it came to "resetting the optics" on Pakistan's foreign fighter program. He invited the resident defense attachés in Islamabad to visit Azad Kashmir and see for themselves that there were no foreigners preparing for jihad against India. The *Hezbul Mujahidin*, he asserted, was 100% Kashmiri, although he neglected to mention HuM, LeT, and the other, decidedly non-Kashmiri terrorist groups.[51]

Terror alliance

ISI's Kashmir strategy was heavily influenced by the Taliban's victories in Afghanistan in the mid-1990s. For instance, ISI transferred parts of its jihadi training program from Pakistan to Afghanistan. There also began a mixing of training responsibilities between ISI on one side and the Taliban and al-Qa'ida on the other. Taliban leader Mullah Omar was said to be especially close to the leadership of the *Harakatul Mujahidin* since both shared ideological roots in the Deobandist madrassas of northern Pakistan. When ISI ramped up its Kashmir campaign in the mid-1990s, it relied on extremists linked to the Taliban and al-Qa'ida.[52] Yet, as US concern about al-Qa'ida grew in the late 1990s, ISI and its Islamist proxies came increasingly under the American microscope. After al-Qa'ida bombed two US embassies in East Africa in 1998, Washington launched cruise missiles at several militant training camps in Afghanistan. Osama Bin Laden was not killed in this attack, but several *Harakatul Mujahidin* militants and their ISI trainers apparently were.[53]

Was it worth it?

From 1988 to 1998, the ISI's proxy war in Kashmir was relatively cost-free. The Americans periodically threatened sanctions but never followed though. India promised military action, but probably was thwarted by the suspected existence of Pakistani nuclear weapons. It did seem as if nuclear weapons were providing an umbrella for Islamabad to escalate its "plausibly deniable" unconventional war against India. The Pakistanis made some tangible gains from their proxy war in Kashmir. India's clumsy and harsh handling of the late-1980s Kashmir revolt meant that its human rights record took a pounding, while the once profitable tourism industry in the Kashmir Valley dried up. Perhaps more importantly from Islamabad's point of view, an estimated 700,000 Indian security forces were tied down in COIN operations in Kashmir. That, of course, meant there were 700,000 fewer soldiers and police facing Pakistan across their international boundary.[54]

The human costs of the Kashmir wars were staggering. An estimated 150,000 Kashmiri civilians were killed between 1988 and 2010 in addition to 6,000 security personnel.[55] The bulk of the Hindu Pandits fled the valley for safety either in Jammu or India proper, potentially bringing a thousand years of a Hindu presence in the valley to an end. The material costs were considerable too. In 1998, an Indian parliamentary report estimated that ISI actions alone cost India the equivalent of $14.5 billion over the previous decade.[56] On the other hand, after ten years of insurgency and terrorism, of training and arming, of deflecting international criticism, ISI had failed to change the facts on the ground. If the ultimate objective of the campaign was obtaining control over Indian Kashmir, New Delhi still showed absolutely no sign it was reconsidering its position.

Sikh militancy

Most accounts of ISI UW operations focus on Afghanistan and Kashmir, since those were the largest programs under ISI control. Yet ISI actions were not restricted to these areas alone for, as we have seen, it had stoked the flames of Naga and Mizo unrest as early as the 1950s and 1960s. Another odd partner of the ISI in the 1980s and 1990s was the militant Sikh nationalist movement. The Sikhs are a religious community concentrated in northwestern India. Their conflict with Muslims goes back centuries, and it was further aggravated by the traumas of Partition, when the Sikh Punjab homeland was divided between India and Pakistan. Very few Sikhs opted to stay in Pakistan, although several historically important Sikh *gurdwaras* – or temples – remained.[57]

Sikh nationalism was predicated on the belief that the Sikhs constituted a nation based on faith, language, customs and shared history. Therefore, nationalists argued, the Sikhs deserved an independent state of their own in northeastern India called Khalistan. In the mid-1980s, tensions between Sikh militants and New Delhi reached a crescendo, when an armed group led by a charismatic leader named Jarnail Singh Bhindranwale seized the Golden Temple complex in Amritsar. In response, the Indian government launched operation BLUE STAR, a military assault on the Golden Temple that killed Bhindranwale but also badly damaged the Sikh holy of holies, the *Akal Takht*. Rather than suppress the uprising, BLUE STAR only poured more gasoline onto the fire.[58] Violence spread, and four months later, Prime Minister Indira Gandhi was assassinated by her own Sikh bodyguards. Indian COIN tactics in Punjab were about as heavy-handed and counter-productive as they would be in Kashmir a decade later. Some Sikhs managed to flee to Pakistan, where, ironically, the Islamist General Zia ul-Haq was eager to help them out.

Zia took a personal interest in Sikhism since he was originally from East Punjab himself. He personally directed that Sikh *gurdwaras* and related historical sites in Pakistan be restored after years of neglect, and then invited Sikhs to visit them. On occasion, Zia met Sikh expatriate leaders, many of whom were Khalistan proponents. Zia saw potential in the Khalistan movement, for here was an opportunity to weaken and distract the Indian government by miring it in yet another insurgent war "of a thousand cuts."[59] The future DGISI, Hamid Gul, argued that "keeping Punjab destabilized is equivalent to the Pakistan Army having an extra division at no cost to the taxpayers."[60]

It would appear that ISI aid began after BLUE STAR, when New Delhi had burned most of its bridges to the Sikh community. Even though Bhindranwale and many of his fighters were killed in that operation, the Indian army had stirred up a hornet's nest of rage and rebellion, an almost certain invitation to ISI interference.[61] But ISI had very limited leverage over the Sikh militants as the majority of them were based on Indian soil, and many opposed any ISI role in their fight. Over time, ISI's position improved, partly due to Sikh factionalism which the Pakistanis deliberately aggravated in order to gain control. The lead Sikh insurgent group in the mid-1980s, the Khalistan Commando Force (KCF), broke up in 1988 mainly over internal squabbles but also because ISI aggravated leadership rivalries in the way it distributed arms. One of the KCF leaders, Zaffarwal, provided overall guidance and leadership to his faction from his ISI-provided safe haven in Pakistan.[62]

India's protests to the international community about Pakistani interference in Punjab fell on deaf ears. At the time, the US was focused on winning the war in Afghanistan and had little patience for an Indian government that backed the Afghan communists and seemed to favor the Soviet Union. Diplomacy proving insufficient, India fortified its border with Pakistan by building fences, erecting observation towers, and using floodlights to deter Sikh militants from crossing the border in either direction.[63] The security forces were not above discrediting the Khalistanis by employing criminals to rape, loot and extort in the name of a given Sikh resistance group. They also infiltrated the Sikh movements in order to disrupt their operations from within. The real losers in this were the moderate Khalistan proponents, who saw their movement usurped by ISI and then absolutely discredited by the Indians and Sikh extremists.[64]

At the same time, though, it must be conceded that the Khalistan backers were their own worst enemies. Similar to the Afghan mujahidin in this sense, the Khalistanis were highly prone to factionalism. Both ISI and Indian intelligence exploited these rifts for their own ends so that, in the end, the list of militant groups seemed to be taken straight out of a Monty Python movie.[65]

It is difficult to accurately measure the impact ISI backing had on the Sikh insurgency. India was naturally inclined to point fingers at Pakistan for its troubles in East Punjab, but this was ignoring the fact that Indian mismanagement and repression sparked most of the Sikh unrest in the first place. The first mistake was failing to reach a compromise with the moderate Sikhs when New Delhi had the chance. The second, and more egregious one, was the 1984 assault on the Golden Temple complex. After Prime Minister Indira Gandhi was gunned down by her bodyguards, the gloves came off and the already grim human rights situation in Punjab got worse. A senior Indian diplomat who happened to be a Sikh put it this way: "There is no point in blaming Pakistan. Pakistan did not attack the Golden Temple."[66]

ISI operations in India's East Punjab demonstrated a certain pragmatism that often eluded analysts who focused solely on its Islamist clients in Afghanistan and Kashmir. From the Pakistan army's perspective, a weakened, divided, and distracted India was most certainly a desirable objective even if this required alliances with otherwise unlikely parties such as the Khalistan extremists. As an instrument of state policy, it was ISI's mission to exploit the Sikh extremists for Pakistan's national interests.

Notes

1 H. Abbas, *Pakistan's Drift into Extremism*, Armonk, NY: M.E. Sharpe, 2005, 365n20.
2 Ibid.
3 A. Jamal, *Shadow War: The Untold Story of Jihad in Kashmir*, Hoboken, NJ: Melville House, 2009, 112–114; B. Riedel, *Deadly Embrace*, Washington, DC: Brookings Institution Press, 2011, 26; H. Haqqani, *Pakistan: Between Mosque and Military*, Washington, DC: Carnegie Endowment, 2005, 273.
4 Jamal, *Shadow War*, op. cit., 109–114.
5 Ibid., 112–115.
6 Ibid., 123.
7 Ibid., 136–137, 142; Haqqani, *Pakistan*, op. cit., 288; J.R. Schmidt, *The Unraveling: Pakistan in the Age of Jihad*, New York: Farrar, Straus and Giroux, 2011, 80–82.
8 Riedel, *Deadly Embrace*, op. cit., 26; N.C. Behera, *Demystifying Kashmir*, Washington, DC: Brookings, 2006, 148.
9 Quoted in Jamal, *Shadow War*, op. cit., 125–126.
10 Behera, *Demystifying Kashmir*, op. cit., 148.
11 Jamal, *Shadow War*, op. cit., 125–126; O.B. Jones, *Pakistan*, op. cit., 87.

12 Riedel, *Deadly Embrace*, op. cit., 26; I. Gul, *The Unholy Nexus*, Lahore: Vanguard, 2002, 69; Jamal, *Shadow War*, op. cit., 126–127.
13 Quoted in A. Levy and C. Scott-Clark, *The Meadow: Kashmir 1995 – Where the Terror Began*, London, Harper Press, 2012, 88–89.
14 Abbas, *Pakistan's Drift*, op. cit., 141–142; Levy and Scott-Clark, *Meadow*, op. cit., 84–85, 89; Jamal, *Shadow Wars*, op. cit., 129, 154.
15 S.P. Kapur and S. Ganguly, "The Jihad Paradox: Pakistan and Islamist Militancy in South Asia," *International Security* 37: 1, Summer 2012, 11–141.
16 I. Akhund, *Trial and Error: The Advent and Eclipse of Benazir Bhutto*, Karachi: OUP, 2000, 207–208; V. Schofield, *Kashmir in Conflict*, London, I.B. Tauris, 2003, 139.
17 Riedel, *Deadly Embrace*, op. cit., 39.
18 Haqqani, *Pakistan*, op. cit., 287–288.
19 A. Shah, *The Army and Democracy*, Cambridge, MA: Harvard University Press, 2014, 158.
20 Quoted in A. Levy and C. Scott-Clark, *Nuclear Deception: The Dangerous Relationship Between the United States and Pakistan*, New York: Walker & Co., 2008, 182.
21 R.G. Wirsing, *Kashmir in the Shadow of War*, London: M.E. Sharpe, 2003, 160.
22 O.B. Jones, *Pakistan*, op. cit., 83; S. Sahni, *Kashmir Underground*, New Delhi: Har Anand, 1999, 54.
23 Gul, *Unholy Nexus*, op. cit., 69; J.R. Schmidt, *The Unraveling: Pakistan in the Age of Jihad*, New York: Farrar, Straus and Giroux, 2011, 81–82; P. Tomsen, *The Wars of Afghanistan*, New York: PublicAffairs, 2011, 359, 424; S. Coll, *Ghost Wars*, New York: Penguin, 2004, 410.
24 Quoted in Haqqani, *Pakistan*, op. cit., 289–290.
25 Ibid.
26 Levy and Scott-Clark, *Meadow*, op. cit., 82; Jamal, *Shadow War*, op. cit., 149–150; Sahni, *Kashmir*, op. cit., 366, 399.
27 Haqqani, *Pakistan*, op. cit., 290; M.A. Zahab, and O. Roy, *Islamist Networks: The Afghan-Pakistan Connection*, New York: Columbia University Press, 2006, 53–54.
28 Haqqani, *Pakistan*, op. cit., 288–289.
29 Ibid., 138; S. Coll, *Grand Trunk Road*, New York: Penguin, 2009, 173.
30 Tomsen, *Wars*, op. cit., 520; Zahab and Roy, *Islamist Networks*, op. cit., 53–54.
31 Riedel, *Deadly Embrace*, op. cit., 32; J.-L. Bruguière, *Ce Que Je N'ai Pas Pu Dire*, Paris: Editions Robert Lafont, 2009, 465–466; Z. Hussain, *Frontline: The Struggle with Militant Islam*, New York: Columbia University Press, 2007, 55; A. Tellis, "Pakistan Simply Sees no Reason to Stop Supporting Terrorists," http://yale global.yale.edu/content/Pakistan-and-afghanistan-end-game-%E2%80%93-part-ii [accessed 21/3/2010]; Haqqani, *Pakistan*, op. cit., 287–288; Abbas, *Pakistan's Drift*, op. cit., 214.
32 P.C. Joshi, *Main Intelligence Outfits of Pakistan*, New Delhi: Anmol Publications, 2008, 242–243.
33 L. Napoleoni, *Modern Jihad*, London: Pluto Press, 2003, 82–83, 91; A. Mir, "FBI Sees ISI Heroin Trail," *Weekly Independent*, 6 December 2001, 1; S. Nooruzzaman, "How Pakistan's ISI Funds Its Proxy War," *The Tribune*, 28 November 1999, www.tribuneindia.com/1999/99nov28/head6.htm#1 [1/4/13].
34 *Talk Back with Wajahat Khan*, "Interview with Lieutenant General (Retd) Asad Durrani," www.youtube.com/watch?v=DdxZzmldc4s [accessed 14/1/15]; Abbas, *Pakistan's Drift*, op. cit., 148–149; J. Anderson and K. Khan, "Heroin Plan by Top Pakistanis Alleged," *Washington Post*, 12 September 1994, www.washingtonpost.com/archive/politics/1994/09/12/heroin-plan-by-top-Pakistanis-alleged/311942bb-983a-416e-b735-7d71a07ba030/ [accessed 6/8/15]; G. Peters, *Seeds of Terror*, New York: Thomas Dunne, 2009, 62–65.
35 Levy & Scott-Clark, *Meadow*, op. cit., 38.
36 Ibid., 43.

37 Ibid., 45.
38 Akhund, *Trial and Error*, op. cit., 222.
39 Jamal, *Shadow War*, op. cit., 243–244; Schofield, *Kashmir*, op. cit., 154–155.
40 US Department of State, *Patterns of Global Terrorism: 1991*, http://fas.org:8080/ irp/threat/terror_91/asia.html [28/7/15].
41 Haqqani, *Pakistan*, op. cit., 293–294.
42 Hussain, *Frontline*, op. cit., 26–27.
43 Quoted in Haqqani, *Pakistan*, op. cit., 294–295.
44 Ibid., 295–296.
45 Ibid., 296.
46 D. Kux, *The United States and Pakistan, 1947–2000: Disenchanted Allies*, Washington, DC: Johns Hopkins University Press, 2001, 316.
47 Ibid., 322; R.J. Smith, "Pakistan Avoids U.S. Listing as Nation Supporting Terrorism," *WP*, 15 July 1993, www.washingtonpost.com/archive/politics/1993/07/15/ Pakistan-avoids-us-listing-as-nation-supporting-terrorism/0ae5c9ef-4354–4ec8-a274– 6a17c0f378cf/ [accessed 6/8/15]; Hussain, *Frontline*, op. cit., 27; Jamal, *Shadow War*, op. cit., 244–245.
48 Smith, "Pakistan Avoids U.S. Listing," op. cit.
49 Haqqani, *Pakistan*, op. cit., 243–244.
50 Quoted in Levy and Scott-Clark, *Deception*, op. cit., 252.
51 Nawaz, *Crossed Swords*, op. cit., 468–469.
52 Hussain, *Frontline*, op. cit, 27, 72; D. Isby, *Afghanistan*, New York: Pegasus Books, 2010, 74–75; L. Wright, *The Looming Tower: Al-Qaeda and the Road to 9/11*, New York: Knopf, 2006, 250.
53 Riedel, *Deadly Embrace*, op. cit., 51.
54 Kapur & Ganguly, "Jihad Paradox," op. cit., 133.
55 Ibid.
56 A. Rashid, *Pakistan on the Brink*, New York: Viking, 2012, 56; H. Baweja, "Terrorism: ISI Spreads Its Net," *India Today*, 2 December 1998, 20.
57 J.J.M. Pettigrew, *The Sikhs of the Punjab*, London: Zed Books, 1995; C.K. Mahmud, *Fighting for Faith and Nation*, Philadelphia: University of Pennsylvania Press, 1996.
58 Pettigrew, *Sikhs*, op. cit., 6–7, 55–58.
59 Haqqani, *Pakistan*, op. cit., 270–271; R. Khan, *Pakistan: A Dream Gone Sour*, Karachi: OUP, 2000, 95; K.M. Arif, *Working with Zia*, Karachi: OUP, 1995, 345–346; R. Anwar, *The Terrorist Prince: The Life and Death of Murtaza Bhutto*, London: Verso, 1997, 193.
60 "We are walking into the American Trap," The Rediff Interview/Former ISI Chief Hamid Gul, 12 February 2004, www.rediff.com/news/2004/feb/12inter. html [accessed 3/3/13].
61 S. Cohen, *The Idea of Pakistan*, Washington, DC: Brookings, 2004, 89–90, 105, 108–109.
62 Pettigrew, *Sikhs*, op. cit., 70; Joshi, *Main Intelligence Outfits*, op. cit., 322.
63 Pettigrew, *Sikhs*, op. cit., 106.
64 Ibid., 94, 103, 133.
65 R. Vinayak & R. Parihar, "Punjab: Grim Signals," *India Today*, 9 December 1997, 32; A. Jolly, "Pakistan's Plan for Khalistan," *India Today*, 14 November 2011, http://indiatoday.intoday.in/story/isi-khalistan-punjab-militancy-babbar-khalsa-international-operation-bluestar/1/158692.html [accessed 12/2/15]; Joshi, *Main Intelligence Outfits*, op. cit., 320–321.
66 Quoted in Pettigrew, *Sikhs*, op. cit., 106.

13 Escalating Tensions with India

By the mid-1980s, the Indians were aware that Pakistan was on the verge of a nuclear weapons capability. For New Delhi, the challenge was formidable, and the options for dealing with it unappealing. The easiest choice was to do nothing: India would yield its nuclear monopoly in South Asia and surrender whatever vague prospects it had for dominating Pakistan. Alternatively, India could preempt by invading Pakistan with overwhelming conventional military power and disarm its enemy by force. The risks of an escalation to nuclear war depended, of course, on Pakistan's real capabilities. Did they possess the bomb or not? If they did, how would they deliver it to an Indian target: strike fighters or missiles? India could also strike the Kahuta Uranium Enrichment facility with aircraft in order to slow down the Pakistani effort, but the risk was similar Pakistani retaliation against Indian targets.

BRASSTACKS

In autumn 1986, the Indian army conducted its largest military exercise ever with over 500,000 soldiers and thousands of tanks training within one hundred miles of the Pakistan border in Rajasthan. From the outset, this exercise, code named BRASSTACKS, was veiled in secrecy, thereby generating considerable unease in Pakistan once its scale and location became known.[1] ISI and MI spies near the Indian cantonments detected stepped up troop movements and deployment of heavy equipment to forward operation bases closer to the Pakistan border. As much as the Indians tried to disguise vital aspects of their plan, Pakistani and other spies could not miss the tremendous activity underway, including use of the national railway grid to move tanks, mobile artillery and other heavy equipment to the training area.[2] In addition, Pakistani SIGINT undoubtedly picked up signs of the exercise lead-up via unencrypted radio chatter.[3]

The core question which ISI analysts tried to answer was deceptively simple: is BRASSTACKS a military exercise or a prelude to a general invasion of Pakistan? After all, ISI's mission from its inception was forewarning the military and government of a surprise attack in sufficient time to generate an adequate response. The problem in 1986 was that all the applicable warning signals such as mobilization, forward deployment, combat aircraft dispersal, movement of ammunition and fuel supplies, and increased communications traffic applied to *both invasion and a large field exercise*. As with so many other intelligence agencies, ISI tended to worst case enemy intentions and, when it came to BRASSTACKS, the analysts assessed that the Indians were preparing for war with Pakistan.[4]

Meanwhile, Pakistani diplomats and military attachés were anxiously seeking meetings with their Indian counterparts to obtain whatever information they could, but the Indians were either non-responsive or simply issued denials of war-like intent. Another Indian response was to defiantly assert that they could conduct whatever exercises they pleased on their own soil. Clearly the Pakistanis were rattled.[5] When the US Deputy DCI, Robert Gates, met Zia in Islamabad in late 1986, the Pakistanis sought information on BRASSTACKS. What was Indian Army Chief, General Sundarji up to? Was he intent on war? Gates apparently didn't give Zia any real answer to these burning questions, but asserted, unhelpfully, that the US was monitoring the exercise closely.[6]

At one point in the crisis, Prime Minister Junejo, Zia's unpredictably independent prime minister, summoned the Defence Committee of the Cabinet, the most senior security-related organization within his limited purview. In addition to Junejo, others present included the Vice COAS, the other service chiefs, and the DGISI. DGISI Akhtar began the discussion with his agency's assessment of the exercise. BRASSTACKS was cover for a preemptive attack on Pakistan, he said. His analysts believed India wanted to convince Pakistan that BRASSTACKS was an exercise, but the real strategy was to unleash a surprise assault at the right moment. Prime Minister Junejo turned to the Vice COAS and asked him point blank: is war imminent? General Arif replied that he did not doubt ISI's assessment, adding that it was backed by "A1" (highly reliable) sources. Arif tempered his assessment by noting that several warning indicators still were not present to indicate imminent attack.[7]

No one in General Headquarters could be complacent, especially when it was learned that the Indians were building forward depots of arms, ammunition and supplies to sustain an offensive. On 18 December, DGISI Akhtar met CIA Station Chief, Milt Bearden, at ISI headquarters. The Indians were "becoming dangerously provocative" the DGISI intoned, adding that ISI was increasingly concerned that the Indian leadership was about to "do something dangerous." What did the CIA make of BRASSTACKS? What were Indian intentions? Were the Indians moving more forces to the border?[8]

The Pakistanis were not going to wait until more reassuring information came in on Indian intentions. The army began mobilizing and deploying units forward, alarming the Indians who temporarily lost track of Pakistan's First Armoured Division. Now the *Indians* had questions: were the Pakistanis contemplating their own offensive? Moreover, Indian intelligence failed to detect some important aspects of Pakistani mobilization, and it reportedly wasn't until two weeks later that the Indians finally understood the extent of Pakistan's counter-mobilization. This sent a shock wave through India's political and military establishments.[9]

On 23 January 1987, another emergency Defence Committee of the Cabinet was convened at Junejo's residence. According to one participant's account, DGISI Akhtar "beamed with confidence" as he narrated how ISI had been accurate in its assessment of India's motives. In the DGISI's view, the Indian government was generating a crisis to cover up unspecified blunders. For his part, the VCOAS, General Arif, counseled restraint and the use of a hot line between the Directors General of Military Operations on both sides.[10] In any case, Zia realized that both countries were standing toe to toe on the brink of a general war unless the situation was defused quickly. He met secretly with Indian Prime Minister Rajiv Gandhi in New Delhi and then attended a cricket match in India where his presence was widely advertised by the media of both sides.[11] An initial deal was made to jointly withdraw 150,000 soldiers from their respective parts of Kashmir. India invited diplomats and journalists to review the final phases of BRASSTACKS as a confidence-building measure.[12]

On 29 August, as the crisis began to abate, a triumphant Akhtar summoned the CIA Station Chief for another meeting at ISI HQ. The DGISI alleged that it was Zia who successfully stared down Indian Prime Minister Rajiv Gandhi, and that India had blinked first. He also claimed that ISI had fed disinformation to the Indians over open lines they knew were being monitored. When the Station Chief asked Akhtar how close the countries were to all-out war, Akhtar figuratively pulled a gun trigger with his hand: "It was that close. All it would have taken was some junior commissioned officer along the border – their JCO or ours – getting nervous, pulling his trigger and setting all off."[13] In the aftermath of the BRASSTACKS crisis, the Pakistani Vice COAS, General Arif, praised ISI's performance:

> The Inter-Service Intelligence Directorate had its fingers firmly placed on the sources of information. The process of collection, collation and dissemination of information worked smoothly in clock-like precision.[14]

On a broader, policymaking level, there were lessons in the 1986–1987 BRASSTACKS showdown that were not absorbed well by either side. For example, the lack of mutual confidence was especially dangerous when both sides probably possessed nuclear weapons at the time. The lack of transparency on India's part during the early stages of the exercise was meant to intimidate, but instead of being cowed, Pakistan assumed the worst and began mobilizing forces in its own right. But it was the frustratingly incomplete intelligence picture that baffled both sides and could have led to serious miscalculations and possibly a war. Confidence-building mechanisms were required by both sides to keep the chances of such miscalculations at a minimum.

1990 and 1998 crises

Unfortunately for both Pakistan and India, the war scares did not end with BRASSTACKS; three years later, in 1990, both were once again poised on the verge of war. The 1990 crisis shared many features with its predecessor: if anything, the shadow of nuclear weapons loomed ever larger here but, unlike 1986, the standoff was not caused by an exercise, but by Pakistan's unconventional war against India. In spring 1990, tensions reached a new high when New Delhi blamed ISI for escalating violence in Kashmir, and both sides exchanged artillery fire across the Kashmir Line of Control (LOC). ISI began picking up signals that Indian fighter jet dispersals were underway so its analysts war-gamed possible Indian moves. Among those considered were cross-LOC attacks, the blockade of Pakistan's ports, an air strike on the Kahuta nuclear facility or an Indian conventional offensive into Pakistan.[15]

In the middle of this escalating crisis, the US found itself mediating between both sides. US military attachés in India and Pakistan respectively were allowed into some deployment areas of their host countries to determine if war preparations were underway. The information they collected was then exchanged with the US Defense Attaché's Office in the other country for forwarding to the host nation MI service. By having American military attachés shuttling to and from the sensitive border areas, rumors could be debunked and confidence gradually restored. Eventually, US diplomats helped ease both contestants out of the crisis as they withdrew forces from forward positions to their cantonments.[16]

The 1990 Indo-Pakistan crisis again emphasized the pivotal role that intelligence must play if both sides are to avoid miscalculation that could lead to all-out war. The US Defense Attaché Offices in Islamabad and New Delhi served as the eyes and ears of both parties to the conflict, because the Americans were seen as impartial and trustworthy. But the circumstances in 1990 were unique and not readily transferable to future crises, where one side might not view the US as a disinterested third party. In such a case, both India and Pakistan would be relying on their own intelligence capabilities to guide them with all the pitfalls this would entail. What BRASSTACKS and the 1990 situation demonstrated was that both sides needed better intelligence and improved confidence-building measures, including notifications prior to exercises, observers at exercises, and more hotline facilities. One US observer of the 1990 crisis summarized these points concisely and bluntly:

> A lesson the Indians and Pakistanis can take out of this is their need for better intelligence and confidence-building measures to get over these misperceptions. The '87 and '90 crises are classic examples of just dreadful intelligence.[17]

Bearing the above in mind, it is disturbing to discover that Pakistani intelligence deficiencies helped trigger another standoff with India in 1998. On 11 and 13 May of that year, India surprised the world by testing five nuclear weapons at its Pokhran site in the Rajasthan desert. The test was conducted in response to Indian domestic politics rather than any specific action on Pakistan's part, but the onus obviously was on Islamabad to respond. For two tense weeks between the Indian tests and those conducted by Pakistan on 27 May 1998, rhetoric escalated to alarming levels while rumors circulated that India alone or in concert with Israel might attempt air strikes on the Kahuta enrichment facility or the Balochistan test site. Unfortunately, some within ISI were prone to take these rumors – no matter how unlikely – as fact until proven otherwise.

Sometime before the Pakistan tests, the ISI Chief of Station in London passed on unevaluated intelligence from a single unidentified source that 10–15 Israeli fighters were missing from their home base. Fearing that these aircraft might be in India preparing for a preemptive attack on Pakistan, ISI ordered its spies to step up monitoring near all of the likely Indian Air Force bases.[18] On 27 May, only hours before Pakistan's first nuclear test, the Saudi GID (possibly the source of the original London report) informed ISI that Israeli F-16s were en route to Pakistan from Chennai, India with the mission of destroying Kahuta and the test site. In the crisis atmosphere of Pakistan's GHQ, it seemed only prudent to scramble F-16s over the targets, activate early warning radars and alert ground-based air defenses. The decision was also taken to disperse Pakistan's nuclear-capable ballistic missiles lest they be hit in a preemptive Indian first strike.[19] Inevitably, the Indians picked up signals of unusual Pakistani air activity and radar activations. When the Indians discovered that Pakistan was dispersing ballistic missiles too, the situation took on an even more worrying aspect. What were the Pakistanis up to? Were they dispersing in order to conduct a preemptive strike against India? As a result of these unanswered questions, India began dispersing her own nuclear-capable ballistic missiles. The escalation cycle had begun in earnest.[20]

In the meantime, the Pakistani Foreign Ministry was alerting diplomats from the US, China, Russia, Britain and France of a possible Indian and/or Israeli attack on Pakistan. Pakistan's Permanent Representative to the United Nations went on CNN and publicly accused India of preparing an imminent attack:

> The world must understand that Pakistan is ready ... the reaction would be massive and dissuasive and that it would lead us into a situation that would bode ill for peace and security not only in the region and beyond.[21]

Things reached a point where the Israel Defense Forces Chief of Staff contacted the Pakistani ambassador in Washington to personally assure him that Israeli fighters were not about to strike Pakistan.[22] In the end, though, Pakistan ended up conducting its nuclear tests in Balochistan without interference, triggering international sanctions and opprobrium.

The 1998 crisis drove home four key lessons for both protagonists. First, they needed better intelligence collection and, in the case of Pakistan, a more rigorous analytical process to sort out fact from fiction. Second, poor intelligence made confidence-building measures imperative. Third, Pakistan seemed to have a poorly coordinated crisis command system where different elements of the government were handling the crisis independent of the others. One result was an irresponsible statement by a senior diplomat that probably wasn't approved by the government and only aggravated matters. Fourth, ballistic missiles added a formidable new complexity to each of the three lessons listed above, because they compress warning times to minutes and seconds, creating an atmosphere where hair-trigger responses may be seen as necessary to avoid losing control of one's own nuclear weapons in a surprise attack.

Kargil

Some Pakistani leaders apparently drew some very different conclusions about how the 1998 nuclear crisis impacted on stability, security and Pakistan's proxy war strategy. Now that Islamabad demonstrated a nuclear weapons capability, they reasoned, India could now be deterred from waging conventional or even nuclear war against Pakistan. India's considerable advantages in manpower and weapons were effectively nullified. This meant Pakistan was free to escalate her proxy war in Kashmir, since she now had nuclear cover to deter any Indian retaliation.[23] It was with this perspective in mind that a cohort of army generals dusted off a plan to create a fait accompli in Kashmir. Among them were the COAS, General Pervez Musharraf, a former ISI Deputy Director General, Lieutenant General Mohammed Aziz, and a future DGISI, Lieutenant General Mahmud Ahmed. In an eerie replay of the 1965 Indo-Pakistan war, the planning for this operation was tightly compartmented; the Navy and Air Force chiefs, the Joint Staff, the Foreign Ministry and even ISI were excluded.[24]

In February 1999, forces from Pakistan's Northern Light Infantry, leavened with SSG veterans, occupied some mountain peaks in the Kargil sector of Indian Kashmir. This is a forbidding region of 16,000 foot peaks, frequent avalanches, sub-zero temperatures and extreme weather conditions. Indian forces routinely abandoned their highland pickets in autumn and returned again in spring. Having observed this pattern over the years, Pakistani planners decided to steal a march on the Indians and occupy the pickets first. It wasn't until 3 May when Indian forces discovered that armed individuals were occupying outposts on the Indian side of the LOC.[25] Moreover, intercepted communications revealed that some of these trespassers on the peaks spoke Pashto. Unbeknownst to the Indians, the intercepts were taped conversations planted by the Pakistanis to make it appear as if it was Pashtun "mujahidin" who had occupied strategic peaks.[26] It was the old plausible deniability cover again: "some Pashtun tribesmen" from western Pakistan and Afghanistan had managed to climb up into the mountain fastness of central

Kashmir in the last, but still frigid, weeks of winter, with tons of weapons and equipment to declare a "liberated space." All of this was done, of course, with neither the knowledge nor the backing of the Pakistan military.

Musharraf and the other generals recognized that occupying the peaks conferred a significant strategic advantage if the Pakistanis could pull it off, for these heights dominated the one road linking Srinagar with points further north in Ladakh. If the road were routinely shelled or otherwise rendered unusable, it would cut off supplies to the formidable array of Indian forces based on or near the disputed Siachen Glacier in northern Kashmir. India would have to join the negotiating table, the Pakistani planners reckoned, because to oust the mujahidin from their mountain sanctuaries would be too costly for the Indian military in terms of blood and treasure.[27]

As events were to demonstrate, the plan's obvious shortcoming was its assessment of how India would respond to the intrusions. Just as in 1965, the Indians surprised the Pakistanis by doing the unexpected: they mobilized forces, deployed them to the Kargil area and then proceeded to systematically blast the Pakistani soldiers off the peaks by using aircraft, artillery and infantry assaults. Musharraf's plan also unraveled because it failed to accurately gauge how the US government would respond to Pakistan's misadventure. In retrospect, it appears as if Islamabad was hoping Washington would intervene to prevent crisis escalation and in so doing would mediate a solution to the Kashmir imbroglio. But Washington did not do what was expected of it either. Instead of mediation, the US demanded that Pakistan remove its forces from the Indian side of the LOC. Moreover, the Clinton White House made it clear that it considered Pakistan responsible for the crisis by acting provocatively, even in the face of possible nuclear war.[28]

Pakistan was forced literally and figuratively to climb down from the Kargil peaks, and the result was a bitter humiliation for the army. India could crow that the US had sided with it for the first time on a Kashmir issue, leaving Pakistan more isolated and mistrusted than ever before. A more accurate read of US and Indian responses to Kargil in advance of operations would have helped Islamabad avoid yet another embarrassing defeat. This, of course, was the job of ISI analysts. It is still difficult to obtain a clear picture of ISI's involvement in the Kargil War. Major General Shahid Aziz, Deputy Director General of ISI's JIB at the time, has argued in his memoirs that ISI itself did not learn about the Kargil operation until intercepted Indian communications alerted them to an incursion of armed "militants" into India's Kargil Sector. General Aziz wrote that he took these reports to the DGISI, Ziauddin Butt, who told him to hold onto the reports but do nothing with them. It was an army operation, the DGISI said. Since ISI was excluded from the planning, Shahid asks, who wrote the intelligence estimates on India's thinking and possible responses to the incursion? Who assessed how the US or China might respond to the Pakistani power play? According to General Aziz:

An unsound military plan based upon invalid assumptions, launched with little preparation and in total disregard to the regional and international environment was bound to fail. That may well have been the reason for its secrecy. It was a total disaster.[29]

When Pakistan entered the "nuclear club" in May 1998, its leadership had irreconcilable objectives. On the one hand, they calculated that nuclear weapons would deter Indian attack and boost Pakistan's international prestige. On the other, they apparently believed that nuclear weapons gave them carte blanche to ramp up proxy wars against India. The end result, however, was that New Delhi was willing and able to fight Pakistan below the nuclear threshold and secure a conventional victory. Moreover, rather than earning Pakistan respect, its possession of nuclear weapons spurred the great powers to insist that it act more responsibly on the world stage. In this context, the Kargil fiasco dealt a significant blow to Pakistani prestige, and the country found itself more isolated internationally.

Notes

1 K.M. Arif, *Working with Zia*, Karachi: OUP, 1995, 242.
2 M. Krepon and M. Faruqee, eds., "Conflict Prevention and Confidence-Building Measures in South Asia: The 1990 Crisis, Henry L. Stimson Center," Occasional Paper No. 17, April 1994, www.stimson.org/books-reports/conflict-prevention-and-confidence-building-measures-in-south-asia-the-1990-crisis-1/ [accessed 17/1/14].
3 S.P. Kapur and S. Ganguly, "The Jihad Paradox: Pakistan and Islamist Militancy in South Asia," *International Security* 37: 1, Summer 2012, 396.
4 K.M. Arif, *Khaki Shadows*, Karachi: OUP, 2001, 257–260.
5 Ibid., 259–260.
6 M. Bearden, and J. Risen, *The Main Enemy*, New York: Random House, 2003, 258.
7 Arif, *Khaki Shadows*, op. cit., 259–261.
8 Ibid., 265; Bearden & Risen, *Main Enemy*, op. cit., 291–292
9 A. Levy and C. Scott-Clark, *Nuclear Deception: The Dangerous Relationship Between the United States and Pakistan*, New York: Walker & Co., 2008, 148–149; Bearden & Risen, *Main Enemy*, op. cit., 291–292; Arif, *Khaki Shadows*, op. cit., 265.
10 Arif, *Khaki Shadows*, op. cit., 269–270.
11 J. Singh, *In Service of Emergent India*, Bloomington: Indiana University Press, 2007, 295.
12 Bearden & Risen, *Main Enemy*, op. cit., 269–271.
13 Ibid., 269–271.
14 Arif, *Khaki Shadows*, op. cit., 257–258.
15 Krepon & Faruqee, "Conflict Prevention and Confidence-Building Measures," op. cit., 17; I. Akhund, *Trial and Error: The Advent and Eclipse of Benazir Bhutto*, Karachi: OUP, 2000, 213–214.
16 Krepon and Faruqee, "Conflict Prevent and Confidence-Building Measures," op. cit., 13, 19.
17 Quoted in Ibid., 27.
18 O.B. Jones, *Pakistan: Eye of the Storm*, New Haven: Yale University Press, 2003, 190; G.A. Khan, *Glimpses into the Corridors of Power*, Karachi: OUP, 2007, 301–302.
19 O.B. Jones, *Pakistan*, op. cit., 187–188; Singh, *In Service of Emergent India*, op. cit., 109.

20 O.B. Jones, *Pakistan*, op. cit., 188.
21 Quoted in Ibid., 188.
22 B. Riedel, *American Diplomacy and the 1999 Kargil Summit at Blair House*, Philadelphia, PA: Center for the Advanced Study of India, 2002, http://citeseerx.ist.psu.edu/viewdoc/download?doi=10.1.1.473.251&rep=rep1&type=pdf [accessed 12/10/12] 4.
23 S. Jones and C.C. Fair, *Counterinsurgency in Pakistan*, Santa Monica, CA: Rand, 2010, 6; H. Abbas, *Pakistan's Drift into Extremism*, Armonk, NY: M.E. Sharpe, 2005, 172–173; N.C. Behera, *Demystifying Kashmir*, Washington, DC: Brookings, 2006, 81.
24 A. Rashid, *Descent into Chaos*, New York: Viking, 2008, 29; R. Laskar, "Musharraf Hid Kargil Intrusions from ISI: Former General," PTI 3 February 2013 www.rediff.com/news/report/musharraf-hid-kargil-intrusions-from-isi-former-general/20130203.html [accessed 17/8/14]; K. Kiyani, "Kargil Adventure was Four-Man Show: General," *Dawn*, 28 January 2013, www.dawn.com/news/782010/kargil-adventure-was-four-man-show-general [accessed 17/8/14].
25 V. Schofield, *Kashmir in Conflict*, London, I.B. Tauris, 2003, 208–209; Riedel, *American Diplomacy*, op. cit., 2.
26 S. Aziz, "Putting Our Children in Line of Fire," *The Nation*, 6 January 2013, http://nation.com.pk/columns/06-Jan-2013/putting-our-children-in-line-of-fire [accessed 17/8/14]; Kiyani, "Kargil Adventure," op. cit.; Singh, *In Service of Emergent India*, op. cit., 170.
27 Aziz, "Putting our Children in Line of Fire," op. cit.
28 Riedel, *American Diplomacy*, op. cit., 4–5.
29 Aziz, "Putting our Children in Line of Fire," op. cit.

14 Pakistan's Afghan Quagmire

After a bloody decade of bombings, beheadings, abductions, pillaging and rape, Pakistan and its jihadi proxies had at the end of the 1990s little to show for their goal of assimilating Kashmir into Pakistan. But Afghanistan seemed to promise a different story. After nine years of a brutal occupation, the last Soviet soldiers left the country on 15 February 1989. ISI and CIA analysts predicted that the Afghan communist regime would collapse within six months of the Soviet withdrawal because it was divided and unpopular.[1] The army was demoralized, despondent and all but defeated. Yet once again, Afghanistan defied the prognostications of outsiders. Najibullah's government survived for another three years; it even outlived the Soviet Union before succumbing to the resistance in April 1992. The biggest reason for its survival was the inability of the Peshawar-based Afghan political parties – the ISI-7 – to remain unified once the Soviets were gone. The closer they sensed victory, the more fractious the ISI-7 leaders became.

Mujahidin quarreling

ISI struggled to keep its mujahidin alliance together. On 10 February 1989, DGISI Hamid Gul held a *shura* in Rawalpindi that included representatives from each of the ISI-7 parties. His ambitious goal was to forge a viable, credible and above all *unified* political alternative to Najibullah in Kabul. Predictably the process was a "chaotic circus" as US Ambassador to the Afghan Resistance, Peter Tomsen, put it years later.[2] The *shura* dragged on for two weeks as every leader of the ISI-7 staked his claim to leadership of the proposed coalition government. Eventually, Saudi intelligence chief, Prince Turki al-Faisal, mediated a temporary solution sweetened by a $25 million reward. The only odd man out in this compromise was the power hungry and ruthless warlord, Gulbuddin Hekmatyar, who resented being shunted aside by the other parties.[3]

In the end, though, no matter how much ISI and the Saudis manipulated the process, none of the ISI-7 parties demonstrated any popularity among Afghans in general, nor did they represent the interests of Afghanistan's many minorities. They retained the support of guerrilla commanders inside Afghanistan only for as long as they could pay and arm them.[4] As for Pakistan, it was never interested in sponsoring a true Afghan government of national reconciliation because this might jeopardize its own goals for Afghanistan. These included: (1) an Islamist government beholden to Islamabad; (2) eventual formation of an Afghan-Pakistani confederation; (3) using Afghanistan as "strategic depth" in the event of war with India; and (4) Afghanistan's formal renunciation of claims on Pakistani territory. Of the ISI-7 leaders, only Hekmatyar was willing to comply with each of the objectives listed above. Peter Tomsen puts a finer point on this when he states that the Afghan interim government "was, in fact, a façade for the ISI's covert strategy to put Hekmatyar in Kabul through military force."[5]

Jalalabad setback

On 6 March 1989, shortly after the Soviet withdrawal, Prime Minister Benazir Bhutto convened a meeting of the Afghan Cell with Hamid Gul, Foreign Ministry representatives, and others to debate the next political steps in Afghanistan. When should Pakistan formally recognize its own creation, the Afghan interim government (AIG)? DGISI Gul urged immediate recognition while Foreign Minister Sahabzada Yaqub Khan emphasized that the AIG must occupy a piece of Afghan territory first before it could be recognized. Benazir concurred with her foreign minister on this point, compelling the DGISI to further develop a plan to seize the eastern Afghan city of Jalalabad. Brigadier Afzal Janjua of ISI's Afghan Bureau worked out the details, which relied on ISI's Islamist allies to spearhead the assault.[6] Gul predicted the city could fall within a week, but he also informed the civilian leadership that wavering was not an option: "There can be no ceasefire in a jihad against the Marxist unbeliever ... war must go on until *darul harb* ('house of war') is cleansed and becomes *darul aman* ('house of peace')."[7]

On the eve of the 1989 Jalalabad offensive, ISI's plan rested on several assumptions that were eventually shown to be quite far off the mark:

- The Afghan army suffered from low morale.
- Afghan army conscripts were likely to defect en masse.
- The Afghan army would be unable to send reinforcements to Jalalabad once the mujahidin offensive began.
- The Afghan military's advantages in airpower would be negated by the insurgents' effective use of cover and advanced air defense systems.
- The rebel alliance would remain unified.[8]

At first, the mujahidin did make good progress against the Jalalabad garrison; their ISI advisors were ebullient, predicting that the city would fall at any time.[9] But then the momentum shifted quickly. The Afghan army stiffened its resolve because stories were circulating that the mujahidin were executing those soldiers who had surrendered to them.[10] In addition, the army was well-entrenched and well-equipped; these advantages came to the fore as the initial assault turned into a stalemate. In meetings with senior military leaders, Hamid Gul was forced to concede that his early estimates were "optimistic," but nonetheless held to his prediction that Jalalabad would fall.[11]

But Jalalabad didn't fall, and as the days turned into weeks, morale in the Afghan army soared while mujahidin unity disintegrated. At the same time, mujahidin resentment of ISI manipulation reached new heights.[12] Even the marginalized Pakistan Foreign Ministry sensed ISI's vulnerability, with one official confidently asserting that "we told ISI policies must be predicated on reality, not wishful thinking."[13] A British Foreign Office diplomat spun it a different way:

> This is what happens when those providing intelligence are also deciding policy. Rather than basing strategy on intelligence coming in, they are providing intelligence to fit their own goals.[14]

It was fair criticism, but ISI is certainly not the only intelligence agency to mix intelligence with policy. As for the Jalalabad offensive, the fault lay in mistaken assumptions about Afghan government weakness and mujahidin unity. In the end, Afghanistan proved yet again that it is a quicksand for any outsider in a hurry, Pakistan included.

Turmoil in the south

Still, Pakistan was continually frustrated by its inability to control events inside Afghanistan. Its ISI-7 political coalition wasn't of much help either because none of the parties commanded much of a following inside Afghanistan. They were especially weak in southern Afghanistan, where their presence was minimal at best. Some of this came to light in Kandahar, where the provincial governor tried forging a separate peace with elders from the historically dominant Durrani tribal confederation. Throughout the anti-Soviet war, ISI had neglected the south, which it regarded as a backwater full of unreconstructed royalists and the old Pashtunistan crowd.[15] Therefore, when ISI tried thwarting the Kandahar peace process, it had very few Afghan allies on hand to accomplish its objectives. So it flew in Hekmatyar, who as a northerner had zero influence in the south. When ISI's Quetta Detachment commander, Colonel Faizan, attempted to chaperone Hekmatyar around refugee camps in the Quetta area they were stoned by an angry mob. An attempt to "introduce" the ISI's favorite warlord to Kandahar also failed when his convoy was ambushed, and he was forced to return to Quetta. No one liked or trusted Gulbuddin Hekmatyar: his grim reputation preceded him wherever he went.[16]

Still, when it came to southern Afghanistan, ISI did have certain advantages, which it exploited to the fullest extent possible. The southern Pashtun tribes take division, feud and fractiousness to a whole new level, even for

Afghans. Moreover, the old tribal system had broken down as a result of the Soviet war, which destroyed centuries-old irrigation canals, leveled parts of Kandahar city and sprinkled the countryside with landmines and unexploded ordnance. ISI's policy here was the classic one of divide-and-conquer, aggravating the tribal divisions that plagued the Durrani Confederation.[17] ISI's Quetta Detachment began tightening up on the distribution of aid so that only those who joined Gulbuddin Hekmatyar's *Hezb-e-Islami* could obtain weapons and assistance. Only pro-Hekmatyar commanders were allowed to use the border roads leading into Afghanistan or access Pakistani medical facilities without being questioned.[18] ISI also created an Islamist *shura* consisting of Arghestan area mullahs, who were supposed to offer an "Islam-sanctioned alternative" to tribal authority. With a dose of hyperbole, Colonel Faizan asserted that this Islamist *shura* "decisively reversed three hundred years of Durrani rule in Afghanistan."[19]

ISI's efforts at manipulating Afghan tribal politics offer useful insights into Pakistan's overall Afghan policy. Islamabad's approach was inherently revolutionary, because it sought to overturn a centuries-old system of tribal rule and replace it with an Islamist leadership dominated by mullahs. This attempt to break tribes in favor of a fundamentalist Islam was to have dangerous consequences for the future stability of Afghanistan and Pakistan.

Tanai coup attempt

ISI wasn't ready to give up on Hekmatyar just yet. In late 1989, it facilitated secret negotiations between the warlord and then Afghan Defense Minister Shahnawaz Tanai to overthrow Najibullah and replace him with a new regime consisting of Tanai's men plus some *Hezb-e-Islami* representatives.[20] ISI and the Saudi GID provided the money to grease the skids in Kabul and lay the necessary groundwork for the coup. [21] Tanai launched his coup on 6–7 March 1990, but Najibullah managed to rally regime security forces and beat off the rebellious military units, forcing Tanai to flee for Peshawar along with five of his generals. As for the other ISI-7 members excluded from the ISI–Tanai–Hezb negotiations, their mistrust of both Hekmatyar and ISI had been validated once again. ISI was clearly intent on imposing Hekmatyar on Afghanistan.[22]

Indeed, ISI and Hekmatyar opposed any attempt by Afghan commanders on the "inside" to forge independent solutions to their country's problems. For instance, when some of the more prominent Afghan guerrilla leaders created a Commanders' Shura in 1990, ISI saw this as an attempt by the rebels to slip free of its controls. Colonel Faizan of the Quetta Detachment made it clear to *his* mujahidin that their commanders should not attend the shura. In the end, of course, ISI still had leverage over many commanders in Afghanistan because it had a near-monopoly on weapons deliveries. No one could stray too far from the ISI fold lest they jeopardize their ability to prosecute the "bigger war" against Najibullah, who stubbornly clung to power.[23]

Najibullah's fall

Yet Najibullah's downfall was coming, and even he must have realized this when the Soviet Union was formally dissolved in December 1991. Up to this point, the Afghan government had been relying heavily on the USSR for discounted weapons, subsidized fuel and food; however, newly independent Russia, cash-strapped in its own right, cut all subsidies. Najibullah definitely was looking weak, and the Afghan communists were splitting apart on political, ethnic and tribal lines.[24]

As Najibullah's throne seemed increasingly shaky, ISI was active both in the Afghan expatriate community in Pakistan and also in Kabul. Early in 1992, the former Frontier Corps officer, Naseerullah Babar, and the former DGISI, Asad Durrani, went secretly to Afghanistan where they met Najibullah and tried to broker a power-sharing deal or a graceful exit for the besieged Afghan president. Najibullah was not interested.[25] Since the negotiated approach had failed, ISI reverted to the Hekmatyar–Tanai alliance, which was preparing for another attack on Kabul from Charasyab on the southern outskirts. Supervised by ISI officers, Tanai reached out to some allies within the regime, encouraging them to break with Najibullah.[26]

But Afghanistan stymied ISI once again. Ahmed Shah Massoud, the Panjshir commander, who had no love for ISI, quietly worked his own deal with a vital prop of the Najibullah regime: powerful Uzbek militia leader General Rashid Dostum. Together, Massoud and Dostum brought their units into positions along the Shomali Plain north of Kabul, while Hekmatyar's forces made an initial foray into the capital accompanied by several former and current ISI stalwarts like Hamid Gul, Afzal Janjua and Colonel Imam.[27]

Even as the Massoud/Dostum forces were preparing to battle Hekmatyar for Kabul, the ISI-7 was predictably quarreling over the spoils. DGISI Javed Nasir eventually had to call on the support of Prince Turki al-Faisal, the JI leader, Qazi Hussain Ahmed, and the COAS to help create another Afghan interim government. But once again, Hekmatyar refused to sign because he wanted to be president rather than accept the lowly post of prime minister in the new regime. In any case, the Afghan capital fell into the hands of Massoud-Dostum, leaving Hekmatyar once more on the outside looking in.[28]

Afghan civil war

On 29 April, Prime Minister Nawaz Sharif flew to Kabul on a quick visit to celebrate the mujahidin victory over Najibullah. Accompanying him were the COAS, General Asif Nawaz Janjua (no relation to Afzal Janjua), Prince Turki and DGISI Nasir, who surprised his companions with an Islamic war cry when their plane entered Afghan airspace. In the meantime, Hekmatyar sulked in his base south of Kabul while his ISI advisors supervised the transfer of new weapons to his militia, including artillery rockets that later killed thousands of Kabul residents. It was the start of a civil war that would virtually level much of the Afghan capital.[29] In fact, over the next two years, ISI tried all sorts of political combinations to try and hoist Hekmatyar onto the Afghan throne but to no avail. It gave him a formidable arsenal, it tried buying off his opposition, and it induced defections in the ranks of Massoud's and Dostum's forces with limited success. In late 1993, Dostum did switch sides and joined Hekmatyar in an assault on Kabul, but even that bid failed.

By early 1994, it was clear to all but a few ISI stalwarts that the Hekmatyar strategy had reached a dead end. Some ISI officials recognized that neither force nor diplomacy could leverage the Rabbani–Massoud clique out of Kabul. Block after block of burned out homes and thousands of graves were grim testimony to ISI's failed campaign to seize the Afghan capital. ISI's Quetta Detachment was among the earliest to question the viability of the Hekmatyar alliance, especially since Gulbuddin had virtually no support in southern Afghanistan.[30] But ISI's Afghan Bureau, the Peshawar Detachment, as well as headquarters still clung to Gulbuddin's *Hezb-e-Islami* partly because it was affiliated with the *JI*, ISI's longtime domestic ally. In response to Quetta Detachment's suggestion that a new "southern strategy" be considered, ISI headquarters staff reverted to the old critique of the southern Pashtuns as royalists or Pashtun nationalists. Besides, these officers argued, if ISI dumped Hekmatyar, Massoud would consolidate his position in Kabul regardless of what took place in the south. India was bound to gain in this circumstance, since many ISI officers believed Massoud and his political ally, Rabbani, were close to New Delhi. In the zero-sum game of South Asian power politics, any "gain" by India would automatically be at the expense of Pakistan.[31]

The Taliban option

While ISI debated Afghan strategy, other Pakistani forces were pursuing their own approach to Afghanistan that would overtake and replace ISI's pro-Hekmatyar policy. When Benazir Bhutto was elected prime minister for the second time in October 1993, she named Naseerullah Babar as Interior Minister. Babar had never lost his interest in Afghanistan since he helped train many of the same insurgent leaders in the 1970s who were now killing each other in the 1990s. After the fall of Najibullah, Babar and other Pakistani officials were drawn to the potentially lucrative trade with the newly independent states of the former Soviet Central Asia. In their vision of the future, Pakistan could grow rich as the maritime outlet for Kazakh oil, Turkmen gas, Afghan copper and other, as yet untapped, natural resources. The only irritant in this grand view of Pakistan's future was, of course, eternally chaotic Afghanistan. Babar and his allies argued that the best option was southern Afghanistan: restore stability there, and Pakistan could work with international investors to lay down road, rail and pipeline networks linking Central Asia to the Indian Ocean across Afghan and Pakistani soil.[32]

Stabilizing southern Afghanistan for trade was the major obstacle. As noted, ISI had few options here because it had coddled Hekmatyar for years without paying much attention to the south. One thing that ISI did have in the south, though, was some local contacts, and to manage these it turned to an ISI veteran of Afghanistan, Colonel Imam. Colonel Imam knew several of the important players in the Kandahar area because he had supervised their training as mujahidin in Pakistan during the 1980s. In fact, he later claimed that he knew many of the Taliban leaders, including Mullah Omar from their stints in ISI training camps. He also was acquainted with many prominent mullahs who were pivotal to the Taliban's rise.[33] But the south was not going to be easy. In addition to its complex tribal politics and years of neglect, ISI had paid scant attention to the Pakistani political party that possessed deep roots here, the *JUI*.[34] JUI had long resented ISI's support for the rival *JI* according to the prominent headmaster of the JUI-affiliated Haqqania madrassa, Samiul Haq:

> The ISI always supported Hikmetyar [*sic*] and [JI leader] Qazi Hussain Ahmed while we were ignored, even though 80 per cent of the commanders fighting the Russians in the Pashtun areas had studied at Haqqania. Hikmetyar had 5 per cent of the popular support but 90 per cent of the military aid from the ISI.[35]

Putting Mullah Omar in power

By June 1994, rumors were reaching Pakistani Interior Minister Naseerullah Babar of a new militia that had emerged in the tortured chaos that was Kandahar. Babar queried the ISI about this "Taliban" militia, but presumably they didn't tell him what he wanted to know so he went to have a look for himself. In September 1994, Babar and Colonel Imam, conducted a discreet reconnaissance of southern and western Afghanistan to better understand the lay of the land and the nature of the Taliban.[36] Upon their return to Quetta, Colonel Imam drafted a report analyzing developments in Afghanistan and offering policy recommendations such as sending humanitarian aid to southern Afghanistan to win the hearts and minds of the population. Babar bought into it immediately.[37]

Having completed his reconnaissance mission, Naseerullah Babar began assembling a truck convoy that would begin its journey in Quetta, pass through Kandahar and head west for Herat and Turkmenistan. The purposes of this convoy were to (1) win the hearts and minds of Afghans by distributing humanitarian aid; (2) collect intelligence; (3) cultivate ties with the Taliban; (4) establish a trade link to Turkmenistan; and (5) create a provocation to help put the Taliban in power. At first, Babar's plan encountered considerable resistance: Colonel Imam was wary of the turbulence in Kandahar while the Taliban leader, Mullah Omar, thought the timing was not right; reportedly both the Foreign Ministry and ISI were opposed. But, in the end, Babar had his way.[38]

Phase one of Babar's plan gave the Taliban access to a vast weapons dump located in the border town of Spin Boldak. Originally these stockpiles were intended for Hekmatyar but now, with ISI's concurrence, they were handed over to the Taliban instead.[39] According to DGISI Ashraf Qazi the arsenal was substantial: "This was seventeen tunnels! Seventeen tunnels full of arms and ammunition. Enough to raise almost half the size of Pakistan's army."[40] Phase two involved the recruitment of madrassa students, sectarian militants from *Sepah-e-Sahaba Pakistan* and *Lashkar-e-Jhangvi*, Arab jihadis, ex–Afghan communists and undercover ISI logisticians. The Saudis supplemented all this with cash and pickup trucks.[41] The final phase was Naseerullah Babar's convoy which consisted of 30 trucks loaded with rice, flour, medical supplies and other necessities. It was joined by an escort of former ISI officers, including Colonel Imam and a Pashtun known only as "Colonel Gul."[42] On 2 November 1994, the convoy was halted by some warlords 35 kilometers east of Kandahar city. Colonel Imam called Mullah Omar on his satellite phone and asked the Taliban leader for help. The Taliban rescued the convoy, and on 4 November, they accompanied it into Kandahar, which was immediately put under their particularly harsh version of Islamic law.[43]

Colonel Imam was obviously a prominent player in the Taliban's capture of Kandahar. On paper, Sultan Amir Tarar (his real name) was accredited by the Rabbani government in Kabul as Pakistan's Consul General to Herat, but in late October, he showed up to help Naseerullah Babar's convoy reach Kandahar. Undoubtedly, Colonel Imam greased more than a few palms in Kandahar to facilitate the convoy's passage and aid the Taliban's takeover of the city. After the Taliban victory it seemed as if he was appointed Consul General to Kandahar, where he helped the Taliban set up their emirate.[44]

We have already seen how "retired" ISI officers were used in the 1980s and early 1990s to provide political and technical guidance to Afghan insurgents. The use of the retired Colonel Imam in 1994 to spearhead the Taliban takeover of Kandahar is another example of this system. Ambassador Peter Tomsen describes what has since been called the Directorate S in this way: "While pretending to exist outside the government, [Hamid] Gul's 'virtual ISI' in reality operated as part of the ISI. It grew in size as more and more ISI officers and NCOs retired and joined its ranks."[45]

Internal debates

Though ISI's Quetta Detachment endorsed a "southern option" after it lost faith in Hekmatyar's ability to shoot his way into Kabul, the Afghan Bureau and the Peshawar Detachment were reluctant to ditch Hekmatyar's *Hezb-e-Islami* even when the surging Taliban refused to join the *Hezb* in any kind of alliance. ISI HQ was now worried that abandoning Gulbuddin could derail the Kashmir proxy war, since many of the militants fighting in Kashmir had been trained at *Hezb* camps in Pakistan and Afghanistan.[46] In an effort to address their skeptics at ISI HQ, a Taliban delegation met DGISI Ashraf Qazi shortly after their capture of Kandahar. Whatever their sales pitch, the DGISI apparently was not overly impressed:

I was horrified to see that they had emerged literally from the villages. They had very little clue about international affairs or anything like that. They had their own peculiar set of ideas. The only thing I found was that they were well-intentioned.[47]

Still, the Taliban were unequivocal about two things: ISI must drop Hekmatyar and all mujahidin leaders "should be hanged." Then they asked Qazi for logistics aid over and on top of the considerable assistance they had already received from Pakistan. The DGISI agreed, but he was keeping his options open just the same.[48]

In addition to debating the merits of the Taliban, ISI was immersed in another dispute concerning the relative merits of intelligence missions versus UW. Traditional espionage advocates argued that UW was consuming far too much of ISI's limited resources and hampering the agency's ability to spy on India. Moreover, the single-minded pursuit of "victory" with jihadis in Afghanistan and Kashmir was jeopardizing Pakistan's relations with many of its foreign intelligence partners like the US, Egypt, Algeria and China. The UW supporters emphasized that Pakistan could not lose in Afghanistan because India would inevitably gain. As for the war in Kashmir, they argued that it was being fought for a principle. Anyway, the Kashmir war forced India to expend considerable resources just to retain the place. The debate was ultimately settled in favor of the UW proponents because the army saw more utility in proxy wars than collecting intelligence.[49]

ISI and Taliban success

The Taliban made it plain from the outset that their program was not restricted to Kandahar or southern Afghanistan, but it would include the entire country plus points beyond. Against ISI advice, the Taliban advanced on Kabul and Herat in early 1995, but were defeated.[50] An operational pause ensued during which the militia was substantially improved in terms of its military capabilities with ISI advisors and Saudi cash. As one expert on Afghanistan put it, the Taliban suddenly and suspiciously became adept in technical areas usually neglected by Afghan guerrillas:

> Tactically the Taliban operated with a flexibility that hinged on a notably efficient communications and command and control network.... Strategically, meanwhile the student-led army displayed an unwavering direction combined with disconcerting speed and mobility.[51]

The slew of Taliban victories in Afghanistan in late 1995 and 1996 that followed the ISI overhaul generated a new round of debates within Islamabad regarding the wisdom of using this austere militia as the stalking horse for Pakistani ambitions. While ISI had shed its earlier misgivings about the Taliban, the same could not be said for others, such as COAS Jehangir Karamat, who advised ISI against aiding the Taliban because Pakistan's international image was suffering. The Deputy Director General of ISI, Major General Aziz Khan, pressed the case for backing the militia. "These people will make Pakistan strong," he insisted, "[t]here is nothing we need to fear from them. All they will do if they take over Afghanistan is spread Islam."[52] Karamat's objections were overridden, for DGISI Nasim Rana had beaten a well-worn path to Benazir Bhutto's door with a proposal to increase aid to the Taliban and help them finally capture Kabul. According to one account, Benazir was ready to grant "unlimited covert aid" to sustain ISI's latest ally in Afghanistan.[53]

The Taliban swept into Herat in September 1995 just before winter put an end to the fighting season. The following summer, the militia carried out a series of well-planned and sustained assaults that culminated with the fall of Jalalabad and Kabul in September 1996. From ISI's perspective, it was a stunning pair of victories, marred only by the fact that Ahmed Shah Massoud was able to extract his forces from Kabul and retreat north to the Panjshir Valley.

New Taliban offensives

Kabul was the official capital of the Taliban Emirate; however, the movement's leader, Mullah Omar, preferred Kandahar, and it was from this city that he ruled much of Afghanistan. The Taliban had no lack of mullahs, but they were deficient in administrators, bureaucrats and technical experts necessary to run a government. ISI pitched in here as well, drawing on a deep bench of serving and retired Pakistani military officers who helped staff the ministries of the Interior, Foreign Affairs and Defence. Some ISI officers even served in Mullah Omar's personal secretariat. ISI also helped the Taliban set up an intelligence facility near Kandahar, where Taliban intelligence officers were trained according to the standard ISI curriculum.[54]

As the Taliban expanded further into Afghanistan, ISI built intelligence bases in Herat, Kabul and Bamiyan. While some ISI officers like Colonel Imam operated openly, others operated under cover as mullahs, *Tablighi Jama'at* missionaries, businessmen or mujahidin. Many spoke Pashto as their native tongue.[55] This ability of ISI officers to blend in with their surroundings made it exceedingly difficult for the Afghan opposition to prove ISI's presence inside their country. It also let some US officials dismiss allegations of Pakistani interference in Afghanistan's internal affairs.

With the 1997 fighting season approaching, a key player in campaign planning was the ISI Chief of Station in Kabul, Brigadier Ashraf Afridi. A veteran ISI Pashtun officer, Afridi had earlier served as Military Attaché in Kabul until the pre-Taliban government declared him persona non grata for interfering in internal Afghan affairs. Afridi's plan for the 1997 campaign focused on capturing the northern city of Mazar-e Sharif, then under the control of the Uzbek warlord, Abdurrashid Dostum.[56]

In May 1997, as the Taliban was entering Mazar-e Sharif, ISI urged Pakistani Prime Minister Nawaz Sharif to recognize the Taliban as the legitimate government of Afghanistan. But the Foreign Ministry hesitated, drawing a complaint from the irritated DGISI, Naseem Rana, who insisted that Pakistan be first to recognize the Taliban. Consequently, on 27 May, Pakistan announced its official recognition of the Taliban Emirate.[57]

But Afghanistan has been notoriously cruel to foreign occupiers, the ISI-led Taliban included. When the militia entered Mazar-e Sharif, it was ambushed by the city's Hazara and Uzbek population and lost hundreds of experienced fighters. Unfortunately for Mazar-e Sharif, it was a short respite because the following summer a mixed Taliban force of madrasa students, foreign fighters, sectarian Pakistani militants, ISI and SSG advisors invaded the city again. This time they were here to stay with lethal consequences for the city's Hazara population in particular.[58]

ISI backing

The Taliban's string of victories in the north triggered renewed suspicions among foreign observers about the Taliban's formidable military capabilities. Wrote one:

> This was mobile warfare at its most effective. To suggest that semi-literate Taliban commanders whose military experience had never extended beyond the hit-and-run attacks of guerrilla warfare could have risen to this level of planning and execution defies belief.[59]

Islamabad's response to reports that its military and intelligence officers were aiding the Taliban was boilerplate: there were no Pakistani army officers inside Afghanistan, and Pakistan was not providing military aid to the Taliban. When, on 9 February 1996, US officials raised these issues with a senior Pakistani delegation consisting of Foreign Minister Asif Ali, ambassador to the US, Maleeha Lodi, and DGISI Rana, the Pakistanis fervently denied that ISI provided military assistance to the Taliban. "Not one bullet," Rana insisted. Pakistan's only mission in Afghanistan, they claimed, was to provide "relief supplies" for "all factions."[60]

Some US officials took Pakistani assertions at face value:

> Pakistani aid to the Taliban is ... probably less malign than most imagine ... [evidence] does not seem to support persistent rumors of large amounts of military aid ... military advice to the Taliban may be there, but is probably not all that significant since the Taliban do quite well on their own.[61]

ISI couldn't have said it any better.

Still, the ISI–Taliban relationship was not an easy one. In the end, most of the Taliban fighters were Afghans and thus shared the stubborn and notoriously independent characteristics of their people. Friction was inevitable, especially when the Pakistanis were perceived as too overbearing. On one occasion, Colonel Imam was advising a Taliban commander on how he should limit his losses. The commander asked his ISI advisor how many wars Pakistan had fought against India. Colonel Imam answered: three. The commander then asked how many of those wars had been won by Pakistan. No answer was necessary.[62] Another ISI officer advising Taliban operations in the Hazara province of Bamiyan was frustrated at his inability to stop the Taliban from slaughtering the civilian population.[63]

Because the ISI–Taliban relationship was not an equal one, there was a fundamental lack of mutual trust. When a Taliban delegation went to the US in 1997, it was accompanied by an ISI minder. Apparently, Islamabad was worried that its protégés might cut a separate deal with the Americans.[64] In his memoirs, a senior Taliban official named Mohamed Zaeef details numerous examples of the friction and frustration that plagued the ISI–Taliban alliance. At times, the Taliban were convinced the ISI was secretly negotiating with the movement's adversaries such as Hamid Karzai, Abdul Haq, the CIA and even Ahmad Shah Massoud.[65] According to Zaeef:

> The wolf and sheep may drink water from the same stream, but since the start of the jihad the ISI extended its roots deep into Afghanistan like a cancer puts down roots in the human body; every ruler of Afghanistan complained about it, but none could get rid of it.[66]

Zaeef went on to describe an ISI that tried bribing him to provide information on the Kandahar Shura, an odd request since ISI had well-placed agents within the shura. ISI also offered to mediate Zaeef's relations with other Pakistani government agencies when he served as ambassador there. In fact, Zaeef wrote that he preferred working with the Foreign Ministry rather than ISI even though the former was relatively ineffectual.[67]

Afghanistan could be a deceptive morass. Just when ISI sensed victory was almost within sight, the unexpected would take place, whether the 1989 setback in Jalalabad, Hekmatyar's failure to capture Kabul in 1992 or the Taliban's 1997 defeat in Mazar-e Sharif. But in late summer 2001, there were plenty of signs that ISI's 20-year-old campaign to control Afghanistan by proxy was about to be crowned with success. A Taliban army reinforced with Pakistani officers and foreign jihadis was poised to break into Ahmed Shah Massoud's Panjshir Valley fortress and eliminate the last resistance to Taliban rule in Afghanistan.

Notes

1 K.M. Arif, *Working with Zia*, Karachi: OUP, 1995, 328; R.M. Khan, *Untying the Afghan Knot*, Durham, NC: Duke University Press, 1991, 243–244.
2 P. Tomsen, *The Wars of Afghanistan*, New York: PublicAffairs, 2011, 258.
3 Ibid., 257–260; I. Akhund, *Trial and Error: The Advent and Eclipse of Benazir Bhutto*, Karachi: OUP, 2000, 173–174; S. Coll, *Ghost Wars*, New York: Penguin, 2004, 191.

4 Tomsen, *Wars of Afghanistan*, op. cit., 320.
5 Ibid.
6 Coll, *Ghost Wars*, op. cit, 192–193; H. Abbas, *Pakistan's Drift into Extremism*, Armonk, NY: M.E. Sharpe, 2005, 140; Akhund, *Trial*, op. cit., 176–177; D. Kux, *The United States and Pakistan, 1947–2000: Disenchanted Allies*, Washington, DC: Johns Hopkins University Press, 2001, 297–298.
7 Quoted in Akhund, *Trial*, op. cit., 176–177.
8 C. Lamb, *Waiting for Allah: Pakistan's Struggle for Democracy*, London: Hamish Hamilton, 1991, 237–238.
9 M. Ahmed, *Stinger Saga*, Xlibris, 2012, 79.
10 R. Khan, *Untying the Afghan Knot*, op. cit., 305.
11 Akhund, *Trial*, op. cit., 176–177.
12 B. Riedel, *Deadly Embrace*, Washington, DC: Brookings Institution Press, 2011, 39.
13 Lamb, *Waiting for Allah*, op. cit., 240.
14 Ibid., 238–239.
15 Tomsen, *Wars of Afghanistan*, op. cit., 332; A. Rashid, *Taliban: Militant Islam, Oil and Fundamentalism in Central Asia*, New Haven: Yale University Press, 2000, 89.
16 Tomsen, *Wars of Afghanistan*, op. cit., 332–333.
17 Ibid., 333.
18 Coll, *Ghost Wars*, op. cit., 182.
19 Quoted in Tomsen, *Wars of Afghanistan*, op. cit., 333.
20 Coll, *Ghost Wars*, op. cit., 212.
21 Rashid, *Taliban*, op. cit., 198.
22 Coll, *Ghost Wars*, op. cit., 212; Tomsen, *Wars of Afghanistan*, op. cit., 361–362; Lamb, *Waiting for Allah*, op. cit., 255.
23 Tomsen, *Wars of Afghanistan*, op. cit., 402–404.
24 Ibid., 435.
25 I. Gul, *The Unholy Nexus*, Lahore: Vanguard, 2002, 15–16; R. Khan, "Babarnama: Interview with Naseerullah Babar," *The News*, 18 Feb 2007; www.qissa-khwani.com/2013/12/babarnama-interview-with-naseerullah.html [accessed 10/12/14].
26 H. Haqqani, *Pakistan: Between Mosque and Military*, Washington, DC: Carnegie Endowment, 2005, 227; Coll, *Ghost Wars*, op. cit., 235.
27 Tomsen, *Wars of Afghanistan*, op. cit., 489–490.
28 Ibid., 479–480, 487, 491.
29 Ibid., 489–491.
30 Coll, *Ghost Wars*, op. cit., 292.
31 Ibid., 282; Tomsen, *Wars of Afghanistan*, op. cit., 313; J.R. Schmidt, *The Unraveling: Pakistan in the Age of Jihad*, New York: Farrar, Straus and Giroux, 2011, 103.
32 Rashid, *Taliban*, op. cit., 26–29, 45–46
33 Cable from Amconsul Peshawar, "New Fighting and New forces in Kandahar," 3 November 1994, no. 01030, http://nsarchive.gwu.edu/NSAEBB/NSAEBB97/tal1.pdf [accessed 2/6/10]; C. Lamb, "The Taliban Will 'Never be Defeated,'" *The Sunday Times*, 7 June 2009.
34 A. Davis, "How the Taliban Became a Military Force" in W. Malley, ed., *Fundamentalism Reborn?* New York: New York University Press, 1998, 44; Tomsen, *Wars of Afghanistan*, 532–533; A. Rashid, "Pakistan and the Taliban," in Malley, *Fundamentalism Reborn?* op. cit. 75–76.
35 Quoted in Rashid, *Taliban*, op. cit., 91.
36 Gul, *Unholy Nexus*, op. cit., 134–137; Steve LeVine, "Helping Hand," *Newsweek*, 13 October 1997.
37 Gul, *Unholy Nexus*, op. cit., 136–139.
38 Ibid., 136–139; I. Gul, *The Most Dangerous Place*, New York: Viking, 2010, 149.
39 Davis, "How the Taliban Became a Military Force," op. cit., 49–50; Cable from Amembassy Islamabad, "Subject [Excised] believe Pakistan is backing Taliban,"

no. 011584, 6 December 1994, http://nsarchive.gwu.edu/NSAEBB/NSAEBB97/tal5.pdf [accessed 2/6/10].

40 Quoted in Coll, *Ghost Wars*, op. cit., 612n26.

41 Tomsen, *Wars of Afghanistan*, op. cit., 535; Cable from Amconsul Peshawar, "New Fighting and New Forces," op. cit.

42 K. Matinuddin, *The Taliban Phenomenon: Afghanistan, 1994–1997*, Karachi: OUP, 1999, 63–66; A.S. Zaeef, *My Life with the Taliban*, ed. Alex Strick van Linschoten and Felix Kuehn, New York: Columbia University Press, 2010, 273n15; Tomsen, *Wars of Afghanistan*, op. cit., 536.

43 Davis, "How the Taliban Became a Military Force," op. cit., 47–48; Gul, *Unholy Nexus*, op. cit., 17–18, 136–139, 277; Tomsen, *Wars of Afghanistan*, op. cit., 536.

44 Matinuddin, *Taliban Phenomenon*, op. cit., 62; M.A. Zahab and O. Roy, *Islamist Networks: The Afghan-Pakistan Connection*, New York: CUP, 2006, 55n3; Davis, "How the Taliban Became a Military Force," op. cit., 49; Rashid, *Taliban*, op. cit., 28–29; Z. Hussain, *Frontline: The Struggle with Militant Islam*, New York: Columbia University Press, 2007, 29.

45 Tomsen, *Wars of Afghanistan*, op. cit., 522.

46 Coll, *Ghost Wars*, op. cit., 292.

47 Quoted in Ibid., 292–293.

48 Ibid.; Schmidt, *Unraveling*, op. cit., 103.

49 Rashid, "Pakistan and the Taliban," op. cit., 86.

50 Ibid., 78; Davis, "How the Taliban Became a Military Force," op. cit., 61.

51 Davis, "How the Taliban Became a Military Force," op. cit., 53–54.

52 D. Frantz, "Pakistan Ended Aid to Taliban Only Reluctantly," *NYT*, 8 December 2001, www.nytimes.com/2001/12/08/world/nation-challenged-supplying-taliban-Pakistan-ended-aid-taliban-only-hesitantly.html [accessed 30/7/15].

53 Coll, *Ghost Wars*, op. cit., 331.

54 Tomsen, *Wars of Afghanistan*, op. cit., 541, 790n72; Gul, *Unholy Nexus*, op. cit., 18–19.

55 Zaeef, *My Life*, op. cit., 124–125.

56 P.C. Joshi, *Main Intelligence Outfits of Pakistan*, New Delhi: Anmol Publications, 2008, 216; Talk Back with Wajahat Khan, "Interview with Lieutenant General (Retd) Hamid Gul," www.youtube.com/watch?v=U1PCeSiMjAo [accessed 15/1/15].

57 G.A. Khan, *Glimpses into the Corridors of Power*, Karachi: OUP, 2007, 289; Coll, *Ghost Wars*, op. cit. 349.

58 Frantz, "Pakistan Ended Aid," op. cit.; Coll, *Ghost Wars*, op. cit., 429.

59 Davis, "How the Taliban Became a Military Force," op. cit., 68–69.

60 Telegram from Secretary of State, "Pak Foreign Minister Asks U.S. Cooperation on Afghanistan," 21 February 1996, no. 034053, http://nsarchive.gwu.edu/NSAEBB/NSAEBB97/tal13.pdf [accessed 2/6/10].

61 Cable from Amembassy Islamabad, "Scenesetter for your visit to Islamabad: Afghan angle," 16 January 1997, no. 436, http://nsarchive.gwu.edu/NSAEBB/NSAEBB97/tal21.pdf [accessed 2/6/10].

62 Gul, *Unholy Nexus*, op. cit., 31–32.

63 Abbas, *Pakistan's Drift*, op. cit., 195.

64 Coll, *Ghost Wars*, op. cit., 365.

65 Zaeef, *My Life*, op. cit., 125–126.

66 Ibid., 124–125.

67 Ibid.

15 ISI and Osama Bin Laden

11 September 2001 must have been the epitome of a bad day for Lieutenant General Mahmud Ahmed, Director General of Pakistan's ISID. First of all, he wasn't at home but abroad, in Washington, DC, no less, where it seemed as if US officials never tired of badgering him about his government's support for the Taliban. But then things got worse – much worse. That morning he was having breakfast with some US politicians when he learned that al-Qa'ida-hijacked planes had slammed into both of the World Trade Center towers and the Pentagon. A fourth plane was apparently heading for Washington when it plowed into the Pennsylvania countryside. He must have known that the relationship between his agency and the CIA had changed dramatically and that this change was not necessarily going to be good.

ISI and al-Qa'ida

The historical irony is that the US government probably would have tolerated a Taliban regime in Afghanistan were it not for Osama Bin Laden. Up until the 1998 al-Qa'ida bombings of two US embassies in East Africa, the Clinton Administration was willing to facilitate negotiations with the Taliban on an oil pipeline from Turkmenistan to Pakistan and ignore the group's human rights abuses.[1] But al-Qa'ida terror "spectaculars" of the late 1990s created insurmountable difficulties for those in the State Department backing engagement because the Taliban repeatedly rebuffed US demands to hand over Bin Laden. By 2000, Afghanistan was a pariah state despite ISI's efforts to obtain international recognition for it.

As Bin Laden gained notoriety for the embassy bombings and the October 2000 attack on the USS *Cole* in Yemen, some questioned Pakistan's links to the "terror mastermind." What did ISI know about him? To what extent had ISI cooperated with Bin Laden in the past? Was such cooperation still ongoing? How much did ISI's "Kashmiri" clients rely on Bin Laden for training courses inside Afghanistan? These were questions Washington hesitated to address publicly because doing so might have forced the State Department to make tough policy decisions including putting Pakistan on the US list of terrorism sponsors and cutting off US aid.[2]

Obviously there is a major difference between contacts with an unsavory individual like Bin Laden and providing him with assistance or guidance. Pakistani officials constantly raised this point when allegations of ISI–Bin Laden contacts arose. Historically, there is no reason to doubt that ISI was aware of Bin Laden back in the early 1980s, when he worked for Abdullah Azzam's *Maktab al-Khidamat* (Office of Services) in Peshawar. Bin Laden was a young, wealthy and fervent jihadi willing to spend some of his wealth on the Afghan jihad. He forged links to several of the Afghan Islamists close to ISI such as Hekmatyar, Abd al-Rasul Sayyaf, Yunus Khalis and Jalaleddin Haqqani. In fact, Osama Bin Laden's agenda closely matched that of Pakistan's "jihadi ISI directors" such as Hamid Gul, Javed Nasir and Mahmud Ahmed: all agreed that sanctioned religious violence (jihad) was justified in establishing Islamic states in Afghanistan, Chechnya, Xinjiang, Palestine, the Philippines and other areas.[3]

When Osama Bin Laden was expelled from Sudan in 1996, he returned to familiar turf in eastern Afghanistan, where ISI facilitated a meeting for him with the local Nangarhar Shura.[4] But shortly after Bin Laden's arrival in Jalalabad, the city fell to the Taliban, and he quickly allied his al-Qa'ida terrorist organization with Mullah Omar. It was Bin Laden and the Taliban together who took over Gulbuddin Hekmatyar's militant training camps in eastern Afghanistan so that ISI's Kashmir jihad would not be disrupted. Indeed, Bin Laden helped ISI train militants from various groups ostensibly formed to fight India in Kashmir such as *Harakatul Mujahidin, Lashkar-e-Taiba*, and *Jaish-e-Mohamed*.[5] Al-Qa'ida also fought alongside the Taliban during the late 1990s against the anti-Taliban resistance – the so-called Northern Alliance. Its fighters earned a reputation for a fanaticism that was rare among Afghans up to that point.[6]

The Taliban's offensives against the Northern Alliance were facilitated by Pakistani SSG men, who were embedded with Taliban units and provided combat experience and advice. Regular Pakistani army officers also assisted with artillery, armor, communications and logistics.[7] Stage-managing all of this was ISI's Afghan Bureau in Rawalpindi, the ISI Station in Kabul, and senior ISI advisors in the Kabul and Kandahar Shuras. Human Rights Watch, for one, harbored no doubts about who masterminded the Taliban's final victory drives:

> Official denials notwithstanding, Pakistan has provided the Taliban with military advisors and logistical support during key battles, has bankrolled the Taliban, has facilitated transshipment of arms, ammunition, and fuel through its territory, and has openly encouraged the recruitment of Pakistanis to fight for the Taliban.[8]

Yet even when the ISI–Taliban alliance was on the cusp of final victory over the Afghan resistance, al-Qa'ida was creating problems for ISI in Washington. CIA assessments detailed a complicated web of individuals and groups clustered around Bin Laden, including the Taliban, Kashmiri extremists, Pakistani sectarian militias, and the ISI. There were at least eight camps run by ISI and staffed by current or retired ISI officers in Afghanistan. The CIA determined that ISI officers "above the Colonel level" (ISI never seemed to suffer from a shortage of brigadiers) met Bin Laden, primarily to negotiate access for "overflow" Kashmiris who couldn't be trained in ISI camps. Even so, CIA analysts cautioned, there was no evidence of ISI "operational support" for al-Qa'ida.[9]

ISI's snatch team

ISI's extensive if discreet contacts with al-Qa'ida at multiple levels convinced some US officials that the road to capturing Bin Laden ran through Islamabad: either it could serve as intermediary between the US and the Taliban for Bin Laden's handover or it could aid a US mission to capture Bin Laden. Prime Minister Nawaz Sharif and his DGISI, Ziauddin Butt, were apparently willing to consider these options provided they did not jeopardize the all-important ISI–Taliban alliance. It was with this context in mind that Sharif and Ziauddin met President Clinton privately in December 1998 during a visit to Washington, and proposed that an ISI-trained team snatch the al-Qa'ida leader if the US could provide his whereabouts.[10] But pinpointing Bin Laden's location in Afghanistan was the crux of the matter. The CIA tried using the liaison channel to obtain ISI information on the al-Qa'ida leader, but the Pakistanis insisted they had nothing of importance on him. Bin Laden didn't trust ISI, the Pakistani argument went, so ISI lacked access to him and his inner circle.[11] Still, in September 1999, DGISI Ziauddin was back in Washington for a new round of talks with the CIA Counterterrorism Center and State Department. The Bin Laden snatch team of retired SSG soldiers was ready to go, he said, if the US could provide the Saudi's location. The CIA turned this around by asking ISI to pressure the Taliban to hand over the fugitive.[12]

On 7 October, DGISI Ziauddin met Mullah Omar in Kandahar, and requested that the Taliban surrender members of the fanatical Pakistani anti-Shi'a group, *Sepah-e-Sahaba Pakistan* hiding out in Afghanistan. Mullah Omar seemed amenable to this, but he rejected any suggestion that he hand over Bin Laden to American justice.[13] Ziauddin subsequently narrated part of this discussion to Nawaz Sharif:

OMAR: 'He [OBL] is like a bone stuck in my throat. I can't swallow it nor can I get it out!'

ZIAUDDIN: 'Is it a question of money?'

OMAR: 'He hasn't given me even one Rupee!'

ZIAUDDIN: 'Would you be willing to countenance a trial of Bin Laden with four judges from Saudi Arabia, Pakistan, Afghanistan, and another Muslim state still to be determined?'[14]

Mehmud Ahmed

Mullah Omar rejected the Muslim jurists option too. In any case, all hopes for Ziauddin's commando team ended in October 1999 when Nawaz Sharif was ousted in a coup. The new DGISI, Mehmud Ahmed turned out to be a strong supporter of the Taliban, who had rediscovered Islam and become something of a "born again" Muslim; however, it was difficult for US officials to gauge this side of his personality because he didn't grow a beard nor did his wife wear a veil.[15]

In April 2000, DGISI Ahmed went to the US for an official meet-and-greet with the DCI, George Tenet. Picking up on Ahmed's interest in US Civil War history – he had written his staff officer's thesis on the Battle of Gettysburg – the CIA took him to the battlefield where a US Army War College professor served as his personal guide. This was a savvy move on CIA's part: in the words of one participant, Ahmed "came alive and talked animatedly about battle tactics, personalities, and the fateful turning points of the American Civil War."[16] But the American message to Mahmud was a mixed one, for even though CIA capably wooed him at Langley and Gettysburg, Thomas Pickering at the State Department played bad cop by criticizing ISI for its support of the Taliban.[17]

The American Civil War interest and his outwardly secular appearance aside, Ahmed had no intention of becoming a friendly US liaison partner. He fervently believed that the Taliban represented Afghanistan's best hope for the future. Indeed, it became apparent that he dealt with the CIA on sufferance: a dirty job that nonetheless had to be carried out for appearances' sake.[18] With the CIA–ISI relationship frozen for the moment, George Tenet flew to Islamabad in spring 2001 to try and break down the walls between the two agencies. He pleaded for ISI's help in penetrating al-Qa'ida, insisting the Pakistanis could do more because of their contacts inside the international jihadi movement and close ties with the Taliban. DGISI Ahmed responded with meaningless platitudes and the saccharine vows of "partnership," "friendship," and "fruitful talks."[19] DGISI Ahmed ended up serving as a courier of American messages to the Taliban leadership, but he did so reluctantly, and some doubt whether he really urged Mullah Omar to surrender Bin Laden.[20] According to one account, the DGISI's meetings with Mullah Omar went poorly, with the Taliban leader accusing Ahmed of being [President George W.] Bush's "errand boy." "You want to please the Americans," Omar continued, "and I want to please God."[21]

The DGISI was in an awkward position from both a personal and professional standpoint. He was implementing his government's policy, which was to help the Taliban seize control of Afghanistan, and use that country as "strategic depth" from which to escalate ISI's proxy war against India. But American policy was to capture Bin Laden via ISI's extensive links to the Taliban, and for a number of reasons, Islamabad simply could not say "no" to Washington. As for Ahmed's personal beliefs, it was obvious that he backed the Taliban in their cause to Islamize Afghanistan, yet, at the same time, he had to put up with American accusations and threats with a straight face for his country's higher interests. No wonder he found all this difficult to reconcile.

Kandahar hijacking

The network of ties linking ISI, the Taliban, al-Qa'ida, and Kashmiri jihadis came to light when Indian Airlines Flight 814 was hijacked on 24 December 1999 en route to New Delhi from Kathmandu. On board were 149 passengers, including five *Harakatul Mujahidin* hijackers, who led the plane on a circuitous journey from Amritsar to Lahore and then on to the United Arab Emirates before arriving in Kandahar on Christmas Day, where they were greeted by "Colonel Gul," head of ISI's Quetta Detachment. Gul spoke to the hijackers shortly after the plane taxied to a halt, then ordered food packages sent to them; buried in these were additional guns and ammunition. Two other unidentified ISI officers joined Gul in mediating between the hijackers and the Indian authorities because the hijackers were demanding the release of militants from Indian prisons. Among these were Masood Azhar and Ahmed Omar Sheikh, both previously involved in ISI's Kashmir program.[22]

On 1 January 2000, India caved to the hijackers' demands and handed over the militants to ISI custody while the hijackers released the hostages. Later it was alleged that Osama Bin Laden feted the hijackers at his compound in Kandahar. ISI's role in the hijacking generated a flurry of rumors that were promptly denied by Islamabad and, curiously enough, by the U.S. State Department too. The line out of Washington was that the US government did "not have reason to believe that the government of Pakistan had foreknowledge, supported or helped carry out this terrorist hijacking."[23] President Clinton reiterated this position three weeks later in a press conference. For its part, New Delhi harbored no doubts about the perpetrators, and shared its findings with the US. It alleged that ISI's Kathmandu Station supplied the hijackers with the weapons used to take over the aircraft. While the plane waited on the Kandahar runway, the Indians reportedly intercepted communications from the hijackers to ISI HQ asking for additional instructions.[24]

One of those exchanged for the hostages was a prominent Pakistani jihadi named Masood Azhar, who returned to his homeland as a national hero. The government not only refrained from restricting his movements, it also let him travel across country drumming up support for the anti-India jihad. On 30 January, he announced the formation of yet another jihadi group for Kashmir's wretched war, the *Jaish-e-Mohamed* (Army of Mohammed) (JeM), which was more virulent than any of its predecessors. ISI undoubtedly had a hand in forming JeM because the Kashmir jihad was lagging, and Azhar's new group could give it a badly needed boost. JeM was indeed more brazen in carrying out operations against India, including attacks on the Srinagar State Assembly in October 2001 and the Indian parliament two months later. Like HuM or *Lashkar-e Taiba*, JeM was only nominally "Kashmiri" since its rank-and-file tended to be comprised of Punjabis and Pashtuns.[25]

The end of an era

On the eve of 9/11, ISI knew more about al-Qa'ida than it was willing to share with the CIA thanks to its numerous sources inside Afghanistan, not the least of which was the Taliban itself. As noted, during the 1990s, ISI officers coordinated Kashmiri militant training with al-Qa'ida when ISI lacked facilities to handle the overflow. In addition, ISI officers must have worked with al-Qa'ida to plan and coordinate operations in northern Afghanistan in the late 1990s against the resistance. All that being said, it is highly unlikely that Bin Laden and his lieutenants were ever willing to take ISI guidance – if it were indeed offered, because Bin Laden had his own money and his own agenda. He undoubtedly mistrusted ISI for its double talk, its tendency to play all sides of the game, and ISI's well-known ties to the CIA. There was no trust in this relationship only a few shared objectives, but the riddle of how he ended up in Abbottabad remains.

On 9 September 2001, the anti-Taliban resistance leader Ahmed Shah Massoud was assassinated when a bomb placed inside a journalist's camera exploded during a press interview. The "journalists" were Arabs recruited by al-Qa'ida with the specific objective of killing the one figure capable of keeping the anti-Taliban resistance afloat.[26] With Massoud out of the picture, ISI officers could rejoice that a long-standing thorn in their side had been finally removed. The road to Taliban victory seemed wide open.

DGISI Mahmud and 9/11

On 11 September 2001, the long-anticipated and much-feared big attack by al-Qa'ida took place when four hijacked passenger jets crashed into the World Trade Center, the Pentagon and a Pennsylvania farm field. With nearly 3,000 people killed, the US was instantly on a war footing, and the Taliban's lease on power in Afghanistan had less than 90 days left. The pro-Taliban DGISI, Mahmud Ahmed happened to be in Washington carrying out a ten day official visit to the CIA, the State Department, the NSC and Capitol Hill. On 9 September, he found himself again on the defensive as he tried defending the Taliban against CIA accusations of harboring al-Qa'ida. The DGISI pleaded for Mullah Omar, whom he described as a "pious and peaceful man." As George Tenet wrote later, the DGISI was stubborn and inflexible:

> As gracious as he could be over the lunch table, the guy was immovable when it came to the Taliban and al-Qa'ida. And bloodless too. After the USS Cole was attacked by Bin Laden's suicide bombers, Mahmood sent

our senior officer in Islamabad a very precisely worded message that conveyed his condolences for the loss of life without offering a single word of support for our going after al-Qaida in its Afghan lair.[27]

The DGISI could barely conceal his disdain for the whole process. His only recommendation to the CIA was to try bribing the Taliban into handing over Bin Laden, but even then, he added, ISI would not facilitate such a transaction. If the US lifted sanctions imposed on Pakistan after the May 1998 nuclear tests, then ISI would be willing to pressure the Taliban on Bin Laden. It was a simple take-it-or-leave-it deal.[28]

On the morning of 11 September, the DGISI was having breakfast at the US Capitol with Senator Bob Graham, Chairman of the Senate Select Committee for Intelligence (SSCI), Senator Jon Kyle, also of the SSCI, and Representative Porter Goss, Chairman of the House Permanent Select Committee on Intelligence. The breakfast was a reciprocal gesture for a "nighttime tribal feast" that Mahmud Ahmed had hosted for the Americans at ISI HQ just two weeks earlier. The DGISI was still spinning a soft line on Mullah Omar, arguing that the Taliban "emir" was not as bad as portrayed by the media. He also dangled the possibility that Mullah Omar might get rid of Bin Laden if the right incentives were offered. At that point, a SSCI aide informed the gathering that one of the two World Trade Center towers had just been hit by an airplane. Upon receiving word of the second tower being struck by another airliner, the breakfast meeting broke up, and the DGISI returned to his Georgetown hotel, where he could see the smoke billowing into the sky from the burning Pentagon.[29]

The following day, DGISI Mahmud and the Pakistani Ambassador to Washington met Deputy Secretary of State Richard Armitage at the State Department. General Ahmed offered the condolences of his government, adding that President Musharraf had asked him to stay longer than planned to aid the Americans in any way that he could. But it turned out to be a difficult meeting for the Pakistanis. Ahmed later described Armitage to historian Shuja Nawaz as a "big hulking bully" who was clearly showing "anger, frustration, and resentment." The former naval officer had dispensed with diplomatic niceties: the Pakistanis had a simple choice to make, he said, they were either with the Americans or they weren't; there were no gray areas. Ahmed retorted that both sides had to get past the "myth" that the Pakistani government was "in bed" with anti-US militants. Pakistanis were adamantly against terrorism, he insisted. The events of 9/11 were a "crime against humanity."[30]

The DGISI's Via Dolorosa wasn't over yet, though. The next stop was the CIA, where DCI Tenet reiterated that if the Taliban continued sheltering al-Qa'ida, then it was "going to pay a terrible price." Even now, Ahmed pleaded for the Taliban, which, although it may have demonstrated Pakistani "steadfastness" of a sort, nonetheless egregiously irritated the Americans who needed no further provocation at this point. Later,

Mahmud was to liken the US public reaction to 9/11 to a "wounded animal," but this understanding apparently wasn't being expressed in meetings with US officials at the time.[31]

On 13 September, the DGISI had a second meeting with Armitage, during which the American passed a list of demands that included granting the US "blanket over flight and landing rights," access to Pakistani facilities, intelligence that would "help prevent" future terrorist attacks, and cutting off "all logistical support for Bin Laden" and the Taliban. Once again Ahmed insisted that Pakistan would side with the US against "non-Muslim behavior;" however, with a little chutzpah, he urged the US take measures to protect Pakistani nationals in the United States.[32]

Revisiting the Taliban option

With unfortunate consequences for the future, the Pakistanis emerged from these meetings apparently convinced that the US was focused only on al-Qa'ida and quite willing to ignore the Taliban except where al-Qa'ida was concerned. Therefore, ISI officials reasoned, while they would aid the Americans against Bin Laden, their cooperation was not required when it came to the Taliban. As for US officials, either they were willing to let the Taliban go at this point while they tackled the greater al-Qa'ida threat or they did not see the Taliban as much of a military threat. One US official later conceded that the Taliban was regarded by Washington as something of a "spent force."[33] It is here that we see the differences in national perspectives. Whereas the US focused on the immediate objective of defeating al-Qa'ida, Pakistan looked to its long-term goals, which included a pro-Pakistan regime in Afghanistan and the use of that country as strategic depth against India. Pakistan's stance on the Taliban did not change as a result of 9/11 nor did it alter course later. This would create serious misunderstandings in the future between Pakistan and the US.[34] As Islamabad Station Chief, Robert Grenier, put it in his memoirs:

> We would see the occasional report to indicate that members of the Taliban shura were pitching up in Karachi, and we sought ISI help in investigating these leads. Somehow, though, the effectiveness which characterized ISI's pursuit of al-Qa'ida did not apply where the Taliban was concerned.[35]

Not long after 9/11, the Taliban ambassador to Pakistan, Mullah Zaeef, was visited by the ISI leadership at his Islamabad residence. According to Zaeef, the DGISI started the meeting by noting reports of a Taliban plot to assassinate Musharraf and warned of the consequences if the Taliban pursued this. At the same time, Mahmud Ahmed emphasized that the Pakistani government would not abandon the Taliban in its fight with the Americans. This was Zaeef's take on the meeting:

When I looked at General Mahmud, tears were running down his face. [DDGISI] Jailani was crying loud with his arms around my neck like a woman. I was puzzled by their reaction. A few moments later they excused themselves and left.[36]

DGISI Mahmud did not limit his meetings to the Taliban ambassador. On 17 September, barely two days after returning from the United States on a CIA jet, he went to Kandahar for talks with the Taliban leadership. Ostensibly, Mahmud's goals were to convince Mullah Omar to hand over Bin Laden and open up al-Qa'ida camps to international inspectors.[37] Yet, as Mullah Zaeef's recollections demonstrate, the ISI chief had no intention of threatening the Taliban, and several accounts report that Mahmud told Mullah Omar to resist the American demands. According to Mullah Mohamed Khaksar, Taliban Deputy Interior Minister at the time, the DGISI urged the Taliban to hide Bin Laden and that ISI would aid them in doing so.[38] In a later interview with Shuja Nawaz, Ahmed declared that his objective was in fact to thwart American military action against the Taliban. "I am a Muslim," he told his interviewer, "why would I go against another Muslim?"[39]

Upon his return from Kandahar, the DGISI pleaded with the Americans for more time. He believed Mullah Omar might still be persuaded to hand over Bin Laden, but further meetings would be necessary. US Ambassador Wendy Chamberlin replied that Washington would not alter its military planning to accommodate the DGISI's ongoing – and disappointing – dialogue with the Taliban. According to the official US transcript of the exchange, Mahmud urged the US government "not to act in anger" and that "real victory will come in negotiations." In Pakistan's view, the DGISI continued, it would be better for all concerned if the Taliban ousted al-Qa'ida instead of the "brute force" approach taken by the Americans. "We will not flinch from a military effort, but a strike will produce thousands of frustrated young Muslim men," he warned. "It will be an incubator of anger that will explode two or three years from now."[40]

28 September found DGISI Ahmed back in Kandahar for another meeting with the Taliban leadership, only this time he brought eight Islamic scholars and judges from Deobandist madrassas in Pakistan. Again, the purpose of his visit was to convince Mullah Omar to hand over Bin Laden to the US and avoid an American invasion of Afghanistan. Accounts vary on what really occurred during this crucial meeting.[41] According to one, Mufti Niazmuddin Shamzai, head of the hardline Binori Town madrassa in Karachi, told Mullah Omar to declare a jihad if the US attacked the Taliban.[42] According to another, the DGISI told Mullah Omar to resist American pressure.[43] Whatever really took place in Kandahar, Mahmud Ahmed afterwards informed the US Ambassador that the Taliban were inflexible on surrendering Bin Laden to justice.[44]

While these dilatory talks took place in Kandahar, the US was gearing up for war against the Taliban. As numerous memoirs of US officials during this era attest, the prevailing mood in Washington was fear, with many anticipating another big terrorist attack. It is with this context in mind that we can better understand the next recorded meeting between American diplomats and DGISI Mahmud. The US Ambassador had been instructed to pass a message to the DGISI for onward delivery to Mullah Omar. The message noted that information of more al-Qa'ida attacks was circulating while the Taliban still refused to hand over any al-Qa'ida leaders or shut down terrorist training camps. The sting was in the tail, however, as the message concluded:

> We will hold leaders of the Taliban personally responsible for any such actions. Every pillar of the Taliban regime will be destroyed.[45]

The DGISI must go

In the lead-up to the US-led Operation ENDURING FREEDOM, there must have been intense behind-the-scenes wrangling between the Americans and the Pakistanis that was reported at a more restricted classification level than has been declassified so far. Undoubtedly, one of the more contentious topics was American insistence that DGISI Mahmud Ahmed had to go since he had been demonstrably hesitant to cooperate with the US against the Taliban. It is also possible that the US intelligence community had learned more details of Ahmed's duplicity during his two visits to Kandahar. This put Musharraf in a bind. The US was pressuring him to get on board their war on terror and remove pro-Taliban allies like the DGISI from their posts in his government; however, the DGISI had been a valuable Musharraf ally during the 1999 coup. In the end, the president settled for a face-saving piece of trickery. On 8 October, he promoted Lieutenant General Mohamed Aziz Khan to the four-star post as Chairman of the Joint Chiefs of Staff Committee (CJCSC). He did so with the full knowledge that this appointment would force Mahmud Ahmed into retirement because the unwanted DGISI was senior in rank to Aziz Khan and had been superseded. That is what happened.[46] The new ISI chief, Ehsan ul-Haq, was a Pashtun from the NWFP, who had served as DGMI at the time of the 1999 coup. Described by one journalist as "dapper and suave," Ehsan maintained a lower profile than Mahmud and tried to preserve the fraying relationship with the CIA.[47]

Although they could not express this publicly, ISI's foreign liaison partners must have been quietly relieved that Mahmud was gone. In addition, rumors floating around the cocktail circuit were quite positive about Ehsan ul-Haq. The army wanted to restructure ISI, it was said, and prevent unspecified "independent operations." Twenty-five percent of ISI officers were to be purged, including "dozens" with Taliban sympathies. The ISI Afghan Bureau was to be improbably shut down while its Kashmir counterpart would be downsized. In retrospect, all of this "winds of change" talk was little more than old wine in new bottles.[48] ISI did not fundamentally change under Ehsan ul-Haq because Pakistan's goals and strategies regarding Afghanistan remained unaltered. The DGISI wasn't going to challenge these, nor would he be given the authority to do so. In brief, his job was to present a "moderate" face to the West.

Searching for a new government

The US-led air operation against the Taliban commenced on 17 October. Now that the bombs were falling and the Americans clearly meant business, Islamabad switched gears in a bid to salvage what remained of its Afghan interests. The new policy embraced the idea of so-called moderate Taliban supposedly willing to negotiate a power-sharing arrangement. In their meetings with US officials, the Pakistanis emphasized the negative things that would ensue if the "war lords" and "drug lords" of the Northern Alliance were allowed to take power again in Kabul. They warned that the lack of Pashtuns in the Northern Alliance was a sure recipe for renewed civil war. This implied that only the Taliban represented the Pashtuns, and therefore they should be given a share of power in the new Afghan government.[49]

ISI's proposals for a future Afghan government created fissures within the CIA. The Station Chief in Islamabad, Robert Grenier, argued that the Pakistanis had an undeniable role to play in Afghanistan so it would be wiser to include them in the discussions rather than leave them embittered and angry on the margins. Grenier noted how Musharraf had removed the "religiously conservative director general" of ISI indicating Islamabad was clearly moving in the right direction. Grenier recommended that US air operations focus on southern Afghanistan and leave the north alone until Pakistan's moderate Taliban option could be fleshed out. In his view, there was no sense permitting the Northern Alliance to reenter Kabul and reopen the old ethnic and sectarian wounds of the early 1990s.[50] Other CIA players contested Grenier's advice. Gary Schroen, the CIA officer who led the first US post-9/11 team into the Panjsher Valley, recorded his disagreement in his memoir, *First In*:

> I read that message [from Grenier] with total dismay. It was a blueprint for failure and political confusion. This push to allow the Pakistanis back into the Afghan game was disturbing and a real mistake. They had their own specific agenda for the country, and it did not track with anything the U.S. Government would want to see emerge there.[51]

CIA's Counterterrorism Center (CTC) wanted the US to back the Northern Alliance, push the Taliban out of Kabul and defeat them in the rest of the country. Some CTC analysts and operators felt that Islamabad Station had been afflicted by "clientitis" at the hands of their ISI liaison partners. These conflicts would reemerge time and again over the next decade.[52]

As for ISI, it had to execute two essential tasks in a time urgent manner. The first of these was to stall for time, ward off further US military action and try to salvage what was left of Pakistan's position in Afghanistan. The second imperative was cobbling together a "Taliban light" government composed of some token Taliban "moderates" and tribal commanders like Jalaleddin Haqqani.[53] Haqqani was an old ISI ally from the 1970s, when he was part of that group of Islamists recruited, trained and armed to fight against the Afghan leader, Daoud Khan. In the 1990s, he had served as a Taliban cabinet minister, although he was never part of Mullah Omar's inner circle. The DGISI met Haqqani in Islamabad and asked whether he would be willing to serve in a new, moderate Taliban government. Haqqani refused, saying that the US was no less an occupier in Afghanistan that the Soviets were. The Americans would never be able to control the Afghan countryside, he reasoned, "so we will go to the mountains and we will resist, just like we did against the Soviet Union."[54]

ISI's attempt to stall for time and put together a Taliban government "with a human face" failed mainly because the CIA found its southern Pashtun option in two men: Hamid Karzai and Gul Agha Shirzai. The former, who was from a prominent tribal family, was trying to spark an anti-Taliban rebellion in Uruzgan. As soon as ISI caught wind of Karzai's initiative, it tried to poison the well by informing the CIA that Karzai lacked credibility. The second of the southern Pashtun leaders was Gul Agha Shirzai, a notoriously corrupt former Kandahar governor who lived in Pakistan during Taliban rule. After 9/11, Shirzai assembled a tribal force that would help put him back in power.[55]

Throughout the rest of November, Pakistan's spy masters witnessed the accelerating collapse of their position as city after city was liberated, and the forces of Karzai and Shirzai closed in on Kandahar, the Taliban's last redoubt. All of this was disturbing enough, but another crisis at ISI HQ concerned the fate of Pakistani officials, Taliban commanders and foreign fighters who were surrounded by the Northern Alliance in the city of Kunduz. Among the Pakistanis were ISI advisors, SSG commandos, Frontier Corps soldiers, and armor and artillery specialists. Pakistan wanted to evacuate its people, so Islamabad made a deal with Washington at the highest levels. On 18 November, Musharraf called either President George W. Bush or Vice President Dick Cheney stating that he wanted to extract Pakistani officials from the Kunduz pocket. Obviously, from Pakistan's viewpoint, it would be most humiliating if the Northern Alliance captured ISI, SSG and other army officers since Islamabad had been denying for years that any Pakistani military personnel were serving inside Afghanistan. Consequently, Pakistani transport planes ferried out Pakistani officials; but it wasn't just Pakistanis. The planes also carried out some al-Qa'ida and parts of the Taliban's Northern Command.[56]

The end game was played out on 6 December, when Kandahar fell to Shirzai and Karzai's forces. But it wasn't quite the decisive victory that the

US had sought, for most of the surviving Taliban leaders, including the group's leader, Mullah Omar, escaped to Pakistan where they were sheltered by the *Jamiat Ulema-e- Islam* or ISI. Much of the rank-and-file fighters simply hid their weapons and melted back into the civilian population. All the ingredients for renewed insurgency were on hand should ISI give the green light.[57]

Notes

1 A. Rashid, *Taliban: Militant Islam, Oil and Fundamentalism in Central Asia*, New Haven: Yale University Press, 2000, 45–46.
2 P. Tomsen, *The Wars of Afghanistan*, New York: PublicAffairs, 2011, 544, 550; J. Randal, *Osama: The Making of a Terrorist*, New York: Knopf, 2004, 311n40; J. Hammond and S. Siddiqi, "Ex-ISI Chief Says Purpose of New Afghan Intelligence Agency RAMA is to 'destabilize Pakistan,'" *Foreign Policy Journal*, 12 August 2009; D. Filkins, "The Journalist and the Spies," *The New Yorker*, 19 September 2011, www.newyorker.com/magazine/2011/09/19/the-journalist-and-the-spies [accessed 31/7/15]; A. Rashid, *Descent into Chaos*, New York: Viking, 2008, 113; I. Gul, *The Most Dangerous Place*, New York: Viking, 2010, 152; S. Coll, *Ghost Wars*, New York: Penguin, 2004; 410; B. Riedel, *Deadly Embrace*, Washington, DC: Brookings Institution Press, 2011, 51.
3 Coll, *Ghost Wars*, op. cit., 212, 341, 407; Riedel, *Deadly Embrace*, op. cit., 55; Randal, *Osama*, op. cit., 243; Z. Hussain, *Frontline: The Struggle with Militant Islam*, New York: CUP, 2007, 44; G. Schroen, *First In*, New York: Presidio, 2005, 361; Gul, *Dangerous Place*, op. cit., 154–155; Tomsen, *Wars of Afghanistan*, op. cit., 543; Rashid, *Descent into Chaos*, op. cit., 17.
4 Coll, *Ghost Wars*, op. cit., 341.
5 Ibid.; Riedel, *Deadly Embrace*, op. cit., 55; Hussain, *Frontline*, op. cit., 44; Schroen, *First In*, op. cit., 361; Gul, *Dangerous Place*, op. cit., 154–155.
6 Riedel, *Deadly Embrace*, op. cit., 54; Journeyman Pictures "ISI: The Secret Government of Pakistan," www.youtube.com/watch?v=cwwcDGjTXo0 2001 [accessed 26/3/13]; Coll, *Ghost Wars*, op. cit., 531–532; Gul, *Dangerous Place*, op. cit., 152–153; R. Gunaratna, *Inside al-Qaeda*, New York: CUP, 2002, 42–43; A. Rashid, *Jihad: The Rise of Militant Islam in Central Asia*, New Haven: Yale University Press, 2002, 174–175.
7 Human Rights Watch, *Afghanistan: Crisis of Impunity, The Role of Pakistan, Russia and Iran in Fueling the Civil War*, Vol. 13, No. 3, July 2001, www.hrw.org/reports/2001/afghan2/ [accessed 27/11/10]; Gunaratna, *Inside al-Qaeda*, op. cit., 42–43; A. Rashid, *Jihad*, op. cit., 174–175; I. Gul, *Unholy Nexus*, Lahore: Vanguard, 2002, 47–48, 152–153; Coll, *Ghost Wars*, op. cit., 440, 531–532; Cable from Amconsul Peshawar, "Afghanistan: a report of Pakistani military assistance to the Taliban," 24 March 1998, no. 00242, http://nsarchive.gwu.edu/NSAEBB/NSAEBB97/tal25.pdf [1/6/13].
8 Human Rights Watch, *Afghanistan*, op. cit.
9 Coll, *Ghost Wars*, op. cit., 439.
10 Ibid., 442–443.
11 Ibid., 443.
12 Ibid., 477–478.
13 Tomsen, *Wars of Afghanistan*, op. cit., 552; Hussain, *Frontline*, op. cit., 31; A. Jamal, *Shadow War: The Untold Story of Jihad in Kashmir*, Hoboken, NJ: Melville House, 2009, 202.
14 Quoted in S. Nawaz, *Crossed Swords*, Karachi: OUP, 2008, 536–537.

15 T. McGirk, "Has Pakistan Tamed Its Spies?" *CNN*, 6 May 2002, www.cnn.com/ALLPOLITICS/time/2002/05/06/spies.html [accessed 1/8/15]; Coll, *Ghost Wars*, op. cit., 510.

16 Coll, *Ghost Wars*, op. cit., 508; R. Grenier, *88 Days to Kandahar*, New York: Simon & Schuster, 2015, 70.

17 Nawaz, *Crossed Swords*, op. cit., 543; Coll, *Ghost Wars*, op. cit., 509.

18 P. Constable, "Pakistani Agency Seeks to Allay U.S. on Terrorism," *WP*, 15 February 2000, www.washingtonpost.com/archive/politics/2000/02/15/Pakistani-agency-seeks-to-allay-us-on-terrorism/6800570b-84e3-42e4-a6e4-170eb6dea414/; Riedel, *Deadly Embrace*, op. cit., 66.

19 Coll, *Ghost Wars*, op. cit., 551–552.

20 Riedel, *Deadly Embrace*, op. cit., 66.

21 M. Mazzetti, *The Way of the Knife*, New York: Penguin, 2013, 32.

22 Tomsen, *Wars of Afghanistan*, op. cit., 517; Hussain, *Frontline*, op. cit., 61–63; "Editorial: Who Could it Be?" *Daily Times*, 29 December 2003, http://archives.dailytimes.com.pk/editorial/29-Dec-2003/editorial-who-could-it-be [accessed 1/8/15].

23 Quoted in Tomsen, *Wars of Afghanistan*, op. cit., 518.

24 J. Lancaster, "U.S. Pressures Pakistan to Cut Ties with Extremist Groups," *WP*, 26 January 2000, www.washingtonpost.com/archive/politics/2000/01/26/us-pressures-Pakistan-to-cutties-with-extremist-groups/bbbf4c72-6acf-475e-a78c-4aa5161ce98d/ [accessed 1/8/15].

25 A. Rashid, *Descent into Chaos*, New York: Viking, 2008, 114, 220; Hussain, *Frontline*, op. cit., 65; Tomsen, *Wars of Afghanistan*, op. cit., 518.

26 "Taliban Foe Hurt and Aide Killed by Bomb," *NYT*, 10 September 2001, www.nytimes.com/2001/09/10/world/taliban-foe-hurt-and-aide-killed-by-bomb.html [accessed 1/8/15]; J. Burns, "Threats and Responses: Assassination; Afghans Too, Mark a Day of Disaster: A Hero Was Lost," *NYT*, 9 September 2002, www.nytimes.com/2002/09/09/world/threats-responses-assassination-afghans-too-mark-day-disaster-hero-was-lost.html [accessed 1/8/15].

27 G. Tenet, *At the Center of the Storm*, New York: Harper Perennial, 2007, 141–142.

28 Ibid., 142; Rashid, *Descent into Chaos*, op. cit., 26.

29 B. Graham, *Intelligence Matters: The CIA, the FBI, Saudi Arabia and the Failure of America's War on Terror*, New York: Random House, 2004, ix–xi; Nawaz, *Crossed Swords*, op. cit., 145, 539.

30 Cable from SecState, "Subject: Deputy Secretary Armitage's Meeting with Pakistan Intel Chief Mahmud: 'You're either with us or you're not,'" 13 September 2001, no. 157813, http://nsarchive.gwu.edu/NSAEBB/NSAEBB358a/doc03–1.pdf [accessed 1/8/15]; Shuja, *Crossed Swords*, op. cit., 539–540.

31 Tenet, *Center*, op. cit., 180.

32 Cable from SecState, "Subject: Deputy Secretary Armitage's Meeting with General Mahmud: Actions and Support expected of Pakistan in fight against terrorism," 14 September 2011, no. 158711, http://nsarchive.gwu.edu/NSAEBB/NSAEBB358a/doc05.pdf [accessed 1/8/15].

33 S. Jones, *Graveyard of Empires*, New York: W.W. Norton, 2009, 101.

34 A. Rashid, *Pakistan on the Brink*, New York: Viking, 2012, 47.

35 Grenier, *88 Days*, op. cit., 362.

36 A.S. Zaeef, *My Life with the Taliban*, ed. Alex Strick van Linschoten and Felix Kuehn, New York: CUP, 2010, 147–148.

37 Cable from SecState, "Subject: Deputy Secretary Armitage-Mamoud Phone Call – Sept. 18, 2001," no. 161279, http://nsarchive.gwu.edu/NSAEBB/NSAEBB358a/doc09.pdf [accessed 1/8/15].

38 K. Gannon, "Pakistani Intelligence: Friend or Foe?" Associated Press, 11 May 2011; Journeyman, "ISI;" McGirk, "Has Pakistan Tamed its Spies?" op. cit.

39 Quoted in Nawaz, *Crossed Swords*, op. cit., 542–543.
40 Cable from Amembassy Islamabad, "Subject: Mahmud plans 2nd Mission to Afghanistan," 24 September 2001, no. 005337, http://nsarchive.gwu.edu/NSAEBB/NSAEBB358a/doc11.pdf [accessed 1/8/15].
41 Rashid, *Descent into Chaos*, op. cit., 77.
42 H. Abbas, *Pakistan's Drift into Extremism*, Armonk, NY: M.E. Sharpe, 2005, 221.
43 Hussain, *Frontline*, op. cit., 43.
44 Cable from Amembassy Islamabad, "Subject: Mahmud on Failed Kandahar Trip," 29 September 2001, no. 005452, http://nsarchive.gwu.edu/NSAEBB/NSAEBB358a/doc12.pdf [accessed 1/8/15].
45 Cable from SecState, "Subject: Message to Taliban," 7 October 2001, no. 175415, http://nsarchive.gwu.edu/NSAEBB/NSAEBB358a/doc16.pdf [accessed 1/8/15].
46 Grenier, *88 Days*, op. cit., 158–159.
47 M. Mazzetti, *The Way of the Knife*, New York: Penguin, 2013, 33–34, 111; Rashid, *Descent into Chaos*, op. cit., 79; Hussain, *Frontline*, op. cit., 46.
48 Rashid, *Descent into Chaos*, op. cit, 79; S.S. Saleem, "Pearl a Victim of Pakistan's Grim Legacy," *Asia Times Online*, 26 February 2002, www.atimes.com/ind-pak/DB26Df01.html [accessed 1/8/15].
49 Mazzetti, *Way of the Knife*, op. cit. 33; Zaeef, *My Life*, op. cit., 150.
50 Grenier, *88 Days*, op. cit., 186–188; Schroen, *First In*, op. cit., 163–164.
51 Schroen, *First In*, op. cit., 163–164.
52 Mazzetti, *Way of the Knife*, op. cit., 32–33.
53 Zaeef, *My Life*, op. cit., 150; Rashid, *Descent into Chaos*, op. cit., 72–73.
54 Mazzetti, *Way of the Knife*, op. cit., 35–36; Rashid, *Descent into Chaos*, op. cit., 243; J. Warrick, *Triple Agent*, New York: Vintage, 2012, 111–112.
55 Rashid, *Descent into Chaos*, op. cit., 89, 95.
56 Tomsen, *Wars of Afghanistan*, op. cit., 606; A. Rashid, *Jihad: The Rise of Militant Islam in Central Asia*, New Haven: Yale University Press, 2002, 174–175; S. Hersh, *Chain of Command*, New York: HarperCollins, 2004, 128–130, 133; Rashid, *Descent into Chaos*, op. cit., 91; M.A. Zahab and O. Roy, *Islamist Networks: The Afghan-Pakistan Connection*, New York: Columbia University Press, 2006, 55–56; BBC, *Secret Pakistan, Part 1: Double Cross*, 2011.
57 Rashid, *Descent*, 77, 241; Mazzetti, *Way*, 34–35.

Part V

Confrontation

16 Intelligence and Nuclear Weapons in South Asia

In the last two weeks of May 2002, India and Pakistan teetered on the edge of their first general war since 1971. One million soldiers had been mobilized on both sides of the border. Pakistan was conspicuously testing nuclear-capable ballistic missiles. Parts of the Indian Navy were at sea. But this was not going to be a reprise of 1971, because both antagonists possessed nuclear weapons, and there was much talk of their use being proclaimed in shrill polemics. It was Pakistan's relentless use of proxies that had brought these two South Asian giants to the brink. On 14 May, militants belonging to the ISI-linked *Lashkar-e-Taiba* attacked an Indian cantonment in Kashmir, killing 34, most of them wives and children of active duty soldiers. A week later, Indian Prime Minister Atal Bihari Vajpayee visited Kashmir and warned his soldiers that it was "time to fight a decisive battle." Rather than winning in Kashmir, ISI and its jihadi allies were on the brink of destroying Pakistan itself.[1]

Operation PARAKRAM

The Indian government viewed 9/11 with a certain degree of grim satisfaction. After all, had they not been telling the Americans for years that the Pakistanis were up to their necks in terrorism? For New Delhi, America's global war on terrorism was a golden opportunity to neutralize Pakistan's proxy strategy once and for all. For their part, the Pakistanis weren't doing themselves any favors after 9/11. On 1 October 2001, the Kashmiri legislature in Srinagar was attacked by militants belonging to the ISI proxy, *Jaish-e-Mohamed* (JeM), killing 38. On 13 December, a five-man JeM suicide squad attacked the Indian parliament in New Delhi, murdering four before the terrorists themselves were killed. A subsequent Indian investigation determined that the perpetrators were Pakistani citizens. Indian intelligence assessed that JeM took its orders directly from ISI.[2]

So how much did ISI know about the JeM attacks in Srinagar and New Delhi? ISI's links to this group are indisputable, although definite evidence of involvement in either attack was lacking. Moreover, there were some outstanding questions concerning Pakistani motives. Why would Pakistan stoke a conflict with India in the immediate aftermath of 9/11 and the US declaration of war on terrorism? Was the intent to drag the Americans into an Indo-Pakistani war? Was it a bid to get the US involved in Kashmir diplomacy or a sop to angry jihadists who felt that Pakistan had sold them out? If ISI did not know about these attacks, then why did it subsequently do very little to rein in these groups? If Islamabad was behind the attacks, it dangerously misjudged the nature and scale of the Indian response.[3]

Within hours of the New Delhi attack, the Indians activated Operation Parakram, mobilizing some 700,000 soldiers and deploying many of these to forward operating bases on the Pakistani border. Skirmishes escalated sharply along the Kashmir LOC and the Siachen Glacier region. India recalled her ambassador from Islamabad for the first time since 1971, while bus and rail links between the two countries were cut.[4] ISI could not miss the danger signals coming from the Indians, but its analysts still sought more indications of Indian intent. What was the status of Indian armored forces and mobile infantry? Had aircraft dispersals taken place? What about movements of heavy equipment by road or rail? At 0200 on 18 December, the head of ISI's JCIB called the US Station Chief at his residence and asked whether the CIA could verify the mobilization of Indian forces. The Station Chief, Robert Grenier, recalling some press articles on the mobilization, replied in the affirmative. After the ISI official had hung up, Grenier realized with a shock what had just happened: "I knew exactly what was happening. Given what he thought he knew about CIA technical capabilities, Jafar had to assume that we would know instantly if the Indians were mobilizing."[5]

This incident is another example of the vital role that ISI and its Indian counterparts play, for better or worse, in Indo-Pakistani tensions. The lack of good human and technical intelligence in this case meant that ISI resorted to foreign liaison information, press reports, and hearsay to try and understand alarming developments on the Indian side of the border. This was repeating a cycle previously seen in the 1986–1987 BRASSTACKS Crisis and the 1990 flare-up where both sides failed to accurately assess what the other was doing and contributed to growing tensions and fears of all-out war. The consequences of inaccurate information in an India–Pakistan crisis could be war and, possibly, the exchange of nuclear weapons with the horrific consequences that this would entail.

In 2002, when reports of Indian mobilization began filtering in, Pakistan responded by mobilizing and deploying units of her own army to pre-positioned areas closer to the border. Unlike the BRASSTACKS episode and 1990 tensions, the stakes were even higher in 2002 because the contestants had publicly tested their nuclear weapons only three years earlier and developed ballistic missile delivery systems as well. By spring 2002, up to one million soldiers were poised for war on both sides of the border.[6]

Musharraf was under strong pressure by India, the West and other influential states to rein in the terrorist groups that had instigated the crisis. Indeed, there was a widely shared perception that Pakistan was dangerously irresponsible and even reckless in its sponsorship of terrorist groups against a nuclear-armed neighbor. On 12 January 2002, Musharraf announced that *Jaish-e-Mohammed*, *Lashkar-e-Taiba* and several other "Kashmiri" groups were "banned," adding that Pakistani territory would not be used for terrorism. Some 2,000 extremists were (temporarily) arrested nationwide, but Musharraf also tried to save some face: "Kashmir runs in our blood," he thundered, "no Pakistani can afford to sever links with Kashmir. We will continue to give all diplomatic, political and moral support to the Kashmiris."[7] Of course, such language had previously been used as cover for covertly training and arming Kashmiri rebels.

ISI produced a code of conduct for those jihadi groups now banned by the president: they were to lie low, avoid the media, refrain from mass rallies, tone down their rhetoric and stay out of Islamabad for a while. Furthermore, they were to stop wearing combat fatigues, scale back infiltrations and cease claiming credit for violence in Kashmir. A final layer of subterfuge was added when these groups were instructed to drop the more obvious monikers like "jihad," "harakat," and "jaish" from their names. Some reports suggested only indigenous Kashmiris would be infiltrated across the LOC in the future.[8] But it was difficult to keep all the disparate jihadi organizations in line. For example, in May 2002, a *Lashkar-e-Taiba* fundraiser informed a Western journalist that

> [t]raining is underway in Azad Jammu and Kashmir and we are not under pressure by any government agency to stop. When this training is going on do you think these agencies are not aware? Of course they are![9]

On 14 May, the Indian army cantonment described at the beginning of this chapter was attacked. New Delhi responded immediately by putting its forces on higher alert and ratcheting up its anti-Pakistan propaganda. There was widespread speculation that the Indians were girding for some sort of retaliation strike, which probably compelled Musharraf to issue clear orders that all cross-LOC infiltrations had to stop immediately. Of course, Musharraf left it up to the ISI to deliver his decision to the jihadis.[10]

A few days later, militant commanders convened a United Jihad Council in Muzaffarabad, capital of Azad Kashmir, where the ISI Deputy Director General informed them that the government had to "stop all cross-border operations." One unidentified militant leader asked whether this decision marked a permanent shift in Islamabad's policy toward the Kashmir issue. The DDGISI replied that the policy had not changed, but all infiltrations were to cease for the next three months. In order to keep the groups under wraps, ISI paid off the commanders as an incentive.[11]

None of this placated the Indians, who had seen this show too many times before to take it seriously. Moreover, there was considerable public pressure on Indian Prime Minister Vajpayee to respond aggressively to Pakistani provocations once and for all. On 22 May, he toured the LOC and delivered an alarming speech that was widely broadcast in India and abroad. Part of that speech affirmed that "[t]he time has come for a decisive battle … and we will have a sure victory in this battle."[12]

Vajpayee's words must have resonated in Islamabad, because the Pakistanis sent a signal of their own resolve by conducting surface-to-surface missile tests on 25 May.[13] A week later, Musharraf repeated his order that all infiltrations across the LOC cease. On 6 June 2002, US Deputy Secretary of State Richard Armitage was in Islamabad on an urgent mission to ease tensions between India and Pakistan. In a meeting with Musharraf and DGISI Ehsan ul-Haq, Armitage asked whether Musharraf was willing to make his "no infiltration" pledge permanent. The president assented, so Armitage took this as a sweetener for talks in New Delhi that followed. Though the Indians were suspicious of Pakistani pledges, the crisis was already subsiding, especially when the Indians noticed a sharp reduction in infiltrations across the LOC. Of course, this only confirmed the degree to which ISI could regulate jihadi violence in Kashmir.[14]

By late 2002, however, the Pakistanis sensed an opportunity to slowly escalate cross-LOC infiltrations again. Some 1,500 militants from JeM, LeT and *Harakatul Mujahidin* were quietly released from prison and allowed to ramp up jihad activities under different names.[15] It was Zia ul-Haq's old boiling pot analogy: during the 2002 Indo-Pakistan crisis, the pot had boiled over and scalded the Pakistanis, so the heat was lowered, tensions eased and tranquility restored. But ISI continued to allow the proxy war in Kashmir to simmer.

The nuclear dimension

From an intelligence warning perspective, nuclear tipped ballistic missiles represent a daunting, perhaps insurmountable, challenge. They offer little or no warning prior to hitting their targets because of their speed and the compressed distances between Islamabad and New Delhi or Mumbai. Neither side has a well-developed early warning radar system capable of detecting ballistic missiles early in their trajectory; even if they did have such capabilities, the time between warning and response would be measured in minutes or even seconds. The bottom line is that India and Pakistan are highly vulnerable to surprise attack. This leaves them in the unenviable position of "use 'em or lose 'em'" if there is even a hint that the other side had launched first.[16]

As far as the Indian military was concerned, the 1990–1991 and 2002 crises revealed a disquieting pattern where India was unable to leverage its natural advantages in geography, population and military strength because of the delays in deploying conventional forces to the Pakistan border. The pattern ran like this:

1   Pakistani proxies stage a high-profile attack against Indian Kashmir or India proper.

2   Indian intelligence traces the attack back to ISI, exposes Pakistani involvement but then faces the full blast of an outraged Indian public demanding retaliation. Pakistan denies any responsibility for the attack.

3   India starts mobilizing for war. The large, armor-heavy strike corps start moving by road and rail to forward deployment areas near the Pakistan border. Combat aircraft are dispersed to emergency airfields. Surface ships and submarines make preparations to go to sea.

4   Due to the sheer size of the forces involved, Indian mobilization takes weeks. For example, in 2002, it took the army three weeks to mobilize and deploy before it was ready to execute military operations. Moreover, the movements of hundreds of thousands of men and thousands of vehicles are impossible to disguise from spies on the ground or intelligence satellites.

5   The Pakistanis mobilize in response, but they also ask the US to mediate the crisis. During negotiations – which sometimes last for weeks – Indian hardliners chafe at the delay as well as the costs associated with maintaining mobilized forces in forward positions indefinitely.

6   Eventually, diplomats reach an agreement to deescalate the crisis. Discussions continue on "confidence-building measures" until the next militant provocation occurs.

7   The deployed forces are pulled back to garrison and demobilized.

This pattern frustrated the Indians because they could not translate their overwhelming conventional military power into tangible political benefits. Existing army doctrine was inadequate to handle political crises generated by Pakistani proxy attacks on Indian soil. Not surprisingly, the Indian army searched for a new doctrine that would compress the time delay linked to mobilization and deployment and enable the Indians to strike before Pakistan could counter-mobilize and seek US diplomatic intervention. Throughout the first decade of the new millennium, the Indians experimented with different operational concepts under a rubric loosely called COLD START. This evolving doctrine entailed breaking up the large, unwieldy strike corps into several independent operational maneuver groups permanently positioned near the border along with their supply depots and ammunition dumps. In the event of hostilities, these "armored packets" would conduct rapid attacks across the border aimed at seizing Pakistani airfields, military bases, rail links, and command, control and communications (C3) nodes. The goal would be to paralyze the Pakistani army's ability to mobilize and defend while breaking the C3 link between GHQ and the nuclear forces.[17]

As of 2015, COLD START (or whatever its new appellation might be) was still under development, but it is a logical response to a long-standing Indian conundrum. It also poses a formidable intelligence challenge for both ISI and the MI, in that it increases the potential for strategic surprise by reducing warning time. Indeed, ISI and MI would be hard-pressed to detect, correctly analyse and warn the leadership that an attack was imminent. Because it would be by no means certain that the Indians *would* attack – this could be a military exercise or a misreading of the intelligence – the likelihood for miscalculation would be high. Doubt, uncertainty, rapid response, preemption and miscalculation are not conducive to confidence-building in a volatile, nuclear-armed region like South Asia.[18]

Loose nukes

In 2000–2001, two retired Pakistani scientists met Osama Bin Laden and his deputy, Ayman al-Zawahiri, in Afghanistan. Both were affiliated with a Pakistani non-governmental organization called *Umma Tamer-e-Nau* (UTN), which ran a charity in Afghanistan; however, the real purpose of their visit was not charity work but nuclear weapons. Disturbingly, one of the scientists, Sultan Bashiruddin Mahmood, was fascinated by the role nuclear weapons might play in Judgment Day, and he was eager to transfer nuclear technologies to fellow Muslim states.[19] The CIA learned about this meeting shortly after 9/11 from a foreign intelligence service and shared this with ISI. Apparently, ISI had already been informed of the meeting through its own sources – possibly Hamid Gul, a UTN board member. ISI told the CIA Station that both scientists were forced into retirement in 1999 after openly voicing radical ideas about nuclear technology. Apparently, ISI did not monitor them after their retirement.[20]

On 23 October 2001, ISI detained seven UTN members and questioned them closely about the Bin Laden link; however, little came from these interrogations, and the detainees denied any wrongdoing. But as far as CIA was concerned, ISI's investigation was flawed, especially when ISI concluded that the Bin Laden meeting was inconsequential since neither scientist had direct access to the weaponization side of the nuclear program.[21] The post-9/11 US government was not going to let an issue like this drop, because it combined the two most lethal ingredients of the "global war on terrorism": weapons of mass destruction and terrorists eager to use them. In November 2001, DCI George Tenet flew to Islamabad on short notice to lay out the UTN case before President Musharraf and urge more action. Tenet recorded part of the conversation in his memoirs:

> Mr. President, you cannot imagine the outrage there would be in my country if it were learned that Pakistan is coddling scientists who are helping Bin Ladin [*sic*] acquire a nuclear weapon. Should such a device ever be used, the full fury of the American people would be focused on whoever helped al-Qa'ida in its cause.[22]

Musharraf retorted that al-Qa'ida simply did not possess the technology to produce nuclear weapons, especially since they were living in caves and dodging bombs at the moment. Tenet disagreed and had a CIA analyst lay out the US position in greater detail; he also asked Musharraf to investigate "certain elements" inside ISI and the military establishment with suspected UTN links. In his memoirs, Tenet wrote that "[i]t appeared that UTN's contacts with the Taliban and al-Qa'ida may have been supported if not facilitated by elements within the Pakistani military and intelligence establishment."[23]

Presumably with an extra nudge from Musharraf, ISI allowed the CIA to interrogate the UTN suspects more thoroughly at an ISI safe house using polygraphers and rotating interrogation teams. Eventually, one of the scientists admitted to meeting the al-Qa'ida leaders as late as August 2001, and that they discussed nuclear weapons. The scientist even drew a crude schematic of a nuclear weapon for Bin Laden. But the case stalled there: neither scientist was put on trial, although the US leaked the story to the press to pressure Islamabad into doing more.[24] The UTN case was alarming enough, but at least it was nipped in the bud. The same could not be said of Abdul Qadir Khan, who, if the Pakistani government's story is accurate, single-handedly took a wrecking ball to the Nuclear Nonproliferation Treaty by selling sensitive nuclear enrichment and weaponization technology to Iran, Libya, North Korea and possibly others.

By the late 1990s, A.Q. Khan was a rich man jet-setting around the world selling nuclear technologies to whomever was willing to pay for them. The CIA and ISI had been trailing him for some time, steadily gathering more information about his network. Apparently, ISI was following the nuclear expert as well, for back in the early 1990s, it had prepared an assessment of Khan's activities that revealed his extensive property holdings at home and abroad as well as his constant travel throughout Asia. ISI added that Khan was "selling documents" on nuclear technology to foreign governments. Then Prime Minister Nawaz Sharif apparently ignored the problem.[25] Still, ISI continued monitoring the scientist as former DGISI Asad Durrani explained later:

> We had a man who ran the garages for official events who would give us useful bits and pieces. This humble garage man was humbled by [A.Q.] Khan's chattering. He said to us, "Khan's job is secret, so what business does this chap have to be at every single reception where he blabs to everyone?" The garage man had tried to tell Khan, "You can't talk so much all over the place." But being a lowly garage man he had been ignored. I tried to warn Khan too. "Keep quiet. Your project is supposed to be secret." But it was difficult to censor a person whom we needed more than he needed us.[26]

ISI monitored Khan throughout summer 2000, reporting to Musharraf that the scientist had made an unauthorized trip to Dubai. Musharraf summoned Khan to inquire about his travel and his refusal to answer questions posed by ISI investigators; however, as Asad Durrani points out, A.Q. Khan was nearly untouchable in a country where he had become a national hero. He even escaped censure when ISI reportedly raided a PAF plane before it took off with nuclear technologies for North Korea. How Khan managed to single-handedly commandeer a PAF transport aircraft from under the noses of the military authorities was never clarified.[27]

But 9/11 changed everything. Flying passenger jets into buildings was bad enough, but the dominant fear in the US was that the next al-Qa'ida attack might well involve a chemical, biological or nuclear weapon. Overnight, the US government shifted from a "collect and wait" approach regarding A.Q. Khan's nuclear proliferation network to a dismantle-and-destroy one. In late 2003, the White House decided to take action, starting with a 23 September meeting between Bush and Musharraf in New York City. A.Q. Khan's proliferation activities must be stopped immediately, the US President emphasized, but he left it up to his DCI, George Tenet, to fill in the gaps the following day.[28]

After receiving an extensive CIA briefing on Khan's activities in Iran, Libya and North Korea, Musharraf ordered ISI to investigate Khan more thoroughly. Subsequently, ISI investigators flew to Dubai, Malaysia, Libya and Iran to uncover details of his network. The scientist and several of his associates were hauled in for questioning by the DGISI and Lieutenant General Khalid Kidwai, Director General of Pakistan's Strategic Plans Division, the office responsible for the nuclear program.[29] ISI also raided Khan's residences in search of incriminating material, but the scientist had prepared for this contingency. One of his daughters had already departed Pakistan, he told his interrogators, and she was carrying sufficient documentation on Pakistani nuclear proliferation to implicate senior officials in selling nuclear-related technologies abroad. In other words, A.Q. Khan had blackmail material and intended to use it as insurance against reprisals by the state.[30]

The A.Q. Khan affair required delicate handling. On the one hand, Musharraf had the Americans breathing down his neck, but on the other, he had a scientist with the capability of airing Pakistan's dirty laundry before the whole world. Apparently, some sort of deal was made, for on 26 January 2004, the government blamed Khan for unilaterally selling the most sensitive secrets of the Pakistani state. He was placed under house arrest and drafted a 12-page "confession" that he delivered in a nationwide address on 4 February. His admission of guilt didn't fool many, and there was a general perception that he was being sacrificed to salvage the reputations of his superiors. Khan himself did nothing to dispel those suspicions and later insisted that he never acted alone when it came to selling nuclear technologies abroad. Given the circumstances of the case, it is much easier to believe him than the government on this score.[31]

So where does ISI come in with all this? Above all else, ISI is responsible for conducting background checks on employees involved in the nuclear weapons program, from the Lieutenant General who directs it and the scientists and engineers who make it happen to the sweepers who keep the premises clean.[32] Bearing this in mind, is it fitting to ask how the UTN scientists could conduct meetings with the two most wanted terrorists in the world without ISI either knowing or doing something about it? Arguing that the scientists were forced to retire on account of extremist beliefs or that they did not have access to the weapons side of the program is hardly reassuring. The possibility of nuclear weapons theft – the infamous "loose nukes dilemma" or "Empty Quiver" as the US military calls it – is probably higher in Pakistan than any other known nuclear-armed state if only because of the alarming history narrated above and the ongoing instability plaguing that country. As one of the primary guardians of Pakistan's nuclear arsenal, ISI would shoulder a great deal of the blame if these weapons fell into the wrong hands.

Notes

1 S. Left, "Indian PM calls for 'decisive battle' over Kashmir," *Guardian*, 22 May 2002, www.theguardian.com/world/2002/may/22/kashmir.india [accessed on 1/8/15]; S. Nawaz, *Crossed Swords*, Karachi: OUP, 2008, 549; Z. Hussain, *Frontline: The Struggle with Militant Islam*, New York: CUP, 2007, 107; R. Grenier, *88 Days to Kandahar*, New York: Simon & Schuster, 2015, 345.

2 H. Haqqani, *Pakistan: Between Mosque and Military*, Washington, DC: Carnegie Endowment, 2005, 302–303; M.A. Zahab and O. Roy, *Islamist Networks: The Afghan-Pakistan Connection*, New York: CUP, 2006, 55; S. Hersh, *Chain of Command: The Road from 9/11 to Abu Ghraib*, New York: HarperCollins, 2004, 300; B. Riedel, *Deadly Embrace*, Washington, DC: Brookings Institution Press, 2011, 69; A. Rashid, *Descent into Chaos*, New York: Viking, 2008, 220.

3 J.R. Schmidt, *The Unraveling: Pakistan in the Age of Jihad*, New York: Farrar, Straus and Giroux, 2011, 97; B. Woodward, *Obama's War*, New York: Simon & Schuster, 2010, 45.

4 Nawaz, *Crossed Swords*, op. cit., 549; Hussain, *Frontline*, op. cit., 107; R.G. Wirsing, *Kashmir in the Shadow of War*, London: M.E. Sharpe, 2003, 121.

5 Grenier, *88 Days*, op. cit., 308–309.

6 Ibid., 345.

7 Quoted in Hussain, *Frontline*, op. cit., 107; I. Gul, *The Most Dangerous Place*, New York: Viking, 2010, 159.

8 A. Jamal, *Shadow War: The Untold Story of Jihad in Kashmir*, Hoboken, NJ: Melville House, 2009, 231–232; Wirsing, *Kashmir*, op. cit. 121.

9 R. McCarthy, "Dangerous Game of State-Sponsored Terror that Threatens Nuclear Conflict," *Guardian*, 25 May 2002, www.theguardian.com/world/2002/may/25/Pakistan.india [accessed 1/8/15].

10 Hussain, *Frontline*, op. cit., 109; H. Abbas, *Pakistan's Drift into Extremism*, Armonk, NY: M.E. Sharpe, 2005, 226–227.

11 Hussain, *Frontline*, op. cit., 111–112; Gul, *Dangerous Place*, op. cit., 159; Haqqani, *Pakistan*, op. cit., 306.

12 Left, "Indian PM calls for 'decisive battle' over Kashmir," op. cit.

13 Grenier, *88 Days*, op. cit., 346.

14 Ibid., 352; Hussain, *Frontline*, op. cit., 109–110; Rashid, *Descent into Chaos*, op. cit., 119; Gul, *Dangerous Place*, op. cit., 159; A. Tellis, "Pakistan Simply Sees no Reason to Stop Supporting Terrorists," yaleglobal.yale.edu, 21 March 2010.

15 Abbas, *Pakistan's Drift*, op. cit., 227.

16 O.B. Jones, *Pakistan: Eye of the Storm*, New Haven: Yale University Press, 2003, 211.

17 W. Ladwig III, "A Cold Start for Hot Wars," *International Security*, 32:3, Winter 2007/2008, 158–190; S. Paul Kapur and Sumit Ganguly, "The Jihad Paradox: Pakistan and Islamist Militancy in South Asia," *International Security* 37: 1 (Summer 2012) 11–141.

18 Ladwig, "Cold Start," op. cit.
19 A. Levy & C. Scott-Clark, *Nuclear Deception: The Dangerous Relationship Between the United States and Pakistan*, New York: Walker & Co., 2008, 310; G. Tenet, *At the Center of the Storm*, New York: Harper Perennial, 2007, 262–264.
20 Levy & Scott-Clark, *Nuclear Deception*, op. cit., 309–311.
21 R. Suskind, *One Percent Doctrine*, New York: Simon & Schuster, 2006, 48–49; Tenet, *Center*, op. cit., 263.
22 Tenet, *Center*, op. cit., 265–267.
23 Ibid.
24 Ibid., 267–268; Grenier, *88 Days*, op. cit., 171.
25 Nawaz, *Crossed Swords*, op. cit., 474–475.
26 Quoted in Levy & Scott-Clark, *Nuclear Deception*, op. cit., 234–235.
27 D. Frantz & C. Collins, *The Nuclear Jihadist*, New York: Hachette, 2007, 257–259; Hussain, *Frontline*, op. cit., 164.
28 Hussain, *Frontline*, op. cit., 67.
29 Ibid.; Rashid, *Descent into Chaos*, op. cit., 289.
30 Frantz & Collins, *Nuclear Jihadist*, op. cit., 341–342.
31 Levy & Scott-Clark, *Nuclear Deception*, op. cit., 389–391.
32 Hussain, *Frontline*, op. cit., 167; D. Sanger, *Confront and Conceal*, New York: Crown, 2012, 10–11.

17　ISI–CIA Liaison after 9/11

Khalid Sheikh Mohamed was sound asleep when the ISI officers burst into his room in the early hours of 1 March 2003. As he was dragged out of bed, the al-Qa'ida leader offered a bribe to his captors if they would let him go, but the Pakistanis were in no mood to bargain. KSM – his unofficial shortened name given to him by US intelligence officials – was still groggy, apparently from sleeping pills, when a CIA officer snapped the infamous picture of him in an undershirt with body hair spilling out in all directions.[1] The *9/11 Commission Report* stated that KSM was the "principal architect of the 9/11 attacks."[2] He was also believed to be the individual who personally beheaded Daniel Pearl, the abducted *Wall Street Journal* correspondent.[3] When he was captured in Rawalpindi and handed over to US custody, the CIA and ISI were at the pinnacle of their post-9/11 alliance. Little did either know that their relationship was about to unravel quickly and ultimately end up in a state bordering on outright hostility.

Hunting al-Qa'ida

As the Taliban regime was collapsing in November and December 2001, its al-Qa'ida allies were fleeing to safe houses in Iran and Pakistan. The US–Pakistan "understanding" drawn up immediately after 9/11 was focused on shutting down al-Qa'ida through a capture or kill policy, but the Taliban and Kashmir-linked groups were largely ignored unless they were involved in combat with US soldiers. This was a game that ISI and its army masters were willing to play as long as the Taliban and the India-focused jihadis were not directly threatened by the Americans.[4]

In the weeks immediately following 9/11, ISI set up a counter terrorism cell that worked closely with the CIA and FBI in locating and arresting al-Qa'ida fugitives. US intelligence was anxious to access ISI knowledge and expertise on al-Qa'ida, although its optimism was no doubt tempered by past experience. It seems as if the Pakistanis were still hesitant to share this kind of information, but there is no denying that ISI was cooperative in late 2001 and 2002 rounding up al-Qa'ida suspects and handing them over to the US.[5] According to George Tenet this early phase in the new CIA–ISI partnership showed promise: "In this period, Pakistan had done a complete about-face and become one of our most valuable allies in the war on terrorism."[6] In truth, ISI tolerated a considerable amount of CIA activity on its turf, and this was going to come back and haunt both agencies later in the decade. Of course, ISI did not do this out of altruism or any fear of al-Qa'ida; the main incentives to cooperate were money, technology and intelligence sharing. Left unsaid was the fact that ISI had little choice other than cooperation at this stage in the war.[7]

In 2002, joint CIA–FBI–ISI teams were active throughout Pakistan, rolling up al-Qa'ida suspects, interrogating them in ISI safe houses and shipping many to CIA-run prisons overseas.[8] Robert Grenier was Station Chief in Islamabad during this frenetic period, and he describes the CIA–ISI relationship in these terms:

> We and the Pakistanis had perfected a methodology for conducting raids to capture these people, and it was a series of rolling raids almost night after night ... and that was the way we did business in those early days.[9]

One of the first al-Qa'ida figures rounded up after 9/11 was Abu Zubayda, a logistician who had been tracked by the CIA transiting in and out of Pakistan in 2000 and 2001. Indeed, the US government had asked the Pakistanis to apprehend him, but ISI took no action. Former US Ambassador to Pakistan, William Milam, put it this way: "The Pakistanis told us they could not find him, even though everyone knew where he was. The ISI just turned a blind eye to his activities."[10] One explanation for ISI inaction during this period may be that Abu Zubayda helped the Pakistanis vet militants for the Kashmir jihad, although, if this were indeed the case, it seems unlikely ISI would have ever handed him over to the Americans. In any case, the post-9/11 environment meant that the US was less tolerant of Pakistani brush-offs when it came to al-Qa'ida.[11] On 28 March 2002, Abu Zubayda was apprehended in a joint ISI–CIA–FBI raid. According to one unidentified CIA official, the reward from the US government for his capture was considerable.

"We paid $10 million for Abu Zubayda ... [ISI] built a new headquarters on thirty-five acres they bought outside of Islamabad, and they got themselves a helicopter. We funded the whole thing."[12]

One year later, the self-described "mastermind" of September 11, Khalid Sheikh Mohamed, was arrested by ISI officers in Rawalpindi. His arrest and subsequent rendition to a CIA "black site" represented the high-tide mark of this phase in ISI–CIA relations. By late 2003, US officials were noticing a drop-off in ISI cooperation, and some attributed this to Washington's preoccupation with Iraq.[13]

At least one ISI officer has a fond memory of this phase in CIA–ISI relations. Brigadier Asad Munir was chief of ISI's Peshawar Detachment when he noticed the substantial numbers of US diplomats, military, and intelligence personnel flowing into Peshawar after 9/11. He also noticed how the

American Consulate was sprouting new wires and antennae adding wryly that it was "a spy station posing as a diplomatic outpost."[14] Munir admits there was considerable mutual suspicion between ISI and the Americans at the outset, but this began to dissipate as US–Pakistani teams worked together against al-Qa'ida in the Peshawar area.[15] In its 2003 appraisal of global terrorism, the State Department echoed the generally positive spin concerning Pakistan's role:

> Pakistan remained a key partner in the war on terror and continued its close cooperation with the United States in law enforcement, border security, and counterterrorism training. In 2003, the Musharraf government began to increase pressure on terrorists seeking refuge along the border with Afghanistan, conducting antiterrorist operations in the Federally Administered Tribal Areas for the first time.[16]

Subsequent events demonstrated that some of this optimism was misplaced as the US and its allies slowly accumulated reports of ISI double-dealing. Take Fida Mohamed, for example. Arrested in 2007 by Afghanistan's National Directorate of Security (NDS), Mohamed told his interrogators that he was an ISI civilian employee hired for his extensive knowledge of the frontier area. He revealed that he was part of an ISI operation in late 2001 aimed at evacuating ISI training camps in Afghanistan and helping the trainees escape to Pakistan. As he explained to a US interviewer: "We told them, 'Shave your beards, change your clothes, and follow'.... We led them to the border with Pakistan and told them they were on their own. And then we went back for more."[17]

Bin Laden's own escape from Afghanistan has yet to be explained. One scenario is provided by Zahir Qadir, a Pashtun warlord hired by the CIA and US Army Special Forces to help flush out al-Qa'ida from the Tora Bora cave networks. He later alleged that a fellow warlord participating in the coalition assault named Haji Zaman was not only a former Taliban commander – many Afghan militia chiefs were at one time or another – but an ISI asset too. It was Haji Zaman who imposed a controversial 12-hour ceasefire at the height of the Tora Bora battle that enabled many al-Qa'ida leaders to escape to Pakistan. As Zahir later put it:

> Whatever Haji Zaman did was instructed by the ISI. They were given the chance and 175 al-Qa'ida members escaped. I strongly believe Osama Bin Laden was among them. The ceasefire was a pre-planned thing. Haji Zaman was the ISI's special person. At Tora Bora he was their man.[18]

Another controversial case involves the al-Qa'ida number two, Ayman al-Zawahiri. In 2004, US intelligence agencies believed they had located him in Wana, South Waziristan, and passed that information to ISI for action. When Pakistani ground forces reached the site it was empty, leading some US officials to believe ISI had tipped off al-Zawahiri in advance.[19] If ISI did tip off the al-Qa'ida fugitive, the next question is why? Was it out of sympathy for his cause? Was ISI afraid he knew too much? Was there an understanding of sorts between the Pakistanis and al-Qa'ida? For his part, by late 2002, DCI George Tenet was starting to change his mind about the ISI and its willingness to aid the Americans in their war on terror:

> For years, it had been obvious that without the cooperation of the Pakistanis, it would be almost impossible to root out al-Qa'ida from behind its Taliban protectors. The Pakistanis always knew more than they were telling us, and they had been singularly uncooperative in helping us run these guys down.[20]

The murder of Daniel Pearl

As far as ISI was concerned, there were implicit limits to cooperating with the Americans from the beginning. While there was a commitment to rounding up al-Qa'ida figures on Pakistani soil (with perhaps an exception or two), this did not include the Taliban nor the various proxies trained for terrorism in Kashmir. When a *Wall Street Journal* correspondent named Daniel Pearl began researching the links binding ISI to terrorist groups like JeM and LeT, he got too close to Pakistan's "Deep State" and paid for it with his life.

Pearl was investigating several stories in Pakistan that ISI would have regarded as especially sensitive. One was the UTN nuclear scientists' case, and another was the infamous Bombay gangster, Dawood Ibrahim, whom the Indians held responsible for bombings in 1993 and believed to be hiding in Pakistan. Pearl was also investigating JeM, learning that it was quite active during a visit to its headquarters even though the government had supposedly banned the group.[21] At the time of his abduction, Pearl was investigating Richard Reid, the "shoe bomber," who tried to bring down a transatlantic flight on 22 December 2001 with explosives hidden in his shoes. Pearl was trying to run down Reid's Pakistan links by working with knowledgeable intermediaries like Khalid Khwaja, an ISI officer during the 1980s.[22] Described by Pearl's wife as a "fascinating but dubious character" Khwaja was known for his connections to the jihad community, including Bin Laden.[23]

On 23 January 2002, Pearl believed he had finally arranged an interview with a religious scholar named Sheikh Mubarak Ali Shah Gilani. Working the interview arrangements was none other than Omar Saeed Sheikh, who had been freed from an Indian prison thanks to the December 1999 hijacking of the Indian Airlines plane. In fact, Gilani never knew he was going to be interviewed. It was a setup carefully planned and implemented by Sheikh, a British national previously involved in the abduction of Western tourists in India during the 1990s.[24]

An intense manhunt involving various police forces, the Sindh Special Branch, the IB and ISI failed to locate either Pearl or his captors. As for Omar

Saeed Sheikh, it appears that he handed over his captive to al-Qa'ida's Khaled Sheikh Mohamed and then fled to a relative's home in Lahore. That relative turned out to be a retired Brigadier named Ijaz Shah, former chief of ISI's Lahore Detachment, and at the time of Pearl's abduction, Punjab Home Secretary. Omar Saeed Sheikh was held incommunicado between 5 and 12 February during which he was interrogated by ISI. It has not been revealed what transpired between Sheikh and his "captors"; however, given his extensive involvement in ISI's Kashmir proxy wars, it stands to reason that he enjoyed some leverage over his interrogators. Some sort of entente was likely forged before Sheikh was handed over to the police.[25] Later, under interrogation by US and Pakistani investigators, Omar Saeed Sheikh confessed to being an ISI agent and named two Special Service Group officers who trained him for his missions in Kashmir. He admitted to a role in the October 2001 Srinagar Assembly bombing as well as the December 2001 attack on the Indian parliament. In revealing such information, Omar Saeed Sheikh apparently skated too close to the edge because ISI soon obstructed further interrogations by the Americans.[26]

Daniel Pearl was beheaded on 1 February 2002, allegedly at the hands of Khaled Sheikh Mohamed himself, and his body dumped in a Karachi suburb. At times, the Pakistani government's involvement in Pearl's case was inept, raising more questions than answers. In addition to alleging that the journalist's abduction was an Indian "black operation," Pervez Musharraf issued a strange statement that hinted at official complicity: "Perhaps Daniel Pearl was overinquisitive; a media person should be aware of the dangers of getting into dangerous areas; unfortunately, he got over-involved in intelligence games."[27]

There is no evidence that ISI aided or directed Pearl's murder; operating on its own turf, the agency would have been careful to cover its tracks. Even so, there is considerable smoke and not a few mirrors to add just enough doubt to any assurances of ISI innocence. First, there is Khalid Khwaja, another one of those mysterious "former ISI" officers like Colonel Imam, who pop up from time to time in matters involving militants. Then there is Omar Saeed Sheikh's previous stint in India and Kashmir, where he worked for a terrorist organization with unambiguous ties to ISI. According to British reporting, Sheikh confessed to being an ISI asset since 1993. In addition, Omar Saeed Sheikh's sojourn at Ijaz Shah's Lahore residence raises other questions about government knowledge of – if not involvement in – the Daniel Pearl affair. Some suggested without elaboration that Ijaz Shah was Sheikh's former ISI case officer. Was it mere coincidence that the Pakistani government announced Sheikh's capture one day before President Musharraf was scheduled to visit the US?[28] What about the abduction itself? Where were the usual IB or ISI informants tracking Pearl, especially when he was prying into no-go zones like ISI's links to al-Qa'ida? The Pakistani critic-in-exile, Tariq Ali, puts it this way: "The notion that Danny Pearl, beavering away on his own, setting up contacts with members of extremist groups, was not at the same time being carefully monitored by secret services is incredible. In fact, it is unbelievable."[29]

Robert Grenier, CIA Station Chief in Islamabad at the time of Pearl's murder laid bare his own frustrations in dealing with ISI during this period:

> We had reason to believe he [Omar Saeed Sheikh] had been detained, and specifically by the ISI, and so I went to a very trusted counterpart within the ISI and said: "How about it? Do you have him?" And he said: "Well, let me look into it." And he came back to me a few hours later and said, "No, we don't have him," and I knew he was lying to me.[30]

Taliban revival

All things considered, there was clearly demonstrated cooperation between the intelligence services of the United States and Pakistan in the early wars against al-Qa'ida. The keystone of that cooperation was tracking down and arresting al-Qa'ida fighters taking refuge in the remote Pashtun tribal areas or in Pakistan's cities. That early burst of cooperation enabled the US to get its hands on a number of al-Qa'ida leaders and functionaries, including Khalid Sheikh Mohamed and Abu Zubayda. But the partnership ultimately foundered on two issues. One was the suspected ISI propensity to tip off al-Qa'ida's "biggest fish" like Ayman al-Zawahiri prior to capture. The other, more important, one was a growing misunderstanding over the Taliban, whom the US had all but written off in late 2001 as a spent force. Pakistan was determined to restore the defeated Taliban and make them capable of implementing Islamabad's agenda.

The Taliban's rapid collapse in late 2001 deceived the US and its allies into thinking it had been essentially destroyed as a political and military movement. The reality was somewhat different. Most of the movement's core leaders – those comprising the Kandahar Shura – escaped to Pakistan, where they no doubt were rounded up by ISI and put in safe houses far from prying eyes. Rank-and-file Taliban fighters had been killed in the hundreds, but a larger number simply melted back into the civilian population, weapons and all. A few clung stubbornly to remote sanctuaries inside Afghanistan.[31]

Pakistan's definition of its core national security interests did not change much as a result of 11 September. True, Islamabad had to join the American war on terror if only to avoid the sanctions that would have followed if it hadn't. Above all, there was India to consider, and the last thing Musharraf and his cohort wanted was an energized Washington-New Delhi axis aimed at Pakistan and its proxies. At the same time, Afghanistan was going to be an unstable neighbor whatever form its government took in the future. Until the Taliban seized Kabul in 1996, Pakistani decision-makers sensed nothing but hostility from the Afghan government whether it was a monarchy, a republic, a communist state, or an Islamic republic.

Thus, having a Pakistan-friendly government in Kabul was imperative from Islamabad's standpoint. Pakistan security experts believed their country's very existence was at stake: to the east and south was an India that was considerably larger in land area, population, economy and military strength. To the west was an implacably hostile and dangerously unpredictable Afghanistan that contested the legitimacy of its border with Pakistan, not to mention voicing occasional irredentist claims on Pakistan's Pashtun and Balochi populations. It is only with this context in mind that we can comprehend why Pakistan continued supporting the Taliban even when it was widely pilloried for its atrocious human rights record, its war on women and its retrograde worldview. Therefore, after 9/11 and the collapse of the Taliban, ISI quietly granted sanctuary to its leadership and, over time, allowed it to construct a government-in-exile in Quetta complete with its own insurgent army. Islamabad needed options when it came to Afghanistan, and the Indian-educated Afghan President, Hamid Karzai, did not fit the bill.[32]

It was not long before the army and ISI felt vindicated in their continued support for the Taliban, even after the Americans invaded Afghanistan. In early 2002, Pakistan was not alone in sensing that America's priorities in the war on terror were shifting. To put it bluntly, as far as Washington was concerned, Afghanistan was out (if it was ever "in"), and talk was now being heard of an invasion of Iraq. In addition, US officials, including the president and his Secretary of Defense, were adamant that they would neither engage in "nation-building" in Afghanistan nor maintain a large military presence there. The Pakistani foreign policy establishment read the American press and watched the 24-hour news channels. The obvious decline in US interest in Afghanistan was being expressed by the withdrawal of Special Forces units and air assets from that country in preparation for Iraq. An Afghan Transitional Administration was installed in Kabul, but its authority did not extend much beyond the city outskirts. Little or no work was being done to build local and national police forces let alone a new army. Insecurity was the top complaint of Afghans polled after 9/11.[33]

Islamabad's approach to Afghanistan in 2001–2002 was wait-and-see, but in 2003, ISI began creating a new Taliban capable of filling the power vacuum and securing Pakistan's interests. The Taliban leadership was conveniently on hand, sheltering in safe houses run by the ISI in Quetta, while the insurgent training infrastructure from the 1980s and 1990s was quietly reactivated. ISI and Taliban recruiters resumed trolling the fifty-plus Deobandist madrassas in the greater Quetta area to fill the ranks of their new army. Once a month, the heads of many of these religious schools met with ISI officials in Quetta, where recruitment quotas were agreed. Thus trained and armed, the new Taliban began infiltrating into southern Afghanistan, establishing a presence in the weaker and more impoverished provinces like Zabul before linking up with existing Taliban pockets in Uruzgan and Helmand. As with any effective insurgency, the Taliban offered things that the Afghan government was manifestly incapable of doing such as security, justice and basic social services.[34]

The architect of the Taliban revival was the DGISI, Lieutenant General Ashfaq Parvez Kayani, variously described as "taciturn" and "unpretentious" with "sad, hollow eyes and stooped shoulders."[35] Some American officials entertained the idea that Kayani would be more partial to US concerns because he had attended the US Army's Command and General Staff College in 1988. Tellingly, his thesis there was entitled "Strengths and Weaknesses of the Afghan Resistance Movement," which examined the utility of proxy wars in Pakistan's national security strategy.[36] Kayani was posted as DGISI in October 2004, while his predecessor, Ehsan ul-Haq was given his fourth star and appointed Chairman of the largely powerless Joint Chiefs of Staff Committee.[37] Western diplomats, intelligence officers, and journalists speculated that Kayani was another "reformer" who would clean out the "rogue" elements and restore government control over the spy service.[38] Of course, the same things had been said of Ehsan ul-Haq and several other ISI chiefs extending back into the early 1990s.

It was under Kayani's watch that existing ISI proxy operations began to expand in scope and lethality. More districts in Afghanistan fell under Taliban control mainly because the government and its foreign allies were unable to address security deficiencies.[39] Still, the coalition could take some justifiable pride in holding Afghanistan's first national elections in 2004, which resulted in Hamid Karzai becoming president. It was neither in the army's nor ISI's interest to allow successful elections to take place in Afghanistan, for this would jeopardize the prospects for a pro-Pakistan regime in Kabul. Consequently, ISI tried to derail the elections either indirectly via the Taliban or directly by intimidating the international observers. On 9 August 2004, for instance, ISI officials met with representatives of the United Nations Assistance Mission in Afghanistan (UNAMA) and warned them that the Taliban were preparing for a big offensive in Kandahar. ISI kindly offered to evacuate UNAMA personnel who were supposed to be observing the elections. The offer was politely rejected. A post-elections UNAMA report stated that ISI's intent was "to create panic and lead the UN to leave Afghanistan in order to disgrace the elections."[40]

In Summer 2006, the full impact of ISI's efforts to revive the Taliban was being felt inside Afghanistan, especially in the south. For the first time, Taliban forces were standing their ground, catching the NATO-led coalition by surprise. Although the Taliban incurred heavy losses as a result of their temporary resort to conventional military tactics, they nonetheless delivered a strong signal to their enemies that they were back and constituted a force to be reckoned with.[41] Former US NSC official, Bruce Riedel, highlights 2006 as a milestone in Pakistan's more assertive approach toward Afghanistan:

> By 2006 it was abundantly clear that the Pakistani intelligence was orchestrating the revival of the Taliban and to me that was the moment when it was clear we had been double dealt. We had our suspicions before then, but in 2006 it was unequivocal: the Afghan Taliban were back, they were surging across southern Afghanistan and they could only do that if they had the support of the Pakistani intelligence service.[42]

US soldiers who had done multiple tours in Afghanistan noticed improved Taliban capabilities in preparing sophisticated ambushes and devising improvised explosive devices that cost the lives of many civilians and soldiers alike.[43] Other assessments indicated that Pakistan allowed the Quetta Shura to operate without restrictions, and ISI was listed as supplying intelligence and money to Afghan insurgents. US policymakers, war fighters, and analysts debated the question of who or what was behind the Taliban's new-found capabilities. Was it Afghan National Army soldiers who had defected to the Taliban, bringing their weapons and military skills with them? Was it captured US training manuals? Was the Taliban far more adaptive than anyone had previously assessed? Were the ISI and SSG behind these improvements?[44]

The next debate in Washington, London, and Brussels was the extent to which so-called ISI rogue elements were aiding the Taliban. This was assuming there *were* rogue ISI officers working without the knowledge or approval of their superiors and implementing policies that just happened to dovetail nicely with Pakistan's long-term national security interests. In fact, the "rogue agent" theory has been used for years by Western diplomats to explain Pakistani behavior that would, in most circumstances, put the country in the same league as other pariahs like Iran, Libya and Syria. Interestingly, Pakistani officials rarely brandish the rogue agent theory themselves as an alibi for state policy.

Directorate S

Still, waging proxy warfare against a US-led coalition does require enough plausible deniability to undercut the legitimacy of retaliation against Pakistan. This played out before when the ISI was fighting another superpower, namely the Soviet Union, without fear of significant reprisals. To be effective, plausible deniability relies on cut-outs and go-betweens who provide sufficient distance between the sponsors (i.e., ISI) and the person or group ultimately committing the act. We have already examined how ISI used "retired" officers like Hamid Gul or Colonel Imam to advise Gulbuddin Hekmatyar and the Taliban in their attempts to obtain control over Afghanistan. In those circumstances where foreign governments can point fingers at a specific individual – Hamid Gul's name was often invoked, much to his delight – the Pakistani authorities resort to the excuse that such individuals are "retired" army officers. As such, neither the government nor the army is responsible for acts committed by those with a "passion" and "sympathy" for the Taliban. It's a somewhat crude tactic, but it has worked well for over 20 years.

In this way, we arrive at the elusive Directorate S. Although cited in many press articles and secondary sources, this author could not determine the primary source(s) substantiating the existence of an actual ISI directorate called "S" or even the origin of the name itself. Reporting suggests Directorate S is a highly compartmented branch within ISI, and few ISI employees are allowed direct knowledge of it.[45] Sir Sherard Cowper-Coles, the former British Ambassador to Kabul, described the Directorate in this way:

What we're talking about here is a small cell in the ISI never knowingly exposed to Western eyes, who are in touch with the Taliban, the Haqqani Network. It is the most secret of the many secrets in Pakistan.[46]

Directorate S – or whatever its real name might be – has been a part of ISI's modus operandi for years. Sometimes called the "virtual ISI," it handles ISI's most sensitive relationships with jihadi organizations like *Lashkar-e-Taiba* and possibly al-Qa'ida. Since the collapse of the Taliban Emirate at the end of 2001, it has also been responsible for ISI's relationships with the Taliban, the Haqqani Network, the Islamic Movement of Uzbekistan and Chechen groups among others. It recruits insurgents and terrorists from Pakistani madrassas and provides them with training in insurgent warfare courtesy of "retired" SSG men or Frontier Corps officers. It ensures that the insurgents are provided with sufficient weapons, ammunition, food and other supplies to enable extended operations inside Afghanistan. It most likely provides intelligence and operational guidance as well.[47]

ISI support for the insurgency

ISI's support for the Taliban embraces virtually every facet of insurgency from military operations to establishing shadow governments for many Afghan provinces. Absent this assistance, it is highly unlikely that the Taliban could have been rejuvenated after 2001 and sent back into Afghanistan in large numbers to combat a US-backed coalition. This is not to suggest that Afghanistan would have automatically thrived and prospered without a reborn Taliban; indeed, the sources of conflict in that country extend well beyond ISI malfeasance. But it is unlikely that any organized, trained, supplied and unified insurgency would have emerged without ISI aid, and it is precisely those areas of organization, training, logistics and relative unity that make the Taliban such a potent threat to the Afghan government today.

Sanctuary is Pakistan's single greatest contribution to the Taliban cause. One of the key tenets of COIN doctrine holds that, historically, few insurgencies have been defeated if the guerrillas enjoyed easy access to a foreign sanctuary. In the case of Pakistan, both the mujahidin of the 1980s and the Taliban of the early 2000s relied heavily on Pakistani territory to base their leadership and allow fighters to rest, heal and reequip before returning to the fight.[48] Ahmed Rashid puts the safe haven argument this way:

> Quetta is absolutely crucial to the Taliban today. From there they get recruits, fuel and fertilizer for explosives, weapons, and food. Suicide bombers are trained on that side. They have support from the mosques and madrassas.[49]

In addition to safe haven, ISI allows the Taliban to recruit on Pakistani soil largely free of any constraints. In fact, a new Taliban could not have been reborn after the 2001 debacle were it not for easy access to a new generation of recruits in Balochistan, the tribal areas and the NWFP.[50] According to one expert "[t]he sanctuary of Pakistan provides a seemingly endless supply of potential recruits for the insurgency."[51]

In the months and years after 9/11, ISI and the SSG fell back on the same infrastructure employed in the 1980s and 1990s to organize, train and sustain guerrilla operations in Afghanistan. These camps are scattered throughout the NWFP, the tribal agencies and northern Balochistan, and their primary missions are to create resilient, tough and effective guerrilla fighters.[52] One Taliban commander codenamed Mullah Azizullah told the BBC in 2011 that:

> They are all the ISI's men. They're the ones who run the training. First they train us about bombs. Then they give us practical guidance. Their generals are everywhere. They are present during the training.[53]

In 2006, ISI training was being felt in Afghanistan in other ways too. Again, the evidence is not definitive, but there are numerous allegations that ISI sponsored the training of suicide bombers for Afghanistan.[54] According to Lieutenant General (retd) David Barno, who served as Commander of Military Operations in Afghanistan, there was a noticeable increase in suicide attacks inside Afghanistan during his tenure there from 2003 to 2006:

> The numbers on suicide attacks: 2003 in Afghanistan there were 2 suicide attacks; 2004 there were 5 suicide attacks; 2005 there were 17 suicide attacks in Afghanistan.... The following year, in 06, there were 139 suicide attacks. That leads me to suspect that our friends in Pakistan may have decided to reenergize the Taliban so that they would have a proxy force in whatever was going to happen after the Americans were gone.[55]

ISI aids the insurgents in other ways as well, including the supply of arms, ammunition, explosives, fuel, vehicles and cash. US officials have complained repeatedly that ISI leaked intelligence to the Taliban and al-Qa'ida that allowed their leaders to escape from drone strikes and Special Forces raids. Eventually, as the attack against Bin Laden demonstrated, US officials lost all trust in ISI's ability to keep a secret and conducted the operation unilaterally.[56]

ISI assistance to Afghan insurgents also extends to oversight and guidance of strategy and operations. According to a British researcher, ISI has assigned three to seven representatives to the Taliban's Quetta Shura, although it is not clear if they are participants or just observers. Still, this distinction may not be all that significant since ISI can exercise a substantial degree of control over the Taliban leadership by virtue of the latter's residence on Pakistani soil. In either case, ISI enjoys direct access to Taliban decision-making and provides input into upcoming campaign plans. An unidentified Taliban commander confirmed ISI's influence over the movement's leadership:

Every commander knows about the involvement of the ISI in the leadership but we do not discuss it because we do not trust each other, and they are much stronger than us. They are afraid that if they say anything against the Taliban or ISI it would be reported to the higher ranks – and they may be removed or assassinated. Everyone sees the sun in the sky but cannot say it is the sun.[57]

It has also been asserted that ISI advisors accompany Taliban units on missions inside Afghanistan, disguising themselves as mullahs, Islamic scholars or insurgents.[58] This is consistent with earlier information that ISI routinely sent its officers under cover into Afghanistan during the 1980s and 1990s. According to one account, a female ISI officer was captured by US forces in the company of a larger Taliban group in Afghanistan. Caught in an awkward diplomatic quandary, the US allegedly handed her back to the Pakistanis rather than risk possible retaliation from Islamabad.[59]

Several years passed before the US and its allies obtained a clearer understanding of what Pakistan was doing in Afghanistan. In the meantime, a key opportunity had been lost after 2001 when the international community could have invested far more time and resources in Afghanistan, enabling it to stand on its own feet. Unfortunately, by 2007, that opportunity had slipped away.

Notes

1 T. McDermott and J. Meyer, "Inside the Mission to Catch Khalid Sheikh Mohammed," *The New Yorker*, 2 April 2012, www.theatlantic.com/international/archive/2012/04/inside-the-mission-to-catch-khalid-sheikh-mohammed/255319/ [accessed 1/8/15]; S. Shane, "Inside a 9/11 Mastermind's Interrogation," *NYT*, 22 June 2008, www.nytimes.com/2008/06/22/washington/22ksm.html?_r=0 [accessed 1/8/15].

2 National Commission on Terrorist Attacks against the United States, *The 9/11 Commission Report*, www.9–11commission.gov/report/911Report_Ch5.htm [accessed 6/8/15].

3 J. Burke & R. McCarthy, "Journalist's Killing 'Link to Pakistan Intelligence,' " *Observer*, 24 February 2002, www.theguardian.com/world/2002/feb/24/Pakistan.pressandpublishing [accessed 1/8/15].

4 R. Grenier, *88 Days to Kandahar*, New York: Simon & Schuster, 2015, 318–319; G. Tenet, Tenet, G., *At the Center of the Storm*, New York: Harper Perennial, 2007, 229.

5 Z. Hussain, *Frontline: The Struggle with Militant Islam*, New York: CUP, 2007, 16–17, 125.

6 Tenet, *Center*, op. cit., 181.

7 BBC, *Secret Pakistan*, Part 1: Double Cross.

8 I. Gul, *The Most Dangerous Place*, New York: Viking, 2010, 175; T. McGirk, "Has Pakistan Tamed Its Spies?" CNN, 29 April 2002; A. Rashid, *Descent into Chaos*, New York: Viking, 2008, 308.

9 Quoted in BBC, *Secret Pakistan*, Part 1, op. cit.

10 Quoted in Rashid, *Descent into Chaos*, op. cit., 48.

11 Ibid.

12 J. Mayer, *The Dark Side*, New York: Doubleday, 2008, 140–142.
13 Rashid, *Descent into Chaos*, op. cit., 225; B. Riedel, *Deadly Embrace*, Washington, DC: Brookings Institution Press, 2011, 73.
14 Quoted in M. Mazzetti, *The Way of the Knife*, New York: Penguin, 2013, 38–40.
15 Ibid.
16 US Department of State, *Patterns of Global Terrorism 2003*, www.state.gov/documents/organization/31937.pdf [accessed 6/8/15].
17 D. Filkins, "The Journalist and the Spies," *The New Yorker*, 19 September 2011, www.newyorker.com/magazine/2011/09/19/the-journalist-and-the-spies [accessed 1/8/15].
18 BBC, *Secret Pakistan*, Part 1, op. cit.
19 Ibid.
20 Tenet, *Center*, op. cit., 139–140.
21 A. Rashid, *Pakistan on the Brink*, New York: Viking, 2012, 136–138.
22 Ibid., 137; J. Burke and R. McCarthy, "Journalist's Killing 'Link to Pakistan Intelligence,'" *Observer*, 24 February 2002.
23 M. Pearl, *A Mighty Heart*, New York: Scribner, 2003, 26–28.
24 M.A. Zahab and O. Roy, *Islamist Networks: The Afghan–Pakistan Connection*, New York: Columbia University Press, 2006, 58–59.
25 Pearl, *Mighty Heart*, op. cit., 181–182; A. Jamal, "Former Pakistani Army Chief Reveals Intelligence Bureau Harbored Bin Laden in Abbottabad," *Terrorism Monitor* 9:47, 22 December 2011, www.jamestown.org/single/?no_cache=1&tx_ttnews%5Btt_news%5D=38819&tx_ttnews%5BbackPid%5D=7&cHash=d955a8f dd5bffc0a7b8a6e380d68347f#.Vb1yj_lViko [accessed 1/8/15]; Z. Hussain, *Frontline*, op. cit., 124–125; BBC, *Secret Pakistan*, Part 1, op. cit.
26 Rashid, *Pakistan on the Brink*, op. cit., 142.
27 R. McCarthy, "Underworld where terror and security meet," *Guardian*, 16 July 2002, www.theguardian.com/world/2002/jul/16/Pakistan.rorymccarthy [accessed 1/8/15].
28 Pearl, *Mighty Heart*, op. cit., 183–184.
29 T. Ali, *The Duel*, New York, NY: Scribner, 2008, 151–152.
30 Quoted in BBC, *Secret Pakistan*, Part 1, op. cit.
31 Ibid.; Rashid, *Pakistan on the Brink*, op. cit., 50; Rashid, *Descent into Chaos*, op. cit., 240.
32 BBC, *Secret Pakistan*, Part 1, op. cit.; Gul, *Dangerous*, op. cit., 184–185.
33 Mazzetti, *Way of the Knife*, op. cit., 40–41, 111–112; Rashid, *Descent into Chaos*, op. cit., 222; P. Tomsen, *The Wars of Afghanistan*, New York: PublicAffairs, 2011, 593.
34 Rashid, *Descent into Chaos*, op. cit., 222, 252, 250; BBC, *Secret Pakistan*, Part 1, op. cit.; Tomsen, *Wars*, op. cit., 593; A. Giustozzi, *Koran, Kalashnikov, and Laptop*, New York: CUP, 2008, 21–28.
35 Mazzetti, *Way of the Knife*, op. cit., 110–113; P. Constable, *Playing with Fire: Pakistan at War with Itself*, New York: Random House, 2011, 117; D. Walsh, "Mixed Legacy for Departing Pakistani Army Chief," *NYT*, 29 November 2013, www.nytimes.com/2013/11/29/world/asia/mixed-legacy-for-departing-Pakistani-army-chief.html?_r=0 [accessed 6/8/15].
36 Mazzetti, *Way of the Knife*, op. cit., 112–113.
37 B. Cloughley, *War, Coups and Terror: Pakistan's Army in Years of Turmoil*, New York: Skyhorse, 2008, 179
38 Gul, *Dangerous*, op. cit., 171,174.
39 Giustozzi, *Koran*, op. cit., 52.
40 Quoted in Rashid, *Descent into Chaos*, op. cit., 259.
41 Giustozzi, *Koran*, op. cit., 123–129
42 Quoted in BBC, *Secret Pakistan*, Part 1, op. cit.
43 Ibid.

44 Ibid.; M. Mazzetti & E. Schmitt, "U.S. Study is Said to Warn of Crisis in Afghanistan," *NYT*, 8 October 2008, www.nytimes.com/2008/10/09/world/asia/09afghan.html?pagewanted=all [accessed 6/8/15].

45 L. Wright, "The Double Game – The Unintended Consequences of American Funding in Pakistan," *The New Yorker*, 16 May 2011, www.newyorker.com/magazine/2011/05/16/the-double-game [accessed 2/8/15]; A. De Borchgrave, "Pakistan's Paranoia Created bin Laden," *Washington Times*, 3 May 2011, 1.

46 Quoted in BBC, *Secret Pakistan: Part 2: Backlash*.

47 A. De Borchgrave, "Commentary: Pakistan: Cutting to the Quick," UPI, 6 May 2011; Rashid, *Descent into Chaos*, op. cit., 221–222; S. Coll, *The Grand Trunk Road*, New York: Penguin, 2009, 304; Rashid, *Pakistan on the Brink*, op. cit., 50–51; M. Waldman, "The Sun in the Sky: The Relationship Between Pakistan's ISI and Afghan Insurgents," Crisis States Research Centre, Discussion Paper 18, June 2010, www.lse.ac.uk/internationalDevelopment/research/crisisStates/Publications/discussion/dp18.aspx [accessed 2/8/15]; Tomsen, *Wars*, op. cit., 474; M. Mazzetti & E. Schmitt, "Afghan Strikes by Taliban get Pakistan Help, U.S. Aides Say," *NYT*, 25 March 2009, www.nytimes.com/2009/03/26/world/asia/26tribal.html?_r=0 [accessed 2/8/15]; E. Lake, "Enemy of the State," *New Republic*, 19 May 2001, www.newrepublic.com/article/world/magazine/88623/Pakistani-intelligence-osama-bin-laden-cia [accessed 1/8/15]; Mazzetti, *Way of the Knife*, op. cit., 168.

48 Mazzetti & Schmitt, "Afghan Strikes by Taliban"; S. Chayes, LAT, 23 November 2011, http://articles.latimes.com/2011/nov/23/opinion/la-oe-chayes-Pakistan-role-in-afghanistan-20111123 [accessed 2/8/15].

49 Quoted in P. Constable, "U.S. Says Taliban Has a New Haven in Pakistan," *WP*, 29 September 2009, www.washingtonpost.com/wp-dyn/content/article/2009/09/28/AR2009092803751.html [accessed 2/8/15].

50 Mazzetti & Schmitt, "Afghan Strikes by Taliban," op. cit.; Giustozzi, *Koran*, op. cit., 38–40.

51 Quoted in Rashid, *Descent into Chaos*, op. cit., 368.

52 Ibid., 222; Mazzetti & Schmitt, "Afghan Strikes by Taliban," op. cit.; Waldmann, *Sun in the Sky*, op. cit., 15–16.

53 BBC, *Secret Pakistan*, Part 1, op. cit.

54 BBC, *Secret Pakistan*, Part 2, op. cit.

55 BBC, *Secret Pakistan*, Part 1, op. cit.

56 D. Walsh, "As Taliban Insurgency Gains Strength and Sophistication, Suspicion Falls on Pakistan," *Guardian*, 13 November 2006, www.theguardian.com/world/2006/nov/13/afghanistan.declanwalsh [accessed 2/8/15]; S. Jones, *In the Graveyard of Empires*, New York: W.W. Norton, 2009, 266–267; Gul, *Dangerous*, op. cit., 163–167; E. Shmitt & T. Shanker, *Counterstrike*, New York: Times Books, 2011, 121–122; "Both Sides Against the Middle," *The Economist*, 2 October 2008, www.economist.com/node/12341689?zid=301&ah=e8eb01e57f7c9b43a3c864613973b57f [accessed 2/8/15]; E. Bumiller, "C.I.A. Director Warns Pakistan on Collusion with Militants," *NYT*, 11 June 2011, www.nytimes.com/2011/06/12/world/asia/12Pakistan.html [accessed 2/8/15]; E. Schmitt and M. Mazzetti, "In a First, U.S. Provides Pakistan with Drone Data," *NYT*, 13 May 2009, www.nytimes.com/2009/05/14/world/asia/14drone.html [accessed 2/8/15].

57 Waldmann, *Sun in the Sky*, op. cit., 6.

58 BBC, *Secret Pakistan*, Part 1, op. cit.

59 Ibid.

18 Friction in ISI–CIA Relations

It was around 1730 on 10 September 2011 when the suicide bomber plowed his truck into the outer perimeter of US Combat Outpost (COP) Sayed Abad in the Afghan province of Wardak. Fortunately for those US Marines and soldiers inside the COP, the HESCO barriers absorbed much of the blast; nonetheless, 77 Marines were injured. Unfortunately for Afghan civilians, though, the bomb killed five, including a woman hit by shrapnel half a mile away. A huge pillar of smoke rose above the COP as helicopters scrambled to evacuate the wounded.[1]

It wasn't supposed to happen this way. Back in July, the US Chairman of the Joint Chiefs of Staff, Admiral Mike Mullen, had passed intelligence to his Pakistani counterpart, COAS, General Ashfaq Pervez Kayani, that the Haqqani Network was preparing two truck bombs in North Waziristan. Kayani said he would look into the matter. On 8 September – two days before the bombing – General John Allen, coalition commander in Afghanistan, contacted General Kayani and warned that at least one of the truck bombs was on the move again. Kayani enigmatically promised to "make a phone call."[2] Incompetence or duplicity? Once again, Pakistan's reliability as an ally was being called into question, and many US officials, including Admiral Mullen, were tired of giving Pakistan the benefit of the doubt for its proxy war in Afghanistan. The ISI had to be "outed," and Mullen decided to do this in open testimony before the Senate Armed Services Committee. It was another turning point in US–Pakistan relations.

Name your price

By 2009, coalition forces in Afghanistan were implementing a consistent COIN strategy which combined force with negotiations to bring about a political settlement. American, Afghan, German and other negotiators made an honest effort at holding talks with the Taliban to achieve peace; however, ISI was not going to allow any settlement that did not include Pakistani interests. At a minimum, those interests included resolving the Afghan–Pakistan border dispute, creating a pro-Pakistan (i.e., Taliban-type) government in Kabul and sharply reducing the Indian presence in Afghanistan.[3]

For those interested in a settlement, whether coalition or Taliban, the obstacle was the ISI itself in its role as handmaiden of Pakistani state policy. Given that the entire Taliban Shura lived in guest houses on Pakistani soil and was subject to constant ISI surveillance, no peace talks were possible absent ISI buy-in. Indeed, ISI occasionally arrested shura family members just to drive home the point that they – and no one else – controlled the peace process in Afghanistan.[4] The Taliban number two, Mullah Abdul Ghani Baradar, discovered this in February 2010 when he was arrested by ISI near Karachi. At first, the US trumpeted Baradar's capture as an unalloyed success, for here was the first time that a very senior Taliban official had actually been arrested on Pakistani soil. Gradually, the real story leaked out that Baradar had been secretly negotiating with Hamid Karzai's half-brother, Ahmed Wali Karzai, behind Islamabad's back.[5]

ISI denied the CIA and FBI access to Baradar for weeks after his arrest, prompting doubts in both agencies about whether the Pakistanis had in fact turned over a new leaf. The US media faithfully echoed some of the debates occurring within US policymaking circles. An unidentified US "counterterrorism official" insisted that Mullah Baradar's arrest was "positive, any way you slice it" while another admitted that Washington had a "very limited understanding" of ISI.[6] When the US was finally granted indirect access to Baradar on 10 April, he divulged little in the way of "actionable intelligence." Once again, ISI signaled that the "solution" to the Afghan war lay in Islamabad and not Kabul – or Quetta for that matter. The disappointing implication of this, though, was that any Afghan peace deal probably would have to be part of an even more problematic regional settlement that included disputed Kashmir.[7]

Pakistan's role in Afghanistan generated disagreements within the US government. ISI held many of the cards necessary for an Afghan settlement, including a captive Taliban leadership and a capability to sustain and even enhance insurgent capabilities against coalition forces. On the other hand, the White House was caught on the horns of a dilemma: publicly accusing Pakistan of backing militants would undoubtedly push the Congress to reduce or even cease bilateral aid. It could also destabilize Pakistan, trigger ISI retaliation in the form of ramped up aid to the Taliban or cut NATO's vulnerable supply lines to Afghanistan that ran through Pakistan. Some US officials even pondered if Pakistan's price for peace in Afghanistan might be too steep for Washington to pay. Apparently, the American Ambassador to Islamabad was of this opinion, which she conveyed to the State Department in a 2009 cable:

> There is no chance that Pakistan will view enhanced assistance levels in any field as sufficient compensation for abandoning support for these groups, which it sees as an important part of its national security apparatus against India.[8]

The "name your price" approach had its own limitations. If the Taliban were integrated into a future Afghan government via a Pakistan-leveraged settlement, how would the US and West European public opinion respond, especially if the Taliban did not renounce its most controversial human rights policies? If Pakistan tied an Afghan deal to the Kashmir problem then all bets for a successful peace process were off because New Delhi would categorically resist US pressure on Kashmir for the sake of the Pakistanis. Money alone was not going to buy Pakistan's agreement to peace in Afghanistan either. After all, as of 2009, the US had given Pakistan the equivalent of $26 billion in humanitarian and military aid since 2001.[9]

Rogue theory

By 2009, even the most optimistic Western officials were starting to concede that the Afghanistan conflict could not be resolved by diplomacy or force. Yet it was difficult for US policymakers to concede defeat on a conflict that had consumed the lives of thousands of American soldiers not to mention the investment in national treasure to make Afghanistan viable. US prestige was on the line, and no president would pull out of the morass without some sort of face-saving measure. Consequently, Washington stalled for time by demanding that the US intelligence community provide "definitive proof" that ISI was backing militants in Afghanistan. Given the nature of the "plausible deniability" business, such proof was nearly impossible to obtain, a fact that suited many policymakers just fine. Essentially, the US was accepting the façade offered by ISI's use of cut-outs to wage proxy wars in Afghanistan.[10]

Some US officials also revived the time-tested accusations that ISI was a "rogue agency" or that it had "rogue agents" operating within it. For those who were more partial to Islamabad's perspective, the rogue agent argument also helped explain – if incorrectly – how the Pakistanis could be double-dealing their ally. Ahmed Rashid puts it this way: "If Washington had determined that support to the Taliban came from the top rather than from a few rogues, the United States would have had to take Musharraf to task, and neither Bush nor Cheney was prepared to do that."[11] This policy crossed over party lines too. When Secretary of State Hillary Clinton was asked in November 2009 if "leading members" of ISI backed the Taliban or had links to al-Qa'ida her response was boilerplate wishful denial: "Not at the highest levels. I am convinced that at the highest levels, we have a good working relationship ... I would like to see a real effort made on the part of the top leadership to make sure that no one down the ranks is giving any kind of support to the al-Qaida leadership."[12]

US officials used the "rogue" theory to explain Pakistani duplicity and give Islamabad a way of saving face; however, the Pakistanis publicly rejected any suggestion that they did not control ISI. In a 2002 press conference, Musharraf insisted that ISI served the state: "The government formulates policies and tells the ISI what to do. They do not do [anything] on their own. Hence, if there is anything wrong, the government is to be blamed, not the ISI."[13] Musharraf reiterated this argument during a January 2007 meeting with a congressional delegation when he affirmed that Pakistan was "not a banana republic and the ISI is not a rogue agency."[14]

Of course, what other options did Musharraf have? Accepting the rogue theory, however spurious, would be an admission that neither he nor his DGISI had a grip on what their own intelligence agency was doing. At times, some Taliban officials made it clear through their own "leaks" to Western journalists that rogue ISI agents were a myth. As one told the BBC in 2011,

> Senior Taliban leaders meet regularly with ISI personnel, who advise on strategy and relay any pertinent concerns of the government of Pakistan. Pakistan knows everything. They control everything. I can't [expletive] on a tree in Kunar without them watching.[15]

Nevertheless, ISI's Afghan allies sometimes forced Washington to adopt a tougher line toward Pakistan. In June 2008, the National Security Agency intercepted communications between ISI officers and the Taliban indicating planning was under way for a big attack in Afghanistan. Unfortunately, the target was not revealed, but on 7 July 2008, suicide bombers struck the Indian Embassy in Kabul, killing 54 including the Defense Attaché. Both the CIA and the Afghan NDS linked the attack to ISI via its Haqqani Network terrorist proxy. As evidence, they noted that a cellphone found in the embassy wreckage enabled investigators to trace phone calls made by the perpetrators to an ISI officer in Peshawar.[16] The CIA Deputy Director, Stephen Kappes, and Chairman of the Joint Chiefs of Staff, Admiral Mike Mullen, were dispatched to Islamabad where they presented evidence of ISI involvement in the embassy bombing to Pakistani officials. The message to Islamabad was clear: ISI aid to the insurgents must cease.[17]

Admiral Mullen served as the White House's de facto front man when it came to engaging the senior Pakistani military establishment. He logged in over 30 face-to-face meetings with General Kayani and made 21 visits to Pakistan during his tenure, leading him to comment later that he had traveled to that country more than any other as Chairman.[18] At the outset, Mullen believed he had established a rapport with the COAS; it was a flag officer-to-flag officer understanding that supposedly permitted a frank exchange of views.[19] Inevitably, however, irritation set in because Mullen's close connection with Kayani did not translate into any tangible gains, such as reduced ISI support for Afghan insurgents.[20]

Admiral Mullen's breaking point came in the summer of 2011, shortly before he was due to retire. As the introduction to this chapter details, US intelligence had picked up signals that the Haqqanis were planning a major suicide attack using two fertilizer trucks. Mullen passed this information on to Kayani, who assured him the trucks would not be allowed to cross into Afghanistan. In fact, the trucks languished in the Haqqani Network's North Waziristan safe haven for two months, before US intelligence picked them up moving toward the Afghan border. US officials approached Kayani once again, and once again the COAS promised that he would take care of the matter. On 10 September 2011, as we have seen, one of the trucks was detonated outside a US base in Wardak Province, wounding 77 US Marines and killing several Afghan civilians.[21] Three days later, suicide bombers assaulted the US Embassy in Kabul killing 20. On 22 September, Admiral Mullen left no doubt who he believed was ultimately responsible for both attacks in testimony before the Senate Armed Services Committee:

> With ISI support Haqqani operatives planned and conducted that truck bomb attack, as well as the assault on our embassy ... [T]he Haqqani network acts as a veritable arm of Pakistan's Inter-Services Intelligence Agency.[22]

The Chairman was giving voice to what everyone in the US Administration knew but refused to publicize: a country that was receiving billions of dollars in US aid every year was waging a not-so-covert guerrilla war that was killing US military personnel and disrupting international efforts to stabilize Afghanistan. The "official" response to Mullen's blunt statements was swift in coming. A "senior Pentagon official" stated that Mullen's declaration "overstates the case," and that there was "scant evidence" to back the Chairman's claim.[23] Then there was a more nuanced critique from yet another "unidentified" official:

> This is not new. Can [ISI] control [the Haqqanis] like a military unit? We don't think so. Do they encourage them? Yes. Do they provide some finance for them? Yes. Do they provide safe havens? Yes.[24]

Islamabad's response to these and other accusations was equally predictable. It claimed Pakistan was "fighting a common enemy" in terrorism and that it represented "part of the solution." This was true as far as it went; no one could deny that Pakistan's backing of jihadis in the past was now rebounding against it in the 2000s.[25] What was more troubling was the fact that neither the army nor ISI was convinced that the proxy strategy now threatened Pakistan itself. Many observers noted how ISI still tried to differentiate between "good jihadis" like the Taliban and the Haqqanis, who were targeting coalition forces in Afghanistan, and "bad jihadis" who were waging war against Islamabad.

But there were other official responses that did not use the "Pakistan-as-a-victim-of terror" line. An unidentified "senior Pakistani military officer" told one journalist that contacts with undesirables was part of the espionage business: "In intelligence, you have to be in contact with your enemy or you are running blind."[26] True, but contacts with insurgents and terrorist groups are one matter; aiding, training and sheltering them is obviously something else altogether. Another argument was that Washington was "scapegoating" Pakistan for the coalition's failures to stabilize Afghanistan, which resonated in Pakistani politics, but avoided the counterargument that ISI was making Afghanistan unstable in the first place.[27] One frequently employed rebuttal was to question the authenticity of the intelligence. Pervez Musharraf employed this from time to time:

> Afghan intelligence, Afghan President, Afghan Government. Don't talk of them. I know what they do. They are, by design, they mislead the world. They talk against Pakistan, because they are under the influence of Indian intelligence, all of them.[28]

All things considered, the outlook for Afghanistan is bleak. Leaving ISI's proxy war aside, the country is beset by an exploding population, grinding poverty, low literacy rates, lack of an effective central government, corruption, and inter-ethnic and sectarian violence. Each of these problems represents an Everest in its own right, and if Afghanistan were afforded breathing room, time and plenty of foreign aid it might, just might, surmount some of them. But Afghanistan does not exist in a vacuum, and as one of the weaker states in Central and South Asia, it inevitably gets sucked into the power struggles of its larger neighbors. If it's not Pakistan versus India, then it's Saudi Arabia versus Iran or even Pakistan versus Iran. Afghanistan has the unfortunate distinction of being the battleground of choice for regional power struggles.

2008 Mumbai terrorist attacks

In 2006, a man by the name of David Coleman Headley could be seen cruising the streets of Mumbai, India's largest city, its financial capital and, of course, home to the Indian film industry. Headley would not have attracted much attention: he appeared to be a tourist, recording the city's landmarks on a hand-held video camera. The truth was that Headley worked for ISI and *Lashkar-e-Taiba* (LeT), one of the most notorious Pakistan-backed terrorist groups. The purpose of his visits to Mumbai was to lay the groundwork for a terrorist "spectacular" that would leave 168 dead and hundreds more injured.[29]

Who was David Coleman Headley, and how did he get mixed up with LeT and ISI in the first place? Born in Washington, DC as Dawood Sayed Gilani to an American mother and a Pakistani father, he moved to Pakistan with his father when his parents divorced. At the age of 17, Headley returned to the United States, trafficked in narcotics, was arrested and eventually struck a deal with the Drug Enforcement Agency (DEA), based upon his knowledge of Pakistan's heroin trade. Around the same time, Headley joined *LeT*, which trained him in Pakistan on small arms, explosives and guerrilla warfare. In addition, Headley was transferred to ISI for training in espionage and counter-surveillance techniques. How a small-time pusher became a recruitment prize for ISI and LeT undoubtedly was due to his American passport, which made him much less suspicious casing targets in India.[30]

Headley wanted to fight alongside LeT fighters in Kashmir; however LeT and ISI regarded this as a waste of his passport and the access it provided to the Indian target. Headley was going to work inside India, they decided, but first he would have to change his name so he would be less suspicious to Indian immigration officials. Consequently, Dawood Sayed Gilani became David Coleman Headley – he used his mother's maiden name – and he was soon reconnoitering targets in Mumbai.[31] Later, while under interrogation by the FBI, Headley disclosed that ISI officers directed the overall planning of the Mumbai operation and provided financial and logistics support as well as weapons. His ISI contact was an as yet unidentified "Major Iqbal"; it was Iqbal who selected the targets and arranged the safe houses while Headley was in India.[32] Bruce Riedel, formerly of the NSC and the CIA, believes that the intensive planning behind Headley's assignment demonstrates senior officials must have been at least aware of the Mumbai plan:

> Running an American citizen like Headley for years was a major ISI operation that would have been overseen and monitored, if not micro-managed, by the top brass of the service. They knew what the plan was and they approved it.[33]

What remains uncertain is why Pakistani officials decided to stage a big ter-rorist attack in Mumbai. Of course, the Pakistani government denies any connection to the Mumbai assault. Therefore, the following is an attempt to understand the motive behind Mumbai and place it in the context of Indo-Pakistani relations at the time. It is based on Headley's testimony, US official communications and numerous press reports.

At the beginning of the twenty-first century, Pakistani national security decision-makers were increasingly worried about the growing network of ties binding India and Afghanistan. The Indian government was one of the largest aid donors to Afghanistan; it was also opening new consulates in several Afghan and Iranian cities near the Pakistani border such as Jalalabad, Zahedan and Kandahar. The Pakistanis accused the Indians of using these consulates as "spy dens" to destabilize and weaken Pakistan.[34] It was further alleged that India's RAW worked closely with the Afghan NDS to fund, arm and train Balochistan separatists as well as anti-Islamabad elements of the Pakistan Taliban in the FATA.[35] In June 2009, former President Musharraf publicly pointed the finger at RAW as the source of much of the internal violence afflicting Pakistan:

> Indian intelligence service RAW is interfering in our country.... One of the most brutal insurgents against our forces, Brahamdagh Bugti ... is sitting in Kabul, protected by the Afghan government and provided with weapons and money by [RAW]. He has his own training camps and sends his fighters to Balochistan where they terrorize people and damage the civil infrastructure. RAW is also interfering in the Swat Valley....

> Where do all these Taliban fighters in Swat get their arms and money from? From Afghanistan. The Indian consulates in Jalalabad and Kandahar only exist to be a thorn in the side of Pakistan.[36]

Pakistani fears of subversion by India and Afghanistan were compounded by growing frustration that the Kashmir dispute remained frozen, even though Islamabad had scaled back cross-LOC infiltrations after the near-war of 2002. Islamabad had few leverage points over India, and the most useful tool against New Delhi, namely the Kashmiri proxies, had been shelved for the time being. The jihadis were restless and dissatisfied as well, since they had been languishing in camps since 2002 with no prospect of renewed anti-India operations in sight.[37] When the Pakistani government cracked down on militants during the 2007 Red Mosque incident, LeT ranks reportedly were divided over how to respond. Fighting the government was out of the question, but what about joining the fight against the Western coalition in Afghanistan? Other LeT commanders felt that Afghan operations would distract the organization from its main enemy: India. According to David Coleman Headley's testimony, ISI's Major Iqbal tried preventing further LeT demoralization by giving it the green light on Mumbai.[38]

Headley was nowhere near Mumbai when LeT launched its terrorist attacks on 26 November 2008. Apparently, ISI's JCIB harbored doubts about his reliability, amid speculation that he was a double agent working for the Americans.[39] Consequently, ISI gradually cut Headley out of the planning for Mumbai, and he was put on ice for the duration of the operation. As for the attack itself, it proved devastatingly effective. The ten attackers infiltrated the city from the sea, split up and attacked several high visibility targets, including the Taj Mahal Palace Hotel, the Trident Oberoi Hotel, a hospital, and a Jewish hospice. Apparently, the last target was especially chosen by Major Iqbal himself.[40] The attack revealed major deficiencies in India's counter terrorism forces, including lack of coordination, communications, intelligence and transportation. In fact, it took two days for them to finally secure the Taj Mahal Palace, one of Mumbai's iconic landmarks. Unfortunately for LeT and ISI, one of the gunmen survived. Amir Ajmal Kasab was wounded in the assault and taken to the hospital where he was interrogated by police and intelligence officers. He revealed that LeT was behind the attacks and that the whole operation had been planned in Pakistan.[41]

In its response to the Mumbai attacks, Islamabad followed a predictable script. President Asif Ali Zardari and Prime Minister Gilani condemned the attack in strident terms.[42] At the same time, the Pakistanis made preparations for possible Indian attack. As DGISI Shuja Pasha put it:

> At first we thought there would be a military reaction. The Indians, after the attacks, were deeply offended and furious, but they are also clever.... We may be crazy in Pakistan, but not completely out of our minds. We know fully well that terror is our enemy, not India.[43]

The Pakistani government then moved into denial mode. The terrorists were not Pakistan citizens, it insisted, although how it knew this was not specified. COAS Kayani complained that New Delhi had made a "rush to judgement" when it blamed Pakistan for the attack.[44] Islamabad also expressed outrage that others even suspected it of links to the attack. A Zardari spokeswoman piously asserted that "this nation has paid in blood for its commitment against terrorism."[45] Indeed, as Pakistan spiraled downwards into sectarian violence, it became easier to point out that it too suffered from terrorism even if this was partly a result of its own policies. The authorities also preempted journalists who tried contacting the families of the Mumbai assailants. Almost all family members had been approached by ISI and told to stick to the official line that their sons, brothers and husbands had been killed fighting in Kashmir against India.[46] Rumors were also circulated that Mumbai was in fact a US and Indian plot to further discredit and isolate Pakistan.

At first, Islamabad offered to assist in the investigation. Foreign Minister Mehmood Qureshi wisely proposed establishing an ISI–RAW hotline to help ease misunderstandings in a future conflict.[47] But as with so many other matters concerning ISI, what the civilian leadership wanted and the army staff were willing to grant were two different things. At one point, Prime Minister Gilani overstepped his authority when he offered to send the DGISI to India to assist with the investigation. The army promptly intervened, and within hours, Gilani had to make a humbling retraction:

> We had announced a director will come from my side. That is what was requested by the Indian Prime Minister, and that is what we have agreed. It is too early for the director generals to meet at the moment. Let the evidence come to light, let the investigation take its course. The [Director General] is too senior a person to get into who overall looks into the investigation.[48]

The Pakistanis demanded proof that their nationals took part in the Mumbai attacks. India's unwillingness to budge much on this issue allowed Islamabad to sit back and try and wait the crisis out. Indeed, months after the attack, the Pakistanis were still waiting for some public evidence of ISI involvement in Mumbai other than Amir Ajmal Kasab's confession.[49] As information from Kasab leaked out, Pakistani officials resorted to the "contacts" and "rogues" explanations. The official line was that ISI no longer backed LeT, but did maintain "informal contacts" with the group. As one ISI official told a journalist, "we don't operate in a safe part of the world. It's our job to know what they are doing."[50]

In late December 2008, DGISI Shuja Pasha visited CIA headquarters in Langley, where he reportedly insisted that Mumbai was a rogue operation carried out by two army officers linked to ISI. "There may have been people associated with my organization who were associated with this," he explained, "[t]hat's different from authority, direction and control."[51] Another leak from "anonymous officials" in Pakistan revealed that ISI's Karachi Detachment "might have been aware" of LeT's plans concerning Mumbai but that ISI HQ had not been informed of this.[52] These partial confessions were not doing much to dampen speculation.

When all other methods failed to turn unwanted attention away from ISI's involvement in Mumbai, there was always the tried-and-tested "reforming ISI" routine. In meetings with foreign officials, President Zardari promised that things would change at ISI and that the agency would no longer "run with the hares and hunt with the hounds."[53] He had appointed a new DGISI Shuja Pasha in September 2008, and as far as British diplomats were concerned, Pasha was a "new broom" who would clean up ISI and make it presentable to the world.[54] For its part, Washington seemed more interested in exculpating the Pakistani government than digging deeper to find the truth behind Mumbai. It was a "rogue" effort hinted some – as always unidentified – officials, who added that the attacks were "not on orders" from Islamabad.[55] How the US government independently knew this was not clarified at the time. In fact, within 48 hours of Mumbai, the CIA Director, Michael Hayden, contacted Pakistan's Ambassador to Washington, Hussain Haqqani, and reassured him that the CIA had found no direct link between ISI and the Mumbai attackers. Those who planned the operation, Hayden added, were "former people who are no longer employees of the Pakistani government."[56] Of course, as has been noted earlier, "retired" or "former" ISI employees are exactly the kind of cover that ISI uses to disguise some of its most sensitive jihadi operations. Finally, why was the DCIA telling the representative of a foreign country that his national intelligence service was not behind a major terrorist incident? The US–Pakistan relationship has had its share of bizarre twists, but this was definitely out of the ordinary.

By February 2009, Washington's willing suspension of disbelief appeared to be lifting as more intelligence about Mumbai flowed in. According to investigative journalist Bob Woodward, the CIA had obtained intelligence revealing direct ISI involvement in training the Mumbai terrorists.[57] Around the same time, a cable from the US Embassy in Islamabad was admitting that "it is unclear if ISI has finally abandoned its policy of using these proxy forces as a foreign policy tool; we need to continue pressing them to realize this strategy has become counter-productive in Kashmir, Afghanistan and FATA."[58]

A major US interest in the immediate aftermath of the Mumbai attacks was to prevent the mobilization and counter-mobilization cycles of armies that had nearly dragged both countries into war six years earlier. This fact alone could account for why Washington policymakers were so eager to deny an official Pakistani role in the terrorist attack if only to calm the waters. In any case, just as it had done in the 1990 crisis, the US served as an intelligence conduit for both India and Pakistan. After a December 2008 meeting with DCIA Hayden in Islamabad, DGISI Pasha agreed to share sanitized information with India regarding Pakistan's investigation into Mumbai. The condition was that such information be restricted to intelligence channels in India.[59] Again, this was a situation where a direct ISI–RAW emergency communications channel would have come in handy.

Ultimately, India did not retaliate against Pakistan for sponsoring the Mumbai attacks, though elements within the Indian military establishment were upset by the government's passivity in the face of yet another Pakistani provocation. It was obvious to the Indian military that its conventional and nuclear force structure was not deterring Pakistan from executing high-risk UW operations against civilian targets in India. For the army, Mumbai confirmed the need for a COLD START-type military doctrine that would provide more of a deterrent and credible retaliation against future Pakistani attacks of this nature.

Meanwhile, the Indians continued to gather additional evidence implicating both LeT and ISI in the Mumbai attacks. Some of it came from a LeT operative named Sayed Zabiuddin Ansari (aka Abu Jundal), who was deported from Saudi Arabia to India to stand trial. According to the Indian government, Ansari confessed to having a role in planning and executing the Mumbai operation. He also revealed that two ISI officers, a Major Iqbal and a Major Sameer Ali, were present when the Mumbai plan was being fine-tuned in Azad Kashmir. When the LeT terrorists attacked the two hotels in Mumbai, Ansari said he was in a special operations headquarters in Karachi along with ISI officers, who remained in constant contact with the surviving attackers. The Pakistani government's tepid response to Ansari's revelations was that these were "speculative allegations."[60]

There is no public "firm and hard" evidence linking ISI directly to the 2008 Mumbai attacks; however, there is a considerable amount of circumstantial evidence indicating an ISI hand. Leaving aside the issue of proof for a moment, it must be asked why the leadership of the Pakistani army was willing to risk Indian retaliation and world outrage by sponsoring a dramatic, high visibility terrorist attack against a nuclear-armed neighbor. It was almost easier to accept the "rogue" agency theory than ponder the seemingly irrational thinking that lay behind the assault on India's commercial and cultural capital.

Notes

1 "77 Americans Wounded in Afghan Truck Bombing," Associated Press, 11 September 2011, www.cbsnews.com/news/77-americans-wounded-in-afghan-truck-bombing/ [accessed 1/8/15]; M. Mazzetti, *The Way of the Knife*, New York: Penguin, 2013, 294.

2 D. Walsh & J. Boone, "US bomb warning to Pakistan ignored," *Guardian*, 22 September 2011, www.theguardian.com/world/2011/sep/22/us-bomb-warning-Pakistan-ignored [accessed 2/8/15]; Mazzetti, *Way of the Knife*, op. cit., 294.

3 A. Rashid, *Pakistan on the Brink*, New York: Viking, 2012, 132,166; A. Rashid, "What Will It Take to Talk to the Taliban?" *Globe and Mail*, 27 January 2010, www.theglobeandmail.com/globe-debate/what-will-it-take-to-talk-to-the-taliban/article4311630/ [accessed 2/8/15]; M. Waldman, "The Sun in the Sky: The

Relationship Between Pakistan's ISI and Afghan Insurgents," Crisis States Research Centre, Discussion Paper 18, June 2010.

4 Rashid, *Pakistan on the Brink*, op. cit., 132, 166; Waldmann, *Sun in the Sky*, op. cit., 8; B. Woodward, *Obama's War*, New York: Simon & Schuster, 2010, 356; A. Rashid, *Descent into Chaos*, New York: Viking, 2008, 73.

5 Rashid, *Pakistan on the Brink*, op. cit., 114–115; G. Miller, "U.S. Officials Say Pakistani Spy Agency Released Afghan Taliban Insurgents," *WP*, 10 April 2010, www.washingtonpost.com/wp-dyn/content/article/2010/04/10/AR20100410021 11.html [accessed 2/8/15]; M. Rosenberg, "Afghan Taliban Leaders Flee Possible Arrest," *Wall Street Journal* [Hereafter *WSJ*], 10 March 2010, www.wsj.com/articles/SB10001424052748703701004575113741711001292 [accessed 2/8/15].

6 Miller, "U.S. Officials Say Pakistani Spy Agency Released Afghan Taliban," op. cit.

7 Mazzetti, *Way of the Knife*, op. cit., 269; "Pakistan Allows U.S. to Question Taliban Leader Baradar," *BBC News*, 22 April 2010 http://news.bbc.co.uk/2/hi/south_asia/8637780.stm [accessed 2/8/15]; "Afghan Spy Agency Accuses Pakistan Agency in Suicide Bombing," *NYT*, 26 May 2010, www.nytimes.com/2010/05/25/world/asia/25afghan.html [accessed 2/8/15]; E. Lake, "Pakistan Seen Restricting Data from Mullah Baradar," *Washington Times*, 26 May 2010.

8 J. Perlez, D. Sanger, E. Schmitt, "Nuclear Fuel Memos Expose Wary Dance with Pakistan," *NYT*, 29 November 2007, www.nytimes.com/2010/12/01/world/asia/01wikileaks-Pakistan.html?pagewanted=all [accessed 6/8/15].

9 K. DeYoung, "U.S. Offers New Role for Pakistan," *WP*, 30 November 2009, www.washingtonpost.com/wp-dyn/content/article/2009/11/29/AR2009112902934.html [accessed 1/8/15].

10 Rashid, *Descent into Chaos*, op. cit., 222.

11 Ibid.

12 "Our Goal is to Defeat al-Qaida and Its Extremist Allies," *Der Spiegel*, 15 November 2009.

13 Quoted in P. Tomsen, *The Wars of Afghanistan*, New York: PublicAffairs, 2011, 624.

14 Quoted in M. Rubin, *Dancing with the Devil: the Perils of Engaging Rogue Regimes*, New York: Encounter Books, 2015, 167.

15 Quoted in R. Leiby, "Pakistan Denies Claims in NATO Report of Spy Service Still Aiding Taliban," *WP*, 1 February 2012, www.washingtonpost.com/world/nato-report-Pakistan-spy-service-still-aiding-taliban-in-afghan-war/2012/02/01/gIQACr5XhQ_story.html [accessed 1/8/15].

16 D. Sanger, *The Inheritance*, New York: Harmony, 2009, 250; "The Spy who Quit: A Conversation with Amrullah Saleh," *PBS Frontline*, 17 January 2011; I. Gul, *The Most Dangerous Place*, New York: Viking, 2010, 161; Woodward, *Obama's War*, op. cit., 5.

17 Gul, *Dangerous Place*, op. cit., 188; Sanger, *Inheritance*, op. cit., 250; E. Shmitt & T. Shanker, *Counterstrike*, New York: Times Books, 2011, 121–122; Rashid, *Pakistan on the Brink*, op. cit., 67.

18 K. Brulliard & K. DeYoung, "U.S. Efforts Fail to Convince Pakistan's Top General to Target Taliban," *WP*, 3 January 2011, www.washingtonpost.com/wp-dyn/content/article/2010/12/31/AR2010123103890.html [accessed 2/8/15].

19 Woodward, *Obama's War*, op. cit., 100–101.

20 G. Miller & K. DeYoung, "Adm Mullen's Words on Pakistan Come under Scrutiny," *WP*, 28 September 2011, www.washingtonpost.com/world/national-security/adm-mullens-words-on-Pakistan-come-under-scrutiny/2011/09/27/gIQA HPJB3K_story.html [accessed 2/8/15].

21 Mazzetti, *Way of the Knife*, op. cit., 294.

22 "Pakistan 'Backed Haqqani Attack on Kabul' – Mike Mullen," BBC, 22 September 2011, www.bbc.com/news/world-us-canada-15024344 [accessed 2/8/15]; E. Bumiller & J. Perlez, "Pakistan's Spy Agency is Tied to Attack on US Embassy,"

NYT, 22 September 2011, www.nytimes.com/2011/09/23/world/asia/mullen-asserts-Pakistani-role-in-attack-on-us-embassy.html [accessed 2/8/15].

23 Miller & DeYoung, "Adm Mullen's Words on Pakistan," op. cit.

24 Ibid.

25 "US Slams Pakistan for 'supporting' Haqqani,'" *Al Jazeera*, 22 September 2011, www.aljazeera.com/news/asia/2011/09/2011922151047307196.html [accessed 2/8/15].

26 M. Mazzetti and E. Schmitt, "Afghan Strikes by Taliban get Pakistan Help, U.S. Aides Say," *NYT*, 25 March 2009, www.nytimes.com/2009/03/26/world/asia/26tribal.html?_r=0 [accessed 15/10/10].

27 B. Plett, "American Leverage in South Asia," *BBC News*, 30 March 2009, http://news.bbc.co.uk/2/hi/south_asia/7971128.stm [accessed 2/8/15]; E. Schmitt & J. Perlez, "Pakistan Objects to U.S. Expansion in Afghan War," *NYT*, 21 July 2009, www.nytimes.com/2009/07/22/world/asia/22pstan.html?_r=0&gwh=31CC097 C4A6D1E8A55D6445E7796021D&gwt=pay [accessed 2/8/15]; K. Brulliard & K. DeYoung, "Pakistan, Afghanistan Begin Talks About Dealing with Insurgents," *WP*, 19 June 2010, www.washingtonpost.com/wp-dyn/content/article/2010/06/18/AR2010061805638.html [accessed 2/8/15].

28 "Afghan is Under Influence of Indian Intelligence: Musharraf," *The Economic Times*, 8 November 2009, http://articles.economictimes.indiatimes.com/2009-11-09/news/27649280_1_afghan-intelligence-isi-Pakistani-president-pervez-musharraf [accessed 2/8/15].

29 *Frontline*, "A Perfect Terrorist," 22 November 2011, www.pbs.org/wgbh/pages/frontline/gunned-down/ [accessed 8/2/15].

30 Ibid.; C. Scott-Clark and A. Levy, *The Siege: 68 Hours inside the Taj Hotel*, New York: Penguin, 2013, 42–4.

31 Frontline, *Perfect Terrorist*, op. cit.; B. Riedel, *Deadly Embrace*, Washington, DC: Brookings Institution Press, 2011, 92.

32 S. Protella, "David Headley, Witness in Terror Trial, Ties Pakistani Spy Agency to Militant Group," *WP*, 23 May 2011, www.washingtonpost.com/national/david-headley-witness-in-terror-trial-ties-Pakistani-spy-agency-to-militant-group/2011/05/23/AFEEb99G_story.html [accessed 2/8/15].

33 B. Riedel, "Killers in the Neighborhood," Brookings Institution, 22 November 2013, www.brookings.edu/research/opinions/2013/11/22-mumbai-terror-attack-architects-roam-free-riedel [accessed 2/8/15].

34 J. Thottam, "Afghanistan: India's Uncertain Road," *Time*, 11 April 2011, http://content.time.com/time/magazine/article/0,9171,2062364,00.html [accessed 6/8/15]; S. Jones, *In The Graveyard of Empires*, New York: W.W. Norton, 2009, 271–272; Gul, *Dangerous*, op. cit., 164.

35 Gul, *Dangerous*, op. cit., 204; J. Hammond & S. Siddiqi, "Ex-ISI Chief Says Purpose of New Afghan Intelligence Agency RAMA is to 'destabilize Pakistan,'" *Foreign Policy Journal*, 12 August 2009, www.foreignpolicyjournal.com/2009/08/12/ex-isi-chief-says-purpose-of-new-afghan-intelligence-agency-rama-is-%E2%80%98to-destabilize-Pakistan%E2%80%99/ [accessed 2/8/15].

36 "Obama 'Is Aiming at the Right Things,'" *Der Spiegel*, 7 June 2009, www.spiegel.de/international/world/spiegel-interview-with-pervez-musharraf-obama-is-aiming-at-the-right-things-a-628960.html [accessed 2/8/15].

37 Gul, *Dangerous*, op. cit., 171–172.

38 Scott-Clark & Levy, *Siege*, op. cit., 52–53.

39 Ibid., 58, 110–111.

40 *Frontline*, "Perfect Terrorist," op. cit.

41 Scott-Clark & Levy, *Siege*, op. cit., 170.

42 "World Leaders Condemn Mumbai Attacks," CNN, 27 November 2008, www.cnn.com/2008/WORLD/asiapcf/11/27/mumbai.world.reaction/index.html?iref=newssearch [accessed 6/8/15].

43 "I Was Ready to Visit Delhi: ISI Chief," *The Nation*, 7 January 2009, www. nation.com.pk/Pakistan-news-newspaper-daily-english-online/Politics/07-Jan-2009/ I-was-ready-to-visit-Delhi-ISI-Chief [accessed 20/4/11].

44 "No drone attack support ever sought: ISPR," *The News*, 21 May 2011, www. thenews.com.pk/Todays-News-13–6155-No-drone-attack-support-ever-sought-ISPR [accessed 6/8/15].

45 M. Rosenberg, "Pakistan's Ties to Terror Group are Unclear," *WSJ*, 22 July 2009, www.wsj.com/articles/SB124820050290269319 [accessed 2/8/15].

46 Scott-Clark and Levy, *Siege*, op. cit., 288.

47 "FM proposes Pak-India intel hotline," *The Nation*, 28 November 2008, http:// staging.nation.com.pk/politics/28-Nov-2008/FM-proposes-PakIndia-intel-hotline [accessed 6/8/15].

48 H. Nawaz, "ISI to Help India," *The Nation*, 29 November 2008, http://nation. com.pk/Politics/29-Nov-2008/ISI-to-help-India [accessed 3/8/15].

49 P. Constable, "Mumbai attacks in 2008 still divide India and Pakistan," *WP*, 6 April 2011, www.washingtonpost.com/world/mumbai-attacks-in-2008-still-divide-india-and-Pakistan/2011/04/03/AFJjDUoC_story.html [accessed 6/8/15].

50 M. Rosenberg, "Pakistan's Ties to Terror Group are Unclear," op. cit.

51 Woodward, *Obama's Wars*, 46–47.

52 Gul, *Dangerous*, 170.

53 R. Cohen, "The Most Dangerous Job on Earth," *NYT*, 29 September 2008, www.nytimes.com/2008/09/29/opinion/29cohen.html?pagewanted=print&_r=0 [accessed 3/8/15].

54 "Pak Army overruled proposal to send Pasha to India post 26/11," *The Hindu*, 2 December 2010, www.thehindu.com/news/international/pak-army-overruled-proposal-to-send-pasha-to-india-post-2611/article927304.ece [accessed 6/8/15].

55 M. Rosenberg, "Pakistan's Ties to Terror Group are Unclear," op. cit.

56 Woodward, *Obama's War*, op. cit., 46.

57 Ibid.

58 "26/11 closed door for talks on Kashmir US envoy told Holbrooke," *The Deccan Herald*, 1 December 2010, www.deccanherald.com/content/117173/2611-closed-door-talks-kashmirus.html [accessed 6/8/15].

59 A. Baruah, "Pakistan shared Mumbai Attacks Research with India," BBC, 4 December 2010, www.bbc.com/news/world-south-asia-11917514 [accessed 6/8/15]; Rashid, *Pakistan on the Brink*, op. cit., 67.

60 A. Khan, "New Evidence of Pakistan's Role in the Mumbai Attacks?" 28 June 2012, PBS *Frontline*, www.pbs.org/wgbh/pages/frontline/afghanistan-Pakistan/ david-headley/new-evidence-of-Pakistans-role-in-the-mumbai-attacks/ [accessed 3/8/15]; K. Tare, "Terrorism: Ansari Nails Pakistan," *India Today*, 9 July 2012, http://indiatoday.intoday.in/story/abu-jundal-mumbai-terror-attacks-isi-Pakistan/1/203056.html [accessed 2/8/15].

19 ISI's Internal Security Missions

ISI's power over domestic and foreign policy peaked during the Musharraf and Zardari presidencies. Even as it was waging covert wars in neighboring countries, ISI was also rigging elections, intimidating and bribing politicians, illegally incarcerating and torturing dissidents, not to mention silencing critics – sometimes literally. As we have seen over the course of this study, numerous promises have been made by military and civilian leaders to dismantle ISI's Internal Wing, yet these promises have never been kept. It is difficult to imagine an enduring, healthy democracy emerging in Pakistan's future unless ISI and MI are either stripped of their domestic powers or, in the case of ISI, disbanded altogether.

Stifling the press

Sometimes it takes an emblematic case to galvanize opinion and put a glaring spotlight on the actions of secret police agencies. Orlando Letelier's 1976 murder at the hands of Chile's notorious *Dirección de Intelligencia Nacional* highlighted the ruthlessness of the Pinochet regime in eliminating opponents both at home and abroad. Similarly, the world learned a great deal more about Iran's Ministry of Intelligence and Security in August 1991 when its agents stabbed to death the former Prime Minister, Shahpour Bakhtiar, in his Paris home. For Pakistan, the murder of Syed Saleem Shahzad, a brave, if sometimes rash, journalist highlights the perils of trying to report the truth in a country regarded as the most dangerous in the world for journalists.[1]

It was Shahzad's reporting for *Asia Times Online* that drew the attention of many, including ISI. Like Daniel Pearl before him, Shahzad wrote about Pakistan's "Deep State" – the murky, secretive world of Pakistani politics, where backroom deals are made far from the public eye. But it wasn't just reporting on the Deep State that attracted ISI's attention: Shahzad wrote on links between foreign jihadis, Pakistani sectarian groups, al-Qa'ida, the Afghan Taliban and ISI. His writings revealed what the Americans had been privately accusing Pakistan of for years: that ISI sheltered the Taliban leadership. [2]

As far as ISI was concerned, Washington could complain about the Afghan Taliban as much as it wanted, but this was an issue of national interests and Pakistan's survival. When a Pakistani journalist repeatedly wrote about how the state was collaborating on some level with al-Qa'ida and the Taliban even as it aided the US war on terror, this was crossing a red line. In October 2010, Rear Admiral Adnan Nazir, the Director of ISI's Media Wing, and his assistant, Commodore Khalid Pervaiz, summoned Shahzad to ISI HQ and demanded that he retract a recent story on links between the Afghan Taliban and the ISI. They also wanted to know the names of his sources.[3] Shahzad refused, and Nazir let him go with this parting threat:

> We have recently arrested a terrorist and have recovered a lot of data, diaries and other material during the interrogation. The terrorist had a hit list with him. If I find your name in the list, I will certainly let you know.[4]

Shahzad certainly saw the warning for what it was. He quickly drafted up notes of his meeting with ISI and sent them to Human Rights Watch and the All Pakistan Newspapers Society with a cover note: "I am forwarding this email to you for your record only if in case something happens to me or my family in future."[5] In doing this, Shahzad undoubtedly hoped to buy himself some extra protection from ISI reprisals, but on 25 March 2011, he was summoned for another meeting with Rear Admiral Nazir. This time, he was ordered to retract a story on al-Qa'ida. "We want the world to believe that Osama is dead," Nazir added, which is an interesting revelation given that the US operation to kill Bin Laden was less than five weeks away. Once again, Shahzad refused to comply.[6]

On 27 May 2011, three weeks after Osama Bin Laden had been killed in Abbottabad, Shahzad wrote his last story. It was about al-Qa'ida's apparent infiltration of the Pakistani Navy as evidenced by a 22 May militant attack on Mehran Naval Base that left 16 dead and 27 wounded. The incident sparked a lot of questions inside Pakistan and abroad about the security of the country's military installations; some noted that Mehran was close to another base that reportedly housed nuclear warheads.[7] Two days after Shahzad's story appeared, a new Mehran commander was named: it was Commodore Khalid Pervaiz, previously of ISI's Media Wing and one of the journalist's interrogators.[8] Then Shahzad disappeared, and it wasn't until 29 May 2011 that his body was found in an irrigation ditch 100 miles from his home. The autopsy results showed that he had died slowly with two smashed ribs and a ruptured liver and lungs. In the aftermath of Shahzad's murder, many fingers pointed to ISI as the culprit, especially after Human Rights Watch released his notes on meetings with ISI media officials.[9] ISI's response was of course denial: these "[b]aseless accusations against the country's sensitive agencies for the alleged involvement in Shahzad's murder are totally unfounded."[10] A defensive ISI spokesman demanded that those making the allegations show proof of the agency's involvement in Shahzad's death, "otherwise, it's totally absurd."[11] The government set up an "independent commission," but it predictably failed to come up with any perpetrators or motives.[12]

Shahzad's murder did trigger outrage in an unexpected quarter. According to one account, the Chairman of the Joint Chiefs of Staff (CJCS), Admiral Mike Mullen, read a National Security Agency (NSA) intercept that supposedly proved that Shahzad's murder had been "sanctioned by the government."[13] Based on this and other intelligence, the US intelligence community assessed that it was DGISI Pasha who had ordered the journalist murdered.[14] This was yet another sign for the CJCS that the Pakistan army and its intelligence services were up to their necks in human rights abuses and double-dealing. As noted earlier, Admiral Mullen made his views plain a few months later in Senate testimony where he alleged that the Haqqani Network was an "arm" of the ISI.

Few cases better illustrate the rot that has eaten away the heart of the Pakistan state and army than that of Syed Saleem Shahzad. The vaunted Pakistani military portrays itself as the guardian of Pakistan, yet that same military intimidates, incarcerates and executes its own citizens without trial. Shahzad's murder also demonstrates the utter powerlessness of the civilian elected government to prevent the murder of citizens at the hands of their army, let alone find and punish the culprits. Syed Saleem Shahzad was an intrepid journalist who tried to speak truth to power; but the power didn't want those truths revealed, and he paid for this with his life – as did Daniel Pearl. Of course, one of the primary objectives behind Shahzad's murder was to "décourager les autres" – make him an example of the fate that could befall other journalists intent on probing the military's secrets. Journalist Ahmed Rashid, puts a finer point on this:

> There is a red line in Pakistan – there has always been a red line. But, after Saleem Shahzad, no one knows where the red line is anymore. It's debilitating, you can't really go out and report.[15]

This is exactly the way ISI wants it to be. For its part, Amnesty International has noted that:

> The spy agency has been implicated in several abductions, torture and killings of journalists, but no serving ISI official has ever been held to account – allowing it to effectively operate beyond the reach of the law. Human rights violations against journalists by the ISI often follow a familiar pattern that starts with threatening phone calls and escalates into abductions, torture and other ill-treatment, and in some cases killings.[16]

It is no secret today in Pakistan that ISI cultivates print and TV journalists to impart the official "line" on controversial matters to the public. It is known, for example, that ISI bribes some with cash or cars.[17] But, as with recruited assets, accepting these "payments" ensnares the recipient in a never-ending cycle of patronage mixed with hints of blackmail. Political analyst Ayesha Siddiqui wrote that cooperating with ISI is a slippery slope: "Once you go into the headquarters, they have you. They can photograph you there, they can put out the word that you were visiting, they can blackmail you."[18] ISI sometimes uses its media contacts – willing or otherwise –to generate anti-US sentiment among the public or to send not-so-subtle threats to designated "enemies of the state."[19]

When it came to intimidating domestic critics, ISI certainly made Saleem Shahzad into a grim warning for others who would dare follow in his footsteps. As we have seen, Shahzad was repeatedly harassed and warned by ISI officers. On at least two occasions, he was summoned to the lion's den, so to speak, where he was personally threatened by senior Media Wing officials. But Shahzad was not alone in receiving this kind of treatment. Umar Cheema is an intrepid journalist for *The News International* who used to write frequently on the army's internal battles with jihadis in its own ranks. Just as it did with Shahzad, ISI warned Cheema to cease reporting on these sensitive issues, but he did not, and on 4 September 2010, he was abducted, stripped, beaten, photographed naked and repeatedly threatened with rape. Just to make it clear that his abductors were not interested in money, they notified him that he was being "punished" for reporting on delicate issues.[20]

A more recent case of overt ISI meddling in Pakistan's media is that of Hamid Mir, a popular TV talk show host on Geo News, one of Pakistan's most popular news channels. He too is a frequent critic of the army, MI and ISI, highlighting their human rights abuses in Balochistan. He told his colleagues on several occasions that ISI was threatening him, but this did not induce him to stop his reporting. On 19 April 2014, Mir was shot six times while on his way to the Karachi studios. As Mir was rushed to hospital, his brother went on Geo News and openly accused the ISI of trying to kill Mir.[21] ISI "was eating up Pakistan like termites" he complained, adding that the DGISI personally intended to kill his outspoken brother.[22] For ISI, this was throwing down the gauntlet, and the spy chiefs promptly tried to shut down Geo News on the pretext that it was dispensing "false" news and had an "anti-Pakistan agenda."[23] Dispensing "false" news is, of course, an ISI specialty, so apparently they knew what they were talking about. ISI alone apparently has the power to determine what is "anti-Pakistan" and what is not. All this took place under a democratically elected government led by Prime Minister Mian Nawaz Sharif.

But the Hamid Mir affair wasn't over yet. Observers soon noticed that posters were suddenly appearing in Islamabad praising DGISI Zaheer ul-Islam and the COAS. Some alleged that "a traitor of Pakistan army is a traitor of the country" while others declared "We love Pakistan army and ISI."[24] Little imagination was required to determine who was behind those posters. As for Mir, the investigation into his assassination attempt predictably came up empty. He told the Committee for the Protection of Journalists that "[t]hese agencies should be answerable to the elected parliament but in my case it was proved that one intelligence agency was more powerful than the government."[25]

As the Daniel Pearl case shows, ISI does not restrict its harassment to Pakistani journalists alone. When it comes to foreign journalists, ISI often selects a more indirect approach, where its agents routinely intimidate local fixers and translators either to cease working for the journalist or to obstruct his or her work.[26] Moreover, foreign journalists are denied access to certain "sensitive" areas like Balochistan and the tribal agencies on the pretext that these are "unsafe." This would be a reasonable enough explanation were it not equally apparent that ISI sought to cover up whatever abuses the government was committing in those same areas. Foreign journalists have reported being subjected to near-constant surveillance both on foot and via tapped telephones.[27] This is yet another reason why the Daniel Pearl case raises so many intriguing questions: if he was followed (as seems likely given the topics he was investigating), why didn't his "shadows" intervene to prevent his abduction? Why didn't they follow his abductor's car to the safe house where he was interrogated and later murdered?

ISI and human rights abuses

ISI's war on journalists is but one facet of a much broader assault on human rights. Indeed, part of ISI's "mystique" is wrapped up in its notorious reputation for torture, murder and seeming omnipotence. Some observers believe ISI deliberately cultivates its own negative image, both to induce fear and intimidate those who would bravely cross its path:

> ISI has honed its reputation as a force to be feared by anyone who falls into its bad graces. Its acronym sends chills through people.... The agency cultivates a reputation for omniscience, omnipresence, and impunity, and it floats rumors of horrific punishments in secret prisons, where men are said to be thrown into dungeons and tormented by rats, snakes, or starving dogs.[28]

Pakistan's atrocious human rights record cannot be attributed to ISI and its sister agencies alone, for they are, after all, instruments in the hands of the country's all-powerful army. Human rights abuses are the unfortunate consequence of decades of military rule, ineffectual civilian governments, lack of transparency, a politicized judiciary, a corrupted civil service, paranoia about India, and chronic ethnic and sectarian instability in places like Karachi, Balochistan and the FATA.

Some human rights observers see a ray of hope on the horizon for Pakistani human rights. The Supreme Court, often a willing supplicant of whatever government is in power, has at times exhibited a surprising assertiveness on human rights. For instance, it has demanded ISI explanations for the "mysterious" deaths of hundreds of detainees and the proper accounting for thousands of missing persons.[29] While it is unlikely ISI will ever fully cooperate with the judges, a moral standard has been reaffirmed and a strong message delivered to those who give themselves the power of life and death over every Pakistani citizen.

ISI and elections "management"

Under Pervez Musharraf, ISI continued its practice of manipulating local, provincial and national elections. Indeed, the dictator leaned heavily on the head of ISI's notorious "Internal Wing," Major General Ehtesham Zamir, to ensure that the domestic political scene conformed more or less to what Musharraf and the senior army leadership wanted. For example, the Internal Wing helped stuff ballot boxes during the April 2002 referendum on Musharraf's "presidency" whereby 97.7 percent of those who voted selected the general for a five-year presidency. Oddly enough, Musharraf acknowledged Zamir's role in election fixing when he dismissed him some months later for election abuses.[30]

After his "triumph" in the referendum, Musharraf ordered new elections for the National Assembly in October 2002. Of course, he was not a general for nothing, and the results had to be determined with a comfortable degree of accuracy long before the voting took place. Disqualifying his two greatest political opponents, Benazir Bhutto and Nawaz Sharif, was an integral part of the elections manipulation process. Next came an ISI-engineered split within Nawaz Sharif's Pakistan Muslim League out of which emerged a pro-Musharraf faction called Pakistan Muslim League – Quaid (after Mohammed Ali Jinnah). ISI not only helped create this party, it also vetted PML-Q candidates at the national and provincial levels for their competence and loyalty to the army and Musharraf. As necessary, ISI "bought" candidates from other parties if they looked especially promising, and this continued after the election itself. Finally, some politicians were blackmailed by material culled from Musharraf's notorious NAB, which was originally intended to root out official corruption.[31]

As in previous cases where military regimes attempted to manipulate elections, the outcome of the October 2002 voting produced some unexpected surprises, one of which was the extent of the electoral victory by Islamist parties. A coalition of six such parties led by the JI and the JUI won 45 seats in the National Assembly, double the pre-election ISI estimate. Perhaps more importantly, this coalition also won control of the Assembly in the NWFP, where several of the parties enjoyed substantial popular support. Still, the "shocking" victory of the Islamist coalition was created in large part by the government's own attempts to defang the leading political parties, the PPP and the Pakistan Muslim League – Nawaz Sharif faction. ISI did cobble together a Musharraf-friendly National Assembly using generous amounts of cash plus certain other "incentives" including NAB information to create a PPP break-away faction that sided with Musharraf.[32]

When Musharraf was up for reelection in 2007, he ensured his victory by putting the election not in the hands of the Pakistani people but their "elected" representatives instead, many of whom happened to be PML-Q members. This had to be something of a rush job, because the current Assembly had only five weeks left before the December 2007 general elections.

According to several accounts, international pressure plus a looming fear that the military was losing popularity at home convinced the army and ISI to refrain from elections interference.[33] As a result, the PML-Q took a big hit as did the Islamist coalition. In fact, the PPP was able to form its first ministry since 1996.

Death of Benazir Bhutto

Benazir Bhutto should have been Prime Minister of that new PPP government, but she had been assassinated three months earlier in Lahore. Her murder is yet another in a long string of political crimes in Pakistan that have never been adequately investigated let alone solved. It also raises valid questions about the long-term viability of Pakistani democracy. Bhutto had been a thorn in the army's side ever since General Zia ul-Haq hanged her father in April 1979. Although she was allowed to form two governments in the 1990s, they were cut short by the army and civilian bureaucracy in Deep State political maneuvers. After the 1999 coup, Bhutto opted for self-exile in Dubai and London to escape Musharraf's NAB. She continued to snipe at Musharraf from the sidelines, and in 2001, she demanded a South African-style "truth and reconciliation commission" to investigate the role of the PIC in human rights violations and elections interference.[34] Benazir Bhutto could not live without the drama, intrigue and endless scheming of Pakistani politics. In 2006, she began negotiating with then DGISI Ashfaq Parvez Kayani, who happened to be her former military secretary but was now leading the talks on Musharraf's behalf. As part of their bargaining, Kayani promised no election rigging in what would turn out to be the rescheduled February 2008 elections. He also negotiated the timing of her return to Pakistan and important details of the elections such as voter rolls.[35] These talks continued in September 2007 at an ISI safe house in Islamabad. This time President Musharraf and representatives from the PML-Q and PPP were also in attendance. True to his nature, Musharraf threatened Bhutto if she parted from the planned script. He reportedly told her that "I'll only protect you if you are nice to me.... You should understand something: your security is based on the state of our relationship."[36]

On 5 October, Musharraf implemented his end of the bargain when he signed the National Reconciliation Ordinance, which provided a blanket amnesty for politicians previously charged with corruption. Although never explicitly stated, it appears that the PPP conceded Musharraf an unopposed presidency in return for letting Bhutto participate in the upcoming elections.[37] At this point, Bhutto believed she had been given the green light to return home, and on 18 October she landed at Karachi's Jinnah International Airport to a tumultuous welcome party generated by her PPP political machine. An estimated half a million followers lined the streets as Bhutto's cavalcade made its way to the Jinnah monument where she was scheduled to give a speech. As her convoy crawled through the crowds, people began noticing that the street lights were being switched off. For many attuned to the ways and wiles of Pakistan's "take no prisoners" political system, this was an ominous portent.[38]

Up to this point, Benazir had received numerous warnings from several Gulf Arab intelligence agencies, the CIA and even ISI that her life would be in danger once she returned to her homeland. It later transpired that ISI had deliberately fed some of these warnings to Saudi Arabia's General Intelligence Directorate for forwarding to Bhutto since it was believed she would take a GID warning more seriously than an ISI one. In any case, the intelligence reporting noted that at least four separate cells linked to the Pakistani Taliban and/or al-Qa'ida were planning to assassinate the PPP leader in Pakistan.[39] Still, Benazir suspected there was more to the alleged plots than met the eye: "there is another structure that is giving them succor, that is giving them encouragement," she said without elaborating further.[40]

In any case, Bhutto used these warnings as the basis for her 16 October letter to Pervez Musharraf in which she alleged that three people were out to kill her, all of whom were connected to ISI: former DGISI Hamid Gul and Ejaz Shah, currently DGIB and formerly involved in the Pearl investigation as the person to whom Omar Saeed Sheikh surrendered. She also identified Qari Saifullah Akhtar, a leader of an Islamist group called HUJI as a person of concern who was also linked to the ISI.[41] We don't know if some or any of these individuals were behind the 18 October suicide bombing in Karachi that ruined Bhutto's homecoming by killing 139 and wounding more than 400.[42]

The 18 October bombing rattled Bhutto. She wanted more security, but who could provide this? Musharraf showed no interest in her plight; in fact, he had already issued a memorandum to provincial officials that Benazir not be given VIP treatment normally extended to former prime ministers.[43] On 23 October, Bhutto met the US Ambassador in Karachi and pleaded for US assistance, especially in the area of technical intelligence. She had a long list of enemies who were out to do her in, she noted, and ISI was allegedly complaining to the Sindh government about her security needs. Could the US help? The ambassador politely turned her down, but gave Bhutto a list of private security firms that might provide the type of protection she needed.[44]

Procuring additional security was going to take time and, as far as Benazir Bhutto was concerned, she didn't have time. The elections were approaching and she simply could not remain tied to her residence while negotiating with a hostile government for more protection. On 26–27 December, Bhutto was in Islamabad preparing for a big speech at Liaquat Bagh, the same park where Pakistan's first Prime Minister, Liaquat Ali Khan, had been assassinated in 1951. In the early morning hours of 27 December, Bhutto met DGISI Nadeem Taj at her Islamabad residence. He asked her to avoid Liaquat Bagh, noting that emissaries from Saudi Arabia and the United Arab Emirates had recently passed credible information to ISI of multiple plots underway to assassinate her. For its part, he added, ISI had reports from SIGINT that at least three Pakistan Taliban cells were independently plotting to kill her.

Unfortunately for Benazir, her political antennae were perhaps too acute this time, for she thought ISI was not only trying to intimidate her but also throwing a wrench into her election campaign by keeping her homebound. She told the DGISI that it was up to him to ensure that her rally in Liaquat Bagh was adequately protected. Then the two briefly discussed the election. Bhutto once again sought assurances that ISI would not rig elections, and Taj replied that he would follow COAS Kayani's instructions and refrain from elections interference.[45]

On the morning of her assassination, Bhutto told Afghan President Hamid Karzai she was certain the ISI was trying to derail her campaign. Karzai responded that his NDS possessed intelligence of multiple plots against her life, adding that during a recent meeting of the Pakistan Army Corps Commanders, Musharraf discussed how Bhutto must be killed. Karzai wanted the NDS to give Bhutto an armored car complete with jammers against improvised explosive devices (IED), but this would take time to arrange. Being cautious was not in Benazir's election plan, certainly not now when elections were only weeks away.[46] After her meeting with Karzai, Bhutto returned to her residence and reportedly instructed one of her aides to put together a brief on Pakistan's intelligence agencies for the US government. Washington had to be informed that Pakistan's spy masters "were directly interfering in the elections," and she wanted to cite specific examples to buttress her case.[47]

It was after she had finished her speech and was exiting Liaquat Bagh that one or more assassins approached her car, fired shots at her and then exploded a bomb that killed 24. Bhutto was rushed to Rawalpindi General Hospital where at 1816 she was pronounced dead. The ISI Rawalpindi Detachment Commander, Colonel Jehangir Akhtar, was hovering nearby when the news came out of the operating room, but his exact role there has never been fully explained. There were other ISI officials inquiring about Bhutto too, including the then Deputy Director, Major General Nusrat Naseem, who reportedly phoned Dr. Mussadiq Khan, part of the emergency team that tried to revive Bhutto. At first, Naseem told the UN Commission investigating the murder that he made no such call. Then he reversed himself and said he had called Dr. Mussadiq to find out about Bhutto's condition. This information, he added, was then passed on to the DGISI.[48]

As news of the bombing rapidly spread, Musharraf chaired a meeting at GHQ, whose participants included the DGISI, DGIB and the DGMI. Musharraf was quickly brought up to date on the medical evidence and a telephone intercept of Pakistan Taliban leader Beitullah Mehsud allegedly claiming responsibility for the hit. Meeting participants agreed that the DGISI would handle the government's spin on the murder. Consequently, when he returned to ISI HQ, Taj summoned BG (retd) Javed Iqbal Cheema, the spokesman for the Ministry of Interior, and ordered him to convene a press conference.[49] During the conference that evening, Cheema told the press corps that Bhutto did not die because of the bomb blast but rather from her head striking a latch located on the escape hatch of her vehicle. He also produced a transcript of

Pakistan Taliban leader Beitullah Mehsud supposedly congratulating a subordinate for performing a "spectacular job," although Bhutto was never mentioned by name. Cheema's revelations didn't convince many of those present. Many were understandably skeptical that a government could discover culprits in less than 24 hours when many other political murders hadn't been resolved in 24 years, if ever. Naturally the PPP cried cover-up, arguing that the veracity of the suspiciously timely intercept could not be ascertained.[50]

There were in fact unmistakable signs of a cover-up that began almost immediately after the assassination took place. The police were astoundingly incompetent in their failure to secure the crime scene and collect adequate evidence, although they were quite proficient in keeping other investigators away from the site. Just as in the 18 October attempt against Benazir, a local fire company was called in and quickly hosed down the site thereby eliminating important evidence. The police also actively thwarted the doctors from conducting an autopsy. As for Bhutto's vaunted security detachment, they inexplicably drove straight to the residence of her husband, Asif Ali Zardari, instead of following the getaway car to the hospital.[51]

It was Zardari who invited the United Nations to set up a commission of inquiry into his wife's death. This was the most prominent sign yet – not that one was needed – that the government could not be trusted with handling another sensitive investigation. The instructions to the head of the commission, veteran Chilean diplomat Heraldo Muñoz, were clear: the inquiry would not determine *who* ordered the assassination but instead investigate *how* she died. The commission encountered resistance from the army almost as soon as it landed in Pakistan. When Muñoz sought an interview with the COAS and the DGISI, he was refused, prompting him to warn that he would depart Pakistan and declare the commission a failure. This seemed to do the trick, because an interview was arranged with DGISI Shuja Pasha.[52] In Muñoz's rendering of their conversation, the DGISI came across as a boastful man, who asserted that ISI was "better than any rival." Shuja Pasha added that ISI was "not an investigating agency," although it did interpret information as part of its analysis mission. He also reminded the commission that his agency had passed threat information directly to Benazir Bhutto, and that she had been warned not to deliver her speech at Liaquat Bagh on the day of her murder. He did confess that ISI had "no firm" evidence that Beitullah Mehsud was behind the assassination, apparently undercutting the alleged "proof" offered by the communications intercept.[53]

The commissioners diverted from talking about the Bhutto killing and asked DGISI Pasha about ISI's role in domestic Pakistani politics. Pasha replied that there were certain unspecified "misconceptions" about this alleged role, that "in the past, political leaders made extensive use of ISI for political tasks. The ISI is no longer involved in political activities. This has changed now." Muñoz later wrote that everybody present smiled wryly at the DGISI's last assertion.[54] It was all a charade, and the frustrated Chilean diplomat understood this even in the early days of his impossible assignment.

Ultimately, the Muñoz investigation concluded that ISI had aided in the cover-up of Benazir Bhutto's assassination and that federal and local security measures were "fatally insufficient and ineffective." The commissioners questioned the ISI intercept of Beitullah Mehsud, arguing that it lacked specificity. They also pointed out that they were never granted access to the original audio recording.[55] The conclusion outlined in the commission report was unusually blunt: "the failure of the police to investigate effectively Ms Bhutto's assassination was deliberate."[56]

So who did it? Recall that the UN Commission was specifically instructed not to determine who committed the crime. As with virtually every other Pakistani political crime, there is no definitive answer to this question. While Beitullah Mehsud denied involvement, his al-Qa'ida ally confirmed its role without adding any detail. The ISI's position is especially confusing. On the one hand, it repeatedly passed warnings to Bhutto of plots against her, including in the early morning hours of 27 December. On the other, ISI made an effort to cover up details of her death by seizing medical records and holding mysterious discussions with one of her presiding doctors. Was the ISI doing this to cover Musharraf's hide or was this for some other motive? As with virtually all the political murders examined in this history, it is unlikely we will ever know for certain who killed Benazir Bhutto.

Return to democracy

When the PPP won its majority in the February 2008 elections, Syed Yusuf Raza Gilani became the first freely elected Prime Minister of Pakistan since 1999. For Musharraf, the defeat was a stunning blow to his own prospects for political survival, for he had assumed that as a newly "reelected" president, he could lead the country with a friendly parliamentary majority. For the West, the PPP victory was a welcome transition from a military dictatorship that had failed to address Pakistan's chronic political and social problems. With a new slate of civilian personalities, US officials hoped ISI could eventually be reined in.

US hopes aside, the new PPP government had to step carefully: ISI "reform" had always been a controversial issue for the army in the past. Even so, when the government finally acted on 26 July it caught everybody off guard by announcing that the Interior Ministry would assume "administrative, financial and operational control" of the ISI and IB "with immediate effect." The news was received in ISI HQ with both shock and derision. As one unnamed ISI brigadier told the journalist Imtiaz Gul, "we were preparing for our Friday prayers when we got to know about the decision – many couldn't help smiling and laughing."[57] Smiling and laughing? Certainly, given that no one believed the decision would stand once the army generals caught wind of it.

On 27 July, the prime minister was en route to Washington when he received two urgent calls from the army. The generals insisted that under no conditions would ISI be transferred to civilian command; this was an issue that could definitely jeopardize the fragile civilian-army relationship. [58] So, in an embarrassing setback, the government had to reverse its decision, and it was the military's spokesman who put a triumphant spin on the whole affair:

> Although there is an ongoing debate that there should be close coordination between all intelligence agencies, placing ISI under the direct control of the interior division was never discussed. When we realised that the decision had been taken, we discussed the issue with the government and are thankful that there was a realisation of ground realities and our position was accepted. [59]

While the ISI transfer issue briefly flared and then faded away, a new political crisis emerged over President Musharraf. Following the February elections, the PPP and the Pakistan Muslim League – Nawaz faction formed a temporary alliance in the National Assembly and initiated impeachment proceedings against Musharraf. Rather than face the ignominy of defeat, Musharraf instead retired on 18 August; three weeks later, Asif Ali Zardari was elected president on the basis of sympathy for his murdered wife. Musharraf's fall left many of his underlings in an exposed position, including DGISI Nadeem Taj and COAS Ashraf Parvez Kayani. Moreover, Washington let it be known through diplomatic and intelligence channels that it wanted DGISI Taj out because of ISI's links to the July attack on the Indian Embassy in Kabul. [60]

On 29 September 2008, Taj was replaced by Lieutenant General Shuja Pasha. Commissioned into the army in 1974 Pasha was fluent in German and had attended the German Staff College. Shuja Pasha proved to be quite adept at handling foreign journalists, a skill that was especially useful given the increasing friction between the US and Pakistan. [61] In one interview, he insisted that the army was in sync with the civilian government:

> It is completely clear to the army chief and I that this government must succeed. Otherwise we will have a lot of problems in this country. The result would be problems in the west and the east, political destabilisation and trouble with America. Anyone who does not support this democratic government today simply does not understand the current situation. I report regularly to the president and take orders from him. [62]

The new DGISI also rebuffed the frequent allegations that his agency harbored rogue agents by arguing that ISI was a military organization and therefore subject to rigorous military discipline. "Many may think in a different direction," he acknowledged, "and everyone is allowed to think differently, but no one can dare to disobey a command or even do something that was not ordered." [63] Given comments like these and others, it is not surprising that DGISI Pasha was seen by some observers domestically and abroad as the long-awaited reformer who would clean out ISI. [64] As in the past, however, these hopes were not borne out by subsequent events.

Notes

1 M. Haider, "Pakistan most dangerous country for journalists," *Dawn*, 4 May 2014, www.dawn.com/news/1104120 [accessed 23/11/15].

2 D. Filkins, "The Journalist and the Spies," *The New Yorker*, 19 September 2011, www.newyorker.com/magazine/2011/09/19/the-journalist-and-the-spies [accessed 1/8/15].

3 Ibid.

4 Quoted in Committee to Protect Journalists, "Roots of Impunity," 23 May 2013, http://cpj.org/reports/2013/05/Pakistan-roots-impunity-saleem-shahzad.php [accessed 7/11/13].

5 Ibid.; K. Brulliard, "Pakistan's Spy Agencies are Suspected of ties to Reporter's Death," *WP*, 1 June 2011, www.washingtonpost.com/world/asia-pacific/Pakistans-spy-agencies-are-suspected-of-ties-to-reporters-death/2011/05/31/AGhrMhFH_story.html [accessed 2/8/15].

6 Filkins, "The Journalist and the Spies," op. cit.

7 Ibid.; "Pakistan 'Approved Saleem Shahzad Murder' Says Mullen," BBC, 8 July 2011, www.bbc.com/news/world-south-asia-14074814 [accessed 3/8/15]; S. Shahzad, "Pakistan's Military under al Qaeda Attack," *Asia Times Online*, 24 May 2011, www.atimes.com/atimes/South_Asia/ME24Df02.html [accessed 3/8/15].

8 Filkins, "The Journalist and the Spies," op. cit.

9 Ibid.; Brulliard, "Pakistan's Spy Agencies," op. cit.; De Borchgrave, "Commentary: Topsy-Turvy Alliance," UPI, 6 July 2011, www.upi.com/Top_News/Analysis/de-Borchgrave/2011/07/06/Commentary-Topsy-turvy-alliance/19701309947558/ [accessed 3/8/15].

10 Quoted in Filkins, "The Journalist and the Spies," op. cit.

11 Quoted in Brulliard, "Pakistan's Spy Agencies," op. cit.

12 "Pakistan 'Approved Saleem Shahzad Murder,'" Says Mullen, op. cit.

13 Ibid.

14 M. Mazzetti, *The Way of the Knife*, New York: Penguin, 2013, 293.

15 Quoted in Filkins, "The Journalist and the Spies," op. cit.

16 Amnesty International, "Pakistan: Journalists under siege from threats, violence and killings," 29 April 2014, www.amnestyusa.org/our-work/countries/asia-and-the-pacific/Pakistan [accessed 27/2/15].

17 D. Walsh, "Attack on Journalist starts Battle in Pakistani Press," *NYT*, 27 April 2014, www.nytimes.com/2014/04/27/world/asia/attack-on-journalist-starts-battle-in-Pakistani-press.html [accessed 3/8/15]; S. Shah, "Pakistani Spy Chief, Crucial to US Aims in Afghanistan, to Stay On," McClatchy Newspapers, 10 March 2010, www.afghanistannewscenter.com/news/2010/march/mar112010.html#7 [accessed 2/8/15].

18 Quoted in Filkins, "The Journalist and the Spies," op. cit.

19 A. Rashid, *Pakistan on the Brink*, New York: Viking, 2012, 146.

20 Filkins, "The Journalist and the Spies," op. cit.; P. Constable, *Playing with Fire: Pakistan at War with Itself*, New York: Random House, 2011, 111–112.

21 Walsh, "Attack on Journalist starts Battle," op. cit.; D. Walsh & S. Masood, "Pakistan Asked to Shut Down News Channel," *NYT*, 23 April 2014, www.nytimes.com/2014/04/23/world/asia/attack-on-journalist-spurs-new-dispute-in-Pakistan.html [accessed 2/8/15].

22 S. Masood, "Critic of Pakistani Military wounded in Karachi Attack," *NYT*, 20 April 2014, www.nytimes.com/2014/04/20/world/asia/critic-of-Pakistani-military-wounded-in-karachi-attack.html [accessed 3/8/15].

23 M. Ahmed, "Pakistan's Army wants TV News Channel Shut Down," Associated Press, 23 April 2014, www.washingtonpost.com/world/asia_pacific/Pakistans-army-seeks-closure-of-tv-channel/2014/04/23/68e6ef8a-cab8-11e3-b81a-6fff56bc591e_print.html [accessed 30/4/14]; Walsh and Masood, "Pakistan Asked to Shut Down News Channel," op. cit.

24 M. Ahmed, "In Pakistan, Signs Praise Spies as Nation Changes," Associated Press, 27 April 2014, www.washingtonpost.com/world/asia_pacific/in-Pakistan-signs-praise-spies-as-nation-changes/2014/04/27/f9c1edac-ce0a-11e3-a714-be7e7f142085_print.html [accessed 30/4/14]; Walsh, "Attack on Journalist starts Battle," op. cit.

25 B. Dietz, "Q&A: Pakistan's Hamid Mir Speaks about Climate for Press Freedom following Attack," https://cpj.org/blog/2014/08/qa-Pakistans-hamid-mir-speaks-about-climate-for-pr.php [accessed 27/2/15].

26 Constable, *Playing with Fire*, op. cit., 111.

27 D. Filkins, "What Pakistan Knew About Bin Laden," *The New Yorker*, 2 May 2011, www.newyorker.com/news/news-desk/what-Pakistan-knew-about-bin-laden [accessed 3/8/15].

28 Constable, *Playing with Fire*, op. cit., 110–111.

29 D. Walsh, "Court Challenges put Unusual Spotlight on Pakistani Spy Agency," *NYT*, 6 Feb 2012, www.nytimes.com/2012/02/07/world/asia/isi-in-Pakistan-faces-court-cases.html [accessed 2/8/15]; I. Malik, *Pakistan: Democracy, Terrorism and the Building of a Nation*, Northampton, MA: Olive Branch Press, 2010, 64.

30 R. McCarthy, "Musharraf Sacks General to Boost Power," *Guardian*, www.the-guardian.com/world/2002/jun/28/Pakistan.rorymccarthy [accessed 27/2/15]; Ayesha Jalal, *The Struggle for Pakistan*, Cambridge: Belknap, 2014, 329.

31 I. Gul, *The Most Dangerous Place*, New York: Viking, 2010, 180–181; H. Haqqani, *Pakistan: Between Mosque and Military*, Washington, DC: Carnegie Endowment, 2005, 259; A. Rashid, *Descent into Chaos*, New York: Viking, 2008, 156; McCarthy, "Musharraf Sacks General to Boost Power," op. cit.

32 Rashid, *Descent into Chaos*, op. cit., 158; A. Riaz, *Islamist Militancy in Bangladesh*, London: Routledge, 2008, 41; A. Mir, "2002 Polls were also rigged by a COAS," 21 October 2012, www.thenews.com.pk/Todays-News-13-18313-2002-polls-were-also-rigged-by-a-COAS [accessed 27/2/15].

33 H. Muñoz, *Getting Away with Murder*, New York: W.W. Norton, 2014, 125, 134, 175; S. Coll, *The Grand Trunk Road*, New York: Penguin, 2009, 292–293;

34 Gul, *Dangerous*, op. cit., 179.

35 Muñoz, *Getting Away with Murder*, op. cit., 119, 125; Coll, *Grand Trunk*, op. cit. 309.

36 Muñoz, *Getting Away with Murder*, op. cit., 184.

37 Ibid., 124.

38 H. Muñoz, "Getting Away with Murder: Benazir Bhutto's Assassination," Talks at Google https://www.youtube.com/watch?v=KFBr3o4cFRk [accessed 27/2/15].

39 Muñoz, *Getting Away with Murder*, op. cit., 128, 196–197

40 Coll, *Grand Trunk*, op. cit., 294–295.

41 Muñoz, *Getting Away with Murder*, op. cit., 171; Z. Hussain, *The Scorpion's Tail*, New York: Free Press, 2010, 138.

42 C. Lamb, "Who Murdered Benazir Bhutto?" *Sunday Times*, 2 May 2010, www.timesonline.co.uk/tol/news/world/middle_east/article7111333.ece [accessed 20/4/11].

43 Muñoz, "Getting Away with Murder: Benazir Bhutto's Assassination," op. cit.

44 B. Till, "Could the U.S. Have Prevented Benazir Bhutto's Death?" *The Atlantic*, 23 May 2011, www.theatlantic.com/international/archive/2011/05/could-the-us-have-prevented-benazir-bhuttos-death/239282/ [accessed 6/8/15].

45 Muñoz, *Getting Away with Murder*, op. cit., 133–134; Lamb, "Who Murdered Benazir Bhutto?" op. cit.

46 Muñoz, *Getting Away with Murder*, op. cit., 134–135; C. Gall, "What Pakistan Knew about Bin Laden," *NYT*, 19 March 2014, www.nytimes.com/2014/03/23/magazine/what-Pakistan-knew-about-bin-laden.html?hpw&rref=magazine [accessed 19/3/14].

47 Coll, *Grand Trunk*, op. cit., 292–293; Rashid, *Descent into Chaos*, op. cit., 378.

48 Muñoz, *Getting Away with Murder*, op. cit., 149.

49 Ibid., 153–154.
50 Ibid.; Muñoz, "Getting Away with Murder: Benazir Bhutto's Assassination," op. cit.
51 Muñoz, "Getting Away with Murder: Benazir Bhutto's Assassination."
52 Muñoz, *Getting Away with Murder*, op. cit., 173–174.
53 Ibid., 174.
54 Ibid., 175.
55 Ibid., 163; "PPP Censured in UN Report," *The Nation*, 17 April 2010, http://nation.com.pk/Pakistan-news-newspaper-daily-english-online//Politics/17-apr-2010/ppp-censured-in-un-report [accessed 21/4/11].
56 Lamb, "Who Murdered Benazir Bhutto?" op. cit.
57 Gul, *Dangerous*, op. cit., 181–182.
58 M. Termizi, "Interior Ministry Gets IB, ISI Control," *The Nation*, 27 July 2008, http://nation.com.pk/politics/27-Jul-2008/Interior-Ministry-gets-ISI-IB-control [accessed 3/8/15]; O. Waraich, "Pakistan's Spies Elude its Government," *Time*, 31 July 2008 http://content.time.com/time/world/article/0,8599,1828207,00.html [accessed 3/8/15].
59 S.I. Raza, "Govt forced to withdraw ISI decision," *Dawn*, 28 July 2008, www.dawn.com/news/313820/govt-forced-to-withdraw-isi-decision [accessed 4/8/15].
60 Filkins, "The Journalist and the Spies," op. cit.
61 "ISI Chief Gets Extension in Service," *The Nation*, 10 March 2010, http://nation.com.pk/politics/10-Mar-2010/ISI-chief-gets-extension-in-service [accessed 4/8/15]; "I Was Ready to Visit Delhi: ISI Chief," *The Nation*, 7 January 2009, www.nation.com.pk/Pakistan-news-newspaper-daily-english-online/Politics/07-Jan-2009/I-was-ready-to-visit-Delhi-ISI-Chief [accessed 20/4/11]. For an interesting Arab perspective on Shuja Pasha's media savvy see "*Yanthar illa al-Istakhabarat al-Bakistania (ISI) beshakl amm bedaraja kabira min al-riba*," al-Majalla, 8 August 2010, www.arb.majalla.com/2010/08/ [accessed 14/11/15].
62 "I was ready to visit Delhi: ISI Chief," op. cit.
63 Ibid.
64 S. Shah, "Pakistani Spy Chief, Crucial to US Aims in Afghanistan, to Stay On," McClatchy Newspapers, 10 March 2010.

20 US Operations in Pakistan

On 13 November 2009 at 0645, a van tried breaking through an army check-point on Artillery Road in the northwestern Pakistani city of Peshawar. Alert guards fired at the van, forcing the driver to explode his bomb prematurely. The ensuing explosion damaged ISI's three-storey provincial headquarters building and left a crater nearly seven feet deep; the shock wave was felt at nearby Army Stadium, leading many to believe that an earthquake had taken place. An enormous cloud of dust and smoke rose above the city as emergency crews rushed to the scene; at least 12 were killed and more than 60 injured.[1] This attack was only the latest in a series aimed at ISI by the *Tehrik-e Taliban Pakistan* (TTP) or Pakistan Taliban, elements of which were targeting the government and the army. Earlier that year, on 27 May, a suicide bomber struck near the Punjab ISI headquarters building in Lahore, leaving 45 dead and some 290 injured. Two years prior to that, in November 2007, a suicide bomber drove his car into a bus carrying ISI employees outside Camp Hamza in Rawalpindi, killing at least 35.[2]

Pakistan's inner wars

What these attacks meant to ISI was starkly evident: the wheel of jihadi violence aimed at India and Afghanistan had come around full circle and was now consuming its own. Nearly three decades after ISI had first dabbled with Islamism to offset Pashtun nationalism, the jihadi Frankenstein had slipped its bonds and was now throttling its master. For years after 9/11, ISI tried distinguishing between "good" versus "bad" militants, but such distinctions were increasingly erroneous and irrelevant. The "good" militants fighting Afghanistan and India such as the Taliban, Haqqanis, and *LeT* were inextricably linked with the "bad" ones seeking to overthrow the Pakistani government. The jihadis were interconnected and often blended together; they formed bonds fighting India and the coalition in Afghanistan. Disentangling them exceeded even the skills of the ISI, and nobody knew regional jihadis better than Pakistan.[3]

Just as the US suffered long-term consequences for backing radicals in the anti-Soviet war in Afghanistan, so too did Islamabad reap what it sowed when it supported these same groups plus the Taliban in the 1990s and beyond. For decades, Pakistan had been shaken by seemingly endemic sectarian and political violence, much of which can be traced back to ISI's proxy wars against Afghanistan and India. Yet the proxies could not be contained, they metastasized in the training camps or the distant battlefields of Kashmir and Afghanistan, and the blowback manifested itself in rising sectarianism inside Pakistan between Shia and Sunni extremists. In this environment, it was the average Pakistani who was bound to suffer the most; indeed, they perished in their thousands.

After 9/11, all the pent up forces that had been building in western Pakistan exploded, and nowhere was this more apparent than the Federally Administered Tribal Areas (FATA). An anachronism from a bygone era, the FATA was run on a British colonial criminal code that included collective punishment and no right of appeal. In return for relative quiescence regarding the Raj, the Pashtun tribes were allowed to run their own show. This arrangement was perpetuated after Pakistan achieved independence; however, the long-term consequences were government neglect, illiteracy, poverty, drug trafficking and the spread of Islamist ideologies.[4]

After 9/11, the FATA was an "escape hatch" for thousands of jihadis fleeing Afghanistan. For years, it was widely believed that Osama Bin Laden and Ayman al-Zawahiri were hiding out here, where they would have enjoyed the protection of the tribes and local mullahs. The FATA was a persistent bone of contention between the US and Pakistan, with the former urging the latter to send military forces into the agencies and roust the militants. When Pakistan finally did so the result was a disaster: significant civilian casualties, tribal resistance and a humbled army which discovered it lacked the necessary doctrine and equipment for COIN. The Pakistan army was reluctant to get mired in what it regarded as a civil war so a pattern emerged where the army would fight an engagement or two and then conclude a truce brokered by local tribal and religious leaders. Such agreements never lasted long, and both parties would be dragged into a new round of fighting with harsh repercussions for the civilian population. According to Pakistani estimates, over 2,300 Army and Frontier Corps officers have died fighting in the FATA, including three generals, five brigadiers, and 4,000 other ranks. For its part, ISI reportedly lost 73 officers in the FATA from 2002 to 2011.[5]

Throughout the decade after 9/11, the extremist monster stalked Pakistan, moving beyond the FATA to the NWFP, Punjab and even the capital. Things got worse in 2007 when Beitullah Mehsud welded together a coalition of extremist groups called the Pakistan Taliban. In 2009, Taliban units entered the idyllic Swat Valley, but rather than evict them, the government chose a ceasefire. The Pakistan Taliban was allowed to implement its "Islamic justice" in Swat with the usual results: burned schools, suicide bomb factories, public executions and beatings, kidnapped "war brides," summary judgments, and thousands of refugees.[6] It was an untenable situation, so in April 2009 another battle for Swat began.

On 25 March 2010, the former ISI Afghan experts Colonel Imam and Khalid Khwaja as well as a UK filmmaker were abducted in North Waziristan while making a documentary on US drone strikes. Their abductors were from a previously unknown group called the Asian Tigers (a probable Pakistan Taliban front), which demanded a $10 million ransom and the release of several Taliban officials from ISI custody, including Mullah Baradar, Mullah Kabir and Mansur Dadullah.[7] Khwaja, a man linked to the abduction of Daniel Pearl, was videotaped by his captors "confessing" to the sins of his past: "I am known among the media and masses as a thoroughbred gentleman," he intoned, "but in fact I was an ISI and CIA mole." He went on to claim that *Lashkar-e-Taiba*, *Jaish-e-Mohamed*, and *Harakatul Mujahidin* received the "financial cooperation of the Pakistani secret services."[8] When the ransom demands were not met, both Khwaja and Colonel Imam were executed in the presence of Pakistan Taliban leader Hakimullah Mehsud.[9] Thus the jihad heroes of one war became the infidel victims of the next.

The government was reluctant to admit that Pakistan was fighting an internal war, a life-and-death struggle for different visions of Islam and state. This was probably due to the fact that the state itself is partly responsible for the escalating violence across much of the country. As handmaiden of the army, ISI is a self-described guardian of Pakistan's national interests, yet in pursuing its proxy wars, ISI has jeopardized the health and stability of the very society it is supposed to protect. We do not know if the army leadership has ever conducted a serious ends-means discussion on Kashmir and Afghanistan or asked the fundamental question: is a "liberated" Kashmir worth a ruined Pakistan?

ISI–CIA cooperation

It has already been noted how the ISI–CIA relationship changed significantly after 9/11, when both agencies found some common ground against al-Qa'ida. When ISI established a formal counter terrorism wing (Directorate C) with US assistance, day-to-day liaison between the two was put on a more solid footing, although the US increasingly suspected Pakistan of double-dealing.[10] At first, ISI was a vital player in the US war against al-Qa'ida and helped arrest several important al-Qa'ida leaders. In addition, it even permitted the CIA to establish small bases within Pakistani army stations, including Quetta, although the movements of CIA case officers were restricted. One CIA officer likened his Quetta assignment to house arrest with ISI wardens holding the keys. Other CIA bases were established in Miram Shah (North Waziristan) and Wana (South Waziristan) with similar restrictions.[11]

By 2007–2008, many observers believed that the coalition was losing the war in Afghanistan. Neither the Afghan government nor its international partners could fill the security and governance vacuum created after the 2001 collapse of the Taliban. Islamabad aggressively pushed back against American insinuations that the Taliban problem was linked to Pakistan policy, arguing that the fault lay with the coalition and its inability to bring security to Afghanistan. The US was searching for a scapegoat, the Pakistanis insisted, because it had bitten off more than it could chew after invading Iraq in 2003.[12]

Still, American frustration with its "major non-NATO ally" grew with each new Haqqani bombing inside Kabul as well as a veritable flood of intelligence reporting of Pakistan-based insurgent training camps. The CIA felt it had been burned too many times by ISI in the hunt for al-Qa'ida, so it stepped up unilateral operations inside Pakistan without ISI consent. Some of these operations gathered intelligence on al-Qa'ida, *LeT* and the nuclear weapons program, while others provided targets for CIA drones. ISI was increasingly aware of CIA unilateral operations on its turf and its resentment grew with each CIA allegation of ISI perfidy.[13] All of this came into the open in early 2011 with the arrest of CIA officer Raymond Davis in Lahore.

Raymond Davis imbroglio

On 27 January 2011, an American named Raymond Davis found himself in a jam on the crowded streets of Lahore. His training in surveillance detection had paid off when he discovered that his Honda Civic was being trailed by two Pakistanis on a motorcycle. The 36-year-old former Special Forces soldier had been working for the Blackwater security company, and lately he had been contracted by CIA to collect intelligence on the Pakistani military. When the motorbike surged past Davis's car, stopped and the Pakistanis pulled out guns, Davis grabbed his 9mm Glock and killed both by pumping five rounds through his windshield. Then he radioed the US Consulate for help. That help came in an emergency vehicle that unfortunately ran over a bystander as it was hurtling through the streets to Davis and had to return to the consulate without stopping. Davis was left to handle matters on his own.

When the police searched Davis's car, they found a black mask, a portable telescope, a satellite phone, 100 bullets for his pistol and a camera full of pictures of Pakistani military facilities.[14] He was charged with double homicide and illegal possession of a firearm. Meanwhile, US diplomats insisted that Davis be released immediately since he had diplomatic immunity, but the Pakistanis refused, noting that Davis had not been declared to the Foreign Ministry as an accredited diplomat.[15] Meanwhile, there was some speculation about Davis's pursuers. Washington accepted that they were robbers who had selected the wrong victim, but there was no explanation of how this conclusion was reached. Others suggested a more plausible alternative: that the pursuers were part of an ISI surveillance team that was overly aggressive in monitoring Davis's movements.[16] The Pakistanis asked themselves how and when Davis managed to get inside their country, and some suspected that in the aftermath of a 2005 earthquake in Gilgit-Baltistan, hundreds of spies entered the country under the guise of disaster relief workers. Among these, ISI suspected, were CIA officers and intelligence teams run by the Joint Special Operations Command in Fort Bragg, North Carolina. The mission of these teams was to collect intelligence on the locations of Pakistani nuclear weapons and the links between ISI and militants.[17]

Raymond Davis became a powerful symbol of the near-collapse in a CIA–ISI relationship that had peaked in the 1980s against the Soviet Union and even enjoyed a brief renaissance in the post-9/11 hunt for al-Qa'ida. But after ten years of fighting in Afghanistan, and a growing divergence in national goals, mutual mistrust had reached the point where the CIA was aggressively conducting unilateral operations inside Pakistan aimed at uncovering ISI's jihadi links. Moreover, ISI was unwilling to treat the Davis case quietly and amicably as it would have in the past. In part this stemmed from ISI's determination to make a public issue out of the CIA's unilateral operations.[18] ISI even sent a letter to the *Wall Street Journal*, spelling out its anger toward its American counterpart: "It is regrettable that CIA leadership on many occasions has failed to show respect to the relationship of the two agencies and has acted with arrogance towards ISI which has resulted in weakening the relationship on which it is entirely dependent."[19] This was an unprecedented public airing of dirty laundry, and it was accompanied by stories in the US media where unidentified ISI officials vented their spleen. As one put it, CIA personnel "have to start showing respect, not belittling us, nor being belligerent to us, not treating us like we are their lackeys."[20] The CIA tried putting a more positive spin on things publicly, hoping to ride out the storm. In an official statement, Langley declared that "the agency's ties to the ISI have been strong over the years, and when there are issues to sort out, we work through them.... That's the sign of a healthy partnership."[21]

The situation was no better behind the scenes. DGISI Shuja Pasha at first tried to handle the Davis case in personal communications with CIA Director Leon Panetta, however, Panetta denied Davis was a CIA employee, and this added to the DGISI's resentment. Pasha decided to wait for the Americans to make an offer; after all, he still had his American captive, and at some point the US would have to make a deal.[22] It didn't help matters that the Davis affair coincided with the recent arrival of a new CIA Station Chief in Islamabad, who apparently did not intend to treat ISI as the occasionally wayward ally that many of his predecessors had done. According to *New York Times* journalist, Mark Mazzetti, the new Station Chief had a different approach:

> Old-school and stubborn, the new chief did not come to Pakistan to be friendly with the I.S.I. Instead, he wanted to recruit more Pakistani agents to work for the C.I.A. under the I.S.I.'s nose, expand electronic surveillance of I.S.I. offices and share little information with Pakistani intelligence officers.[23]

The CIA's more aggressive approach to ISI was not welcome by the US Ambassador, Cameron Munter, who, as a result of the Davis case, found himself embroiled in an unwanted public spat with the Pakistani government. Internally, the ambassador argued that it was wiser to confess to Davis's activities, get him out of Pakistan as soon as possible, and then move on, but the

Station Chief was determined to concede nothing, saying this would demonstrate US adherence to principle. Eventually, Ambassador Munter approached DGISI Pasha himself and confessed that Davis was working for the CIA. This paved the way for a negotiated compromise where the US paid $2.34 million in "blood money" to the families of the three slain Pakistanis in return for Davis's release.[24] The Raymond Davis affair was over, but it cast a pall over an already turbulent intelligence relationship.

The Davis case vividly illustrates the difficulties built into any intelligence liaison arrangement, since both agencies are intelligence collectors by definition and therefore expected to spy on each other in principle. In only rare cases, such as the US–UK–Commonwealth Five-Eyes arrangement, do the parties formally agree to refrain from spying on each other. The Soviet war in the Afghanistan case showed that CIA and ISI could work together only within the narrow interstices of a shared enemy, and even this was subject to change. Therefore, it should come as no surprise that the CIA–ISI relationship was marked by frequent acrimony, especially when national interests clearly diverged. This was certainly true in Afghanistan after 2004, where Islamabad's goals were substantially different from those of the coalition.

CI is the arena where intelligence agencies carry out operations against each other. As discussed earlier, the CIA increased unilateral operations inside Pakistan after the limits of its bilateral relationship with ISI had been reached. ISI certainly detected the influx of undeclared US intelligence officers, and the rising number of Americans inside Pakistan made it more difficult for CI to track them. There are indications that ISI dangled spies in front of suspected US intelligence officers by offering information on Pakistani nuclear weapons, for example.[25] When several of these fishing expeditions were discovered by the CIA, Langley scrubbed its Afghan and Pakistani human sources and reportedly uncovered at least 12 double agents working for ISI. According to unnamed "former US officials" – undoubtedly retired CIA case officers – Pakistani double agent operations are usually aimed at uncovering US intelligence officers instead of feeding disinformation.[26]

In addition to Raymond Davis, there were other signs of decay in the CIA–ISI relationship. The new Station Chief who had arrived just before Davis was arrested was only the latest in a string of chiefs who were less interested in tending the liaison relationship and more concerned about treating the ISI as an adversary. Indeed, according to one report, CIA case officers were instructed to use "Moscow Rules" counter-surveillance techniques in Pakistan, a clear sign that ISI had adopted a more aggressive stance against undeclared US intelligence activities. By 2011, Station Chiefs were cycling through Islamabad Station rapidly, inhibiting the buildup of trust and amicability that had been so valuable in the past. In May 2011, one Station Chief had to leave Pakistan after his name was leaked in a legal complaint sent to the Pakistani police by victims of CIA drone attacks in the tribal areas. Some suspected that this was in retaliation for a civil lawsuit filed in New York City implicating DGISI Shuja Pasha in the 2008 Mumbai attack.[27]

Faisal Shahzad

The US–Pakistan relationship reached another one of its troughs when Faisal Shahzad tried to set off a car bomb in New York City's Times Square on 1 May 2010. Only alert bystanders and a faulty IED prevented this from becoming a mass casualty event. The ensuing US investigation revealed that Shahzad had received IED training at a militant camp in Pakistan, and it was this news that prompted the White House to send DCIA Leon Panetta and the President's National Security Advisor, General (Retd) James Jones to Islamabad. DGISI Shuja Pasha begged off meeting the American delegation, pleading an undisclosed illness, but everyone knew that he was snubbing them.[28]

Shuja Pasha probably acted this way because he knew the Americans were coming to chastise and criticize, and he was tired of hearing it. In fact, on 19 May, Jones and Panetta delivered a blunt message to President Asif Ali Zardari. General Jones warned Zardari that "we're living on borrowed time.... We consider the Times Square attempt a successful plot because neither the American nor the Pakistani intelligence agencies could intercept or stop it." Then Panetta produced a chart outlining the numerous links between Shahzad and the Pakistan Taliban. The US government had additional intelligence that this group was planning further attacks against US interests. Jones chimed in that even the *Lashkar-e-Taiba* leader, Zaki Ur Rahman Lakhvi "continues to direct LeT operations from his [Pakistani] detention center."[29]

The Americans made several demands of Zardari including "full intelligence sharing," improved counter terrorism cooperation, faster visa approvals and access to passenger lists on all aircraft entering and departing Pakistan. Obtaining this kind of cooperation was vital, Jones continued, because if a future bombing like Shahzad's were successful "no one will be able to stop the response and consequences. This is not a threat, just a statement of political fact."[30] Moreover, Jones warned Zardari, the US had already developed a "retribution" plan for any terrorist attacks on US soil that could be traced back to Pakistan. Such a plan included bombing some 150 training camps inside Pakistan, air and missile strikes, as well as the insertion of Special Forces teams presumably from neighboring Afghanistan. Zardari interjected, highlighting the extent of Pakistani assistance on the CT front, but Jones wasn't buying this line any longer:

> You can do something that costs you no money. It may be politically difficult, but it's the right thing to do if you really have the future of your country in mind. And that is to reject all forms of terrorism as a viable instrument of national policy inside your borders.[31]

But "we rejected it," Zardari protested. Did Pakistan not have a strategic partnership with the US? He asked whether the US would aid Pakistan in a crisis like the present one. Jones's response was curt and lacking ambiguity: the US government could no longer tolerate Pakistan's "a la carte approach" to counter terrorism. Pakistan was playing Russian roulette, he concluded, and one day Islamabad might gravely miscalculate and underestimate the US response to another terrorism attack.[32]

Drones

Candidate Barack Obama had promised to refocus American attention on Afghanistan during the 2008 election, and this implied a renewed focus on Pakistan and the broader regional conflict. A surge strategy was employed in 2009–2010 in an attempt to reverse the tide against the Taliban in southern Afghanistan albeit with only limited success. But the most characteristic feature of the new US approach to the so-called Af-Pak Theater was the escalating use of drones against militant targets inside Pakistan. On one level, the drone campaign was very successful since it killed several high-profile militants, including Hakimullah and Beitullah Mehsud, Ilyas Kashmiri and Badruddin Haqqani. On another, though, the campaign was very unpopular in Pakistan and the subject of many protests and demonstrations.

The CIA's drone effort began in June 2004, when a secret deal was forged with ISI that allowed the former to use drones in Pakistani airspace. Yet the Pakistanis also imposed restrictions on this effort: (1) ISI must approve each strike; (2) ISI must have the right to veto the target list; (3) the drones were to fly in designated areas only (Quetta and Balochistan were excepted); and (4) the US would never acknowledge the strikes whereas ISI could take credit or stay silent. The CIA's Pakistan-based drone operations were staged out of Shamsi Air Base in Pakistan Balochistan, but others were undoubtedly flown out of Afghanistan as well.[33]

Although it was to be very successful later on, the drone program did not start out on the right foot. The CIA was frustrated by delays in getting ISI to approve or reject the target list. Often missiles would hit empty targets, leading to suspicions that ISI tipped off the militants in advance.[34] It wasn't until the July 2008 attack on the Indian Embassy in Kabul that the US government authorized the CIA to launch drone strikes without prior ISI notification.[35] Because of this policy switch and the change in US administrations, drone strikes in Pakistan increased significantly with 54 in 2009 compared to 36 in 2008 and 4 in 2007. Between 2009 and 2011, drones killed an estimated 1,500 militants in Pakistan, although an untold number of civilians were killed as well.[36] As the drone campaign reaped its success, ISI quietly fanned a barrage of Pakistani media criticism at the United States.[37] It also demanded an end to the strikes in public forums, even though Islamabad had quietly endorsed them.[38] The US government countered with some media leaks of its own. For example, one article in the *Washington Post* noted how the CIA provided the Pakistanis with routine briefings on the drone attacks and their results. The CIA Deputy Director would meet frequently with Pakistan's Ambassador to Washington, Hussain Haqqani, to discuss drone warfare and ISI's suspected role in tipping off certain militants before attacks.[39]

For all its success, though, the CIA drone effort was on life support, especially after the Raymond Davis affair of 2011. The US Embassy in Islamabad was reporting constantly on the anger being generated inside Pakistan as a result of the drones, and it warned that anti-American sentiments in the country had never been higher. Pakistan forced the operations inside the country to be scaled back, and by June 2011, Islamabad had ordered all drone activity at Shamsi to cease immediately.[40] This latter action was almost certainly retaliation for the May 2011 US raid against Osama Bin Laden.

Notes

1 "Bombers Hit Pakistan Spy Agency," *BBC News*, 13 November 2009, http://news.bbc.co.uk/2/hi/south_asia/8358109.stm [accessed 4/8/15].

2 "Taliban blamed for Lahore attack," *BBC News*, 28 May 2009, http://news.bbc.co.uk/2/hi/south_asia/8070408.stm [accessed 4/8/15]; J. Sturcke, "Deadly bomb blast in Lahore," *Guardian*, 27 May 2009, www.theguardian.com/world/2009/may/27/powerful-bomb-blast-lahore-Pakistan [accessed 4/8/15]; S. Jones & C.C. Fair, *Counterinsurgency in Pakistan*, Santa Monica, CA: Rand Corporation, 2010, 63–64; S. Coll, *The Grand Trunk Road*, New York: Penguin, 2009, 304.

3 D. Rohde & K. Mulvihill, *A Rope and a Prayer*, New York: Viking, 2010, 327; M. Mazzetti & E. Schmitt, "Afghan Strikes by Taliban get Pakistan Help, U.S. Aides Say," 26 March, 2009, *NYT*, www.nytimes.com/2009/03/26/world/asia/26tribal.html?_r=0 [accessed 4/8/15]; D. Ignatius, "Revenge on the Taliban from 10,000 Feet," *WP*, 6 February 2010, www.washingtonpost.com/wp-dyn/content/article/2010/02/02/AR2010020203514.html [accessed 4/8/15].

4 Z. Hussain, *Frontline: The Struggle with Militant Islam*, New York: CUP, 2007, 125; R. Grenier, *88 Days to Kandahar*, New York: Simon & Schuster, 2015, 385; I. Gul, *The Most Dangerous Place*, New York: Viking, 2010, 176.

5 Gul, *Dangerous*, op. cit., 213; A. Rashid, *Pakistan on the Brink*, New York: Viking, 2012, 150.

6 S. Koelbl, "Islamists Triumph in Swat Valley," *Der Spiegel*, 21 February 2009, www.spiegel.de/international/world/islamists-triumph-in-swat-valley-bowing-down-to-the-taliban-a-609575.html [accessed 4/8/15].

7 A. Siddique, "Pakistani Military Faces Decision on North Waziristan," Radio Free Europe/Radio Liberty, 5 May 2010, www.rferl.org/content/Pakistani_Military_Faces_Decision_On_North_Waziristan/2033080.html [accessed 4/8/15]; A. Rodriguez, "Pakistan Tribal Region No Simple Target," *LAT*, 24 May 2010, http://articles.latimes.com/2010/may/24/world/la-fg-Pakistan-militants-20100524 [accessed 4/8/15].

8 T. Wright & R. Mehsud, "Pakistani Islamists Hold Ex-Spy," *WSJ*, 19 April 2010, www.afghanistannewscenter.com/news/2010/april/apr202010.html#14 [accessed 4/8/15]; A. Mir, "Key Jihadi Behind Col Imam's Murder," *The News*, 24 January 20, www.thenews.com.pk/Todays-News-13–3521-Key-Jihadi-behind-Col-Imams-murder [accessed 4/8/15]; S. Shahzad, "Confessions of a Pakistani Spy," *Asia Times*, 27 April 2010, www.atimes.com/atimes/South_Asia/LD24Df04.html [accessed 5/8/15].

9 "Pakistani Taliban Issue Video of Slain Spy Officer," Xinhua News, 19 February 2011, http://news.xinhuanet.com/english2010/world/2011–02/19/c_13740065.htm [accessed 4/8/15].

10 *Abbottabad Commission Report*, http://webapps.aljazeera.net/aje/custom/binladen files/Pakistan-Bin-Laden-Dossier.pdf [accessed 15/4/14]; M. Mazzetti, *The Way of the Knife*, New York: Penguin, 2013, 168.

11 B. Woodward, *Obama's War*, New York: Simon & Schuster, 2010, 286–287; "Pakistan Agrees to Expand CIA Presence in Quetta," *The News*, 21 November 2010, www.thenews.com.pk/Todays-News-13-2183-Pakistan-agrees-to-expand-CIA-presence-in-Quetta [accessed 4/8/15]; Mazzetti, *Way of the Knife*, op. cit., 156–160, 169.

12 B. Plett, "American Leverage in South Asia," *BBC News*, http://news.bbc.co.uk/2/hi/south_asia/7971128.stm [accessed 4/8/15].

13 E. Lake, "Enemy of the State," *New Republic*, 19 May 2001, www.newrepublic.com/article/world/magazine/88623/Pakistani-intelligence-osama-bin-laden-cia [accessed 1/8/15]; Rashid, *Pakistan on the Brink*, op. cit., 171; "CIA and Pakistan Locked in Aggressive Spy Battles," Associated Press, 7 June 2010, http://dailycaller.com/2010/07/06/cia-and-Pakistan-locked-in-aggressive-spy-battles/ [accessed 4/8/15].

14 M. Mazzetti, "How a Single Spy Helped Turn Pakistan Against the United States," *NYT*, 9 April 2013, www.nytimes.com/2013/04/14/magazine/raymond-davis-Pakistan.html [accessed 4/8/15]; "ISI–CIA Ties Hit Rock Bottom," *The Nation*, 25 February 2011, http://nation.com.pk/Pakistan-news-newspaper-daily-english-online/Politics/25-Feb-2011/ISICIA-ties-hit-rock-bottom/1 [accessed 20/4/11]; D. Sanger, *Confront and Conceal*, New York: Crown, 2012, 82–83.

15 Rashid, *Pakistan on the Brink*, op. cit., 171.

16 E. Schmitt & T. Shanker, *Counterstrike*, New York: Times Books, 2011, 244; Sanger, *Confront*, op. cit., 82–83; BBC, *Secret Pakistan*, Part 2: Backlash.

17 Mazzetti, *Way of the Knife*, op. cit., 164–165; M. Ambinder & D. Grady, "The Story of How U.S. Special Forces Infiltrated Pakistan," *The Atlantic*, 15 February 2012, www.theatlantic.com/international/archive/2012/02/the-story-of-how-us-special-forces-infiltrated-Pakistan/253100/ [accessed 4/8/15].

18 Rashid, *Pakistan on the Brink*, op. cit., 171; "ISI–CIA Ties Hit Rock Bottom," op. cit.

19 "ISI–CIA Ties Hit Rock Bottom," op. cit.

20 Ibid.

21 "U.S.-Pakistan intelligence operations frozen since January," Reuters, 9 April 2011, www.reuters.com/article/2011/04/09/us-Pakistan-usa-idUSTRE7381MG20110409 [accessed 4/8/15].

22 Mazzetti, "How a Single Spy Helped Turn Pakistan Against the United States," op. cit.

23 Ibid.

24 Ibid.; Mazzetti, *The Way of the Knife*, op. cit., 274.

25 "CIA and Pakistan Locked in Aggressive Spy Battles," op. cit.

26 Ibid.

27 M. Mazzetti & S. Masood, "Pakistani Role is Suspected in Revealing U.S. Spy's Name," *NYT*, 17 December 2010, www.nytimes.com/2010/12/18/world/asia/18pstan.html [accessed 4/8/15]; Mazzetti, "How a Single Spy Helped Turn Pakistan Against the United States," op. cit; Mazzetti, *The Way of the Knife*, op. cit., 267–268; Rashid, *Pakistan on the Brink*, op. cit., 156–157; Lake, "Enemy of the State," op. cit.

28 Z. Hussain, *The Scorpion's Tail*, New York: Free Press, 2010, 194–196.

29 B. Woodward, "Obama: 'We Need to Make Clear to People that the Cancer is in Pakistan,'" *WP*, 29 September 2010, www.washingtonpost.com/wp-dyn/content/article/2010/09/28/AR2010092805092.html [accessed 4/8/15].

30 Woodward, *Obama's War*, op. cit., 363–366.

31 Ibid.

32 Ibid.

33 "Pakistan Agrees to Expand CIA Presence in Quetta," *The News*, 21 November 2010, www.thenews.com.pk/Todays-News-13-2183-Pakistan-agrees-to-expand-CIA-presence-in-Quetta [accessed 4/8/15]; M. Mazzetti, "A Secret Deal on Drones

Sealed in Blood," *NYT*, 6 Apr 2013, www.nytimes.com/2013/04/07/world/asia/origins-of-cias-not-so-secret-drone-war-in-Pakistan.html [accessed 4/8/15]; Mazzetti, *Way*, 108–109.

34 Woodward, *Obama's War*, op. cit., 4; J. Warrick, *Triple Agent*, New York: Vintage, 2012, 13.

35 Mazzetti, "How a Single Spy Helped Turn Pakistan against the United States," op. cit.; Mazzetti, *The Way of the Knife*, op. cit., 265.

36 A. Antous, et al., "U.S. Tightens Drone Rules," *WSJ*, 4 November 2011, www.wsj.com/articles/SB10001424052970204621904577013982672973836 [accessed 8/4/15].

37 Mazzetti, *Way of the Knife*, op. cit., 268.

38 Sanger, *Confront*, op. cit., 87–88.

39 G. Miller & B. Woodward, "Secret Memos Reveal Explicit Nature of U.S., Pakistan Agreement on Drones," *WP*, 23 Oct 2013, www.washingtonpost.com/world/national-security/top-Pakistani-leaders-secretly-backed-cia-drone-campaign-secret-documents-show/2013/10/23/15e6b0d8-3beb-11e3-b6a9-da62c264f40e_story.html [accessed 4/8/15].

40 F. Bokhari, "Pakistan shuts us out of drone base," *Financial Times*, 29 June 2011, www.ft.com/intl/cms/s/0/dccb8472-a272-11e0-9760-00144feabdc0.html#axzz3hsHCOUOg [accessed 4/8/15].

21 ISI and the Demise of Bin Laden

The drone war in the FATA attracted a great deal of media attention for its novelty and lethality. While Pakistanis focused their attention and outrage on Predator/Reaper strikes on the Pakistan-Afghan border, the CIA was secretly flying another, stealthy drone deep inside Pakistan over a city called Abbottabad. A growing number of intelligence analysts and national security officials were convinced that Osama Bin Laden was hiding there in a complex with few apparent links to the outside world.[1]

The Bin Laden mystery

For ten years after 9/11, the US conducted the most intense manhunt in history, expending billions of dollars in an effort to locate and kill the al-Qa'ida leader, Osama Bin Laden. The last tangible reporting concerning his whereabouts dated back to late 2001, when a US Delta Force team intercepted his communications in the mountains of Tora Bora.[2] But then his trail went cold – stone cold. For a decade, the CIA routinely pressed ISI to share more Bin Laden-related intelligence, and for a decade, the ISI's rote responses included a mix of the following: (1) we told you all we know; (2) we acted on your tips, but they were all based on erroneous information; (3) Bin Laden's dead; and (4) Bin Laden may be dead but, if not, he's living in Iran or Afghanistan.[3]

While this dance of the intelligence agencies continued, Bin Laden moved to a large residence in the garrison city of Abbottabad in 2005. Located 110 kilometers north of Islamabad, Abbottabad enjoys a pleasant climate in the foothills of the Himalayas, and is home to many retired military personnel. By 2010, the CIA and the NSA were starting to close in on Osama Bin Laden after years of false leads and dead ends.[4] As with any terrorist or insurgent leader, Bin Laden's primary weakness was his communications. Thanks to US media leaks in the late 1990s, the al-Qa'ida leader was well aware of the NSA's abilities to intercept his satellite telephones, so he relied instead on human couriers, trusting that US advantages in technology could be neutralized by the simple – if slower – expedient of personal message carriers. Eventually, however, the CIA located one of these couriers, Abu Ahmed al-Kuwaiti, and it was only a matter of time before he unknowingly led them to Abbottabad and the Bin Laden residence.[5]

The US intelligence community increased its intelligence coverage of the compound with stealth drones, imagery satellites, SIGINT and on-the-ground case officers and agents.[6] Locating Bin Laden was the biggest hurdle, but now the policymakers had to decide how they were going to capture or kill him. If Bin Laden was in fact living in that compound, should ISI be informed? Should the US propose a joint mission with ISI to apprehend the fugitive? CIA had no interest in sharing its intelligence with ISI, especially in light of previous failures, where ISI was strongly suspected of leaking intelligence to planned targets and allowing them to escape. Thus was born the unilateral US mission codenamed NEPTUNE SPEAR.[7]

On the night of 1–2 May 2011, a US Navy SEAL team secretly entered Pakistan on modified Black Hawk and Chinook helicopters operated by the Army's 160th Special Operations Aviation Regiment. Upon arrival at the Abbottabad compound, the unit assaulted the residence, killed one of Bin Laden's guards and a son, and then shot the al-Qa'ida leader himself. They also collected a vast haul of information consisting of five computers, ten hard drives, 110 flash drives and Bin Laden's hand-written journal. Upon departure, they had to leave one of their helicopters behind after it had encountered a mishap during landing. It was 0100 on 2 May when the COAS, General Kayani, was informed that a foreign helicopter had crashed in Abbottabad. At 0207, the COAS called Air Chief Marshal Rao Qamar Suleman and asked him to scramble F-16s to "shoot down intruding helicopters." But it was too late: the US helicopters had safely crossed into Afghan airspace, leaving a political crisis and a deeply embarrassed Pakistani military in their wake.[8]

The available information concerning ISI actions during the nighttime hours of 1–2 May comes from an official Pakistani investigation that was leaked to *Al Jazeera*. According to this report, military police arrived at the scene 15–20 minutes after the SEALs had departed. They were followed shortly afterwards by ISI officers from the Abbottabad Detachment, who took over the investigation. Coincidentally, ISI's Abbottabad Detachment was already aware of an al-Qa'ida presence in the Abbottabad area, for on 25 January 2011, they had arrested Umar Patek, who was later convicted for his involvement in the 2002 Bali bombings. ISI never explained why Patek was in Abbottabad, although it is possible he met Bin Laden there. As for the provincial Special Bureau, a civilian police investigation arm, they had no information on Patek's arrest because ISI did not share the relevant information with them.[9]

ISI interrogated the survivors of the raid, including Bin Laden's three wives, who were held incommunicado for several months.[10] A Pakistani doctor named Shakil Afridi was also arrested by ISI, and he "confessed" to working for the CIA while serving under US Agency for International Development (AID) cover. His mission was to try and collect Bin Laden's

DNA sample for positive identification under the guise of a polio vaccination campaign.[11] According to ISI, Afridi met "25 times with foreign secret agents, received instructions and provided sensitive information to them.... The accused was aware that he was working against Pakistan."[12] Later attempts by US diplomats to obtain Afridi's release were met with vehement refusals by the DGISI.[13] ISI retaliated in other ways as well. Within days of the Bin Laden raid, the name of the CIA Station Chief was leaked to the Pakistani press after having served at his post for only five months.[14] This continued the rapid turnover of Station Chiefs in Islamabad in recent years, and the overall CIA–ISI relationship suffered as a result.

ISI's mythology of power

However much the army tried to obfuscate, the raid was embarrassing and deeply humiliating. Indeed, some critics jumped at the rare opportunity to go after the army and ISI while they were down. In a 12 June 2011, *Friday Times* editorial, Najam Sethi bemoaned the lack of accountability inside the armed forces for the Bin Laden debacle. "Heads should have rolled," he wrote. "An angry public wants to know why we are spending half our tax resources on equipping the military with F-16s and BMWs when it can't even protect itself, let alone defend the nation." Nor did Sethi spare the ISI:

> Ominously, the ISI's mythology of power is now being deconstructed and exposed as undeserved. The 'agencies' are out of fashion, the ISI is squarely in the spotlight ... [A] conviction has now taken root in the public imagination that the ISI should not be beyond the pale of the law and accountability.[15]

As we discovered earlier, neither the army nor the ISI like to be kicked, especially when they are down. Not surprisingly, Najam Sethi received death threats after this editorial was published.[16] He certainly had courage in writing it.

But the matter was not going to be resolved with a little press criticism, and on 9 May, military and ISI leaders were summoned to a closed-door National Assembly hearing on the Bin Laden affair. Curiously, the DGISI was not asked how Bin Laden lived unmolested in Pakistan for years, but why the US entered and exited Pakistani air space without being detected. The DGISI asserted that the Americans had kept ISI in the "complete dark" although he did not elaborate on why the CIA might have done this. He also admitted to an "intelligence failure" for not detecting the US operation on Pakistani soil, but his offer to resign was rejected by the prime minister. In fact, many National Assembly members ended up giving the DGISI a standing ovation, although what he did to deserve this was not clear.[17] In the end, no one was held accountable for the seeming failure to detect Bin Laden in Abbottabad and the military's inability to intercept the American "intruders" who killed him. The veteran Pakistani journalist, Ahmed Rashid, noted ruefully that "at the very least Pasha should have resigned, but there were no resignations, no accountability, and nobody took responsibility."[18] Once again, the Pakistani state had failed to hold itself to account, and it was seemingly business as usual as far as ISI was concerned.

The "business as usual" attitude was just a façade. Although no one was going to officially hold ISI responsible for the multiple breakdowns in Pakistani intelligence throughout the Bin Laden controversy, the agency had been badly shamed. As foreign observers noted at the time, either ISI was complicit in sheltering Bin Laden, "rogue" ISI elements were sheltering him or the agency simply failed to detect him living within a kilometer of the Pakistan Military Academy. DCIA Leon Panetta put it best during 4 May 2011 testimony before the US House of Representatives: "either they were involved or incompetent. Neither place is a good place to be."[19]

In the aftermath of the Bin Laden raid, one of the most persistent yet unanswered questions was ISI's links to Osama Bin Laden and al-Qa'ida. There were undoubtedly contacts in the 1980s and 1990s, when ISI, its Islamist allies and al-Qa'ida worked together training militants in Afghanistan. There is the strong possibility that ISI worked with al-Qa'ida from 1999 to 2001 in northern Afghanistan where Bin Laden had contributed his 055 Arab Brigade to fight the anti-Taliban resistance. Yet, as ISI officials remind us repeatedly, such "contacts" – no matter how frequent – do not equate to "operational control." In other words, there is no proof that ISI officers instruct, guide or advise al-Qa'ida in the selection of its targets or otherwise support its operations.[20]

The official line by the US government is that there is no evidence linking al-Qa'ida and ISI. Within two weeks of NEPTUNE SPEAR, unidentified US officials told the press they had no evidence that ISI was aware of Bin Laden's presence in Abbottabad or that they had given him any support during his extended residence there.[21] President Obama's Homeland Security Advisor, John O. Brennan, stated that Bin Laden obviously required some sort of support network inside Pakistan, but "whether or not that was individuals inside of the Pakistani government is not known."[22]

Yet in the face of these denials and careful delineations between contacts and operational control, there was a lingering cloud suggesting something more to ISI's relationship with al-Qa'ida. Some suspected, for example, that Osama Bin Laden was shielded by ISI's secretive, compartmented Directorate S, which, as this study has shown, was created to provide some evidentiary distance between ISI and its militant allies.[23] On 12 May 2011, the Pakistani Ambassador to Washington, Hussain Haqqani, met Lieutenant General Douglas Lute at the NSC to discuss the ongoing blowback from the Bin Laden raid. Lute asked the ambassador why Islamabad was deliberately "raising the level of noise" (criticism) inside Pakistan and inflaming anti-US public sentiment. After all, he added, the SEALs had discovered "a whole treasure trove of material" in the Bin Laden compound, and if the Pakistan government-generated "noise" did not cease, then Washington might be compelled to reveal exactly what it had found. Those revelations, he warned, would be sufficient to spur both the US public and Congress to demand "measures that may go well beyond the past patter of only cutting off aid."[24] Of course, exactly what Lute was threatening Haqqani with has not been revealed in open sources, but it does offer an intriguing clue about a more substantial relationship between the Pakistani government and Bin Laden than has hitherto been revealed.

Then there are the revelations by veteran *New York Times* correspondent Carlotta Gall, who has extensive experience working in both Afghanistan and Pakistan. In her 2013 book, *The Wrong Enemy*, Gall quotes an unidentified Pakistani official as revealing that the US had "direct evidence" that DGISI Pasha knew Bin Laden was in Abbottabad before the raid. When the *New York Times* queried sources in the US government about the claim, "everyone suddenly clammed up." According to Gall, Bin Laden's Abbottabad information treasure trove showed that the al-Qa'ida leader had routine contacts with both the *LeT* leader, Hafiz Mohamed Saeed and the Taliban's Mullah Omar. Both have had a long-term relationship with ISI that includes training, aid and operational guidance. Gall's book contains reporting from a single, unidentified source that the Bin Laden account was handled by a special ISI office that was even more compartmented and secretive than Directorate S.[25]

Bin Laden reportedly warned al-Qa'ida subordinates about his sometimes tense relations with the Pakistani government, but that he relied on it to hide him. Even so, he was under no illusions that, sooner or later, ISI would betray him to the Americans.[26] Other reports have since detailed Bin Laden's wariness of the Pakistanis, especially his sense that ISI was double-dealing him. In her book, Gall also wonders why there were no escape routes in the Bin Laden compound. When the SEALs came to get him, he had nowhere to flee or hide; he was caught in his bedroom and shot unarmed. Gall suspects that the al-Qa'ida leader was depending on receiving prior warning by ISI before an American raid took place, but such warnings never came because the US kept NEPTUNE SPEAR in unilateral channels. As Gall puts it, "I realized U.S. officials had come to the conclusion that someone in the ISI had been protecting Bin Laden too."[27]

Some reports claim Bin Laden was shielded by "some members" of ISI, lending credence to the theory that the organization has "rogues" operating inside it.[28] But other information seems to support a more substantial Bin Laden–ISI link. The Chairman of the House Permanent Select Committee on Intelligence, Congressman Mike Rogers, stated in 2011 that ISI "elements ... knew and looked the other way" when they learned that Bin Laden had an extensive network operating on Pakistani soil.[29] Yet once again we see that Pakistani "institutions" as a whole are exempted, and the rogue actor theory is revived and reinforced.

Then what is one to make of the allegations made by former DGISI, Ziauddin Butt Khwaja, who was put under house arrest after the failed 1999 ouster of Pervez Musharraf? In October 2011, i.e., five months after NEPTUNE SPEAR, Ziauddin disclosed that the former DGIB Brigadier Ijaz Shah had sheltered Bin Laden in the weeks after the Tora Bora operation. He elaborated further on his allegations in December of the same year: "Ijaz Shah had kept this man [Bin Laden] in the Abbottabad compound with the full knowledge of General Pervez Musharraf. Ijaz Shah was an all-powerful official in the government of General Musharraf."[30] Ijaz Shah has cropped up from time to time in this history as one of those mysterious gray eminences who play a role in political life disproportionate to their rank. He was certainly the man who sheltered Omar Saeed Sheikh for several weeks during which Daniel Pearl was murdered. In 2007, Benazir Bhutto repeatedly accused him of trying to kill her. In any case, Ziauddin's assertions cannot be confirmed, and he certainly had an ax to grind against Musharraf and the army.[31] Still, he did have undeniable access at one time to ISI files and undoubtedly knew about more than a few skeletons in the organization's closet.

Overall, it must be admitted that evidence of an ISI–Bin Laden operational link is fragmentary and weak. It is often dependent on single sources of unknown origin or questionable motivations. It cannot be directly corroborated by any information available in open sources. And yet it's there, it stems from multiple, separate sources, and nagging doubts remain. So why would ISI hide Osama Bin Laden? How could it possibly be in the Pakistan army's interests to shelter the world's most wanted man when the consequences of his possible discovery by the US could be disastrous?

At this point, we enter speculation. Bin Laden would have been useful to ISI because of his links to extremist groups worldwide, and his cult figure status would be helpful with the lagging Kashmir campaign. Retaining Bin Laden would have made him a de facto hostage for al-Qa'ida's good behavior on Pakistani territory. Alternatively, perhaps ISI sheltered Bin Laden out of respect for his cause and his faith. We know there are pro-jihadi army and ISI officers; perhaps they guarded Bin Laden out of sympathy for his program and his defiance of the West. This brings us back to the "rogue agent" theory that presupposes that no one higher up in the chain of command in either ISI or the army knew that Bin Laden was being sheltered by junior Pakistani officers. It calls into question army discipline, hierarchy and credibility, and these in a country possessing a growing stockpile of nuclear warheads.

In the end, we are left with disappointingly little evidence that either implicates or exonerates ISI from involvement in Bin Laden's sanctuary. Much remains unanswered years after NEPTUNE SPEAR took place, and the CIA is only parceling out the Bin Laden information hoard in a controlled and graduated process. If there is a "smoking gun" hidden somewhere in all those flash drives, hard drives and computers, it must be one of the best kept secrets in Washington. *Washington Post* columnist David Ignatius sums up the ISI hall of mirrors succinctly:

Osama Bin Laden lived in five houses in Pakistan, fathered four children there, kept three wives who took dictation for his rambling directives to his terror network, had two children born in public hospitals — and through it all, the Pakistani government did not know one single thing about his whereabouts?... And U.S. officials, with the cautious tone of witnesses who hope they won't have to testify at the trial, keep repeating that they haven't found the "smoking gun" that would confirm official Pakistani knowledge about the al-Qaeda chief hiding in Abbottabad ...[32]

The failure to arrive at a conclusive answer to the Bin Laden affair is distinctly dissatisfying and disappointing, but that is often the reality of the intelligence business.

The Abbottabad commission

The Pakistan government did make an honest effort to get to the bottom of the Bin Laden affair, when it set up a commission on 21 June 2011 led by Chief Justice Javed Iqbal. The commission was tasked with answering the following questions: (1) How did Osama Bin Laden manage to live in Abbottabad for six years without being detected by the Pakistani authorities? (2) Why didn't the PIC locate him? (3) How were US forces able to infiltrate and exfiltrate Pakistani airspace without any response from the military? Finally, the commission was asked to issue recommendations on the shortfalls it identified. After interviewing numerous witnesses from the military and intelligence communities, the commission produced a 337 page report that was subsequently leaked to *Al Jazeera*.[33] The commission's revelations aren't so surprising in light of previous investigations of the PIC; many of the same problems were identified and similar recommendations proposed. The witnesses, however, made several observations that are worthy of further examination.

The PAF blamed ISI for failing to detect the US intrusion into Pakistani air space, describing it as a "combined failure at all levels in assessing the intentions of the USA." According to the Deputy Chief of Air Staff, ISI was at fault because it was responsible for all-services analysis of adversaries and presumed allies like the US.[34] For its part, the Army Board of Inquiry blamed the PIC as a whole for failing to detect and warn of the US incursion. Ironically, the army focused on the inadequacies of the civilian services in particular, stating that neither the IB nor the Special Branches collected or analyzed information in a competent manner. The Army Adjutant General complained that Pakistan lacked a real intelligence community, since there was no coordination across the agencies, little or no information sharing, and each agency reported to a different master.[35]

The DGMI tried to clear his name and that of his agency by arguing that "national level" CI and counter terrorism were not specific MI responsibilities except when they concerned the army alone. He agreed that the PIC was inadequate to address Pakistan's many challenges but cautioned that blaming the PIC alone for the Bin Laden raid was "not the right way to address the challenges." He also conceded that information sharing between MI and ISI was not routinized but subject instead to circumstance, specific requirements and relations among the senior staff of both agencies.[36]

The commission's interview with DGISI Shuja Pasha was more revealing. Pasha appeared to be prickly and defensive from the start, arguing that the "real problem" behind the Abbottabad affair was that other PIC agencies were not doing their share of the work. This was especially true of the civilian agencies, he said, since they were under-resourced, over-tasked and too politicized. The CIDs and provincial Special Branches had the best local sources but, he complained, they did not often share their information with the military. Moreover, neither the IB nor the FIA knew "the basics of intelligence," and the IB in particular needed to be shielded from the vicissitudes of Pakistani civilian politics. Since the existing civilian security agencies were inadequate, Pasha requested formal powers of arrest for both the Internal Security and Counter Terrorism wings of his agency.[37]

Pasha also lamented that ISI was performing missions outside its original mandate. The agency was "over-burdened" with ancillary responsibilities for which it had neither the time nor resources. Counter terrorism, for example, was not formally listed in ISI's 1975 charter, yet the agency was asked to take on this difficult mission because the other PIC agencies could not. Chillingly, the DGISI argued that critics of his agency were those "who should fear the ISI" because they were working against the interests of the Pakistani state (as defined by himself). After the events of 2 May, he continued, many Pakistanis "outdid" the country's many enemies in their harsh criticism of ISI when in fact they should have condemned the US. This applied to those civilian leaders who did not stand up for Pakistan and the ISI in the aftermath of NEPTUNE SPEAR.[38]

Shuja Pasha did not spare the CIA either. He alleged that the last time the Americans shared any intelligence on Osama Bin Laden with ISI was the October–November 2005 timeframe when Bin Laden was reportedly sighted in Chitral. This American silence, he added, coupled with the fact that Bin Laden's trail had gone cold, convinced the ISI leadership that the al-Qa'ida leader was dead, especially since he was known to be suffering from several health problems. Despite this silence, ISI nonetheless noted that the US government had publicly discussed ISI's supposed links to al-Qa'ida. When the ISI asked the US for more information on these allegations, none was forthcoming. In the DGISI's opinion, the CIA's "main agenda" was to declare ISI a terrorist organization. Tellingly, he cited the Mumbai terrorist attack civil lawsuit in New York City as a prime example of the CIA's true intentions.[39]

Shuja Pasha was adamantly against putting ISI under civilian control because the agency required direct access to the president in order to be effective. Moreover, it was "no longer involved in the political affairs of the country. We are a very weak state," Pasha continued, governance was "corrupt" and "low grade" and "apathy" afflicted virtually every level of society. He complained that things had reached such a dismal point that

[a] US intelligence officer had the gall to say 'you are so cheap' ... we can buy you with a visa, with a visa to the US even with a dinner ... we can buy anyone.[40]

The bottom line as the DGISI saw it was that ISI was "neither complicit nor incompetent with respect to the presence of [Osama Bin Laden] in Pakistan" for the simple fact that it had played a key role in rendering senior al-Qa'ida figures to the CIA and other foreign intelligence agencies.[41]

Despite – or because of – the DGISI's forceful arguments, the commission leveled the most criticism at ISI in its report. ISI should definitely "stay within the law," the commissioners stressed, and it should certainly not be granted the powers of arrest requested by the DGISI. ISI "must be accountable and answerable to political oversight," and the commissioners found it "unacceptable" that ISI consistently refused to accept any form of civilian control over its activities. ISI might be over-burdened, the commission conceded, but it also took upon itself political missions that distracted it from its more important national security duties. Unfortunately, the ISI was "more political and less professional and the country suffered on both counts."[42] When it came to the Bin Laden raid itself, the report determined that ISI "failed" to supply "correct intelligence" to its military clients "regarding any developing or eminent threat" stemming from the US. The commission concluded that ISI never conducted a "real search" for Bin Laden and the result of this negligence was that "the country suffered military humiliation, national outrage and instrumental isolation." Rather than aiding others in the search for Bin Laden, the commission stressed, ISI did what it could to obstruct their investigations into his whereabouts.[43]

As far as recommendations went, many of the commission's proposals had been aired before in previous attempts at intelligence reform. Civilian oversight of the PIC was an absolute must if Pakistan were to create a truly viable democracy. They recommended the creation of some sort of coordinating body whose sole mission was to supervise the PIC agencies.[44] The commissioners concluded that the intelligence community had simply grown too powerful: "The excessive powers and non-accountability of the Pakistani intelligence establishment have posed the greatest threat of state failure to Pakistan."[45]

After Bin Laden

It has been nearly five years since Osama Bin Laden was gunned down in Abbottabad, and yet we are no closer to understanding how he remained there for so long undetected by the Pakistan authorities. The CIA–ISI feud, if it still exists, has been completely removed from the public eye. This is probably due to the fact that Washington simply is no longer interested in Afghanistan or Pakistan since new crises have emerged in the Middle East and Southeast Asia. The drop-off in Western media coverage on "Af-Pak" parallels the marked reduction in the number of coalition troops in Afghanistan and this, in turn, has taken the spotlight off ISI–CIA interactions and eased tensions in US–Pakistan relations.

If this history teaches us anything, it is that the bilateral intelligence relationship ebbs and flows in accordance with the national interests of both countries. The enduring ISI–CIA relationship has, in retrospect, managed to survive a number of crises, for the fundamental reason that Washington and Islamabad need each other, albeit for different reasons and to varying degrees of intensity. This case certainly validates the old maxim that there are no friends and enemies among intelligence services, only interests.

ISI's Internal Security Wing has supposedly been disbanded, and Pakistan has now enjoyed seven years of uninterrupted civilian rule. Despite these positive developments, the army remains the only effective power in the country, especially when it comes to national security, relations with India and Afghanistan, and taking the fight to internal insurgencies. As the army's watchdog, the ISI continues to exercise its self-assigned role as guardian of Pakistan's identity, a mission whose deliberately ambiguous parameters give ISI the flexibility to meddle in just about any internal matter it deems dangerous to the country. Such an elastic definition of "guardianship" has allowed ISI to go after its domestic critics without any fear of penalty or retribution.

Civilian politicians are still too timid when it comes to curbing ISI's powers via parliamentary legislation. In 2012 one bold (foolhardy?) senator named Farhatullah Khan Babar submitted a bill entitled "Inter-Services Intelligence Agency (Functions, Powers and Regulation) Act, 2012" that would finally place ISI within a legislative framework and make it answerable to the parliament and the prime minister. Parliament would also create a nine person Intelligence and Security Committee with responsibilities for making inquiries into administration, expenditures and policies of the ISI. Included in the language of the bill was the following:

> The absence of appropriate legislation regulating the functioning, duties, powers and responsibilities of the agency is not consistent with the principles of natural justice and accountability of authority and power and has given rise to resentment against the premier national agency.[46]

Given the history covered in this book, it should perhaps come as no surprise that this bill languished in committee and withdrawn by its author. The decades-long campaign to reform ISI by giving it a legal mandate and making it subservient to civilian government continues. The army's dominance may not be as starkly evident as it once was, but this does not mean that the army has relinquished its power to meddle in government policy. Far from it. As long as the army exercises its role as guardian of the Islamic Republic of Pakistan, it will require an ISI handmaiden that responds to GHQ orders and, if forced to do so, obeys the COAS rather than elected leaders.

Notes

1 G. Miller, "CIA Flew Stealth Drones into Pakistan to Monitor Bin Laden House," *WP*, 17 May 2011, www.washingtonpost.com/world/national-security/cia-flew-stealth-drones-into-Pakistan-to-monitor-bin-laden-house/2011/05/13/AF5dW55G_print.html [accessed 4/8/15].

2 D. Fury, *Kill Bin Laden*, New York: St. Martin's Press, 2008, 138, 284–285.

3 Government of Pakistan, *Abbottabad Commission Report* found in "Document: Pakistan's Bin Laden Dossier," *Al Jazeera*, 8 July 2013, www.aljazeera.com/indepth/spotlight/binladenfiles/2013/07/201378143927822246.html [accessed 24/11/15].

4 Miller, "CIA Flew Stealth Drones," op. cit.

5 Ibid.

6 Ibid.

7 A. De Borchgrave, "Pakistan's Paranoia Created bin Laden," United Press International, 3 May 2011, http://defence.pk/threads/Pakistan%C2%92s-paranoia-created-bin-laden.106751/ [accessed 4/8/15]; D. Sanger, *Confront and Conceal*, New York: Crown, 2012, 86; E. Shmitt & T. Shanker, *Counterstrike*, New York: Times Books, 2011, 261.

8 A. Rashid, *Pakistan on the Brink*, New York: Viking, 2012, 7–8; *Abbottabad Commission Report*, op. cit.

9 *Abbottabad Commission Report*, op. cit.

10 *Abbottabad Commission Report*, op. cit., 41, 174; D. Walsh, "A Personal Quest to Clarify Bin Laden's Last Days Yields Vexing Accounts," *NYT*, 7 March 2012, www.nytimes.com/2012/03/08/world/asia/quest-to-clarify-bin-ladens-last-days-in-Pakistan-yields-vexing-accounts.html [accessed 4/8/15].

11 *Abbottabad Commission Report*, op. cit., 115; R. Leiby, "Pakistan Recounts in New Report how Doctor helped US in bin Laden Operation," *WP*, 26 July 2012, www.washingtonpost.com/world/asia_pacific/Pakistan-recounts-how-convicted-spy-helped-us-in-bin-laden-operation/2012/07/26/gJQAGyL1BX_story.html [accessed 4/8/15].

12 Leiby, "Pakistan Recounts in New Report how Doctor helped US," op. cit.

13 Sanger, *Confront*, op. cit., 80–81.

14 E. Lake, "Enemy of the State," *The New Republic*, 19 May 2011, www.google.com/#q=enemy+of+the+state+lake+new+republic [accessed 11/24/15]; K. Brulliardb & G. Miller, "Pakistanis Name CIA Station Chief: U.S. Suspects Retaliation," *WP*, 9 May 2011, www.washingtonpost.com/world/Pakistani-pm-failure-to-locate-bin-laden-not-incompetence-or-complicity/2011/05/09/AFKg0nYG_story.html [accessed 4/8/15].

15 N. Sethi, "Accountability of Military Inc.," *Friday Times*, 10–16 June 2011, www.thefridaytimes.com/10062011/page1.shtml [accessed 4/8/15].

16 "The silencing of the liberals," *The Economist*, 26 April 2014, www.economist.com/news/asia/21601311-shooting-famous-journalist-exposes-worrying-trend-silencing-liberals [accessed 4/8/15].

17 Sanger, *Confront*, op. cit., 107–108; K. DeYoung & K. Brulliard, "Obama Administration is Divided Over Future of U.S.-Pakistan Relationship," *WP*, 15 May 2011, www.washingtonpost.com/world/national-security/obama-administration-remains-divided-over-future-of-us-Pakistan-relationship/2011/05/13/AFOJcj3G_story.html [accessed 4/8/15]; D. Walsh, "Pakistan May Cut Nato's Afghan Supply Line after Osama bin Laden Killing," *Guardian*, 14 May 2011 www.theguardian.com/world/2011/may/14/Pakistan-nato-afghanistan-bin-laden [accessed 4/8/15]; Miller, "CIA Flew Stealth Drones," op. cit.

18 Rashid, *Pakistan on the Brink*, op. cit., 177–178.

19 "Sources: Panetta to Congress: Pakistan Either Incompetent or Involved," CNN, 4 May 2011, http://politicalticker.blogs.cnn.com/2011/05/03/sources-panetta-to-congress-Pakistan-either-incompetent-or-involved/ [accessed 4/8/15].

20 M. Rosenberg, "Pakistan's Ties to Terror Group are Unclear," *WSJ*, 22 July 2009, www.wsj.com/articles/SB124820050290269319 [accessed 4/8/15]; G. Miller, "U.S. Officials Say Pakistani Spy Agency Released Afghan Taliban Insurgents," *WP*, 10 April 2010, www.washingtonpost.com/wp-dyn/content/article/2010/04/10/AR20 10041002111.html [accessed 4/8/15].

21 D. Walsh, "A Personal Quest," op. cit.; Sanger, *Confront*, op. cit., 112–113.

22 Quoted in Rashid, *Pakistan on the Brink*, op. cit., 8.

23 S. Hersh, *Chain of Command: The Road from 9/11 to Abu Ghraib*, New York: HarperCollins, 2004, 131; De Borchgrave, "Pakistan's Paranoia," op. cit.; L. Wright, "The Double Game," *The New Yorker*, 8 May 2011, www.newyorker.com/magazine/2011/05/16/the-double-game [accessed 4/8/15].

24 H. Haqqani, *Magnificent Delusions*, New York: Public Affairs, 2013, 318–319.

25 C. Gall, *The Wrong Enemy*, Boston: Houghton Mifflin Harcourt, 2014, 248–249; C. Gall, "What Pakistan Knew about Bin Laden," *NYT*, 19 March 2014, www.nytimes.com/2014/03/23/magazine/what-Pakistan-knew-about-bin-laden.html?hpw&rref=magazine [accessed 19/3/14].

26 Gall, *Wrong Enemy*, op. cit., 249.

27 Ibid.

28 B. Starr, "NATO Official: Bin Laden, Deputy Hiding in northwest Pakistan," 18 October 2010, CNN, www.cnn.com/2010/WORLD/asiapcf/10/18/afghanistan.bin.laden/ [accessed 4/8/15].

29 B. Gertz, "Inside the Ring," *Washington Times*, 11 May 2011, www.washingtontimes.com/news/2011/may/11/inside-the-ring-320207052/?page=all [accessed 4/8/15].

30 A. Jamal, "Former Pakistani Army Chief Reveals Intelligence Bureau Harbored Bin Laden in Abbottabad," The Jamestown Foundation, *Terrorism Monitor*, 22 December 2011, www.jamestown.org/single/?no_cache=1&tx_ttnews%5Btt_news%5D=38819#.VcGJSk2D6M8 [accessed 4/8/15].

31 B. Reidel, "Pakistan's Musharraf has been Accused of Knowing Osama bin Laden's Hideout," *Daily Beast*, 14 February 2012, www.thedailybeast.com/articles/2012/02/13/Pakistan-s-musharraf-has-been-accused-of-knowing-osama-bin-laden-s-hideout.html [accessed 4/8/15].

32 D. Ignatius, "From Pakistan Answers Needed about Osama bin Laden," *WP*, 3 April 2012, www.washingtonpost.com/opinions/from-Pakistan-answers-needed-about-osama-bin-laden/2012/04/03/gIQAKliytS_story.html [accessed 5/8/15].

33 T. Craig, "Pakistan Faults Self in bin Laden Hunt," *WP*, 8 July 2013 www.washingtonpost.com/world/Pakistan-faults-self-in-bin-laden-hunt/2013/07/08/99970 6d4-e813–11e2–818e-aa29e855f3ab_story.html [accessed 5/8/15]; *Abbottabad Commission Report*, op. cit., 31.

34 *Abbottabad Commission Report*, op. cit., 140, 146.

35 Ibid., 169–172.

36 Ibid., 185–190.

37 Ibid., 198–199.

38 Ibid., 192–194.

39 Ibid., 195–196, 202.

40 Ibid., 207.

41 Ibid., 196.

42 Ibid., 151, 177, 210–211.

43 Ibid., 175–177.

44 Ibid., 213, 310.

45 Ibid., 316–317.

46 S.I. Raza, "Bill Seeking ISI's Accountability Submitted to Senate," *Dawn*, 8 July 2012, www.dawn.com/news/732735/bill-seeking-isis-accountability-submitted-to-senate [accessed 24/11/15];   M.S. Zaafir, "Farhatullah Withdraws Bill in Senate about ISI Control," *The News*, 13 July 2012, www.thenews.com.pk/Todays-News-6–120149-Farhatullah-withdraws-bill-in-Senate-about-ISI-control [accessed 24/11/15].

Conclusions

In this book, we have examined how ISI evolved from a bare-bones outfit responsible for assessments and CI to the multifaceted intelligence and security behemoth it has become today. Indeed, ISI is second only to the army when it comes to power and influence in Pakistan, for it is a servant of the army and implements national security policies formulated by army headquarters. Civilian governments have tried to supplant ISI or assume control of it, but the army has always ensured that these endeavors fail. Therefore, reforming ISI would not address the greater problem, which is the army's propensity to interfere in the political life of the state. ISI is not just an intelligence and security agency, though, for it also plans and implements Pakistan's UW strategy against India and Afghanistan. It is this latter mission that has focused international attention on ISI in recent decades with many accusing it of recklessness, jihadism and endangering a fragile peace in a nuclear-armed South Asia.

Throughout this book, we have explored those themes that permeate the warp and weft of ISI's history, including:

- Its evolving powers and capabilities both domestically and internationally.
- Its role in an underdeveloped PIC.
- Its use of UW to achieve national goals as defined by the army.
- Its record in providing early warning of surprise attack.
- Its decades-old liaison relationship with CIA.
- Its frequent intervention in Pakistan's democratic processes.
- Its unlikely status as a "rogue" agency.
- The failure of numerous Pakistani governments to rein in ISI and reform the larger PIC.

In the introduction, these themes were outlined as distinct questions to be addressed by the research. The following represent the key findings:

How has ISI evolved as an institution exercising intelligence and security responsibilities at home and abroad? What were the driving forces behind that evolutionary process?

ISI's beginnings were very modest indeed, especially when we compare them to the extensive facilities and responsibilities that it enjoys today. Starting out with a simple Karachi office and a small staff, ISI's earliest missions were analysis, armed services CI and limited HUMINT collection. When Ayub Khan established a military dictatorship in October 1958, ISI really came into its own. It flourished under army rule, and as Ayub empowered the federal government at the expense of the provinces, ISI absorbed new missions in UW and manipulating domestic politics. By the late 1960s, ISI had become *primus intra pares* in the PIC.

Ironically, it wasn't until a civilian politician named Zulfikar Ali Bhutto assumed the presidency in late 1971 that ISI became a truly dominant player in both the intelligence and policy arenas. Not only did Bhutto enshrine its formal missions in a 1975 charter that is still in effect, he also promoted the ISI chief to Lieutenant General rank, giving the agency even greater prominence within the army. The paradox is that although Bhutto was highly suspicious of even his closest associates, he inexplicably trusted his ISI Director General with his thoughts, plans and ambitions. That trust cost him both his government and his life.

ISI reached its prime in the 1980s, when it was the most important member of a three-party intelligence alliance that included the CIA and Saudi Arabia's GID. The Soviets had occupied Afghanistan, so Washington and Riyadh provided ISI with cash, weapons, training and technical equipment to recruit and train an Afghan guerrilla army. During this decade, ISI became the second most powerful state institution with the DGISI answering only to the COAS. ISI used the Afghan war as a training ground, where it honed an UW strategy first used against India in the 1950s. After the Soviet Union quit Afghanistan in 1989, ISI was dealt an unexpected setback when its proxies failed to capture Kabul.

The heavy focus on UW meant that ISI was neglecting some of its other missions, including intelligence collection and analysis. A few ISI officers pointed this out in the early 1990s, but their concerns were ignored, and ISI continued to sponsor proxies and expand its domestic authorities as well. Money, expertise and technical surveillance capabilities helped fuel ISI's frequent intervention in Pakistani politics throughout the 1990s and early 2000s. It became the essential pillar of Pervez Musharraf's military government, helping rig referendums and elections to keep him in power. After the 2008 elections, which ushered in Pakistan's first civilian government in nine years, calls were made to rein in this intrusive agency. Promises were made that ISI's so-called Internal Wing had been dismantled, but other events, including the aftermath of the 2008 Mumbai attacks, indicated that this agency remained beyond civilian control.

It would be logical to assume that ISI's power waxes and wanes with the rise and fall of military dictatorships; however, this study reveals that ISI's evolution has been facilitated by military *and* civilian rulers. Ayub Khan launched the agency on the road of domestic interference and UW, but it was the civilian prime minister, Zulfikar Ali Bhutto, who gave ISI a formal charter that included intervening in domestic politics and election forecasting.

Later, in the 1990s, both Benazir Bhutto and Mian Nawaz Sharif were more interested in bringing ISI under *their* control than actually reducing its powers. Military and civilian leaders have both made ISI into the leviathan it is today; only the combined efforts of the major civilian parties and the unlikely consent of army generals will reduce ISI's power and influence.

How does ISI fit into the larger Pakistan Intelligence Community (PIC)?

From its inception to the present day, the PIC has been a loosely organized body with little or no coordination among its members. In fact, there has never been a single, consistent PIC overseer, a managing entity capable of harnessing and synchronizing the various military and civilian agencies. At times, the concept of a Joint Intelligence Committee has been proposed with the goal of at least ensuring a community consensus on key assessments; however, the military agencies have always resisted civilian intrusions on their turf.

The issue of coordinating intelligence is closely linked to civil–military relations in general. Over the years, military leaders have often called for an empowered NSC sanctioned by the constitution and charged with formulating domestic and foreign policies at the highest levels. Some civilian politicians have been wary of such a body, viewing it as an attempt by the army to retain a permanent and constitutionally mandated role at the pinnacle of national decision-making. The Pakistani NSC, as it is currently constituted, has a mixed history. At times, an NSC has been created by one administration only to be disbanded by another. In any case, should a new, empowered NSC be created, ISI would exercise a preponderant role in it as a purveyor of intelligence and custodian of the country's UW programs. The intelligence coordinating agency noted above would presumably be subordinated to this NSC, which would direct intelligence requirements and national intelligence estimates to the PIC.

It remains to be seen whether the new (as of 2014) National Intelligence Directorate (NID) will become a true JIC-type coordinator of national estimates drafted by the civilian and military agencies. History would teach us to be skeptical about the long-term success of such an organization whose fate hinges on the broader issue of civil-military relations. It will be interesting to see if the NID produces estimates of Indian intentions and military capabilities that contradict military assessments. Who will adjudicate such a dispute? Would the army accept a compromise position?

Leaving intelligence coordination aside, we find that, as early as the mid-1950s, the military agencies in general, but ISI in particular, were dwarfing their civilian counterparts in personnel, resources and institutional clout. To be sure, various prime ministers tried to counterbalance ISI by boosting the civilian IB, but the latter never could command the budget and expertise possessed by the former. Ultimately, it came down to control of the military agencies: both Benazir Bhutto and Nawaz Sharif tried wresting ISI away from the military by appointing their own Directors General; however, the army invariably responded by empowering MI as an alternative. After 9/11, ISI's position as uncontested leader of Pakistan intelligence writ large was further cemented by the infusion of CIA resources and ISI's control over the counter terrorism mission.

How has ISI employed UW in support of the state's national security objectives? To what extent has UW been a successful strategy for Pakistan?

In this study, we have seen how ISI gradually assumed responsibility for Pakistan's proxy wars against India and Afghanistan. Successive governments – civilian and military – have viewed UW as the best means of projecting Pakistani power in South and Central Asia given the country's limited military and economic means. When it comes to military strategy, Pakistan is never going to match its Indian adversary in conventional weapons, so it has gravitated toward the two extremes of the conflict spectrum: UW and nuclear weapons.

The fact that Pakistan has clung to the UW strategy for so long is surprising because, to date, ISI's proxy wars have not secured a decisive victory in either Afghanistan or Kashmir. While the Pakistani leadership might still hold out hope for an eventual triumph in Afghanistan, there are few signs of Indian flexibility on the Kashmir dispute despite (or because of) decades of conflict. In fact, ISI's use of extremist groups like *LeT* and *JeM* has probably done more to alienate Kashmiri and international opinion than anything India has done in Kashmir over the last 30 years. Pakistani UW proponents might point out that Kashmir's insecurity has tied down substantial numbers of Indian security forces and that this testifies to the success of the strategy. Still, the goal of tying down Indian forces in internal security is clearly secondary to that of recovering Kashmir in its entirety, and this latter objective remains as elusive as ever.

The Pakistan case shows that a state employing UW as a policy tool must be capable of sustaining it over the long term. It must also synchronize the UW effort with a comprehensive diplomatic and public relations program to ensure that the UW tool doesn't become an end in itself. Pakistan's resources are too meager for its ambitions regardless of which strategy it employs to satisfy them. Indeed, by 2015, Islamabad had arguably overreached in both Afghanistan and Kashmir. Although it had escaped US military retaliation for its covert support of the Taliban in Afghanistan, ISI nonetheless failed to plant its own government in Kabul. As for Kashmir, ISI's extremist proxies and the 1999 Kargil misadventure badly scarred Pakistan's credibility and improved US–India counter terrorism cooperation. Better Washington–New Delhi ties can only be seen by Islamabad as a strategic setback in the zero-sum game of South Asian security.

Perhaps more significantly, ISI's use of UW has been highly risky for both Pakistan and India. On three occasions over the last quarter century – 1990,

2002 and 2008 – Pakistan's use of proxies has come alarmingly close to triggering a general war with India that Pakistan could never win. It has disrupted Pakistan's relations with the US, which remains its single largest donor of military and humanitarian aid. It has even endangered Pakistan–China relations at times due to links between ISI-favored proxies and Uighur militants fighting the Chinese authorities for an independent East Turkestan.

What is ISI's record in providing accurate and timely early warning intelligence to decision-makers?

This history is replete with examples of how India and Pakistan frequently misread each other's intentions as a result of poor intelligence, cultural bias, erroneous assumptions and domestic political concerns. In the early 1950s, a series of mobilization crises convinced one to suspect the other of planning to invade, so counter-mobilization was initiated and tensions increased. Such crises, however, were nothing compared to those that emerged decades later when both militaries were much larger, nuclear weapons were present, and ballistic missiles reduced warning and reaction times. The BRASSTACKS episode of 1986–1987 demonstrated how a large-scale exercise on the India–Pakistan border could have turned into a "hot" war as a result of misunderstandings on both sides. In 1990, US intelligence served as a trusted intermediary passing reliable intelligence to both parties in order to increase mutual confidence. This was necessary because poor intelligence on both sides was pushing them toward confrontation.

The lessons of the US–Soviet strategic arms race are worth noting as we contemplate the role of intelligence in a nuclear-armed South Asia. The inability of the United States to collect reliable and timely intelligence on Soviet strategic developments in the 1950s opened up possible "bomber gaps" and "missile gaps" that subsequently entered domestic political debates and spurred new military spending. In the 1970s, some analysts felt that the Soviet investment in land-based heavy ICBMs and the possibility of "depressed trajectory" submarine ballistic missiles launches close to the US coast gave Moscow the possibility of initiating a crippling, surprise nuclear strike. India and Pakistan at present suffer from many of the same deficiencies in technical intelligence that plagued the US and the Soviets in the early years of the Cold War. Neither Islamabad nor New Delhi has adequate early warning radars to detect and track incoming ballistic missiles, and this raises the possibility that one side could knock out the other in a surprise attack. Moreover, the relatively short distance between Islamabad and New Delhi (as compared with Washington, DC and Moscow) means that even if one or both acquired effective early warning systems, they would still lack sufficient time to retaliate. Consequently, in the event of future clashes triggered by proxies or miscalculation, both countries may quickly transition their nuclear forces to a much more dangerous and risky "launch on warning" status.

In a future India–Pakistan crisis, it will be ISI's responsibility to accurately assess Indian capabilities and intentions, and such accuracy requires technical and HUMINT capabilities that ISI likely does not possess. It will also require an analytical process that strives for "bias free" judgments where long-held assumptions – such as one Pakistani soldier equals ten Indian soldiers – are constantly challenged and tested. There is a possibility that the next use of nuclear weapons in war will be in South Asia because intelligence capabilities are limited, crisis communications remain rudimentary and the perceived vulnerability of nuclear forces to a first strike could create a "use 'em or lose 'em" scenario. Kashmir and other disputes aside, at some point, New Delhi and Islamabad will have to hammer out a verifiable agreement on military exercises and nuclear weapons inventories to reduce the possibility of misinterpretation leading to a war that neither side wants. In this context, it is clear that intelligence is absolutely vital for the maintenance of peace on the Subcontinent and will underpin any future regional arms control initiatives.

What does the decades-old relationship between the CIA and ISI tell us about the larger US–Pakistan security relationship?

Much has been written about US foreign intelligence relationships with European allies, Canada and Australia; however, the literature thins out considerably when we consider US intelligence relationships with non-Western states. It is not as if these non-Western liaison links lacked importance – one need only examine how the US employed its intelligence relationships after 9/11 to see how crucial countries like Egypt, Jordan and even Syria shared intelligence on extremist groups. This history has highlighted ISI–CIA intelligence liaison within the larger US–Pakistan diplomatic relationship from the early 1950s to the 2011 death of Osama Bin Laden. Indeed, such was the extent of this liaison and the resources transferred to ISI after the 1979 Soviet invasion of Afghanistan and, later, the 9/11 terrorist attacks, that the CIA Station Chief in Islamabad was the most powerful American official in Pakistan with privileged access to the most senior Pakistani leaders.

From the outset, national security concerns figured prominently in US–Pakistan relations. We have seen how the Pakistanis tried to parlay their country's strategic location into a means of obtaining American military equipment and a commitment to defend Pakistan from attack. But, more than any other facet of the bilateral relationship, the US technical intelligence facilities in Pakistan drove Washington's interest in Pakistan from 1954 to 1969. The SIGINT/ELINT facilities at Peshawar were vital tools for US arms control since they facilitated monitoring of Soviet strategic weapons developments. For their part, the Pakistanis were well aware of the importance the US government attached to Peshawar and leveraged this for their own gain. To put it bluntly, Pakistan wanted American weapons to offset India's manpower, geographical and economic advantages and Peshawar was offered as the quid pro quo.

By the end of the 1960s, the bilateral relationship lacked the warmth of the early years. This was partly due to the US embargo on weapons and spare parts to Pakistan during the 1965 war with India; another factor was Foreign Minister Zulfikar Ali Bhutto's policy of engaging the People's Republic of China, which greatly irritated the Kennedy and Johnson Administrations. The culmination of this decaying relationship was the shuttering of the last Peshawar intelligence facilities in 1969. It seemed as if CIA–ISI liaison had peaked and both sides were starting to drift in different directions.

During the 1970s, US–Pakistan relations remained strained. Washington was focused on extracting itself from Vietnam while Islamabad licked its wounds after the humiliating 1971 war. Even so, the CIA–ISI relationship continued even if the former was often suspected by the latter of exercising undue influence over Pakistani politics. The nadir in diplomatic ties was reached in 1979 with the execution of former Prime Minister Zulfikar Ali Bhutto and the sacking of the US Embassy in Islamabad. But then help came from an unlikely quarter. The December 1979 Soviet invasion of Afghanistan drove the US and Pakistan back together in a renewed Cold War alliance with the ISI–CIA partnership at its heart. ISI was the beneficiary of billions of dollars in CIA aid while Washington congratulated itself in tying down the Soviet bear in the mountains of Afghanistan. It was an era when a visit to ISI headquarters was almost de rigueur for all visiting US congressional delegations.

When the Soviets withdrew from Afghanistan in 1989, the cement binding the ISI–CIA alliance had crumbled away. American interest in Afghanistan and Pakistan dropped off considerably, the money and weapons stream dried up, and Washington even revived pressure on Islamabad over its nuclear weapons program. By the end of the 1990s, diplomatic and intelligence linkages were all but severed or severely curtailed, especially when the 1999 coup returned the army to power. The ISI-backed misogynist Taliban were committing atrocities in Afghanistan, and the Pakistanis repeatedly rebuffed US demands to extradite or expel Osama Bin Laden from Afghanistan. A new DGISI made it clear that he had no interest in improving relations with the CIA.

But then, just as in 1979, the pendulum swung back for, amid the ruins of the World Trade Center and the Pentagon in Fall 2001 came the realization in Washington that, like it or not, Pakistan was central to the White House's so-called Global War on Terror. Once again, the intelligence relationship was placed front and center as the US money spigots were opened and cooperation on locating al-Qa'ida operatives in Pakistan burgeoned. Indeed, the early years of this revived CIA–ISI alliance should not be overshadowed by later acrimony. Nonetheless, when it became clear that the Bush Administration was focused on invading Iraq, Islamabad was convinced that the Americans had no interest in stabilizing Afghanistan. As a contingency, ISI had put many of the core Taliban leaders in the proverbial Quetta cooler, sensing that the day might come when their favorite Afghan proxies would be needed again.

The 2011 arrest of CIA contractor Raymond Davis symbolized the extent to which the ISI–CIA relationship had devolved into outright hostility by the end of the decade. CIA had secretly infiltrated case officers into Pakistan to try and obtain the intelligence it suspected ISI was hiding, namely the presence of al-Qa'ida and other jihadi leaders on Pakistani soil as well as the status of the nuclear weapons program. The rift was papered over, but only just, and the mutual suspicion lingered for years. It is difficult to envisage how the bilateral intelligence relationship could return to its 1980s prime any time soon, yet as the 1979 Soviet invasion of Afghanistan and the 9/11 attacks on the US have shown, dramatic events can forge unexpected alliances in a remarkably short period of time.

ISI's 60-year liaison with CIA is remarkable when we consider the peaks and valleys of the broader US–Pakistan relationship. With the exception of Israel and Turkey, no other intelligence community in the Middle East or South Asia has the longevity, stability and consistency that characterize the US–Pakistan intelligence relationship. Although much has been made of the hostility between ISI and CIA in recent years, we should not ignore the broader – and more enduring – trend of cooperation that has marked much of their long-standing association.

To what extent has ISI disrupted and abused Pakistan's democratic processes?

This study has highlighted how ISI constitutes a formidable obstacle to Pakistani democracy. From its first hesitant forays into domestic politics in the late 1950s, ISI's capabilities in suppressing free speech, pluralism and human rights grew dramatically in the decades that followed. The apogee was reached in the 1990s and early 2000s, but we should not assume that ISI has given up its domestic political mission for good. After all, as the ill-fated attempt to put it under civilian control in 2008 showed, ISI remains beholden only to the army. Elections interference aside, ISI has stunted the growth of pluralism by suppressing a free media, violating the human rights of Pakistani citizens and rolling back those groups and individuals it deems a threat to Pakistan. Just like secret police apparatuses in Latin America and the Middle East, ISI often brutalizes those it deems "state enemies" or makes them simply "disappear."

One is left with the hope that, over time, successive civilian governments in Islamabad will gradually wrest power from the army and, by extension, the ISI. Such a process will require some sort of rapprochement with India, which, if successful, will undercut the army's claim to a disproportionate share of the nation's wealth. No wonder then that the army is openly dismissive of long-term peace with India. Changing this calculus will take a bold and united civilian leadership (both chronically lacking) with the quiet backing of the US and others to make it viable. In the end, we must keep in mind that ISI is but an instrument (albeit a very important one) in the hands of army generals who often manipulate national politics to suit their own ends. The road to cleaning up Pakistani politics lies through Army GHQ and not ISI.

Is ISI a rogue agency or a "state within a state"?

I do not believe ISI has ever been a "rogue" agency or a "state within a state." This has often been used as an excuse for aberrant and seemingly irrational Pakistani behavior such as the 2008 Mumbai attacks or as justification for not retaliating against Pakistan for its proxy wars. Still, pretending that ISI is something it is not will not make the agency or its deeds disappear. ISI is a military-run organization in a state where the most important national security decisions are made by the army. ISI implements policies set by army-dominated planners who not only view themselves as sole "guardians" of Pakistan's national interests but also define just what those interests are. ISI will pursue a successful peace process in Afghanistan, for example, only if the army leadership determines that the time is opportune to do so.

Since the early 1990s, Pakistan has played a game with the apparent connivance of the US and its allies that runs along these lines. A terrorist outrage takes place. At first, Pakistan fervently denies any involvement but, as indications of ISI links mount, some foreign observers – often "anonymous" in press accounts – suggest that the agency or some of its officers are operating without the knowledge or consent of the government. A DGISI might be removed for unspecified "infractions," but he is often promoted and simply given another assignment. The new DGISI is expected to "clean the place up" by removing pro-jihadi elements that got Pakistan embroiled in the incident in the first place. But over time, nothing substantial takes place on the "reform ISI" front, and it is only a matter of time before an ISI proxy perpetrates another "plausibly deniable incident."

This book details several cases where US officials referenced "rogue" agents inside ISI or hinted that ISI itself may be a "rogue" agency. One wonders if this was a ploy to avoid congressional criticism when billions of US taxpayer dollars were spent on Pakistan every year even though ISI proxies were killing American soldiers in Afghanistan. The "rogue" excuse helps justify inaction, providing the Pakistani government with a convenient alibi to (once again) clean up its wayward intelligence services. Perhaps it also serves as a substitute for policy, because inaction just might be the preferred option where any form of US retaliation could trigger unintended consequences such as the collapse of the Pakistani state and loss of control over its nuclear weapons. Islamabad has been more than willing to invoke such nightmarish scenarios to pressure its friends and enemies into a hands-off policy regarding ISI's proxy wars. Still, the long-term consequences of public denial and apparent willful ignorance should be kept in mind. As Stephen Walt writes:

> One of the things that gets in the way of good national security policy is a reluctance to call things by their right names and state plainly what is really happening. If you keep describing difficult situations in misleading or inaccurate ways, plenty of people will draw the wrong conclusions about them and will continue to support policies that don't make a lot of sense.[1]

Can ISI be reined in and the PIC reformed?

Can ISI be reformed? Can it be made responsive to an elected civilian establishment instead of an unelected and powerful military? Can it become – as US diplomats might put it – a "responsible player" in regional politics: a force for "stability" rather than repeatedly sowing the seeds for a potential Indo-Pakistan war? This history has revealed that Pakistan's record with intelligence reform is poor. Over the course of several decades numerous commissions have examined the PIC, identified problems, recommended solutions and then watched as their reports gathered dust. The Pakistani political system currently cannot accommodate a PIC that is formally subordinated to civilian control and oversight. The army repeatedly rejects civilian "interference" in either ISI or MI, citing the higher mission of "guarding" the state's interests over "political expediency." As discussed earlier, even civilian-led governments have been reluctant to create a Joint Intelligence Council or a NSC, fearing these would become powerful tools in the hands of the military.

Virtually every Intelligence Reform Commission has sought to redress the power imbalance in the PIC between the civilian and military agencies by empowering the civilian-run IB in particular. Yet, with the exception of one curtailed Benazir Bhutto term as Prime Minister, the IB has never benefited from a substantial infusion of new resources, expanded authorities and well-trained personnel. Even when Bhutto tried to make the IB a cocqual to ISI, her efforts were reversed, her government dismissed and IB was subjected to the direct control of army generals. The US government doesn't help matters either because it naturally prefers to work with the only intelligence service that seems to deliver the goods in Pakistan, namely the ISI. This only perpetuates the inordinate amount of power that ISI has accumulated over the years at the expense of its civilian counterparts.

The blueprint for reforming the PIC already exists in the form of various commission reports that were never implemented. But as this history teaches us, intelligence reform will be only one piece in a larger, comprehensive effort to transform civil-military relations in that country.

The imperative of political reform

These conclusions have repeatedly emphasized that the "problem" of ISI and intelligence reform is only a subset of a much greater challenge: transforming an army-dominated state into one where the civilian establishment is allowed to predominate. Nearly 70 years after independence, the army still effectively rules Pakistan. As political scientist Ayesha Siddiqi illustrates in her book *Pakistan Inc.*, army officers not only own a great deal of land, many also run army-linked businesses and industries after retirement.[2] Moreover, with its self-anointed role as Pakistan's guardian, the army has all too often arrogated to itself the right to dismiss civilian governments at will. The costs of undercutting civilian rule are manifested in weak civilian institutions, a corrupt bureaucracy and inexperienced political parties. Using the ISI as its hatchet man, the army intimidates, harasses and sometimes even kills troublesome journalists, lawyers and annoying human rights activists.[3] Its backing of political parties with authoritarian Islamist agendas has helped tilt Pakistan toward extremist vitriol and rising sectarian violence.

Reforming ISI alone would treat a symptom but not the underlying causes of Pakistan's many intractable problems. One of the most challenging of these is Pakistan's interminable identity crisis. *Are we a Muslim state in South Asia?* This was the thesis of the country's founder, Mohamed Ali Jinnah, who envisaged a democratic, secular state that would accommodate its multi-ethnic and sectarian constituencies. *Are we an Islamic state?* This is the alternative identity that has always loomed over Pakistan but never fully implemented because of unending debates over Shari'a and the use of jihad to force societal change. In a phenomenon that is sweeping across many other Muslim societies, a battle is being fought inside Pakistan today over different interpretations of Islam. A modernist, puritanical Islam is attacking a more traditional and tolerant version rooted in local culture on the basis that it is "inauthentic" or "idolatrous."[4] These are civilizational and national challenges that will not be resolved any time soon, certainly not by the West.

Pakistan's civilian political parties must be given an opportunity to govern the country for their constitutionally mandated period without interference from the army. The fact is that until 2012, no elected civilian government had ever been allowed to pass power to its elected successor after completing its full term in office. The bottom line is that, for all their faults, neither the PPP nor the Pakistan Muslim League–Nawaz Sharif faction has ever been given enough time in power to gain both the experience and wisdom involved in governing a state as complicated as Pakistan. But merely stipulating that Pakistani political parties be allowed to form governments if they win elections is not enough. Civilian governance certainly needs improvement, and this involves rooting out corruption, creating stronger party bureaucracies and reducing the proclivity of both the PPP and PML–N for dynastic rule. Accountability and transparency are often cited as *sine qua nons* of modern democracies, yet a fundamental change in Pakistan's political culture needs to take place first.

Other necessary changes include an independent judiciary free from the machinations of political parties or the pressures of army-dominated juntas. Occasionally, there are signs of judicial assertiveness in Pakistan, but this seems to be the exception to the unfortunate rule that many judges can be bought or intimidated. Pakistan would be particularly well served if its Supreme Court finally put an end to the use of the so-called Doctrine of Necessity which affirms "that which is otherwise not lawful is made lawful by necessity." This has been used time and again to put a pseudo-constitutional imprimatur on military coups.[5]

A free press is a crucial element of a healthy democracy. In the case of Pakistan, there is in fact a vibrant and politically diverse media community that includes print journalists, bloggers, cable news stations and Internet websites. Yet we have learned about the existence of certain "red line" topics where public discourse is strongly discouraged. These "no-go" areas, policed by ISI, include the Pakistani nuclear weapons program, the army's suppression of human rights in Balochistan, ISI's links to extremists and ISI's violations of human rights such as unlawful detention. In brief, the army must be taken out of the business of intimidating, harassing and torturing journalists and made more accountable to civilian authority.

Pakistan's history of center-periphery relations has been dismal. Like India, Pakistan has a tendency to attribute minority ethnic and/or religious unrest to "outside forces" while the real causes of discontent lie within the state's mismanagement of its peripheral regions. Thus, Pakistan's interference in Kashmir has allowed New Delhi to ignore thorny political compromises in favor of "military solutions." Similarly, persistent unrest in Pakistan's Balochistan province is usually blamed on Indian intelligence rather than the unmet political, economic and social needs of its people. The post Bin-Laden Abbottabad Commission put this best, noting that the army regards:

> [T]he whole issue of Baloch alienation [as] a problem of external interference and subversion. The Baloch don't count except as suspected agents of foreign forces. The real reasons for Baloch alienation are ignored and the problem is left to fester forever.[6]

This willful ignorance of provincial problems and their causes continues despite Pakistan's tragic history of civil war, secession, five Baloch rebellions, persistent unrest in the Pashtun tribal areas and simmering tensions in Sindh. Addressing those grievances through dialogue, compromise and greater attention to local needs would go much further in alleviating Pakistan's chronic insurgency and terrorism woes than any number of Cobra helicopters and F-16s.

Pakistan also faces a major challenge in accountability. Since its early years, the state has been embarrassingly incapable of holding civilian and military officials accountable for their actions. This includes the pathetic legacy of failed investigations into the assassinations of political leaders such as Liaquat Ali Khan in 1951, Zia ul-Haq in 1988 and Benazir Bhutto in 2007. Botched inquiries erode public confidence in the police and provide fertile ground for conspiracy theories that now metastasize via social media. An important first step toward greater accountability is to give the police more pay and make them less prone to the corruption that permeates Pakistani society. How many travelers to Pakistan have been boldly shaken down by police in the country's international airports? A corrupt, poorly paid police force will never be able to address the core problem of poor accountability.

The natural partner of accountability is oversight. In fact, the latter helps enable the former. As the US learned with its own intelligence agencies in the 1970s, parliamentary oversight of the intelligence community is essential to any healthy democracy because it makes politicians not only knowledge-able but responsible; it helps ensure sound policymaking and provides a necessary check on executive power. Pakistan's National Assembly must be given more responsibility for how the country's intelligence agencies func-tion; it should not be allowed to take a convenient back seat, kibitzing from the sidelines and shamefully cheering on the ISI even as it flouts the funda-mental rights of Pakistani citizens. The 2014 legislation that would have created a parliamentary oversight committee was a step in the right direction. It needs to be revived and resubmitted for consideration with the backing of both the PML–N and PPP.

The most formidable obstacle of all, though, is reducing the powers of the army. Pakistan epitomizes "national security state," and from the very begin-ning it has devoted considerable resources to defense at the expense of eco-nomic, social and political development. Yet it should be emphasized that Pakistan is not alone in this regard, for there are numerous examples of military-run states in similar difficult geopolitical circumstances that managed transitions to democracy. South Korea, Poland and Turkey show the Pakistanis (and international skeptics) that democratic transitions do take place and states can put their security forces under civilian control. "But it's not so easy," critics counter. "How can army power be reduced when Pakistan is constantly threatened by a hostile and much larger India?" A big first step would be a general agreement on the Kashmir dispute based on acknow-ledging the status quo and making the LOC an international boundary. This alone would help undercut many army arguments that deterring India requires enormous outlays of scarce revenues to fund weapons acquisition. Absent fundamental trust-building between India and Pakistan, the army will continue to peddle its usual justifications for larger budgets and the right to have the preponderant voice in national security affairs. It will continue nur-turing extremist parties and employing proxies against neighboring states. In short, the army desperately needs India as an enemy to ensure its own grip on power.

Of course, Kashmir is not the only obstacle on the path to improved Indo-Pakistan relations. Real change must also take place in the attitudes and per-ceptions within the Pakistani political establishment and the army itself. The government has long pursued regional objectives that greatly exceeded the country's resources and capabilities. Take Afghanistan, for example, where the pursuit of an outdated and unrealistic concept of strategic depth motiv-ated Pakistan to repeatedly meddle in the internal affairs of its turbulent neighbor at the expense of long-term Afghan stability and prosperity. Afghan-istan has always been a "bridge too far" for Pakistan. Its politics and its wars demand too many resources for it to ever be stabilized by Pakistan alone, and even when the notionally Pakistan-friendly Taliban were in power, Islamabad obtained few security dividends from its investment. As for ISI's argument that Afghanistan's insecurity is the primary cause of Pakistani instability this is somewhat disingenuous since it is ISI support for the Taliban and the

Haqqanis that helps make Afghanistan unstable in the first place. What ISI sows in Afghanistan it often reaps in the form of terrorism in the FATA, Khyber Pakhtunkhwa and Punjab.

Each of the above represents a daunting challenge for any would-be reformer. Moreover, Pakistani state institutions repeatedly demonstrate that they are quite immune to reform and lack the creative energy necessary for change. The outlook for Pakistani democracy is thus quite bleak. Reforming ISI or even dismantling it would be insufficient because ISI is only a servant of a much more powerful army which endlessly harps on the "wounds" of Kashmir and an "existential" India threat. Even if Pakistani civilian politicians were bold enough to dissolve ISI altogether and achieved this over army objections (two big "ifs"), the COAS could always fall back on his DGMI to pick up the slack. As long as the army dominates the state, directly or indirectly, ISI and/or MI will be there to safeguard army rule. Therefore, meaningful reform in Pakistan must address army supremacy, ineffective civilian governments, pervasive official corruption and a national security state mentality where the ends always seem to justify the means.

Notes

1 S. Walt, "Lessons of two wars: We will lose in Iraq and Afghanistan," *Foreign Policy*, 16 August 2011, http://foreignpolicy.com/2011/08/16/lessons-of-two-wars-we-will-lose-in-iraq-and-afghanistan/ [accessed 5/8/15].

2 A. Siddiqa, *Military Inc.: Inside Pakistan's Military Economy*, London: Pluto Press, 2007.

3 Amnesty International, *"A Bullet Has Been Chosen for You,"* Attacks on Journalists in Pakistan, London: Amnesty International, 2014.

4 A. Hashim, "Deadly warning to Pakistan Liberals," *Al Jazeera*, 7 January 2011, www.aljazeera.com/indepth/features/2011/01/2011141762235392.html [accessed 5/8/15].

5 S. Qazi, "Necessity as the mother of laws," *Herald*, 27 March 2015, http://herald.dawn.com/news/1152911 [accessed 5/8/15].

6 *Abbottabad Commission Report*, 312.

Bibliography

Abbas, H., *Pakistan's Drift into Extremism*, Armonk, NY: M.E. Sharpe, 2005.

Abou Zahab, M. and O. Roy, *Islamist Networks: The Afghan-Pakistan Connection*, New York: Columbia University Press, 2004.

Ahmed, M. *Stinger Saga*, Xlibris, 2012.

Akhund, I., *Trial and Error: The Advent and Eclipse of Benazir Bhutto*, Karachi: OUP, 2000.

Alam, H., *Brave of Heart: the Urban Guerrilla Warfare of Sector-2 during the Liberation War of Bangladesh*, Dhaka: Academic Press and Publishers Library, 2006.

Aldrich, Richard J., *The Hidden Hand: Britain, America, and Cold War Secret Intelligence*, New York: Overlook Books, 2002.

Ali, S.M., *Cold War in the High Himalayas: the USA, China and South Asia in the 1950s*, New York: St. Martin's Press, 1999.

Ali, T., *The Duel*, New York: Scribner, 2008.

Amin, A.H., *The Pakistan Army Till 1965*, Arlington, VA: Strategicus and Tacticus, 1999,

Anand, V.K., *Conflict in Nagaland: A Study of Insurgency and Counter-Insurgency*, Delhi: Chanakya Publications, 1980.

Andrew, C. and V. Mitrokhin, *The World Was Going Our Way*, New York: Basic Books, 2005.

Anwar, R., *The Terrorist Prince: The Life and Death of Murtaza Bhutto*, London: Verso, 1997.

Arif, K.M., *Khaki Shadows*, Karachi: OUP, 2001.

Arif, K.M., *Working with Zia*, Karachi: OUP, 1995.

Bass, G.J., *The Blood Telegram: Nixon, Kissinger and a Forgotten Genocide*, New York: Knopf, 2013.

Baxter, C. ed., *Diaries of Field Marshal Mohammad Ayub Khan 1966–1972*, Karachi: OUP, 2007.

Bazaz, P.N., *Kashmir in the Crucible*, New Delhi: Pamposh Publications, 1967.

Bearden, M. and J. Risen, *The Main Enemy*, New York: Random House, 2003.

Behera, N.C., *Demystifying Kashmir*, Washington, DC: Brookings, 2006.

Bhattacharya, S., *Nothing But! What Price Freedom*, New Delhi: Partridge, 2013.

Bhaumik, S., *Insurgency Crossfire: North-East India*, New Delhi: Lancer, 1996.

Bhaumik, S., *Troubled Periphery: Crisis of India's North East*, New Delhi: Sage Publications, 2009.

Bhutto, B., *Daughter of Destiny*, New York: Simon & Schuster, 1989.

Bhutto, B., *Reconciliation*, New York, NY: Harper, 2008.

Bhutto, Fatima, *Songs of Blood and Sword*, New York: Nation Books, 2010.

Bhutto, Z.A., *If I am Assassinated*, New Delhi: Vikas, 1979.

Bourke-White, M., *Halfway to Freedom: A Report on the New India*, New York: Simon & Schuster, 1949.

Bruguière, J.-L., *Ce Que Je N'ai Pas Pu Dire*, Paris: Editions Robert Lafont, 2009.

Cheema, P.I., *Pakistan Defense Policy, 1947–58*, New York: St. Martin's Press, 1990.

Chishti, F.A., *Betrayals of Another Kind: Islam, Democracy and the Army in Pakistan*, 3rd edition, Lahore: Jang Publishers, 1996.

Choudhury, G.W., *The Last Days of United Pakistan*, London: C. Hurst, 1974.

Clarridge, D.R., *A Spy for All Seasons*, New York: Scribner, 1997.

Cloughley, B., *War, Coups and Terror: Pakistan's Army in Years of Turmoil*, New York: Skyhorse, 2008.

Cohen, S., *The Idea of Pakistan*, Washington, DC: Brookings, 2004.

Cohen, S., *The Pakistan Army*, 1998 edition, Karachi: OUP, 1998.

Coll, S., *Ghost Wars*, New York: Penguin, 2004.

Coll, S., *On the Grand Trunk Road*, 2nd edition, New York: Penguin, 2009.

Constable, P., *Playing with Fire: Pakistan at War with Itself*, New York: Random House, 2011.

Cordovez, D. and S. Harrison, *Out of Afghanistan: The Inside Story of the Soviet Withdrawal*, New York: OUP, 1995.

Crile, G., *Charlie Wilson's War*, New York: Grove, 2004.

Crumpton, H., *The Art of Intelligence: Lessons from a Life in the CIA's Clandestine Service*, New York: Penguin, 2012.

Dil, A., ed., *Strategy, Diplomacy, Humanity: Life and Work of Sahabzada Yaqub-Khan*, San Diego: Takshila Research University, 2005.

Feifer, G., *The Great Gamble: The Soviet War in Afghanistan*, New York: HarperCollins, 2009.

Feldman, H., *From Crisis to Crisis*, Karachi: OUP, 1972.

Frantz, D. and C. Collins, *The Nuclear Jihadist*, New York: Hachette, 2007.

Fury, D., *Kill Bin Laden*, New York: St. Martin's Press, 2008.

Gall, C., *The Wrong Enemy*, Boston: Houghton Mifflin Harcourt, 2014.

Gauhar, A., *Ayub Khan: Pakistan's First Military Ruler*, Karachi: OUP, 1996.

Gerolymatos, A., *Castles Made of Sand*, New York: St. Martin's Press, 2010.

Girardet, E.R., *Afghanistan: The Soviet War*, New York: St. Martin's, 1985.

Giustozzi, A., *Koran, Kalashnikov, and Laptop*, New York: Columbia University Press, 2008.

Glancey, J., *Nagaland*, London: Faber and Faber, 2011.

Government of Pakistan, *Abbottabad Commission Report*, http://webapps.aljazeera.net/aje/custom/binladenfiles/Pakistan-Bin-Laden-Dossier.pdf [accessed 15/4/14].

Government of Pakistan, *Hamoodur Rehman Commission Report*, nd www.pppusa.org/Acrobat/Hamoodur%20Rahman%20Commission%20Report.pdf [accessed 17/5/11].

Graham, B., *Intelligence Matters: The CIA, the FBI, Saudi Arabia and the Failure of America's War on Terror*, New York: Random House, 2004.

Grare, F., *Reforming the Intelligence Agencies in Pakistan's Transitional Democracy*, Washington, DC: Carnegie Endowment for International Peace, 2009.

Grenier, R. *88 Days to Kandahar*, New York: Simon & Schuster, 2015.

Gul, I., *The Most Dangerous Place*, New York: Viking, 2010.

Gul, I., *The Unholy Nexus*, Lahore: Vanguard, 2002.

Gunaratna, R., *Inside al-Qaeda*, New York: Columbia University Press, 2002.

Gundevia, Y.D., *War and Peace in Nagaland*, Dehra Dun: Palit & Palit, 1975.

Hamid, S.S., *Autobiography of a General*, Lahore: Ferozsons, 1988.

Hamid, S.S., *Disastrous Twilight: A Personal Record of the Partition of India*, London: Leo Cooper, 1986.

Hamid, S.S., *Early Years of Pakistan*, Lahore: Ferzosons, 1993.

Handel, M.I., "Intelligence and the Problem of Strategic Surprise," *The Journal of Strategic Studies* 7:3, 1984.

Haqqani, H., *Magnificent Delusions*, New York: Public Affairs, 2013.

Haqqani, H., *Pakistan: Between Mosque and Military*, Washington, DC: Carnegie Endowment, 2005.

Harrison S.S. *In Afghanistan's Shadow: Baluch Nationalism and Soviet Temptation*, Washington, DC: Carnegie Endowment, 1981.

Helms, R., *A Look Over my Shoulder*, New York: Presidio Press, 2003, 154.

Hersh, S., *Chain of Command: The Road from 9/11 to Abu Ghraib*, New York: HarperCollins, 2004.

Holm, R., *The Craft We Chose: My Life in the CIA*, Mountain Lake Park, MD: Mountain Lake Press, 2012.

Human Rights Watch, *Afghanistan: Crisis of Impunity, The Role of Pakistan, Russia and Iran in Fueling the Civil War* 13/ 3, July 2001, www.hrw.org/reports/2001/afghan2/ [accessed 27/11/10].

Hussain, Z., *Frontline: The Struggle with Militant Islam*, New York: Columbia University Press, 2007.

Hussain, Z., *The Scorpion's Tail*, New York: Free Press, 2010.

Hyman, A., *Afghanistan under Soviet Occupation, 1964–1981*, New York: St. Martin's Press, 1982.

Isby, D., *Afghanistan*, New York: Pegasus Books, 2010.

Jalal, A., *The State of Martial Rule*, Cambridge: CUP, 1990.

Jalal, A., *The Struggle for Pakistan*, Cambridge, MA: Belknap Press, 2014.

Jamal, A., *Shadow War: The Untold Story of Jihad in Kashmir*, Hoboken, NJ: Melville House, 2009.

James, M., *Pakistan Chronicle*, New York: St. Martin's Press, 1993.

Jones, O.B., Bennett, *Pakistan: Eye of the Storm*, New Haven: Yale University Press, 2003.

Jones, S., *In the Graveyard of Empires*, New York: W.W. Norton, 2009.

Jones, S. and C.C. Fair, *Counterinsurgency in Pakistan*, Santa Monica, CA: Rand Corporation, 2010.

Joshi, P.C., *Main Intelligence Outfits of Pakistan*, New Delhi: Anmol Publications, 2008.

Kaplan, R.D., *Soldiers of God*, Boston: Houghton Mifflin, 1990.

Kasturi, B. "Military Intelligence in India: An Analysis," *The Indian Defence Review*, 1995.

Khan, A., *Raiders in Kashmir*, 2nd edition, Islamabad: National Book Foundation, 1975.

Khan, A., *Friends Not Masters*, New York: OUP, 1967.

Khan, F.M., *The Story of the Pakistan Army*, 2nd edition, Lahore: OUP, 1964.

Khan, G.A., *Glimpses into the Corridors of Power*, Karachi: OUP, 2007.

Khan, G.H., *Memoirs of Lt. Gen. Gul Hassan Khan*, Karachi: OUP, 1993.

Khan, Jahan Dad, *Pakistan Leadership Challenges*, Karachi: OUP, 1999.

Khan, M.A., *Trumped Up as an Indian Spy*, Lahore: Mohammad Akram Khan, 2002.

Khan, M. Asghar, *Generals in Politics: Pakistan, 1958–1982*, New Delhi: Vikas, 1983.

Khan, Riaz M., *Untying the Afghan Knot*, Durham, NC: Duke University Press, 1991.

Khan, R., *The American Papers*, Karachi: OUP, 1999.

Khan, R., *The British Papers*, Karachi: OUP, 2002.

Khan, R., *Pakistan: A Dream Gone Sour*, Karachi: OUP, 2000.

Khan, Y., *The Great Partition*, New Haven, CT: Yale University Press, 2008.

Kiriakou, J., *The Reluctant Spy: My Secret Life in the CIA's War on Terror*, New York: Bantam, 2012.

Kux, D., *The United States and Pakistan, 1947–2000: Disenchanted Allies*, Washington, DC: Johns Hopkins University Press, 2001.

Lamb, C., *Waiting for Allah: Pakistan's Struggle for Democracy*, London: Hamish Hamilton, 1991.

Levy, A. and C. Scott-Clark, *The Meadow: Kashmir 1995 – Where the Terror Began*, London, Harper Press, 2012.

Levy, A. and C. Scott-Clark, *Nuclear Deception: The Dangerous Relationship Between the United States and Pakistan*, New York: Walker & Co., 2008.

Levy, A. and C. Scott-Clark, *The Siege: 68 Hours inside the Taj Hotel*, New York: Penguin, 2013.

Lohbeck, K., *Holy War, Unholy Victory*, Washington, DC: Regnery, 1993.

Mahmud, C.K., *Fighting for Faith and Nation*, Philadelphia: University of Pennsylvania Press, 1996.

Malik, I., *Pakistan: Democracy, Terrorism and the Building of a Nation*, Northampton, MA: Olive Branch Press, 2010.

Malik, I., *State and Civil Society in Pakistan*, London: Macmillan, 1997.

Malik, T.H., *The Story of My Struggle*, Lahore: Jang, 1991.

Malley, W., ed., *Fundamentalism Reborn?* New York: New York University Press, 1998.

Margolis, E.S., *War at the Top of the World: The Struggle for Afghanistan, Kashmir and Tibet*, New York: Routledge, 2000.

Marker, J., *Quiet Diplomacy: Memoirs of an Ambassador of Pakistan*, Karachi: OUP, 2010.

Marrin, S., "The 9/11 Terrorist Attacks: A Failure of Policy Not Strategic Intelligence Analysis," *Intelligence and National Security*, 26:2–3, 2011.

Matinuddin, K., *The Taliban Phenomenon: Afghanistan, 1994–1997*, Karachi: OUP, 1999.

Matinuddin, K., *Tragedy of Errors: East Pakistan Crisis, 1968–1971*, Lahore: Wajdalis, 1994.

Mayer, J., *The Dark Side*, New York: Doubleday, 2008.

Mazzetti, M., *The Way of the Knife*, New York: Penguin, 2013.

McGehee, R. *Deadly Deceits: My 25 Years in the CIA*, New York: Sheridan Square Press, 1983.

McMahon, R.J., *The Cold War on the Periphery*, New York: Columbia University Press, 1994.

Methven, S., *Laughter in the Shadows: A CIA Memoir*, Annapolis, MD: Naval Institute Press, 2014.

Milam, W.B., *Bangladesh and Pakistan: Flirting with Failure in South Asia*, New York: Columbia University Press, 2009.

Mitha, A.O., *Unlikely Beginnings: A Soldier's Life*, Karachi: OUP, 2003.

Morell, M., *The Great War of our Time*, New York: Twelve Books, 2015.

Mubashir, H., *Mirage of Power: An Inquiry into the Bhutto Years, 1971–1977*, Oxford: OUP, 2000.

Mullick, B.N., *My Years with Nehru: Kashmir*, Bombay: Allied Publishers, 1971.

Muñoz, H., *Getting Away with Murder*, New York: W.W. Norton, 2014.

Musa, M., *Jawan to General: Recollections of a Pakistani Soldier*, Karachi: East and West Publishing Company, 1987.

Musa, M., *My Version: India-Pakistan War 1965*, Lahore: Wajdalis, 1983.

Napoleoni, L., *Modern Jihad*, London: Pluto Press, 2003.

Nasr, V.R., *The Vanguard of the Islamic Revolution: The Jama'at-i Islami of Pakistan*, Berkeley, CA: University of California Press, 1994.

Nawaz, S., *Crossed Swords: Pakistan, Its Army, and the Wars Within*, Karachi: OUP, 2008.

Niazi, A.A.K., *The Betrayal of East Pakistan*, Karachi: OUP, 1999.

Palit, D.K., *The Lightning Campaign*, New Delhi: Thomson Press, 1972.

Pataudi, N.S.A.K., *The Story of Soldiering and Politics in India & Pakistan*, 1st edition, Lahore: Wajdalis, 1978.

Pearl, M., *A Mighty Heart*, New York: Scribner, 2003.

Peters, G., *Seeds of Terror*, New York: Thomas Dunne, 2009.

Pettigrew, J.J.M., *The Sikhs of the Punjab*, London: Zed Books, 1995.

Raina, A., *Inside RAW: the Story of India's Secret Service*, New Delhi: Vikas, 1981.

Rana, M.A., *A to Z of Jehadi Organisations in Pakistan*, trans. Saba Ansari, Lahore: Mashal Books, 2007.

Randal, J., *Osama: The Making of a Terrorist*, New York: Knopf, 2004.

Ranelagh, J., *The Agency: The Rise and Fall of the CIA*, New York: Simon and Schuster, 1987.

Rashid, A., *Descent into Chaos*, New York: Viking, 2008.

Rashid, A., *Jihad: The Rise of Militant Islam in Central Asia*, New Haven: Yale University Press, 2002.

Rashid, A., *Pakistan on the Brink*, New York: Viking, 2012.

Rashid, A., *Taliban: Militant Islam, Oil and Fundamentalism in Central Asia*, New Haven: Yale University Press, 2000.

Raza, R., *Zulfikar Ali Bhutto and Pakistan 1967–1977*, Karachi: OUP, 1997.

Riaz, A., *Islamist Militancy in Bangladesh*, London: Routledge, 2008.

Richelson, J., *The Wizards of Langley*, Boulder, CO: Westview, 2001.

Riedel, B., *American Diplomacy and the 1999 Kargil Summit at Blair House*, Philadelphia, PA: Center for the Advanced Study of India, 2002.

Riedel, B., *Deadly Embrace*, Washington, DC: Brookings Institution Press, 2011.

Riza, S., *The Pakistan Army: 1947–1949*, Dehra Dun: Natraj Publishers, 1977.

Riza, S., *The Pakistan Army: War of 1965*, Dehra Dun: Natraj Publishers, 1977.

Rizzo, J., *Company Man*, New York: Scribner, 2014.

Rodriguez, J., *Hard Measures*, New York: Threshold Editions, 2012.

Rohde, D. and K. Mulvihill, *A Rope and a Prayer*, New York: Viking, 2010.

Roy, O., *Islam and Resistance in Afghanistan*, 2nd edition, Cambridge: CUP, 1990.

Rubin, M., *Dancing with the Devil: The Dangers of Engaging Rogue Regimes*, New York: Encounter Books, 2015.

Sahni, S., *Kashmir Underground*, New Delhi: Har Anand, 1999.

Salik, Siddiq, *Witness to Surrender*, Karachi: OUP, 1997.

Sanger, D., *Confront and Conceal*, New York: Crown, 2012.

Sanger, D., *The Inheritance*, New York: Harmony, 2009.

Schmidt, J.R., *The Unraveling: Pakistan in the Age of Jihad*, New York: Farrar, Straus and Giroux, 2011.

Schofield, V., *Kashmir in Conflict*, London, I.B. Tauris, 2003.

Schroen, G., *First In*, New York: Presidio, 2005.

Scott, L., "Intelligence and the Risk of Nuclear War: Able Archer Revisited," *Intelligence and National Security*, 26:6, 2011.

Scott, L. and P. Jackson, "The Study of Intelligence in Theory and Practice," *Intelligence and National Security*, 19:2, Summer 2004.

Shmitt, E. & T. Shanker, *Counterstrike*, New York: Times Books, 2011.

Sen, L.P. *Slender was the Thread: Kashmir Confrontation*, New Delhi: Orient Longmans, 1973.

Shah, Aqil, *The Army and Democracy: Military Politics in Pakistan*, Cambridge, MA: Harvard University Press, 2014.

Siddiqa, A., *Military Inc.: Inside Pakistan's Military Economy*, London: Pluto Press, 2007.

Siddiqi, A.R., *East Pakistan: The Endgame*, Karachi: OUP, 2004.

Singh, J., *In Service of Emergent India*, Bloomington, IN: Indiana University Press, 2007.

Singh, V.K., *India's External Intelligence*, New Delhi: Manas, 2007.

Sisson, R. and L. Rose, *War and Secession: Pakistan, India, and the Creation of Bangladesh*, Berkeley, CA: University of California Press, 1990.

The Story of the Pakistan Air Force: A Sage of Courage and Honor, Islamabad: Shaheen Foundation, 1988.

Stripp, A., *Codebreaker in the Far East*, Oxford: OUP, 1995.

Suskind, R., *One Percent Doctrine*, New York: Simon & Schuster, 2006.

Swami, P., *India, Pakistan and the Secret Jihad: The Covert War in Kashmir, 1947–2004*, London: Routledge, 2007.

Talbot, I., *Pakistan: A Modern History*, New York: Palgrave Macmillan, 2009.

Tenet, G., *At the Center of the Storm*, New k: PublicAffairs, 2011. York: Harper Perennial, 2007.

Tirmazi, S.A.I., *Profiles in Intelligence*, Lahore: Combined Printers, 1995.

Tomsen, P., *The Wars of Afghanistan*, New Yor

Waldman, M., "The Sun in the Sky: The Relationship Between Pakistan's ISI and Afghan Insurgents," Crisis States Research Centre, Discussion Paper 18, June 2010.

Warrick, J., *Triple Agent*, New York: Vintage, 2012.

West, N., *Historical Dictionary of World War II Intelligence*, Plymouth: Rowman & Littlefield, 2008.

Wirsing, R.G., *Kashmir in the Shadow of War*, London: M.E. Sharpe, 2003.

Wolpert, S., *Zulfi Bhutto of Pakistan*, New York: OUP, 1993.

Woodward, B., *Obama's War*, New York: Simon & Schuster, 2010.

Yousaf, M., *Silent Soldier: The Man Behind the Afghan Jehad*, Lahore: Jang, 1991.

Yousaf, M. and M. Adkin, *Afghanistan: The Bear Trap*, Havertown, PA: Casemate, 2001.

Zaeef, A.S., *My Life with the Taliban*, ed. Alex Strick van Linschoten and Felix Kuehn, New York: Columbia University Press, 2010.

Zahab, M.A. and O. Roy, *Islamist Networks: The Afghan–Pakistan Connection*, New York: Columbia University Press, 2006.

Zaheer, H., *The Separation of East Pakistan*, Dhaka: OUP, 1994.

Zaheer, H., *The Time and Trial of the Rawalpindi Conspiracy, 1951*, Karachi, OUP: 1998.

Ziring, L., *The Ayub Khan Era*, Syracuse: Syracuse University Press, 1971.

Index

Taylor & Francis eBooks

Helping you to choose the right eBooks for your Library

Add Routledge titles to your library's digital collection today. Taylor and Francis ebooks contains over 50,000 titles in the Humanities, Social Sciences, Behavioural Sciences, Built Environment and Law.

Choose from a range of subject packages or create your own!

Benefits for you

» Free MARC records
» COUNTER-compliant usage statistics
» Flexible purchase and pricing options
» All titles DRM-free.

Benefits for your user

» Off-site, anytime access via Athens or referring URL
» Print or copy pages or chapters
» Full content search
» Bookmark, highlight and annotate text
» Access to thousands of pages of quality research at the click of a button.

REQUEST YOUR **FREE** INSTITUTIONAL TRIAL TODAY | **Free Trials Available**
We offer free trials to qualifying academic, corporate and government customers.

eCollections – Choose from over 30 subject eCollections, including:

Archaeology	Language Learning
Architecture	Law
Asian Studies	Literature
Business & Management	Media & Communication
Classical Studies	Middle East Studies
Construction	Music
Creative & Media Arts	Philosophy
Criminology & Criminal Justice	Planning
Economics	Politics
Education	Psychology & Mental Health
Energy	Religion
Engineering	Security
English Language & Linguistics	Social Work
Environment & Sustainability	Sociology
Geography	Sport
Health Studies	Theatre & Performance
History	Tourism, Hospitality & Events

For more information, pricing enquiries or to order a free trial, please contact your local sales team:
www.tandfebooks.com/page/sales

 Routledge
Taylor & Francis Group | The home of
Routledge books

www.tandfebooks.com